CRITICAL ACCLAIM
FOR *TRAVELERS' TALES*

"The *Travelers' Tales* series is altogether remarkable."
—Jan Morris, author of *Fifty Years of Europe*

"*Travelers' Tales* delivers something most guidebooks only promise: a real sense of what a country is all about...."
—Steve Silk, *Hartford Courant*

"For the thoughtful traveler, these books are an invaluable resource. There's nothing like them on the market."
—Pico Iyer, author of *Video Night in Kathmandu*

"This is the stuff memories can be duplicated from."
—Karen Krebsbach, *Foreign Service Journal*

"I can't think of a better way to get comfortable with a destination than by delving into *Travelers' Tales*...before reading a guidebook, before seeing a travel agent. The series helps visitors refine their interests and readies them to communicate with the peoples they come in contact with...."
—Paul Glassman, Society of American Travel Writers

"The *Travelers' Tales* series should become required reading for anyone visiting a foreign country who wants to truly step off the tourist track and experience another culture, another place, firsthand."
—Nancy Paradis, *St. Petersburg Times*

"If there's one thing traditional guidebooks lack, it's the really juicy travel information, the personal stories about back alleys and brief encounters. The *Travelers' Tales* series fills this gap...."
—Jim Gullo, *Diversion*

T R A V E L E R S ' T A L E S

IRELAND

TRUE STORIES OF LIFE
ON THE EMERALD ISLE

TRAVELERS' TALES GUIDES

IRELAND

TRUE STORIES OF LIFE
ON THE EMERALD ISLE

Edited by

JAMES O'REILLY, LARRY HABEGGER,
AND SEAN O'REILLY

TRAVELERS' TALES
SAN FRANCISCO

Cover design: Michele Wetherbee
Interior design: Susan Bailey and Kathryn Heflin
Cover photograph: © Terry donnelly / The Image Bank. Kylemore Abbey, County Galway.
Illustrations: Copyright © 1996, 1997 by Dover Publications, Inc.
Map: Keith Granger
Page layout: Cynthia Lamb, using the fonts Bembo and Boulevard

Distributed by Publishers Group West, 1700 Fourth Street, Berkeley, California 94710.

Library of Congress Cataloging-in-Publication Data

Ireland : true stories / edited by James O'Reilly, Larry Habegger, and Sean O'Reilly. — 1st ed.
    p. cm. — (Travelers' tales)
Includes bibliographical references.
 ISBN 1-885211-94-5 (pbk.)
 1. Ireland—Description and travel—Anecdotes. I. O'Reilly, James, 1953- II. Habegger, Larry. III. O'Reilly, Sean. IV. Travelers' Tales guides.
 DA978.2 .I747 2003
 941.5—dc21

                           2003009758

First Edition
Printed in the United States of America
10 9 8 7 6 5 4

Ireland, Sir, for good or evil is like no other place under Heaven, and no man can touch its sod or breathe its air without becoming better or worse.

—George Bernard Shaw

In loving memory of Sean O'Reilly, M.D. (1922–1982),
a Kerry man.

Table of Contents

Part Two
SOME THINGS TO DO

★ ★ ★

THE NEXT STEP

Ireland: An Introduction

When I was a boy, I remember my father sitting, lost in thought and memory, in view of a painting in our American living room. That painting was of Torc Mountain rising above the Lakes of Killarney in County Kerry, Ireland, which was for my father, home. He always seemed unreachable in this state, but whether or not he was, it was clear to me that he was filled with a longing that I at least in part understood. I loved him then as he loved Ireland—hopelessly, with every fiber of my body.

So for me, my father was Ireland itself, just as he was the Catholic Church, the essence of which he labored mightily to instill in me and my six brothers and sisters. (And of course in Ireland, the two are, as the saying goes, joined at the hip.) What then did my father, as Ireland, represent in these twin roles?

He embodied a love of learning, a love of scholarship, a love of exact speech, of moral laws, of hard work, of looking for and expecting goodness in others but not being surprised if it wasn't forthcoming, of storytelling and reading and music, of sly and lunatic humor. He had a wild streak of sacrifice and charity, a combination of St. Francis-like gentleness and ayatollah-like fierceness. He lanced personal boils with self-denial, revered tradition and rules because they are the stone framework of civilization when the wolves of cruelty and hunger are at the door, as they have been for so much of Irish history, a framework that lasts long after the roof has burned and the residents hanged. My father made me want to be, well, a saint—because it was so transparently the goal and practice in his own life—and it seemed then as it seems now, that nothing else could be as important. What does being a saint mean? Being as close to your Maker as you possibly can, at all times, warts and nose hairs and terrible bleeding mistakes all. That was the gift of my father, and for me was and remains the gift of Ireland.

What does this have to do with modern Ireland? Ireland has changed so dramatically in recent years, you'd hardly recognize the place if you haven't been in a while, or if all you know of Ireland is what Uncle Paddy told you of his childhood. So intellectuals in Dublin may scoff at my characterization of Ireland, cynics in Belfast hoot with derision, geeks in Cork dismiss the bandwidth of my thinking, Eurotrash in Galway snort at my naïvete. They've seen the real Ireland and it doesn't look at all like the romanticized version sloshing over the gunwales of the vast Irish diaspora. The Catholic faith has eroded, the Church is in decline, the famine ships are ancient history, the rural culture is on its last legs, and everything Irish is nothing but a tourist gimmick. But sometimes those who have left, those who are filled with unspeakable longing, as my father was, have something correct to say.

Ireland has in it, in its soil and air and water and sun, something that for want of a better word is alchemical, that no other place on earth seems to have. This is not to say that other peoples don't love their native land as much or as well, or that ancient portals of feeling and wisdom don't exist the world over, not at all. It is just that whatever there is in Ireland is unique. Perhaps this is a genetic thing—my bias is suspect with a name like O'Reilly—but I don't think so. I think the genetic predisposition may be only to love Ireland a bit more fervently, but it is not responsible for the place Ireland holds open on the spectrum of human possibilities. Ireland, it seems to me, is an earth-bound zone between birth and death that has not been de-coupled from either human event, not by Celts, nor Catholics, nor Computers. In Ireland you can sense more clearly the form of your own life, the shape of the little corporal boat that carries you down the river to home and the Eternal. In other words, in Ireland, you can get pretty close to Heaven.

When my father died, we took him back to Kerry. He was borne on the shoulders of his grade school classmates to rest above Killarney in Aghadoe, in a sixth-century cemetery with a breathtaking view of his beloved Lakes and, of course, Torc Mountain.

My brothers and I filled in his grave, taking care with the skulls and bones of other relatives buried there.

When I visit now, especially when I visit my father's grave, and look out over the Kerry Mountains, I am still filled with longing for all the things humans long for. But the heart's home really *is* elsewhere...only in Ireland, you are closer to it than anywhere else.

—JAMES O'REILLY

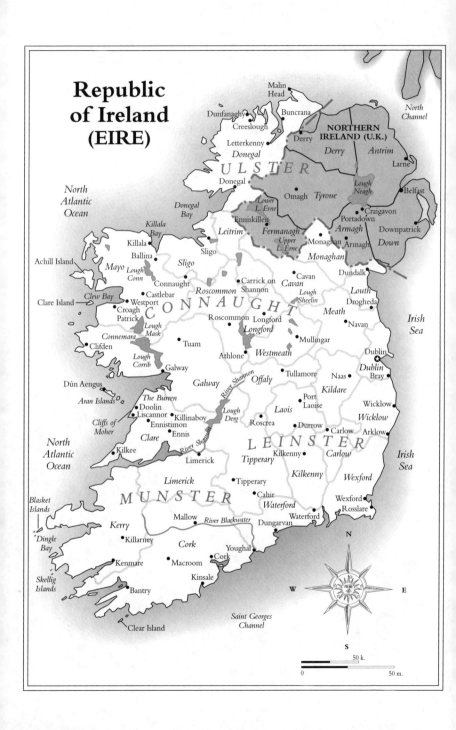

Republic of Ireland (EIRE)

NORTHERN IRELAND (U.K.)

North Channel

North Atlantic Ocean

ULSTER

Malin Head
Dunfanaghy
Buncrana
Creeslough
Letterkenny
Derry
Derry
Antrim
Donegal
Larne
Donegal
Omagh
Tyrone
Belfast
Lough Neagh
Craigavon
Portadown
Armagh
Downpatrick
Armagh
Down

Killala Bay
Killala
Ballina
Donegal Bay
Leitrim
Lower L. Erne
Enniskillen
Fermanagh
Upper L. Erne
Monaghan
Monaghan
Dundalk

Achill Island
Mayo
Lough Conn
Sligo
Sligo
Carrick on Shannon
Cavan
Cavan
Lough Sheelin
Louth
Drogheda

Clare Island
Clew Bay
Connaught
Roscommon
CONNAUGHT
Westport
Castlebar
Meath
Navan
Croagh Patrick
Lough Mask
Roscommon
Longford
Longford
Mullingar

Connemara
Clifden
Lough Corrib
Tuam
Athlone
Westmeath
Dublin
Dublin
Galway
Galway
Offaly
Tullamore
Naas
Bray

Dún Aengus
Aran Islands
The Burren
Doolin
Liscannor
Killinaboy
Ennistimon
Ennis
Lough Derg
Roscrea
Port Laoise
Laois
Kildare
Wicklow
Wicklow

Cliffs of Moher
Clare
River Shannon
Durrow
Carlow
Arklow

North Atlantic Ocean
Kilkee
Limerick
Tipperary
Kilkenny
Kilkenny
Carlow
LEINSTER

Limerick
Tipperary
Cahir
Wexford
Wexford
Rosslare

Blasket Islands
Kerry
MUNSTER
Mallow
River Blackwater
Waterford
Waterford
Dungarvan

Dingle Bay
Killarney
Cork
Youghal
Cork

Skellig Islands
Kenmare
Macroom
Kinsale

Bantry

Clear Island

Irish Sea

Saint Georges Channel

N
W   E
S

50 k.
0   50 m.

PART ONE

ESSENCE OF IRELAND

BRIAN WILSON

* * *

An Unexpected Reception

A kayaker discovers old Ireland.

I COULD HARDLY HAVE PICKED A MORE TORN OR FRAGMENTED section of the entire Irish coast on which to make a lucky-dip landfall. As it runs westward, the coast of Iar Connaught disintegrates, almost dissolves, into a tangle of bulbous peninsulas, convoluted bays, islands, causeways, and, finally, hundreds of tiny islets. There are neither roads, railways, harbours, nor even a lighthouse to provide a coastal way marker. Apart from a handful of dwellings, and long rough tracks snaking down from the nearest road, Iar Connaught meets the sea in a smudge of anonymous, fragmented rock and turf. From the point where a leaden sea could just be distinguished from the slate-grey sky, a band of bile-coloured no man's land appeared and very slowly expanded to become a stretch of featureless coast. It looked more imaginary than real. And yet, if I had imagined it I would surely have endowed it with at least some features or shapes. The coast looked like a grubby smear at the back of a shirt collar, and was just about as inviting. I landed, close to low tide, on a shingle beach within a semicircular bay, fringed by rocky islets which almost entirely absorbed the swell from the sea. The fingers of the sea, seeking, searching among the pebbles and shingles of the beach and rock pools, managed, within a few yards, to pilfer away the vast energy of the open ocean.

3

I thought it likely that I was on the edge of Gorumna Island, but there seemed no way to check. The coastal features I could see were a recurring configuration along the entire coast. And besides, it didn't really matter; it was enough just to be on land; wet through and beginning to shiver, the important thing for the moment was to organise food and shelter. After hauling the kayak above the tidemark, I removed my dry clothes and camp gear from its hatches. Then, following a hedge of brambles laden with irresistible berries, over tumbled dykes and hollows, I found myself half a mile inland, in front of a rickety stone-built haybarn, such as the old books on Ireland used to call a "cabin." Like a prop from *Hansel and Gretel*, it seemed simply to have materialised from the mist. But it was sound and dry inside, and with the entire surrounding countryside smothered in a seeping cloud, it seemed the perfect place to doss down for the night.

Within an hour I was stripped, dried, and snug in warm clothes. My sleeping bag was laid on a pile of dry, sweet-smelling hay, and my wet gear dripped steadily from a drying line at the other end of the barn. The sodden efforts of the day were fast becoming a memory, banished for the moment beyond the solid walls of the little refuge. Outside the wind continued to push, and a dripping grey mist rolled in from the bay to engulf the building; but I read peacefully by the light of a candle, and felt sleep edge ever closer. I was in good spirits: infinitely happier than in a soggy tent at Doolin. I'd gained quite a few unexpected miles, and reached somewhere on the coast of County Galway, perhaps within striking distance of Connemara. It was progress, and to cap it all there was an improved forecast for the following day.

The morning light bled in by an east-facing window, diffusing through a dense golden smokescreen of haydust. Curled in the hay like a dormouse, I lay with one eye watching the day arrive, the other still reluctant to open. From a ball of straw and daub in a high corner of the rafters, came a steady plaintive cheep-cheeping as mother swift darted in and out of the light shafts with acrobatic brilliance, snatching drowsy insects to feed her nest of noisy youngsters. The heavy black clouds of the previous day had been replaced by a fine white mist, wet and swirling. A light breeze blew tiny particles of vapour in through gaps in the walls and windows, and all that they touched—including my jersey and longjohns—quickly became saturated. I rolled my sleeping bag, breakfasted on sausage sandwiches, and pulled on my wet gear. An early start would give me a chance to feel my way through the sea mist to Roundstone or Clifden in Connemara.

The little barn was completely shrouded in cotton-wool cloud, but I could hear the murmuring sea, and was able to retrace my bramble-lined route to the kayak's landing bay from the previous night. I could hardly believe my eyes when I climbed over the last stone wall and saw—no kayak! My gaze darted uneasily around the bay, then back to the shingle beach; and still no kayak. I was stunned. My familiar routine was so dependent on the kayak being there that I hardly knew where to turn. Was this the same bay? Yes, I was certain. Had I dragged the boat high enough? Of course—after seven weeks that had become almost instinctive. But perhaps there had been an unusually high tide? Yet all the signs were that the last tide had risen even less than the previous storm-driven one. How could a heavily laden kayak simply disappear? The gradual process of logical deduction began, and progressed to its almost incredible conclusion. The kayak had been taken; and surely by at least two people. But where had they come from, and where could they have taken it to?

Desperately, I searched the maze of low drystone walls—wanting to believe that some well-wisher had just tucked the kayak away behind a dyke for extra safety—but there was no sign of it. There were no houses visible in either direction, but then I remembered some lights I'd seen farther to the east just before coming ashore, and decided to head in that direction. For about an hour I scoured the rough countryside, clambering over low walls, losing my boots in boggy holes and tearing my clothes in tangles of bramble and dog rose. I hardly knew if I was even heading in the right direction. The first house I reached looked empty. No smoke came from the chimney. And its pebble-dashed gable was flaky and damp with neglect. But from beneath a pile of shore-salvaged timber, driftwood, plastic floats, and wooden fishboxes, I caught a glimpse of a familiar yellow—*Sola's* distinctive under-belly? Yes, there she was—stacked under a mound of stinking flot-sam, the contents of her hatches strewn on the ground, and the paddle missing. There didn't seem to be any damage, and my re-lief at finding her at all was tremendous; but nonetheless I was fu-rious, livid that someone would brazenly lift *Sola* from the shore and cart her away. I hammered on the door loudly enough to wake anyone unfortunate enough to be still sleeping inside; ham-mered again, but there was no reply. I jogged along to the next house and was puffing and hot in my paddling suit when the door opened slowly and a stout, middle-aged woman stood staring at me in a puzzled silence.

"Do you know anything about a big canoe that's sitting beside the next house?" I said, trying to remain civil for just a moment longer.

"Oh, the boat, indeed, yes," she said. "That came out of the sea. It belongs to my son Donal—"

"It certainly does not. It's mine!" I interrupted, beginning to lose my cool.

She looked me up and down—from the wet-suit boots to the hooded pink paddling jacket—then said: "What do you mean, it's yours? It was washed up on our coast, you know, after the storm, and all the wreckage in the bay belongs to us."

"Now, look here—it is *not* wreckage and it was *not* washed up—*I paddled* it up! And what's more it was well above the tide-line. Where is your son now? Let me speak to him. He had a bloody cheek to move it at all," I raved, wondering at the time how to persuade a reluctant Irishman, who was probably twice my size, to carry the kayak back to the bay.

"Well, he is—oh, out hauling creels," she said unconvincingly. "But I daresay he might let you have the boat at a fair price, if you'll just—"

"Might what! I'll—"

"Now, now. You'll come in for some tea and breakfast?" She

added, and I felt my indignation and anger give way to confusion, and even mild amusement at the bizarre situations I seemed regularly to end up in. I could cope with being tent-bound in a gale, or even kidnapped by Sherkin pirates, but to have the kayak taken as wreckage, then offered to me for sale, left me stuck for words. Not for the first time I thought the difficulty in kayaking around Ireland lay not so much in getting to a place, but in getting away from it. There are times when the flotsam analogy comes too close to truth for comfort.

The woman shouted in Irish into the house, and a couple of doors slammed mysteriously before she let me into the warm kitchen. She sat me down beside the range, and seemed well-used to placating angry menfolk by filling their stomachs. Over several cups of tea, and a huge plate of ham and eggs with pancake and beans, and homemade soda bread, the picture became clearer. The rights of wreck and salvage along parts of the Irish coast—perhaps especially those where timber and other resources have traditionally been scarce—are extremely ancient and important, sometimes complicated, and often grimly defended. As in many parts of the British

A valuable and entertaining book might be written about the personality of Irish villages—a volume, which as far as I know, has not yet been written. Why, for example, is one village physically neat and mentally active while another in similar surroundings is untidy and stupid? Why are villages sullen or merry or brutal or benevolent? What is it that makes this village tolerant of a man's donkey cart because of his face, while that village is intolerant of his face because of his donkey cart?

—Harold Speakman, *Here's Ireland* (1925)

Isles, coastal people have looked on most forms of flotsam and jetsam as their legitimate property, a sort of Atlantic providence. Shipwrecks, especially during wars, have played an important part in the economy of Ireland's remoter coasts; even today houses and barns may be seen with mahogany mantelpieces, rafters riddled with shipworm boreholes, and ship's furniture recycled as kitchen units.

There are very subtle differences between wreck and wrack, flotsam and jetsam, smuggling and salvage, and many similar forms of coastal enterprise which have largely slipped through the net of written record-keeping. It is even harder to shed light on some of the shadier aspects of shore life, but it seems that in the past smuggling and deliberate wrecking have almost everywhere been regarded as more or less acceptable methods of obtaining food and supplementing a difficult living from the sea. Almost automatically, unwritten codes of practice have developed regarding aspects such as legitimate targets, division of shoreline, ownership and property, and rights of salvage. Generation after generation of coastal families has inherited rights to its own stretch of shoreline, perhaps demarcated by a stream on one boundary, and a cliff on the other.

In an area with no local woodland, bays that collect driftwood are the most jealously guarded of all. Every such bay has its own particular ideal wind, during which it reaps the optimum harvest from the sea; and wreck seekers keep as close an eye on wind and tide conditions as a Hawaiian surfer, for whatever the sea throws up on the land is theirs for the taking.

The woman pointed out of the kitchen window at stacks of driftwood, crates, baskets, and creels, all of which had been found on "her" shore. Enough new timber had come up last year to build a shed extension to the house; a hen-hut on the corner of her yard looked suspiciously like the wheelhouse of a Spanish trawler; and even the seat I was sitting on had come from a Norwegian whaler wrecked on Slyne Head. "Timber doesn't grow on trees 'round here, you know," she said.

Two days after a westerly storm, she explained, is the time when wreckage—either fresh or old stuff stirred by the sea's movement—generally starts to float and drift onto her beaches. Her youngest son, eighteen-year-old Donal, had checked the beaches at about half past eight the previous night. He had seen the kayak there and looked about in the mist for an owner, but as I was by then in the barn, he found no one. By eleven o'clock he decided that the kayak was now not only legitimate wreck, but one of his best-ever finds, and enlisted his brother Michael to help carry it home.

Pouring me another cup of tea, and perhaps judging that I'd calmed down a little, she admitted that actually Donal was not at the lobsters, but in his room across the hall; but it was best to leave him there. "He has a quick temper, and he wouldn't want you to be taking the boat."

Smiling now, I calmly explained about my journey round Ireland, and that not only would I be taking the canoe away, but that the paddle was also missing, and I needed a hand to carry it all to the bay. "I'll get Michael so," she said.

Shouting in Irish, she opened the kitchen door and Michael, who had obviously been listening at the keyhole, almost fell into the room, sheepishly clutching the missing paddle. A big, stooping, quiet lad of about nineteen, with a neck like an ox, and hands almost as wide as the paddle blades, Michael exuded disappointment rather than temper, and agreed to help carry the kayak, just as soon as we'd finished the tea. All the way to the bay, except to answer me with a yes or no, Michael said nothing.

Then, on the water's edge: "Will you write an' tell us how far you get to. Maybe you'll make it to Galway, God willing."

"O.K. Sure I will. And thanks for the lift," I said, pushing off from the shore. "What's this place called anyway?"

"This is Lettermullan. You'll pass Golam Head soon to the west," he answered, and gave a gentle wave.

"Tell Donal I'm sorry about the canoe!" I shouted.

Michael mumbled a reply, which I didn't quite hear, but I felt sure any hard feelings had already vanished on the Iar Connaught breeze.

Brian Wilson is a writer, adventurer, and environmentalist, living and working in northwest Scotland. A former judo champion and philosophy graduate, he now specializes in drystone walling, thatching, and adventure travel. His previous book, Blazing Paddles, *chronicled his 1800-mile voyage around Scotland. This story was excerpted from his book,* Dances with Waves: Around Ireland by Kayak.

PAUL McGREAL

A Mayo Dog

*In Ireland, it pays to know
the family tree.*

IN MAYO, IN THE WEST OF IRELAND, UNCLE PADDY WAS KNOWN AS a dog man. Other sheep farmers would bring him dogs to train or just to ask his opinion about the pup they carried under one arm while standing in the pub, a pint of Guinness set on the bar within reach of the other arm. Would it make a good sheepdog? Look at the size of its head and paws. Sure, the like of it has never been seen in Ireland before. A champion if ever there was one.

Paddy would give his opinions freely, but the training of a dog was a business matter and was usually arranged after several meetings over a few pints of Guinness and the payment of a fee. The fee was a very private matter and would not be disclosed to anyone in the village. Discretion and secrecy are highly developed arts in Ireland, and both parties would go to the grave without ever mentioning the transaction again.

On my last visit to Westport, several years ago, I was privileged to sit at a table with Paddy and three other men earnestly discussing the sale of a pup that was tied to a post outside the pub. Paddy and Seamus Flanagan were the prospective buyers, and the O'Mara brothers were the sellers.

"He's a fine, strong dog," said John O'Mara. "He put on weight faster than any other pup in the litter."

"And who is the mother?" asked Seamus. "It is always good to know where a dog has come from, is it not?"

"The mother," said John O'Mara, "is my own dog, Kerry. And you both well know that Kerry has won a few prizes at the fairs for her gathering and sorting abilities. She could go into the herd and bring back the sheep you wanted in record time."

"I've seen Kerry at the fairs," said Paddy. "She did fine work."

Now that the dog's mother was known, Seamus wanted to know about the paternal line. His question was short and to the point.

"And the father?"

The O'Mara brothers looked at each other then gazed at the foamy heads of their full beer glasses. After a minute of silence, John O'Mara took a toothpick from the breast pocket of his old, worn suit coat and shoved it into the tiny space between his buck teeth.

"Now that's a bit of a tale," he said.

Paddy looked at the clock on the wall. It was five o'clock.

"We've time to hear it," he said.

"Well, then," said O'Mara, "if you have time to hear it, I have time to tell it. But before I do I will bring the dog in and tie it to the leg of the table so we can all look at it and admire its health and strength and observe what a fine dog it is."

John O'Mara did not move but nodded to his younger, silent brother Vincent who immediately stood up from the table and went to fetch the dog.

It was a small dog and it did not like being pulled through the pub on a string. It shoved its hind legs forward to brake its journey along the wooden floor but it was useless effort against Vincent's pull on the string around its neck. A few barks and whelps leapt out of it while Vincent tied it to the leg of the table. It had a nice collie snout but the rest of the dog was anybody's guess.

John O'Mara pulled the toothpick from his teeth and pointed at the dog.

"That dog," he said, "will be one of the finest sheepdogs that Ireland has ever seen. Mark my words."

"And the father?" said Seamus, again, lifting the glass of Guinness to his lips.

"The father," said John, "is suspected to be one of the finest sheepherding dogs in the county. It came in the night and it was gone before anyone woke up to see it. Kerry was tied up outside, you see. It must have been the first day the heat was on her. Had we known we would have brought her inside. We're usually quite careful about that, you know."

"And where were you when this happened, might I ask?" said Seamus, looking at the pup stretched out on the floor next to the table.

Paddy said nothing but glanced at me and nodded towards the dog. I looked at it and didn't notice anything remarkable. It had a white patch running up its nose and over one eye. It was lying on the floor, its hind legs tucked under its belly and its left forepaw beside its head, the high nail resting on a

---

Alone at the bar one man drank heavily, trembling violently. He introduced himself and told us he had just that evening had a terrible experience with his dog.

"He has the devil in him. I've known it for a long time now. That's why I had to drown him. Do you know how I did it?" he asked, knocking back another whisky. "Well, I took a stone from the wall, beneath my bed, and tied it to his neck with a rope. Then at high tide there I put him off the pier. And wouldn't you think that would be the end of my troubles? But no…" he paused for a sip, with all the art of the natural storyteller, "…I stopped in here for a drop—just the one—and when I got home the blasted dog was in front of the fire. But worse than that—" he rose to his feet with fear in his eyes, and said slowly, "the stone was back in the wall!"

—Brian Wilson, *Dances with Waves: Around Ireland by Kayak*

loose bit of lip at the corner of its mouth. It looked like it was sucking its thumb.

"Well, now," said John O'Mara. "I won't lead you through the brambles on this one, Seamus. From the timing of the birth I reckon Kerry was in one of two places at the time she was mounted. Either tied up next to my house not far from here, like I said, or running loose for half an hour at the last fair in Leitrim while I was talking to Jim O'Donnel, a sheep man down that way."

"Then the father might be a Leitrim dog?" said Seamus, disappointed. "Didn't you say it was one of the finest sheepherding dogs in the county? Will you come straight, John?"

John rolled the toothpick between his first lower molars and called the barman to set the table with fresh pints of Guinness. When the table was set he leaned back in his chair and smiled at Seamus.

"Well, now," he said. "Everyone sitting at this table knows that I did not say which county. I did not say Mayo nor did I say Leitrim. But in either case I did say the father was one of the finest sheepdogs in the county. I was referring to whichever county the father is from. You may wonder why I said that, not knowing the father personally, and I am going to tell you why I said that, Seamus. First of all, if the pup's life began at the fair in Leitrim, you can be sure it was one of the dogs competing at the fair. As you know, the dogs at the fair are brought from all over Ireland for the contest. Any man who is of sound mind will bring his best dog. He will not bring a dog that doesn't know the difference between a sheep and a tree stump. He will not bring a dog that is half deaf or that cannot understand whistle commands. He will bring his best dog and with it try to win the purse and the trophy offered as first prize. Vincent was with me at that fair, weren't you Vincent?"

Vincent, his large, heavy hand curled round his beer glass, looked at us all and nodded solemnly.

"I was," he said.

"If the father was a Leitrim dog, you must lower the price," said Seamus. "They are inland dogs and do not get the benefit of the sea air like the dogs around here. Everyone knows that it is the sea air that makes the Mayo dog strong and intelligent. For lack of sea air, inland dogs must be content with limited capabilities. I do not mean to denigrate the inland dog, but I prefer Mayo dogs and their offspring. I could not bring a dog home that was not a Mayo dog."

"But I did not say it is not a Mayo dog," said John O'Mara. "It may very well be a Mayo dog. As such, the price must stay the same. Look at the dog, Seamus. Does it not look like a Mayo dog? Mark my words, with my Kerry as its mother it will grow to be one of the finest sheepdogs in Ireland. Still, I could lower the price a few pounds if I got one of your dogs in trade, particularly the young black one with the ginger markings on its back and the top of its head."

"You mean my little Redcap?" said Seamus. "No, I would never let Redcap go. Just the other day he went up on the hill and brought down the herd with only three whistles from me. It was dark too. You won't find many dogs that can do that at his age. No, I'm sorry John, even though Kerry is renowned for her abilities, I'd never be able to trade Redcap for an uncertainty. From what you've said so far the pup's father is still a riddle. We all like riddles but I'm not going to pay for one."

John, realizing that one prospective buyer had fallen by the wayside turned his attention to Paddy, who had not shown much interest in the pup.

"And you, Paddy?" said O'Mara. "You've had a look at the pup. What do you think?"

"I think your dog Kerry is one of the best sheepdogs ever to come out of Mayo." said Paddy. "But as Seamus said, it seems the pup is a bit of a riddle, and riddles in Ireland, although they tax the mind, have always been free of financial burden. Still, John, if you will bring the dog outside for a minute, I would like to see how its nose rises to the sea air. When I came in there was a strong breeze from the west."

John untied the dog from the table and walked out with Paddy. Seamus told Vincent it was a shame nobody knew who the father was but it was the same with dogs as with people these days.

Modern life, he said. A man hasn't time to keep an eye out on his dogs, his sheep, the weather, and his daughters all at the same time. What is the world coming to, he said.

Vincent nodded and gazed glumly at the golden harp emblazoned on his beer glass. "Aye, what is the world coming to," he repeated, as he raised the glass to his lips.

When John and Paddy came back inside Paddy was holding the rope. He handed it to me when he sat down.

"I've just purchased a dog," he said. "And a fine dog it is."

Seamus was surprised, curious, and suspicious about the transaction and looked from Paddy to the dog and then at John and Vincent and back to the dog again.

"Well, that is that," he said, in good humour, and called for another round of Guinness.

They talked of other dogs from other times, construction work and large boulders that had to be blasted out of fields, local lads who had gone off to America, and other happenings in the parish.

As we all stood to leave Vincent shook my hand and seemed to be struggling for something to say. He finally nodded towards the pup and looked into my eyes.

"The dog is sold," he said.

On the way home, with the pup sitting between us on the front seat of the Datsun pickup, I asked Paddy why he had bought the dog.

"Because I knew the answer to the riddle before it was presented," he said.

"Do you mean to say you know the father of the pup?"

"Of course, I do," he said. "I would not have bought it otherwise."

"And who is the father of the pup?" I queried, more curious than ever.

"Sure, my own dog, Rover, is the father of the pup," he said. "And I remember the night well. I had stopped the Datsun to take a pee by the side of the road near O'Mara's farm. Rover jumped out and was gone for about half an hour. Rover is the finest sheepdog I've ever had. O'Mara should lock his dogs inside when the heat is on them."

As we turned off the main road onto the dirt track that led to his farm I pulled the pup onto my lap and stroked its head.

"Have you got a name for the pup, yet," I asked.

"Its name will be Finn," said Paddy. "The name came to me as I watched it on the pub floor with the high toe of its paw in its mouth. Are you familiar with the old Gaelic sagas?"

"Not much," I said.

"Finn McCool," said Paddy. "The only man in Ireland who gained wisdom by sucking his thumb."

He dipped his hand into his pocket, pulled out a dog biscuit, and gave it to the pup.

"Well, Finn," he said, scratching the pup behind the ear. "You and I are going to do great things together. I've been watching you since the day you were born."

Needless to say, I left Ireland with a new appreciation of the buying and selling of dogs.

After fifteen years working in Spain as a translator, interpreter, and teacher, Paul McGreal has recently returned home to Canada. He has traveled widely in Europe, Canada, the United States, and Mexico. He is currently working as a technical communicator, "messing with computers and networks" and, during the long Canadian winters, dreaming of southern climes.

THOM ELKJER

A Blackbird Follows the Heat of the Sun

First the music got to him,
then the musician.

YOU CAN DIVIDE THE WORLD INTO THOSE WHO'VE HAD THEIR Irish period, and those who haven't. It can start at any age, and it doesn't matter what nationality you are. Like other human conditions, it varies in degree. Some people discover the poetry of William Butler Yeats, or become furious about the events of 1916, until they find another poet or another political outrage. Others discover an Irish gift shop later in life, and plunder it for Belleek teapots and Nicolas Mosse pitchers until their cupboards are full. These are comparatively mild cases.

My own case came on during the age of greatest susceptibility: late teens and early twenties. It started innocently with a couple of political plays by Brendan Behan and J. M. Synge, then advanced rapidly with exposure to a story by Seán O'Faoláin called "The Heat of the Sun." When I heard early recordings of the Chieftains later that same year, all natural resistance was swept away. By the time I finished college I was drinking Irish tea in the morning, Irish stout in the afternoon, and Irish whiskey at night, wearing a Donegal tweed hat (even though it didn't fit me), and could recite you a dozen of Yeats's poems from memory.

But it was the music that had me by the ear and wouldn't let go. I remember watching a documentary about the Clearing, when the English ran the Irish off their land, cut down the trees, and moved in flocks of sheep. A solo uilleann pipe on the film's sound track intoned melancholy melodies that flushed my system like a fever. For a long while that sound—in any song, in any context—brought me to the verge of tears.

Sometime later I discovered that someone I knew not only sang and played traditional Irish music, he went to Ireland to collect the songs firsthand. My all-time favorite was called "Rathdrum Fair": the melodic line was all plaintive, pentatonic scales, and the lyrics were personal yet sublimely universal. I was sure the song was a century old at least. Then the singer, Danny Carnahan, informed me that he had learned it from the composer a couple years before, in Dublin.

✳

The great Gaels of Ireland
Are the men that God
made mad,
For all their wars are merry,
And all their songs are sad.
—G. K. Chesterton

But I was going to Dublin myself, that summer! Could I hear this genius in person, I wondered? Danny told me where to look for him, a folksinger named Mick Fitzgerald, playing the Dublin music bars. "In fact," he added, "I've got some performance dates set up in the fall. If you see Mick, could you ask

him about coming over to the States?" I agreed immediately. I'd never been outside the U.S., but at that point I knew more about Maude Gonne than I did about Betsy Ross. In the full flower of my Irish period I headed off on a vitally important mission of musical diplomacy.

The first night in Dublin, sitting in a bar, I explained the mission to my traveling companion. This woman was yet to have her Irish period, and there was no prospect in sight. She had just counted thirty-two people in the bar and announced that every one of them was smoking, except for ourselves and the bartender.

Clearly, she needed a new point of attention. I began to sing, softly but audibly, from "Rathdrum Fair."

I rose and tasted the first breath of Spring,
The mist from the grassy land rising.
I set to my grey mare and saddled for the road,
Where the green hills the sun was caressing.
Saw the nest of the blackbird as it took to the air,
Setting off in the direction of Rathdrum Fair.
I come with the dawn bringing silver to buy,
Hoping wits and good fortune would aid me...

I became aware of the bartender, standing nearby. "Mick Fitzgerald," he said.

"Of course," I replied, covering a thrill of pride.

"D'you know him?" the barman asked.

"I know his work," I said, exaggerating suavely. "I'm here to invite him to America. Set up some gigs."

The bartender looked into my face a moment, as if judging my fitness for such a task. "Is that so?" he said finally, then moved slowly back down the bar.

I had not been in Ireland twenty-four hours but already I was revising one preconception: the Irish are not all big talkers, even when they've got something to say. I wanted to know what the bartender was thinking, but my companion urged me outside, away from the smoke. As we walked along on that late summer evening, I sang another verse.

I rode with the sun, took my feet to an inn,
Where the talk was all livestock and memories.
Where old tales were traded for new ones in turn,
And the pipes would lament into the day-o.
Where the faces were old, but the eyes, they were good;
They knew the money in your pocket and they'd have it if they could.
Where the clowns and the streetsellers wandered around,
And the fiddler was lost in the noise of the crowd...

I loved imagining wily villagers, eyeing a naive newcomer and crafting barely fair ways to relieve him of his money. Ah, Ireland!

The next night, after dinner, we took the bus into town and headed for Slattery's, in Capel Street, not far from the General Post Office where Patrick Pearse read out the Proclamation of Independence in 1916. Slattery's was the traditional Irish music bar where Danny had said we were mostly likely to find Mick Fitzgerald. The place was a converted grocery store, which suggested to me that it would be small and cozy, a perfect setting for traditional Irish musicians to sit around a table together and play through the evening. The Gaelic word for this, *seisiúns*, sounds like the English word "sessions," from which I inferred that the musicians were playing mostly for each other, and the rest of us were lucky to be in the same room.

But when we arrived at Slattery's, I could hear loud, amplified guitars and a heavy drumbeat spilling out the door. "Rock and roll downstairs, Irish upstairs," said a man in black. He looked to me just like the doormen at American music clubs. I told him we were looking for Mick Fitzgerald. "Not on tonight," he replied.

When I said I just wanted to talk to him, the doorman shrugged, jerked his thumb toward a stairway behind him, and said, "No cover." We went up. At the top of the stairs we turned into a large, low-ceilinged room, with a bar along one long wall and a small stage in the center of the opposite wall. Except for an aisle along the bar, and the area between the bar and the stairs, the room was packed with tables, low stools, and people. Talking, drinking, smoking, laughing, shouting people.

There was a five-piece acoustic band playing, but their sound was completely lost in the noise of the crowd. We squeezed onto two empty stools at the far end of the room, got drinks, and looked around to assess the situation. I remembered something Oscar Wilde said about *seisiúns*: "If the music is good, no one will listen. If the music is bad, no one will talk." If this remark was as true as the rest of Wilde's aphorisms, then the music that night in Slattery's must have been very good indeed. I just couldn't hear it.

The band finished a song and suddenly there was a man onstage, waving his arms and quieting the crowd. "You've all come here to listen to these fine musicians," he exhorted them. "So please listen!" The crowd quieted, he left the stand, and the band began to play. By the end of the song, I couldn't hear myself think. A little while later, the same man again took the stage and begged people to be quiet. The band's pretty blonde harpist then began to play a solo number, and it wasn't very good. To my surprise, the crowd sat in silence and watched her play.

I seized the opportunity to go up to the bar and ask the whereabouts of Mick Fitzgerald. A barman inclined his head toward the far end of the bar, near the top of the stairs. "Dark hair, got a black jacket on," he said. I walked the length of the bar, my excitement rising. I could see a man, not much older than myself, who fit the description, standing talking to a woman seated at the bar. As I got closer, he began talking to another woman, seated next to the first one. I realized that he was trying to strike up a

My husband Lawrence's music was a hit in the north as it had been in the south. Our hosts, the O'Kanes, persuaded him to bring his fiddle with him one evening. They had a friend named Ann who also played. But Ann hadn't touched her fiddle in months. Her husband had died in an accident and she was expecting a baby. She had withdrawn into her sorrow. Wise in the way of the spirit, the O'Kanes had a plan.

That night at the family's favorite watering hole, Lawrence entertained with waltzes and reels. He poured his heart into hornpipes and jigs. Exhausted, he finally put his instrument down. Elderly Mrs. O'Kane ordered vodka. The pub filled up with music and camaraderie. And then a marvelous thing happened. Of course the O'Kanes had expected it would. As our spirits rose and our group became louder, the gaiety in the room became a force that not even Ann could resist. Reaching over the table, a song most assuredly forming in her mind, she picked up Lawrence's fiddle and played.

—Linda Watanabe McFerrin, "Fiddlin' Around in Ireland"

conversation with one of them, either of them, and they were ignoring him. It seemed to me a shabby way to treat a major musical figure. But I would show them a better way.

"Mick Fitzgerald?" I asked. He spun around, took a step back, and stared at me.

"What?" he demanded.

I was startled by his manner and blurted out something about coming from America to see him, but I didn't get far.

"America?" he bellowed, and clapped me on the shoulder. "God bless America, let's drink to 'er!" I didn't have a drink, and neither did he, but there was a bar not three feet away, and a barman looking my way. I squeezed between the two women, quickly paid for a couple shots of Bushmills, and handed one to Mick. "America," he said, and downed his shot. I hesitated a moment, then did the same. I had found Mick Fitzgerald, and we were drinking together!

The harpist ended her song, the dull roar of the crowd quickly began rising, and there were people jostling around us where we stood near the bar. I had to lean in closer to continue my explanation about him coming to America to play music.

"I can't," he announced abruptly. I asked why. He was looking down into his glass. "Something happened," he said. I asked him again, What? "Something happened to my whiskey," he said, and looked up at me, deadpan. I turned again to the bar, fetched us two more glasses of Bushmills, and asked again what the problem was with coming to America.

"Damn government," Mick stated emphatically. "Took my papers, so I can't leave and I can't go anywhere either." He took his drink and slugged half of it. I didn't feel like celebrating now, with my mission in peril, but I drank too. "We were having this discussion, me and a couple other fellows," Mick complained. "Had to settle it one way or the other. Broke a few chairs, was all. Then the damned government took my papers."

We looked at each other a moment, he cursed the government, and we downed our drinks. This one hit me a little harder than the first, but seemed to have no effect on Mick Fitzgerald. He was eyeing the two women again, but they were focused on the stage. I had my back to the room, and had to strain to hear any trace of the band.

"So how did you find me?" Mick Fitzgerald asked. "Am I famous yet in America?"

I assured him that a select group of true fans of Irish music was hearing his music. This did not seem to Mick to qualify as being "famous in America," because he was again looking down into his glass. I pressed on. "When Danny Carnahan sings 'Rathdrum Fair,' you should see the people's faces!"

Mick looked up. "Danny?" he asked, surprised. "You know Danny?"

"I told you," I said, impatient now. "Remember, that's why I came here, because he has arranged some gigs for you in America!"

Mick Fitzgerald took half a step back. Before my eyes, he seemed to grow larger and taller. "*Gigs?*" he roared. "Why didn't you say so?" He clapped me on the back joyously, then looked about as if trying to remember where he'd put down his calendar. I reiterated my explanation about the performance dates and coming to America. Of course that was impossible now, and I for one was very sorry that—

"Thursday," Mick announced suddenly. "I'll come on Thursday!"

I stared at him. For the first time, it occurred to me that one of us was drunk, but I was not sure if it was him or me. "But what about the problem with the government?" I asked, trying to remember the details. "What about your papers?"

"They love me in America," he answered grandly. Then, in one smooth gesture, he swung his hand with the empty whiskey glass up and then down onto the bar between the two women. When he swung his arm back out, it was holding a nearly full glass. Somehow, in an instant when neither woman was minding her glass, he had swapped his for one of theirs. Before I could react, he winked broadly at me and slipped the whiskey down his throat.

Out of the corner of my eye I could see one of the women look down, discover her empty glass, and look over her shoulder at Mick. He had his back to her, and a choirboy look on his face as insurance. So the woman cut her accusing eyes to me. Fortunately, the glass in my hand was empty. I avoided her gaze, kept my face neutral, and casually turned away from the bar.

"Listen, boyo," Mick was saying, "I've got to get myself in proper order." He wrapped one arm around my shoulder and moved us toward the top of the stairs. I nodded and mumbled some assent. "But listen, I'm a bit short of the ticket." He patted the pocket where my wallet was. Before watching him descend the stairs, I gave him some money and he gave me his promise to re-imburse me in America. Then he was gone. I found my way back to my table and sat down.

In not quite ten minutes, the major musical figure I had come to venerate—that sublime composer of traditional Irish songs—had tapped me for two drinks, made me an accomplice in swiping a third, and taken possession of half the contents of my wallet. And yet I still felt exhilarated, as if I had succeeded in some cloak-and-dagger stratagem. The deafening noise of the crowd washed over me, and through the smoke I watched the fiddler sawing away. My boast to the bartender earlier that evening came back to me, and also his three-word response. I began to wonder if I would ever see Mick Fitzgerald again.

Soon afterward, bouncing sleepily along in the back of the bus, I recalled the final verse of "Rathdrum Fair," the thoroughly contemporary song I had thought so old.

And when business is done you'll adjourn for a dram,
And drink maybe well into the day-o.
But when twilight draws near you will drink your last beer,
And set up your goods to take away-o.
And the old mare will stumble and bite at the wind,
As you sleep in the saddle with your collar turned in.
And the year will grow old when the traders have gone,
And the blackbird will follow the heat of the sun....

Thom Elkjer is wine editor for Wine Country Living *and editor of* Adventures in Wine: True Stories of Vineyards and Vintages around the World. *His work has appeared in* Wine Spectator, WINE *magazine, and many Travelers' Tales volumes. He is also the author of* Escape to the Wine Country *and a mystery novel,* Hook, Line and Murder.

The lyrics to "Rathdrum Fair" are used with the kind permission of their author, Mick Fitzgerald, who writes: "May I reassure the reader that I am a much more mature restless spirit now. Over the years I have taken the many ghosts of Rathdrum Fair to America, to Canada and Australia, and to Hungary and Poland before the Berlin Wall came down. The ghosts of that long ago time are now telling blackbirds of their travels back home in Rathdrum. The song will always have a special place in my heart."

DAVID W. McFADDEN

✦ ✦ ✦

Mr. Looney's Archeological Adventures

He knows his accents, make no mistakes.

HE WAS KNOWN AROUND TOWN AS TIMMY, THE TOWN BEING Cahir, where he had spent his entire life. But he was a man who deserved great respect, and in his demeanour and manner of speech he demanded great respect, and so I called him Mr. Looney. He was also known as Old Looney because he was an octogenarian widower living in a small house with sagging bookshelves on a side street off the old town square. From the age of sixteen he had dedicated himself to studying the history of Ireland, a fervent amateur with no time for the academies. He spoke slowly, evenly, deliberately, and soberly. He never smiled.

"It is not generally known that this is the most historic part of Ireland."

"You mean County Tipperary?"

"I do."

"Why would it be more historic than the other parts?"

"There are many reasons for that. Even the Celts when they came in here to Ireland it was here that they stayed. Just outside the town of Cahir was one of their main bases. That's going back, for they arrived in Ireland in 504 B.C. There were eighteen kings of

Munster who resided just outside of town. And then later they moved to Cashel."

"Is it known where they are buried?"

"It is not."

"No idea at all?"

"Well, I think I know. But it hasn't been excavated yet."

Mr. Looney's main theme was the poverty of knowledge on the subject of the history of Ireland. Very little was officially known because very little had been excavated. For every Newgrange that had been discovered, excavated, studied, written about, renovated, popularized, and put on the tourist maps, there were thousands more that were known only to lonely amateurs like Mr. Looney, who had been exploring the countryside with a passionate eye for six decades.

From his inspired guesses about the nature and meaning of many of the unexcavated mounds of various sizes and shapes that he was familiar with, he wove theories that were potentially disturbing, even revolutionary, and conjectures that were sometimes a bit confusing.

I had driven north from Mount Melleray, back over the Knockmealdown Mountains, along winding roads offering heavenly views of the Tipperary plain bathed in bright cold sunshine, past dead sheep that had been hit by cars, and down to Cahir. Pity the season wasn't a month or so more advanced and that the beautiful rhododendrons, everywhere in bud, weren't in full blossom.

Mr. Looney invited me in. He was dressed in a black pinstriped suit, black shoes, burgundy wool cardigan with matching tie and socks, and a white shirt. He didn't waste time getting down to business.

"The main monument of Ireland is Newgrange. If you were at Newgrange and if you went to the trouble of walking around the mound, you'd find it exactly 300 paces. And it's about 30 feet high. Now I'm working on a mound here—"

He was referring to the burial place of the kings of Munster in a field somewhere just outside of Cahir.

"I have it located. I've had it divined—I don't know if that's a new word for you—"

"No, it's not. You're talking about dowsing."

"I am. Excavation without going underground."

"Well put."

"The place I'm working now is exactly 600 paces to walk around it."

"Double the circumference."

"It is."

"And how tall is the mound?"

"It'd be about fifty or sixty feet."

"Twice as high."

"It is."

"Have you spoken to anyone in charge of excavations about this?"

"I have not. The trouble here is this. Now I've made a number of finds. I've walked in fields and I'm always on the lookout for something. Mounds and that. I reported an important find here in 1961, and they came along and they declared it a national monument—the mound and twenty acres surrounding it. And they haven't come back."

"And what was that find?"

"It was a court cairn. A

Having never been a history buff, I was at first only casually interested in Newgrange and the fact that it was older than Stonehenge and the pyramids of ancient Egypt. I went because fellow travelers insisted that I see it. And I liked the name, too…Newgrange…It struck me as having a certain musicality. I certainly did not expect it to be one of my favorite experiences in Ireland. But it resides in my memory as just that, and I return to it often. I retrieve not only the feel of the place, but also the lessons I learned as I tunneled through its tight walls and felt the beautiful carvings etched upon them. The experience I had there has become a part of defining what I believe about art, what it meant to be alive at the time Newgrange was built, and what it means to be alive now.

—Laurie Young, "A Visit to Newgrange"

mound that's more or less pear-shaped. And there's a *souterrain* passage in that for burial."

"How far back would that go?"

"That would have been built in 4000 B.C."

"And it still hasn't been excavated?"

"It has not; they never came back. Now that's the trouble in Ireland. You report something and that's it, that finishes it. I have found sites around here that they don't know anything about. They haven't money. That's the problem. They'll take the place over all right, but they haven't the money, they haven't the knowledge, and they haven't the people."

At first, when Mr. Looney said the word Tipperary, I thought he was saying "the prairie," because he pronounced it something like that. Tipperary is a relatively flat, prairielike county, bordered by mountains. But the word Tipperary is said to come from the Irish *tiobraid Árann*, meaning "the well of Arann." Mr. Looney tended to pronounce *th* as if it were *t* (and sometimes *d*) and *t* as if it were *th*. He also tended to roll his *r*'s and his *l*'s and to insert an *r* or an *l* where it wasn't required. Water, for instance, was invariably "wortle." And he claimed to be able to tell by accent which county someone came from.

H. V. Morton wouldn't knowingly have had much to do with Mr. Looney, and Mr. Looney could not remember having heard anything about Morton or his books, but I have an uncanny feeling—close to certainty—that their paths did cross at one time. And in such a way that it did no less than seal Mr. Looney's fate. I had asked Mr. Looney how he became interested in studying the history of his region.

It was sixty-five years earlier. Coincidentally, Morton would have been on his whirlwind tour of Ireland—including a brief stop in Cahir. Mr. Looney was sixteen and working as a clerk in an office in town.

"The windows were open and the old characters of the town would sit outside the window on long benches. And I would hear some very interesting stories being told."

One day a very distinguished English visitor stopped and asked one of the old gentlemen for the directions to Cahir Abbey.

"Never heard of it," the old man said.

"Sure now, I thought there was an abbey in this town."

"Oh no, there's nothing like that here."

By this time the young eavesdropper was becoming a little angry. He went out, but the visitor had gone on his way. He approached the old man and asked him where he lived.

"On Abbey Street."

"Abbey Street. I thought so. And when you open the door in the morning, what's the first thing you see?"

"Oh, my God. The Abbey! I never thought of that."

Mr. Looney went back in and went back to work, but he couldn't stop thinking about the incident.

"Later that day, on thinking this thing over, I decided that no man, no matter where he came from or who he was, would come into my district and ask me a question I couldn't answer. And that's how I started to get interested in my parish and the history of it and the history of the whole locality, not only of Cahir and South Tipperary, but of the whole south of Ireland—south of a line run-

---

But over it all—the white houses, the green fields with their stone walls, the long road winding, the slow herds coming along in the knee-deep dust, the sweet smell of turf burning, the little carts with coloured shafts, the soft Irish voices, the quick Irish smiles—over it all, and in it as if imprisoned in the stone and brick of this country, as if buried beneath the grass and hidden in the trees, is something that is half magic and half music.

There is something in a minor key that a man never quite hears. Perhaps no stranger ever hears it. But I think the Irish do. It is something drawn up out of the earth of Ireland, in the fields, something of the sky and of the earth—a something that is mysterious and like a fall of dew over the land.

—H. V. Morton, *In Search of Ireland* (1930)

ning from Dublin to Galway, which is roughly half of Ireland. I've travelled it all, and I know the history and background of all those parts. The unfortunate thing is that very few people ever ask me anything about it."

I didn't ask Mr. Looney anything more about the English visitor. Even if I'd had a picture of Morton to show him, I probably wouldn't have. How reliable would his memory have been after a glimpse of someone more than sixty years ago? Besides, he apparently heard Morton's voice but didn't see his face. As far as I was concerned, the visitor could have been none other than Morton. I was in search of Morton, and I had discovered him, if only in the resounding impact he had unknowingly made on the life of one individual human being.

Morton's visit to Cahir was brief. But it was a lovely day, the sort of day when old men like to sit out on benches and chat, and he liked the town immensely. He found it "bright, clean, hopeful, vaguely busy...peaceful and drenched in the sanity of the eighteenth century." He mentions the castle, the bridge, the river, "the square as wide as a parade ground, and the warm afternoon sunlight."

But he doesn't mention the abbey.

Perhaps because a certain old codger, sitting in a warm afternoon sunlight, had told him it didn't exist.

"The Peloponnesians were the first here," Mr. Looney was saying. "They came from Greece. We did a lot of trade with Greece and with the Middle East in pre-Christian times. There was a big trade with the Mediterranean."

"What about the Celts?"

"The Celtic people originated on the Tibetan-Indian border and moved from there to Ireland along the southern part of the Mediterranean and into Spain. Milesius, the king of Spain, sent his three sons in here to conquer Ireland. They arrived here in 504 B.C."

On the wall of Mr. Looney's house was a painting showing a dolmen, a smaller version of the one at Browne's Hill. Mr. Looney said

A rchaeology presents us with a perplexing picture, one largely at variance with that presented by philology, early Irish history, folklore, and tradition. It seems almost heretical to insist that a Celtic invasion of Ireland never happened. In this regard, however, the archaeologist should bear in mind the deficiencies of his discipline. Perhaps, as in the field of religion, he should adopt a stance akin to that of the agnostics rather than one of atheism. Perhaps there was, indeed, a migration of "Celts" to Ireland. The only problem is, archaeology cannot prove it. As J. R. R. Tolkien wrote:

"To most people outside the small company of the great scholars, past and present, 'Celtic' of any sort is…a magic bag, into which anything may be put, and out of which almost anything may come…Anything is possible in the fabulous Celtic twilight, which is not so much a twilight of the gods as of the reason."

—Barry Raftery, *Pagan Celtic Ireland*

he had discovered the dolmen on a wooded slope just out of town, and the painter, a local crony had painted it for him.

"It's a huge capstone," he said.

You couldn't get a sense of size from the painting. But the capstone looked as it if were just sitting on top of the ground.

"Is it still supported?"

"It is, actually. But poorly. It was interfered with in some way. But it's a very good example of a capstone. Perfect, in fact."

"And you haven't reported it."

"I have not."

He started talking about beehive huts, which he pronounced "hoods" and described as "old drystone buildings of the early Christian period—little huts for living in, monastic cells. There are a lot of them around here, but I haven't divulged the location of any. You can put in a very interesting day around here, I tell you."

Sitting on Mr. Looney's desk was a stack of old leather-bound books that looked as if they had been borrowed from the county registry as part of whatever project he was working on. I picked one up and flipped it open. It showed a town that had a population of 2,000 in 1821.

"The population of that town today is 500," he said.

He offered to take me out to Athassel Abbey on the River Suir. We hopped into his little red Zazen.

"See that church?"

We were buzzing along the Waterford Road, heading east out of Cahir. The church was in ruins and covered with vegetation.

"That's the old parish church. There's a wall down the middle of it like, and it's known as a screen wall. And the screen wall, it divided the Catholic and the Protestant services. The two were held together then. You can see there were two belfries on it."

"Are there a lot of them like that around?"

"You'll have a job finding a second one of them, I tell you. I came across another one of them down outside Killarney. As for this one, the last service held there was Protestant—in 1795. A Catholic service would have been held just before then."

We passed a gloomy-looking crossroads, a T-junction actually, one of those landscapes that make you think inexplicably of death and sorrow, a *crux commissa* or Saint Anthony's Cross, and Mr. Looney said three men had been hanged there a hundred years ago or so.

"And just about four years ago the bloody fellow who didn't know any better took down the posts they were hanged on."

We had pulled over to drink in the gloom.

"He was bulldozing the field. And it's a tradition, even now with the posts removed, that the people will never walk past here. They always went out of their way to avoid walking past here."

"What were the men hanged for?"

"Land agitation."

"Oh dear."

"There was a lot of that in those days."

"So the people around here must have sympathized with them."

"Well, everyone did. Because, see, like if you go back to, say, even up to 1912 or 1913, you'd have a big job going around this, the most prosperous part of Ireland, finding a man with a ten-pound note of his own. There was no money. Even people working, the wages was practically nil. It was a battle of survival. I have copies of the actual paysheets; the wages was one shilling and six-pence per day. Nine shillings a week. And if you were able to supply a cair and box with yourself you got one pound a week."

"A cair and box?"

"By that is meant a horse and cart for drawing stones and that."

Mr. Looney said 160 men were hired in those days to work on the railway in Cahir.

"And that was the wages they were getting. They had to walk in the nine miles from Clogheen and be in by eight o'clock in the morning. And they walked home at six in the evening. And then be in again the following morning. And they fought at one another to get the job. If a fellow fell out, there were dozens waiting to take his place."

We parked the car by a stone wall a mile from the village of Golden and walked 300 yards across a spacious green field down to the River Suir, where the ruins of Athassel Abbey sat quietly in the warm sunlight like a lucid dream.

"This abbey was ruined during the Reformation," said Mr. Looney. "The tourists don't even come here, even in the summer."

"How far are we from the Rock of Cashel?"

"About seven miles."

"That may be why. There's no shortage of tourists there, even this early in the spring."

Mr. Looney had been a teetotaller and nonsmoker all his life, and in spite of his years he scampered up the crumbling stairs of Athassel, leaving me to eat his dust as I stood in the church choir staring at the tomb of a thirteenth-century Norman knight. When I caught up with him, he was breathing quietly and gazing silently out a small window over the mythic countryside. He was about five-eight, and had a sort of Richard Nixon-Barry Fitzgerald look, but without the quivering jowls.

He didn't say anything, but I later realized that the spot at which he'd been gazing had been the site of an ancient town which had disappeared in the fourteenth century and of which no trace remained. "Disappeared" is a euphemism. Brian O'Brien burnt the town to the ground in 1329.

"Powerful weather," said Mr. Looney.

"A brief respite from the cold rain."

"Summer will be a while yet."

Over his bald head he had a few strands of feathery white hair, which were brushed back and which would puff up in a breeze so that they looked like the lonesome arches of a ruined cathedral, like Saint Patrick's on the Rock of Cashel.

"The Normans would come up the Suir in flat-bottomed boats," he said. "They even had their own bakery. But there was a lot of trouble with drink and with women here."

He said Athassel Abbey was also known as Saint Edmond's Priory.

"The terrible thing was, their libraries were destroyed. From all their manuscripts there are just a few scraps remaining at Cahir Abbey. I've had a terrible problem trying to find anything written about Athassel Saint Edmond's."

He said that pigs had been brought into the ruined abbey on three different occasions by three different individuals over the years, and in each case they didn't thrive. It might have had something to do with the consecrated ground.

"Would this be pretty consistent throughout Ireland?"

"It would not. These places aren't usually interfered with in that way."

As we got back in the car, a young man on foot, and with a large backpack with a Stars and Stripes sewn on, was coming along the road. He scarcely glanced at us, and we didn't say anything. He climbed the stone wall and made his way down to the abbey alone.

I hadn't knowingly met any Tinkers yet, but had heard a lot of different shades of opinion about them and was about to hear many more. Also, they had been the focus of a recent spate of unpleasant stories in the country weeklies and small-town dailies, in a mean and amateurish journalistic style that was shockingly one-sided.

"The Tinkers were dispossessed during Cromwellian times and never got resettled," said Mr. Looney.

"This has the ring of truth."

"The Tinkers are the travelling people. They maintain the old Irish customs. The thing is slowly breaking down, but, when they marry, the bride and groom never meet until the wedding day. And the children are looked after first. Not one adult will eat a bite until all the children are fed."

"But they are not liked, the Tinkers."

"The farmers like these people. They are strictly honest. They live by very strict pre-Norman codes."

I was very impressed with Mr. Looney's take on the Tinkers. He thought of them as a somewhat distinct race with ancient values that the rest of us had forgotten. Most others saw them as layabouts, thieves, and vagabonds.

I had no idea where we were by this time—some farmer's lane. A group of smiling, gap-toothed rustics gathered around the Zazen and said, "Hello, Timmy, how're ye bein'?"

They waved us on. We drove slowly past the farm buildings and up a slight hill to an uncultivated area. Slightly below the top of the hill was an ancient, roofless stone chapel, very small, about thirty by fifteen feet. Mr. Looney said it was built in the seventh century. A window over the high altar seemed to be lined up with the spot where the sun would be rising at the spring solstice, which was close at hand. Below the chapel was a small group of stone crosses. Mr. Looney called them high crosses, but they didn't seem tall enough to be called high. On one had been carved six lines of ancient Gaelic.

"No one has succeeded in deciphering it yet," said Mr. Looney.

He said there were no figures of Christ on the crosses, or even in the churches, until the twelfth century.

"See this stone?" he said. A metal bracket had been secured over it so it couldn't be removed. "Saint Bechaum came to this chapel and asked for butter. He was refused, so the butter turned to stone."

"And this is it, Mr. Looney?"

"It is."

Farther down, there was a small *clochán*, a stone beehive hut with an extremely narrow opening, again in the direction of the rising sun. The capstone that might have been on top—or more likely a wood-and-straw roof—had been long missing.

On the floor inside was a large flat rock with two round basins carved into it so smoothly it might have been natural. Mr. Looney said it was a *balaun* stone, that would have been used for baptizing the pagans.

"And in pre-Christian times they were used for grinding corn, is that right?"

"There's another one in Cahir Abbey," he said.

"Saint Bechaum travelled most of Ireland," said Mr. Looney, referring to his favourite saint. "He was an itinerant preacher. He was well-known in Rome, involved in changing the dates for Easter. No one knows where he's buried, but I've found traces of him all over Ireland."

I marvelled at the large number of Irish saints. Morton's book says there had been a veritable army of them.

"And of all the saints we have—hundreds and hundreds of them—only three are registered in Rome," said Mr. Looney. "Even Saint Patrick is not registered in Rome. I guess he didn't pay his fee."

We both felt we'd done enough for the day but agreed to meet again tomorrow. As we slowly walked back to the car, it occurred to me that the area under cultivation had perhaps at one time been the site of an expansive village of stone huts. What we had seen had been merely an untouched remnant of a vast clearing of the huts over the centuries. Mr. Looney enthusiastically agreed.

Emboldened, I asked about the Blarney Stone.

"Would it really cause me to become eloquent? If there's the slightest chance—"

"The Blarney Stone? That's only folk stuff. That's just a gimmick."

"Well, what about the Little People?"

"That's different," he said.

His face softened, and he began to tell a story I was to hear many times on my travels, a story that was part of an extensive living mythology, one that the academics and professional historians were beginning to find in the main correct.

"Now before the Celtic people came here, there was a tribe of people occupying Ireland. They were called the Tuatha Dé Danann. They were small people. Like in early Christian times a tall Irishman would be five feet six inches. But these were small people."

"Smaller than five-six, Mr. Looney?"

"Much smaller. And the Celts were bigger people, and they were all blond. The Tuatha Dé Danann built those forts you see. And when they were under pressure from the Celts, they'd disappear. And that's how this thing came about with the Little People and all disappearing into the earth. They used to go down into their *souterrains,* their underground chambers and passageways. They just disappeared into nowhere. That's how the thing about the Little People came about."

"When did they become extinct?"

"The Celts finally defeated them and slaughtered them all. That's the way it was in those days—even up to Cromwell's time. Massacres. Ach, but the history of Ireland has never been written."

David W. McFadden has published numerous books of poetry and prose, including Anonymity Suite, A Trip Around Lake Ontario, Gypsy Guitar, Canadian Sunset, The Art of Darkness, Animal Spirits, A Trip Around Lake Erie, A Trip Around Lake Huron, My Body Was Eaten by Dogs, On the Road Again, A Knight in Dried Plums, *and* Intense Pleasure. *He lives in Toronto. This story was excerpted from his book,* An Innocent in Ireland: Curious Rambles and Singular Encounters.

DAVID BLAKER

* * *

Irish Roads

*Some insights into the long
memories of the Irish.*

THUMBING RIDES IN IRELAND WAS EASY, THAT SUMMER. I SELDOM
had to wait more than ten minutes at the roadside before a truck
driver or traveler would draw up beside me.

"Where are you going, now? I can take you as far as Ballymena.
Hop in."

And so it went. From Larne to the gray walls of Derry, then on
to the Republic and beautiful empty Donegal. Most of the drivers
were going a short distance only, so I met maybe a dozen new ones
every day. On both sides of the border, my ride-givers were unfailingly polite and friendly.

"Where are you from, then? Africa? What a long way from
home! And how are you liking Ireland?" The chatter would continue in the usual contrived way it did when I thumbed rides.
Anyone who has traveled like this probably knows the slightly
edgy disadvantaged feeling. Not because of physical safety—which
was not an issue at that time and in that place—but because I was
in a partly parasitic relationship with a total stranger. Because of
this, I always felt the need to be extra polite, and unwilling to let
conversation falter.

Despite the spontaneous friendliness of the drivers and my own forced conviviality, I began to dread their almost inevitable question. After a few rides, I learned that within ten minutes of getting in their vehicle, almost every driver would ask me the same question, either directly or in a casual offhand way.

"And what are you then? Catholic or Protestant?"

There never seemed to be any obvious correct way to answer this, and several times the wrong answer resulted in the tiniest chill creeping into the conversation. Even though there was a 50 percent chance of saying the right thing, I could never predict which answer would please my driver most, and there seemed to be no scope for the truthful description of: "semi-lapsed Presbyterian-Anglican."

And so it was, after four days, that I embraced the Jewish faith. Having a Jew as a passenger seemed to satisfy and even please people. I was regarded as a freak; interesting, and perhaps a source of anecdote later. They chose not to detect my false Jewishness, and I had no reliable way of deciding whether each driver was Catholic or Protestant.

On several occasions I felt brave enough to ask: "How can you tell? What sets them apart?"

"Ah, it's in the way they talk. And you can tell it from their names, and what schools they went to." My name and accent gave people no clues whatsoever—which stirred their curiosity about my background.

Gradually, I started to pick up on the subtle and not-so-subtle ways in which Protestants and Catholics each reinforced their suspicion and resentment of the other. That's the way it was, in 1968. But it was one of the rides north from Drogheda that produced my saddest insight into the centuries-old web which had ensnared these charming people.

My lift-givers were two friendly young men. Cousins, they said. Their car was a very small and not very young Fiat, and we traveled at no great speed. They used the time to educate me in Irish history, which gave them scope to build vivid pictures using some very selective detail. I learned of the Drogheda rising, and of Dublin shootings and hangings.

Somewhere near Dundalk, at a curve in the road, the cousins pointed out the spot where, forty years before, They had lain in wait for Them, and shot Them down with machine guns, with all in the car killed. I've forgotten which side was They and which Them, but clearly remember the almost gleeful indignation of the two men.

As the miles reeled slowly by, the cousins filled in outlines of their own lives. Poor, unemployed, and disadvantaged. They were landless gypsies, in fact. This puzzled me, as they certainly did not look at all like Romany gypsies. They just looked Irish.

"Landless?" I said. "That's tough. What happened?"

"Our people were driven off the land!"

"By whom?"

"By Cromwell, that's who! Oliver Cromwell the destroyer!"

They dropped me a short distance from my hostel destination, and we said our farewells. I walked in peace; the mountains of Mourne across the lough, and gray stone walls lining the fields

---

My very first ride pulled over. The "Thank God" I muttered was quite apt, because a nun, polite, elderly, and grave, sat behind the wheel. Inexplicably I told her that I was Catholic.

Now, I'm what you would call a "lapsed Catholic." I went to parochial school and attended religious education classes; I have, however, no concrete recollection of anything I learned.

"And how are you finding the Liturgy here in Ireland?" she asked.

"Pardon?" I had, of course, heard her.

"The Liturgy," she repeated. "Do you find it much different in Ireland than it is in America?"

I'm proud to admit, that despite my spiritual and financial poverty, I did not attempt to bluff my way out. While I consider myself "lapsed," I am no devil and anyway, my ear-stretching experiences with Catholic-school nuns prohibits even lies of omission. I sheepishly admitted that I hadn't been to church… since I'd been in Ireland (O.K., so a teeny lie of omission).

—James Villers, Jr.,
"Connecting the Dots"

all around me. A great place, and fine people. But 300 years is a long time to keep bitterness alive and snapping.

A biologist by training and inquisitive by nature, David Blaker is based in New Zealand.

REX GRIZELL

✦ ✦ ✦

Long Ago in Ireland

*A journalist recalls covering a dispute
involving fairies.*

MY FIRST VISIT TO IRELAND TOOK PLACE A GOOD MANY YEARS
ago. Even at the time there was something of a dream in the whole
business, unfamiliar, outside normality, veering from the poetic to
the incredible, floating somewhere above the common ground of
everyday, touched with beauty. I was a staff writer on a magazine,
not long out of university, not much experienced, not much traveled, new at the job.

One morning the features editor called me into his office and
showed me a short paragraph which he had ringed in the morning's paper.

"Go and find out what that's about," he said, "and see what you
can make of it."

It was an item which reported that some workmen in a remote part of Mayo, itself a remote part of western Ireland, had
gone on strike because they believed the work they were doing
was interfering with the peace of the local fairies, and would
bring the whole community bad luck. In those days fairies were
invariably the gossamer-winged creatures often said to live at the
bottom of gardens.

"Makes a change from '153-year-old man found in isolated

mountain village,'" I said, which was the sort of story that desperate subeditors made up to fill awkward spaces, and put under fictional headings like "From our Hungarian correspondent" or "Kathmandu. Friday."

"No," he said. "It's right. Men don't give up paid work in those parts for fun, and I've checked."

So I went to Ireland and found myself in what, at that time was, and probably still is, and possibly always will be, another world. I hired a small car in Belfast and drove west via Enniskillen and Sligo. The farther I got from Belfast the more empty the roads became, and I bowled happily along in the summer sunshine. The only incident occurred on a narrow stretch of road somewhere in County Sligo. I had been admiring the beautiful contrasting scenery of lakes and glens and steep-sided hills and mountains, when I rounded a bend and, for the first and only time in my life, found the road completely blocked by a herd of baby donkeys. I remember them as being in various shades of gray, pink, and mauve, and not one over two feet tall.

There must have been a hundred of them, delightful creatures, but stubborn, I waited patiently while two ragged boys tried to persuade them to make room. No other car appeared from either direction and eventually I managed to squeeze past. No doubt they were on their way to be sold at some county fair, but I could not help wondering where they had come from. Were there such things as donkey farms and are there still?

In early afternoon, by way of a lonely road between the mountains and the sea, I came to Ballina, a pleasant little town at the estuary of the River Moy. From two stone bridges over the river, boys with homemade rods were fishing optimistically for salmon and trout, which frequently come in from Killala Bay. Otherwise, peace prevailed and there was no one about in what was said to be the best and busiest shopping center in County Mayo. It seemed like a town on the edge of the world to me, but I still had forty miles to go to my destination, Belmullet, on Blacksod Bay. The Mullet is a stony, wind- and rain-swept peninsula, barren and clean as an old skeleton, so exposed that almost nothing grows there. It is in all respects an island, except that it is connected to the main-land by a short neck of land, too insignificant to be described as an isthmus, but big enough to hold Belmullet, sometimes described as the loneliest town in Ireland, and one it seemed where they still believed in fairies.

I drove on towards the westering sun, in this wild and deserted land, Erris, between the mountains and the wide Atlantic Ocean. Belmullet, when I reached it, did nothing to dispel the feeling of being in another world. I found nothing familiar there, nothing English, nothing European, in retrospect a land that might have been designed by Tolkien for *The Lord of the Rings* and *The Hobbit*. Indeed, when I left Ireland I had become convinced that it was the most foreign country in Europe, and I still think so.

I had been given the name of the only hotel, something very Irish like O'Kelly's or Donnelly's, and I drove down the deserted main street in search of it. It was a plain two-story building. From the street you entered directly a room with a wooden floor and a bar counter. There was no one there and nobody came. At the end of the counter I found one of those brass bells that you hit with the palm of your hand for attention. I did so and the bell produced a small cloud of dust as if it had not been touched for years, and a surprisingly loud sound, which vibrated through the building. Nobody came.

After a long pause I went and stood in the doorway, and looked up and down the street. There was nobody in sight. Then I heard a distant, wailing sound, hardly human, which I could not iden-tify. As I wandered down the street, the sound became slightly louder, and from a corner not far from the hotel, I could see, about a quarter of a mile away, between the village and the sea, a long, slow procession of black-clad figures dragging slowly to-wards the cemetery. I had arrived in the middle of a funeral, with the whole village in attendance, and the unearthly sound was the keening of the women.

I drove round for a bit and found a virgin sweep of silver sands that might have been on some undiscovered South Seas island, and waited, contemplating the empty sea. I saw no boat, no ship, only the boundless blue ocean. On the beach a few tatters of dried sea-weed stirred in the wind. I dozed off in the June sunshine. In the evening I went back and got myself installed in the hotel.

In lonely places there are often people who for one reason or another cannot get away though they yearn for other things. Some of them wait in bars and cafés for the world to come to them. I met a young man like this in O'Kelly's bar that evening. He showed me round the "town." There were only a few recognizable shops in Belmullet, but there were quite a number of "shops" in front rooms of ordinary houses. All of them except the draper's and outfitter's had a bar somewhere and sold everything from Guinness to poteen. While leading me from one to the other, he told me about local life, including the strike. There were five men and a "granger" or foreman involved, and it was the biggest thing that had happened in Belmullet for years, perhaps ever, if you didn't count the day in 1794 when the French army came to help the Irish set up a republic, but they landed forty miles away in Ballina.

I had arrived in Belmullet on a Friday. On the Saturday morning there was something called a "horse fair" for which the tinkers came to town, and there were a few horses and donkeys and one or two cows about. Not all of them for sale, according to my bar friend, "they just bring them for the outing." The local pastimes of drinking and fighting were enjoyed, and when I got back to the hotel there was a good deal of excitement going on. The landlord, whom I had not met, had got into an argument with a Tinker who brought it to a sudden end by hitting the landlord on the head with an ancient starting handle of a car, which, according to the well-informed, he always carried in his belt and had been known to use before. The landlord had been taken away to the hospital with a suspected fractured skull, and the tinker had been taken away in custody.

On Sunday morning, clear and sunny, the village was wrapped in silence like a sunken ship. I managed to get a cup of tea from a sleepy girl in the kitchen of the hotel, and was told that the entire village would later attend Mass, no one would dare to be absent.

Not being of a religious turn of mind I did not dare to be present, so I went off exploring.

Eventually, I stopped at a point where there was a magnificent view across the sunlit, almost Homeric sea, to the mountains of Achill Island. It would have been no great surprise if on that deserted ocean Jason and his Argonauts had sailed into view, seeking an Irish Golden Fleece, but nothing disturbed the enchantment. I ate a cheese sandwich. Presently a solitary figure appeared trudging towards me up the hill, and I heard an occasional distant clank. As he approached I thought he might be a peddler or a tramp. He had a frying pan and a couple of saucepans hung from his neck and a leather bag, like an old school satchel, on a sling. He stopped to greet me, as they all do in those parts. I was as strange and unexpected to him as he was to me. It turned out that he was neither tramp nor peddler, but a

A gray stone abbey and cemetery stand on a lonely hill on Clare Island, which dominates the entrance to Clew Bay near Achill Island. It dates to the thirteenth century and is said to hold the former tomb of the legendary Granuaile, or Grace O'Malley, who is known as a queen, a warrior, and a woman of mythological powers who ruled over the area for much of the sixteenth century. Faded frescoes adorn the vaulted ceiling with images of Christian symbols but also of birds, dragons, griffins. What struggles for influence did these images symbolize, what quests for power? The wind whistled through the arches, clouds closed in and a light rain began to fall. Water ran down the abbey walls as it's done for centuries, seeping into the soil around the graves.

—Larry Habegger, "A Wayward Ramble through the Wild West"

poet. Another first, the only wandering poet I had ever met. He told me he walked all over the west of Ireland from Kerry to Donegal, from farm to farm, house to house, offering his poems for sale. Most, he said, were his own composition, but occasionally he would include an ancient lay. Sometimes he got a little money. But more often a farmer's wife would give him a meal, or some bread or potatoes to take away. Or he might be paid for some odd job he could do. He spoke the kind of graceful and picturesque English which is often a literal translation of the Gaelic, but the poems themselves were written in Gaelic. He took some from the leather bag to show me. They were neatly handwritten on good-quality paper. I apologized for not being able to read them but bought one as a souvenir, which pleased him greatly. I watched him into the distance. It had been like meeting a troubadour left over from the Middle Ages.

On Monday I went with my friend from the bar to meet the men on strike. The foreman was a big man with curly black hair and a red face, and he leaned slightly to one side all the time like a tree that has grown in a permanent wind. The problem was, he explained, that the fence they had been asked to put up would go straight through the middle of a "fairy fort."

What was actually happening was that a system of almost feudal land tenure by which different farmers held different strips of land, sometimes miles apart, was being simplified by government order, so that each farmer had more land in one place and could work it more efficiently with less waste of time. All had gone well until they reached this "fairy fort," and, naturally, they had downed tools at once.

"It's not that we are superstitious, you understand," the foreman explained to me, "but if we did that it would bring us bad luck."

"Oh," I said, remembering that this was Ireland. "What sort of bad luck?"

"Well, the cows could go dry. I might be tipped from my bike, like O'Rourke, and get me leg broke. There's no knowing what might befall. They've been here since before the time of the kings. I'll not displeasure them."

I did not know then, but found out later that what he was showing me was almost certainly a rough example of a "ring fort," a kind of primitive Iron Age dwelling, half-buried, with a subterranean room, all overgrown with grass, and of which there are hundreds scattered all over Ireland. This was explained to me by the local MP, himself a Mayo man, who arrived the following day.

"I'll soon have this settled," he told me. "I understand these people." So he did. On the day following his visit the men went back to work and erected the fence so that it made a neat detour round the "fairy fort" and then resumed the correct line. I took a photograph of this inimitably Irish solution, and another of the foreman and his men.

Everybody was happy, and the foreman, overcome with relief, as he happened to live closest to the offended fairies, invited me to lunch. I demurred, he insisted, and not wishing to seem discourteous, I accepted.

His house was a single-story whitewashed cottage with a thatched roof, a door and three small windows, one on one side of the door, two on the other. A no longer threatened cow, hitched to the end wall, meditated in the sunshine. The door led straight into a

---

There is an old belief in Ireland that the Tuatha Dé Dannan, the tribe of Celts banished from the surface of Ireland, now inhabit the underworld beneath the land. From there, they controlled the fecundity of the land above. Consequently, when a king was being crowned, he entered into a symbolic marriage with the goddess. His reign mediated between the visible landscape with its grass, crops, and trees and the hidden subterranean world in which all is rooted. The balance was vital since the Celts were a rural, farming people. This mythological and spiritual perspective has had an immense subconscious effect on how landscape is viewed in Ireland. Landscape is not matter nor merely nature, rather it enjoys a luminosity. Landscape is numinous. Each field has a different name, and in each place something different happened. Landscape has a secret and silent memory, a narrative of presence where nothing is ever lost or forgotten.

—John O'Donohue, *Anam Cara: A Book of Celtic Wisdom*

room containing a rough wooden table and two chairs. A peat fire was smoking in the hearth, and beside it a woman with a red shawl over her shoulders was sitting on a stool. There was a broom of twigs propped in a corner, and she looked like a witch planning her next ride on it. He said something to her in Gaelic, perhaps explaining who I was, but she said nothing, just nodded briefly towards me.

The table was covered with a newspaper, which I noticed was the *Irish Independent*, and the food, which consisted of large potatoes baked in their jackets and taken directly from the peat fire, was placed straight on it without benefit of plates. The woman gave me a knife and a large spoon and placed a bowl of butter, homemade, on the table before resuming her place on the stool. The foreman dug a hole in his potato and filled it full of butter, and I followed suit. With the butter well soaked in, I savored the potato. I don't know whether it was the edge of appetite acquired from the pure, salt air of the Atlantic which I had been breathing all that morning, or whether the fairies, relieved in their turn, had done a little magic, or whether it was the change from the diet of greasy mutton chops which was all O'Kelly's hotel offered at breakfast, lunch, and dinner, but it was a totally satisfying meal. The foreman and his wife exchanged occasional sentences in Gaelic. I don't know what I said to him or what he said to me, but I remember he beamed at me across the table, a happy man, at home, and on the right side of the fairies.

I left Belmullet behind like a dream, bearing with me along the lonely roads of Mayo, where fairies have their forts and ancient kings their tombs, some of the fanciful daze in which the inhabitants appeared to exist, and it took the width of Ireland to bring me back to a more ordinary but, perhaps, no more livable world.

When I had finished this text I showed it to an old Irish friend, now a distinguished psychiatrist in Dublin, who sometimes takes his holidays with us on our farm in France. When he had read it, he said nothing for a while, looking away into the orchard and far beyond.

"That was the Ireland of my youth," he said, at last. "But it's an Ireland long gone."

It seemed to me that there was a touch of regret in his voice.

Rex Grizell spent thirty years as a feature writer and executive on London's Fleet Street. He is the author of Auvergne and the Massif Central *and* A White House in Gascony: Escape to the Old French South. *He lives with his French wife on a farm in Gascony.*

ROSEMARY MAHONEY

The True Face

The author introduces us to some very
interesting denizens of Dublin.

THE CITY OF DUBLIN IS CROWDED WITH CHURCHES. AT THE TURN
of the hour, church bells ring out from every direction, their various tones crossing and colliding, confusing the listener. Some begin a minute too early, some a minute too late, rendering the ringing interminable and the hour unclear.

During the six months I spent in Dublin, I lived in a one-room apartment in a converted Georgian house on Waterloo Road. The apartment was like a waiting room in a dentist's office, a dissolute dentist who had few patients and no assistant to help him. The ceiling was cracked, and the walls, graced with billowing brown and yellow water stains, looked like a nautical chart. My furniture was an armoire, a lamp, and a couch that folded out into a bed. The mattress was the thickness of a paperback novel and had molded itself to the narrow shape of the person who lived there before me. The wall-to-wall carpet—roughly the color of brains—was frayed and worn. The best thing about the place was its proximity to three neighborhood churches, the sound of whose bells drifted through my window each morning, wakening me and reminding me again of the importance of religion in Ireland.

Religion was as pervasive as the currency. It was everywhere. It was embedded deep in the Irish mind, and that seemed most evident in the way Irish people blessed themselves as they passed by a church; an instinctual flutter of the right hand as they studied the headlines of the newspaper they had just bought, or scolded a disobedient child, or made a conversational point to a companion. Sometimes just the fingers moved, twitching above the sternum or passing absently over the face in a barely perceptible wiping motion. Riding in a Dublin bus, I was often gripped by an eerie disorientation at the moment the bus passed by a church (a church I was never quick enough to notice), and I glimpsed, in the periphery of my vision, thirty hands flying into the air in similar fashion. On the streets teenagers' hands leapt reflexively at the sight of a church and then, driven by embarrassment, the hands would inevitably detour to the hair and pat it down, or to an eye to remove a nonexistent cinder. Young people didn't want to be seen to be religious or to be identified with the lack of sophistication that religion had come to signify, but they were unable to rid themselves of the habit. Even red-faced schoolboys could not help raising a hand and passing it absently across their noses as they ran by a church hurling curses at each other. The gesture was as ingrained and superstitious as the national pause for the Angelus.

One of Dublin's distinctions is that it is the birthplace of the Legion of Mary, an international Catholic organization of great power and influence that grew out of a small, informal meeting on Francis Street in 1921. I had heard of the Legion long before I ever set foot in Ireland, had seen it in operation in the United States and in China, but I knew little about its purpose, and it wasn't until I began seeing regular notices in the *Irish Times* about Legion meetings that I took an interest. The notices always said: "'The Legion of Mary presents the true face of the Catholic Church,' Pope John XXIII."

The idea of the "true face" interested me, for at times it seemed difficult to know what the true face of the Church was amid its many politically motivated distortions. The notices listed the various places Legion meetings were held each week, including Myra House at 100 Francis Street. This was the address at which Frank Duff had started the Legion of Mary seventy years before, so I chose to attend that meeting, although on any given night I could have attended five others in the city.

As I walked across the city to Francis Street the next Monday evening, I passed a young girl playing a tin whistle on O'Connell Bridge. The girl was skinny and long-limbed, with red lips, a pretty face, and scraggly black hair that hung to her waist. She seemed oblivious to the five o'clock crush of pedestrians that jostled her from all sides. She held the whistle to her lips and blew violently into it. The whistle squealed out three wild notes, and the girl responded with a little jig of delight. She twirled in place with one leg held up in the air. In one swift motion she spun around and gave a nearby drunk a spontaneous thump in the rear end with her sneakered foot. She howled with laughter at that, pleased by her own unpredictability. She spun again, hair swirling gracefully around her shoulders like the ribbons of a maypole, eyes ablaze with excitement. She hopped, turned, and panted into the whistle, and then, caught up in the momentum of her own soaring spirit, she wound up and flung the whistle into the Liffey. The whistle rocketed high into the pale evening air and came down,

> The moment of the Angelus is, to me, the most touching and the most beautiful in an Irish day. At first a stranger is unaware of the bell. He may be riding in a Dublin tram-car. Suddenly there is a movement. Men and women are making the sign of the cross. Or in a crowded street the man you are talking to becomes silent and lifts his hat. But it is in the lanes and the country towns of Ireland that the Angelus is most beautiful. I do not care how bigoted and anti-Catholic a man may be, how sincerely he believes that all priests are rogues who batten on the superstition of the ignorant, he must, if there is a spark of reverence in him or any feeling for beauty, bare his head at this time and offer up his prayer.
>
> —H. V. Morton, *In Search of Ireland* (1930)

piercing its way into the river, tip first and without a splash. The girl clapped her dirty hands over her mouth. Little bubbles—remnants of her own breath—rose to the surface as the whistle sank to the bottom. Slowly the girl's hands descended to her sides, and her good cheer dwindled visibly as she realized that her whistle was gone for good.

Francis Street, in the old section of Dublin, was a narrow lane of ancient, empty, or burned-out shop fronts, of antique furniture stores and junk shops packed to the ceiling with every imaginable article made from brass. The buildings here were low and old with big windows. I wandered up the gently sloping street, and as I passed one shop I noticed, out of the corner of my eye, scores of photographs of naked people taped in the window. I stopped to look more closely. The photographs, clipped from a Swedish magazine, were not pornographic, but looked more like they had come from the newsletter of some nudist colony. There were shots of women plunging into the ocean, a man and woman walking happily hand in hand along the shore, two young girls with breasts the size of limes playing in the surf—all of them displaying the gawky, hairy, lumpy nudity of real people. It was precisely these physical imperfections never evident in the models that made the photographs seem seedy.

I walked on past several expensive restaurants. A menu propped up in one window announced smoked salmon and medallions of veal at nineteen pounds, money no resident of this neighborhood could possibly spare for a meal. These restaurants, I soon realized, were for patrons of the theater at the top of the street where the old and the new, the affluent and the destitute, the holy and the lewd mixed without friction or conflict.

The Legion's Myra House was a small stucco structure not far from the theater. I sat on one of three empty beer kegs standing in the doorway of the house and waited to see who would arrive for the meeting. The street was empty. I watched the sky. No matter where the sun hung, Dublin's light always seemed to be approaching from a sharp angle, lighting the clouds from the side and lending them great depth of color—orange, purple, and crimson against a field of blue. That evening golden clouds flew in from the west, massing against each other like frightened sheep. At the top of the street I could see the sober spire of Christ Church, and beyond the bottom of the street, toward the south, the green humps of the Dublin Mountains were crowned in bloated clouds. Across the street in a vacant lot an abandoned couch lay sodden and gutted amid the rubbish, tall weeds sprouting from its cushions like hair.

A car pulled up in front of Myra House, and three men climbed out of it, one of them a priest. As he stepped onto the curb, the man who had been sitting in the front passenger seat said happily and loudly to the priest, who had been sitting behind him, "Now I will finally have a chance to look at your face, and you can see mine!"

The priest and the driver said nothing; they seemed not to have heard this happy man, or perhaps they were merely tolerating him. The man had an enormous head. A pair of tortoiseshell eyeglasses dominated his big face. On his feet he wore huge leather basketball shoes. I thought I had heard a trace of Poland in his accent. All three men were elderly, and age had rendered the priest unsteady on his feet. With a large skeleton key the driver let them into the house.

I sat on my keg and waited to see who else would arrive. A moment or two later a fat man in a green polo shirt showed up with a similar skeleton key and a bag of groceries. After him came a man on a bicycle, also with a key. I asked this man if the Legion meeting was open to anyone, and he stared at me. "Well, if you're really interested," he said finally, "of course, you're welcome." But from the way he stared, I could see he was skeptical. Nevertheless, in true missionary fashion he could not refuse me. He smiled nervously. His teeth were a dull matte white, as though the enamel had been filed off them.

I followed him into the house and up some dark stairs to a small room on the third floor, where five men were sitting around a table covered in a cloth that had *Legio Mariae* embroidered in it in red Gothic script. There was a statue of the Blessed Virgin in the center of the table flanked by two vases of flowers and two candles.

Except for the fading sunlight faintly reflected in the eastern sky, the candles were the only source of light here; the corners of the room were veiled in great nets of shadow.

The men looked astonished to see me come into the room on the heels of the bicyclist. They sat gaping for a moment, then politely stood up to introduce themselves. They were Tim Donovan (the driver), Ira Weizmann (the happy man), Aidan Murphy (the man on the bike), Padraig Pearse ("no relation to the martyr"), and Canon Leary (the priest). The fat man in the green shirt introduced himself simply as Bobby. He did not stand up but remained importantly in his seat at the head of the table with his groceries safely by his feet. I guessed correctly that Bobby was the chairman. He was smooth as a porpoise. His black hair, oiled and slicked back, was just beginning to gray over the ears. His gold wedding band was tight on his pudgy finger, and his fat face glistened like porcelain in the candlelight.

I sat in a chair, and Bobby began to speak. He welcomed Ira Weizmann and me as the two newcomers to the meeting. He had a strong Dublin accent, but there was something else in his speech, remnants of another language that had settled in the gutters of his mouth. It sounded faintly like French. "And now we shall say the Rosary," he said, and they all scraped back their chairs and knelt on the floor. Ira Weizmann, looking bored already, watched the men drop to their knees. He stayed seated, conducting a private debate in his mind, then moved to kneel with a great grunting effort, leaning heavily on the table, causing the statue and the candles to teeter. I knelt with them, and we said the Rosary—the five men, the priest, and me in this dark little room. I felt awkward and hot. The candlelight gave the meeting an intimate, cultlike intensity that made me uneasy. I had expected a large meeting where I would be able to hide at the back of the room. I didn't want to have to talk or explain myself or say the Rosary. I heard myself muttering, "Blessed is the fruit of thy womb..." and was thankful that saying the Rosary, like riding a bicycle or skipping rope, is one of those things that once learned is never forgotten. I prayed mechanically, furtively trying to watch the men. Tim Donovan had given Ira Weizmann a child's string of bright red plastic Rosary beads, which dangled prettily over his hairy hand as he said the Our Father. The priest leaned against the table with his narrow forehead pressed into the palm of one hand and the other hand counting his beads. Fine red veins fanned across his nose and cheeks; his lipless mouth was like a mail slot.

Ira Weizmann's eyes roved—like me, he was more interested in studying his companions than in praying. He seemed to be comparing Padraig Pearse, Tim Donovan, and Aidan Murphy, and that made sense, for the three men looked remarkably interchangeable; they had the same slight physique, the same freckled coloring, sharp features, reticence, and stodgy clothing. They were like triplets. It occurred to me that the deeply religious often share a similar stubborn lack of interest in fashion.

Bobby, the pudgy chairman, was different. He had short fingers and very thick red lips, and when my mind began to wander I found myself picturing him raising a forkful of food to his mouth.

As the Rosary came to an end, a middle-aged woman came hurrying into the room. The men said, "Welcome, Sister Keating," and the meeting began in earnest. These people addressed each other as Brother and Sister, though all but Canon Leary were lay members of the Church. Their relationships to one another had obviously solidified long ago. They had a stilted, formal way of relating, and they played their parts in the meeting strictly according to Legion rules. They met to discuss the Legion's efforts—through Social Services and Catholic Action—in their community that week, and they took turns giving presentations and reports. They used words like *praesidium, tessera, concilium, archconfraternity*, and *mediatrix*. They seemed to be following a script, and for a group whose stated mission was to make God loved in His world, a group who saw themselves as a soul-saving army devoted to "crushing the head of the serpent and advancing the reign of Christ," they seemed surprisingly uncomfortable with newcomers. I felt keenly that Ira Weizmann and I were intruding.

Brother Murphy read the minutes of the last meeting. In them were mentioned several visits Legion members had made to the elderly, the sick, and the incarcerated. There was financial business, and the minutes of the Pillar of Fire meeting, a small branch of the Legion dedicated to fostering better understanding between Catholics and Jews.

At the Pillar of Fire meeting a Mrs. Greenberg of the Jewish community had given a presentation on the Holocaust. Brother Donovan read the extensive minutes of that meeting in a monotonous halting voice that began to lull his fellow Legionaries to sleep. Brother Pearse's head tilted onto his right shoulder, and his blue-veined eyelids drooped heavily. Brother Donovan read, "Mr. Nyack, Mr. Weizmann, and Mrs. Tolkin were in attendance.

> One of the regular sights as you drive around Ireland are the roadside grottos with statues of the Blessed Mother. The wayside shrines come in many sizes and shapes (Our Lady of Lourdes seems particularly represented). It is a delight to see fresh flowers or stumble, as I did, on a traffic hold-up, not due to a herd of sheep, but a flock of faithful attending a roadside Mass at their local shrine.
> —Frank O'Reilly, "Across the Generations"

Mrs. Greenberg ran out of the house without the speech she had prepared and realized that instead she had grabbed the rough notes, so her speech was not what it could have been. She talked about the Holocaust…"

Ira Weizmann said suddenly, "May I say one thing about Mrs. Greenberg?" All the heads at the table snapped up, startled by the sound of his loud voice. "Mrs. Greenberg is a great lady and she did an excellent job, but just one thing she got wrong—and I know this from a personal fact—she said the Italians were no good, but I actually know that the Italians took many Jews in and saved them, so Mrs. Greenberg was wrong about the Italians."

Everyone stared politely at Ira Weizmann. It was clearly not protocol for members of the Legion to venture into reminiscences or personal opinion; Ira was confusing the order and demeanor of the meeting. But Ira himself seemed not to notice the disruption.

He made a fist of his big hand and placed it on the table to help further his point. The little red Rosary beads still tangled in his fingers looked edible, like strung cranberries wound around a Christmas tree. Through the window I saw that the light in the sky had faded to a bruised purple, and the room was entirely at the mercy of the two candles. Ira's big face shone. He took a hanky out of his pocket and mopped his brow.

"Only 5,000 Jews died in Italy," he said. The volume of his voice covered the sadness in it. "Now, I know Mrs. Greenberg was in Bergen-Belsen, but I had my own personal tragedy. I lost two sisters and two brothers in the gas chamber. And the reason why I became a Catholic, which I am very proud of, was the element of forgiveness in the Catholic Church. I told the father that if he could prove to me that I could become a forgiving person with the help of his forgiving God, I would become a Catholic."

Ira's revelation was followed by what seemed like a remarkably stingy silence. No one responded. Instead they looked away and resumed the proceedings, as though Ira Weizmann had said nothing at all. Brother Padraig Pearse displayed a plastic bag full of lapel pins he had brought along for distribution throughout the community. Ira took one of the pins and held it up to the candlelight. "What the heck is it?" he said.

"It's the Pioneers," Brother Pearse said; his voice was a tiny lilting peep after Ira's. "You wear it on your coat to show that you practice total abstention from alcohol."

Ira let his hands fall heavily to his lap. He turned and looked affably at Brother Donovan. His big eyeglasses were like a mask on his face; their lenses glinted in the candlelight. "May I say this, Mister? I don't drink and I don't smoke, but I would never wear a pin in my coat about it. Sometimes in the night I get up and make myself a cup of tea—I am an old man now—and I put a drop of whiskey in it. But I don't drink. I had enough problems with people drinking in my family."

I could see the group wondering what to say to this man. His frankness was startling and his self-confidence surprising, even enviable, but the Legionaries clearly had little skill at fostering the exchange of ideas. As the evening progressed I realized that it was not unfriendliness that made them reticent, it was shyness and a complete lack of self-confidence. Though he had professed his fealty to the Catholic Church, and though he had lived in Dublin for years, Ira Weizmann was still alien and therefore an inhibiting presence. I marveled that the Legion of Mary had managed to take root on every continent of the world, that with such markedly uncharismatic foundation as this it had found its way out of Dublin at all.

The members moved on to reports on various people who aspired to be Legion members. Brother Murphy said he had talked to an aspirant recently who seemed to be speaking against the bishops and cardinals. This man also seemed to be worshiping a false god in Assisi and had even said that the pope sometimes made mistakes. "They say he's doing good work," Murphy said, "but he just doesn't seem like a candidate for membership."

Bobby invited Ira Weizmann and me to work for the Legion the following week, and I could see this was something we would be expected to do if we hoped to become members. Bobby asked me to work at the Children's Praesidium, a Catholic Education class for young girls. He asked Ira if he would be willing to talk with the men in the Jewish retirement home and bring them information about the Legion. Ira held onto his eyeglasses with both hands and tilted them slightly, the better to see Bobby. "Bobby," he said, "let me just say I'll be perfectly happy to talk to anybody. But since I converted, the Jews don't like me. My sister hasn't spoken to me in forty years. So if you think the Jews in the Jewish home are going to listen to a convert telling them about Catholics, I don't know. I think it won't work." He mugged a face of indifference and shrugged and threw up his hands as if to say, *But it's your club; you decide.*

Canon Leary cleared his throat and spoke for the first time. "Simon Wiesenthal said the Jews missed a great opportunity when they forgot to mention the 5 million non-Jewish people who were also killed in the Holocaust, that people are tired of hearing the Jews complain, and that if the Jews had co-opted all the other dead souls, they wouldn't be so unpopular with their message today. I think Wiesenthal might be right. Someone once asked where God was when the Jews were being murdered. But the real question is, Where was man?"

All the Legionaries turned and looked at Canon Leary as though God Himself had come into the room. Leary opened the Legion handbook and read this pitying view of the Jews: "St. Michael remains the loyal defender of the Church, but his guardianship of the Jews did not lapse because they turned away. Rather it was intensified because of their need. The Legion serves under Michael. Under his inspiration doctrinal position has been so undermined by the passage of time. According to the Book of Daniel and all the other prophecies the time for the coming of the Messiah is long since expired. The Temple is destroyed and their Sacrifice has ceased, never to be restored. What, then, is the meaning of their depleted worship, and what divine message has the Old Testament for them today?"

When Canon Leary had finished reading, Ira Weizmann blurted, "No kidding! I say that all the time! I agree with that, Father, but I'm telling you I would have one heck of a time making them folks in the home listen to me. They'd roll over in their grave just seeing Ira Weizmann walk through the door!"

I had told Bobby that I would work for two hours at the Children's Praesidium, chiefly because I was curious as to what the Legion was teaching children. The following week I returned to Myra House to fulfill my duty. This time a tiny boy holding a long pool cue opened the door for me. He had a square red crew cut and a square freckled face. "Lookin' for S'ta Keatin', is it?" he cried.

"Yes, I am," I said.

"Grand! Come wit' me den!"

The boy led me up the stairs past a room where Bobby the chairman was leading a lot of young boys in a game of snooker. Through the door I could see Bobby laboriously tipping his big body over the pool table to make a shot.

Sister Keating was in the Legion room chatting with a young priest. She nodded as I came into the room and continued talking.

I listened but failed to follow what she was saying, for she spoke too fast. She was a small woman with a round face, two shining little eyes. And a slight underbite that gave her a disgruntled, faintly canine expression.

Sister Keating left the priest little opportunity to speak, and when finally he left the room she turned to me and put her little face up to mine and began talking at me in the same rapid-fire way. Her breath smelled odd though not unpleasant; it was damp and milky, like curds. She explained that she and I would be giving the children a few religious lessons, that they were rough girls, most of whom came from broken homes, and that they were often "very wicked." She said, "It's never guaranteed that they'll come. One week they're here and the next they're not because their mother wants them to mind the baby for her so she can go out to the pub. And sure, aren't they babies themselves?"

The girls began showing up in twos and threes. They banged through the door and flung their book bags into a corner of the room. They were little and breathless. They wore tin rings on every finger, and their hands and wide, gypsyish faces were shot with copper freckles. Most were dressed in brightly colored nylon running suits. They chewed big wads of bubble gum and stared at me. They had huge green eyes and flaming red ponytails that sprang out of the sides of

> You are Irish you say lightly, and allocated to you are the tendencies to be wild, wanton, drunk, superstitious, unreliable, backward, toadying, and prone to fits, whereas you know that in fact a whole entourage of ghosts resides in you, ghosts with whom the inner rapport is as frequent, as perplexing, as defiant as with any of the living.
> —Edna O'Brien, *Mother Ireland*

their heads like water from an open hydrant. They were irresistible, and I was pleased and surprised when the red-lipped, whistle-playing girl I had seen the week before on O'Connell Bridge blew into the room with her wild black hair streaming out behind her.

The girls inched up to me. One of them whispered, "She's posh lookin'," and the others murmured their assent. They spoke with the dirtiest street accent I had heard in Dublin. They found a way to stretch monosyllabic words into two syllables, sometimes three. They said "ho-wum" for home, "wa-rum" for warm, and for mushroom they said "mush-a-roo-um."

The girl from the bridge elbowed her way to the front of the crowd. Her name was Jane. She pointed at me and said, "S'ta Keatin'? What's she to you?"

"She is nothing to me, Jane," Sister Keating said in an admonishing, correcting tone that stayed with her for the rest of the afternoon.

"She is a Legionary and she is going to be working with us. She is called Sister Rose O'Mahony."

Jane looked disgusted. "A person like yourself isn't after joining out the Legion, are you O'Mahony?" she demanded.

"Not yet," I said.

At the sound of my voice another girl said, *"Lads, did ye hear her?! She's American!"*

Sister Keating brought the meeting to order, and the girls sat in folding chairs arranged in a semicircle. Their knees were bony, and their feet barely reached the floor. Sister Keating prepared the girls for prayer by asking, "Why do we say the Hail Mary, girls?"

With insurrection in her voice a pie-faced girl shrieked, "Dunno, S'ta Keatin'!" and the others tittered wickedly. Sister Keating was unfazed. "Why do we say the Hail Mary, Jane?"

Jane couldn't have been more than nine; on the bridge she had looked older. She had a sardonic sense of humor and the deep, smoky voice of a barmaid. Watching me, but speaking to Sister Keating, she said unctuously, "We say the Hail Mary, S'ta Keatin', to honor Mary, Mother of God!"

The girls began reciting a slovenly rendition of the Hail Mary. They made it sound taunting and lewd, like a jeering chant from an angry crowd at a football game. *Blast art'ou 'mongst wam 'n' blast's da fruit...* Their faces were twisted into postures of sarcasm and mirth, and I could see I wasn't the person for this job; I wouldn't be able to keep from taking their side. I would find it difficult to ally myself with Sister Keating and her stern admonishments. Just as I was thinking how much I wanted a piece of their bubble gum, Sister Keating shouted at them to spit the chewing gum into the bin. Jane, the ringleader, cried with brilliant mimicry, "Girls! Put da choongum out in da bin!" and the girls ran over to the tin wastebasket and shot the gum out of their mouths with such expert force it pinged like bullets against the metal.

Sister Keating said, "Before we begin, I want to get to the bottom of who took the key out of the door lock last week. There was a key in the door and one of you took it. I want the culprit to confess to me immediately. Vicki Corrigan, was it you?"

Vicki, a skinny girl in a torn sweatshirt, held her hands up defensively and said, "Wasn't near that key, S'ta Keatin'!" Then her face crumpled and she began to cry.

A scrappy eight-year old sitting beside me sneered, "Vicki! 'f ya croy it means yar guilty, so for Chrissake don't croy!"

Sister Keating frowned at the girl. "We must never take the name of the Lord in vain, Roisin."

"Oh, right, S'ta Keatin'," Roisin said. "It slipped me mind. I won't never do it again." Roisin batted her bangs out of her eyes and grinned fatuously at Sister Keating. She could not have cared less about the name of the Lord.

Vicki, the guilty party, pulled the sleeves of her running suit over her little hands and pressed them to her damp eyes.

Saucer-eyed with false innocence, Jane said, "Either will I ever again take the Lord in vain, S'ta Keatin'."

Marie suppressed a grin. "Right, S'ta Keatin'," she said, "neither will I."

It was a highly skilled act. They heaped scorn upon Sister Keating by pretending to be the obedient girls she expected them to be. They hammed it up and winked at each other over the simple way they could mock and fool her.

Sister Keating read aloud for us the story of the fishes and the loaves, then asked a girl on my right to repeat the story. The girl

sat silent for a long time, plucking at her lips, then turned plead-
ingly to me. "Rose," she whispered, "could ya ever gimmee the
start at least?"

With all my heart I wanted to give her the start, but I shook my
head, no.

Jane jumped out of her chair. "I can tell your damn story,"
she said.

"Jane, in the Legion we do not say words like damn."

"Course we don't, S'ta Keatin'. It slipped me mind, like. Well,
anyway, once upon a time there was these 5,000 people and they
was all layin' on the ground."

That the people were lying on the ground was a curious detail
not included in the original story. Sister Keating, pleased that Jane
was responding, asked, "And why were the people there, Jane?"

"Lissenin' to Jaysus. And they was starved with the hunger. And
there was this little young fella there, and he had five fishes and two
loafs, and says Jaysus to the little young fella, 'Will we eat the fishes
'n' loafs, Bucky?' and the little young fella says 'Right enough, Jays,
we will.' And they ate till they was burstin'. Then they had a look
at the leftovers and there was twelve loafs now and twelve new
fishes, and Jays says to the little young fella, 'Mind if I have the leftovers, then?' and the little young fella says, ''Tis all the same to me,
Jays,' and Jaysus fed all the 5,000 in the crowd wid' 'em."

Sister Keating said, "And what do we call that, Jane?"

"Dunno, S'ta Keatin'."

"You do know, Jane. Try to remember."

Jane wiggled a loose tooth in her mouth. "Picnic, S'ta Keatin'?"

"Not a picnic, Jane."

Jane wiped her fingers on her shirtfront. "Oh, yeah. Not a picnic. What then, S'ta Keatin'?"

"A miracle."

"Oh, yeah. A miracle."

"And what is a miracle, Jane?"

"Something that happens and you don't know why, S'ta
Keatin'."

"And who knows what holy day Friday is?"

"Frank Duff's birthday!" Siobhan shouted wildly.

"Frank Duff's birthday is not a holy day," Sister Keating said. She went on to read us the story of Martha and Mary, and as she read I felt an arm slide gently around my shoulders and across the back of my neck. It was Una Hennessy, the little girl sitting beside me. She put her knee on my thigh and her mouth up to my ear. "Rose," she whispered, "I'm five years old." *Oy'm foive yeeyars owe-uld.* She brought her face quickly around and positioned it in front of mine to catch my reaction. She was beautiful. She had bangs as black as anthracite, a perfectly round face, and enormous black eyes. On one her cheeks a nasty circular burn was beginning to heal. My arm slipped automatically around her tiny waist. "I believe you," I said.

Una's mouth came down over my ear again; it had the muffled echo of a nautilus shell, the same hiss that mimicked the sea. "H'wold're ya?" she said.

"Thirty," I whispered.

"Hah?"

"Thirty."

The girl's hand was hot on the back of my neck, and her mouth was moist against my ear. "What'd ya say?"

"I said thirty."

I could hear Sister Keating speedily reading, "Lord, don't you care that my sister has left me to do the work by myself? Tell her to help me!"

"Rose! I'm askin' ya how old are ya?"

"I'm thirty, Una," I said.

Una brought her face around to look at mine again. She was utterly puzzled. Abandoning all pretense at a whisper, she screeched, "What are ya sayin' to me, Rose?"

Karen, two seats away, saw the problem. "She said she's *torty*, Una. Are ya feckin' deaf?"

"Torty!" Una exclaimed. "Shite! Older dan me mudder."

Sister Keating put down her book and took Karen and Una out of the room for a disciplinary chat. She asked me to mind the remaining seven girls. On her way out the door, Sister Keating said,

"And when I come back I want to hear everyone recite Joseph Mary Plunkett's poem."

As the door shut behind Sister Keating, Jane gave her the finger. I did my best to appear to disapprove of Jane's gesture. Jane pulled a lock of her long hair across her mouth and sucked on it. "Keatin's a nasty old hoor!"

"She is not," I said. "She cares about you."

Jane made a face, a dog's face, that replicated Sister Keating's with eerie precision. "Why do we say do Hayill Meery, girls!" she jeered.

I couldn't argue with that; I didn't have an answer myself.

The girls were delighted that Sister Keating was gone. They pulled their chairs up so close to mine that our knees were touching and they stared expectantly at me. I was in charge. But I had no idea what to do. I taught them a secret handshake. A hush fell over them as they watched my demonstration. Their mouths sagged open, and I saw in those moments how they must have looked in sleep: pretty and innocent and defenseless. They weren't sure whether they should be evil or good, obstructive or obedient. They didn't know their birthdays, and some of the younger ones didn't know their own last names. I tested the handshake on all of them, and then we took turns reading a catalogue of the various miracles. We practiced our Irish, played guess-the-saints, talked about confirmation, confession, and what a holy day of obligation is. We talked about the Eucharist. They loved the taste of it. "It's brilliant," said one girl. "I love it too," said Marie, and immediately the other girls reminded her that she was too young to have made her first communion, therefore she could not possibly know what the Eucharist tasted like.

I asked them to tell me about Joseph Mary Plunkett, the poet and patriot whose poem Sister Keating wanted them to recite. Kerry Spenser leaned forward in her chair. "Y'see, Rose, he wrote a poem. It goes like this, 'I seen his blood upon da leaf.'"

Roisin gave Kerry a peremptory blow in the chest. "Not *leaf,* stupid! 'Tis rose. I seen his blood upon da *rose!*"

Marie, preoccupied with the effort of peeling the paper jacket from a crayon, murmured feverishly at her hands, "Oy seen his blood upon da rose and in da stars da glory of his oys his body gleams amid etairnal snows his tears fallin' down from da skoys oy seen his face in every flower da toonder and da singin' a da boards an' oy duno da rest a da fookin' pome and how come they called him Mary?"

The Angelus rang out from a church nearby, and the girls faced the statue of the Blessed Virgin and rushed through a prayer. Instead of praying, Jane spun cartwheels across the room, the heels of her sneakers flying past the face of the Virgin. Roisin went to the window and looked out at the couch in the lot across the street. I heard her saying to herself, "'Tis creepy." Margaret, a girl obsessed with her new bra, got up and proved to us all that she could extinguish the candles with her bare fingers. Vicki went one better than Margaret and lit some matches and put them out by holding them half an inch from her gaping mouth and huffing at them. I heard one of the matches sizzle against her wet lip, and then I told everyone to stop fooling around. They heard the order in my voice and looked at me, waiting to see whether this was a joke. Marie put her hand on my thigh and said sweetly, "Rose, are ya playin' at S'ta Keatin'? Is that it?"

Sister Keating returned just in time to hear Jane shout, "Vicki's shirt is sexy."

Sister Keating chastised her. "Don't be saying dirty words, Jane, or other words you don't know the meaning of. It's not nice. It's wrong. If you don't understand a word, go home and ask your mother what it means and is it all right to say."

Jane said bitterly, "Me moodah's dead, S'ta Keatin'."

All the girls looked at Jane with renewed respect.

Karen said, "If I went home and asked my mother what 'sexy' means, she'd slap my face, S'ta Keatin'."

Sister Keating looked at me almost apologetically, obviously unable to control these girls. "They are seeing things and hearing things they shouldn't be seeing," she said. "They know more than they should about the world."

Rosemary Mahoney is the author of The Early Arrival of Dreams, The Singular Pilgrim: Travels on Sacred Ground, *and the memoir* A Likely Story. *This story was excerpted from her book,* Whoredom in Kimmage: Irish Women Coming of Age. *She lives in New York City.*

PAMELA RAMSEY

✶ ✶ ✶

A Pub Fairy Tale

*Perfect moments rarely give
you any warning.*

I COULD FEEL THE EXCITEMENT IN THE AIR AS I SAT PERCHED ON a wobbly wooden bench at the back of the bar, to listen to the music and watch the evening unfold. The atmosphere was electric, pulsating, like a rock concert when everyone is waiting for the warm-up band to begin. Only this wasn't a rock concert, it was an Irish pub filled with old people. But these old folks were wired, and waiting in anticipation for the party, the night music, the dancing to begin. The minute the concertina and fiddle players hit their first notes, the floor was crammed with dancers gyrating in a strange jerky up-and-down motion, dancing an Irish folk dance, a jig.

One gentleman must have been at least eighty. Pale rheumy eyes sparkled out from a face so wrinkled it looked like it belonged on the cover of *National Geographic*—an ancient Indian portrait shriveled by the Southwest sun. A classy blue suit and bright gold tie perfectly fit his small wiry body. And he wore a beret, a black beret situated jauntily on the side of his head.

He was an amazing dancer, dancing every single dance, never seeming to tire, never breaking a sweat. Even between dances, his feet continued to shuffle, a rhythmic kick thrown in periodically to match the beat of his arthritic-gnarled fingers tapping his thigh.

People were curious and friendly towards me—stopping by my bench to ask where I was from, where I was headed, and generously buying me rounds of the room-temperature, lime-flavored ale I was drinking. I wanted to dance. At home, I would have gathered up my moxie and asked someone to dance with me or maybe even danced alone. But I wasn't sure of the rules here, and didn't want to act inappropriately, or offend anyone. Each time someone approached, my heartbeat rose hopefully, and I waited for an invitation to dance. It didn't come.

A few minutes before eleven o'clock closing time, the musician announced the last song of the night. The lovely old man with the pale rheumy eyes walked straight over to me and in a thick brogue asked if I would do him the honor of joining him on the dance floor. I was so surprised, so flustered, I fell all over myself with excuses. I didn't know how. I couldn't possibly. He should ask someone else. I had desperately wanted to dance all evening, but now the idea of exposing myself out on the dance floor terrified me. The old man just smiled and pulled me to my feet.

> The old, dimly lit bars in which, over a pint of Guinness, one ruminated on the meaning of a life are still a dominant feature of rural Ireland, but in Dublin and Cork and Galway the newer drinking establishments make you think you're in such chic European capitals as Paris or Rome or Copenhagen.
>
> —John Boland, "Irish Ironies"

For the first few minutes, I trampled all over his toes. And since I was at least a head taller than he, I felt like a big, awkward, graceless goose. I could feel my face flood with blood and turn beet red. I was back in junior high school.

Thankfully, he kept his steps simple and danced an odd two-step rather than the complicated jig he'd shown off all night. Soon, I was following his lead and relaxing into the rhythm of the music.

I could feel the other dancers watching us, nodding, laughing, giving us encouragement, but the old man and I had eyes only for each other. We were two odd strangers caught in a moment of tenderness. A moment of magic. I was Cinderella, the belle of the ball, dancing with my Prince—an old, almost-blind man wearing a black beret.

Pamela Ramsey lives in Manitou Springs, Colorado, with her husband, two children, and a tortoiseshell cat named Peaches. She is a part-time librarian and writer. This story is excerpted from a book she recently completed, Lightning Bugs and Vagabonds, *about her experiences hitchhiking through Europe.*

FRANK McCOURT

* * *

Holy Communion

The author embarks on a remarkable
rite of passage.

THE DAY BEFORE FIRST COMMUNION THE MASTER LEADS US TO
St. Joseph's Church for First Confession. We march in pairs, and if
we so much as move a lip on the streets of Limerick he'll kill us
on the spot and send us to hell bloated with sin. That doesn't stop
the bragging about the big sins. Willie Harold is whispering about
his big sin, that he looked at his sister's naked body. Paddy Hartigan
says he stole ten shillings from his aunt's purse and made himself
sick with ice cream and chips. Question Quigley says he ran away
from home and spent half the night in a ditch with four goats. I
try to tell them about Cuchulain and Emer, but the master catches
me talking and gives me a thump on the head.

We kneel in the pews by the confession box, and I wonder if
my Emer sin is as bad as looking at your sister's naked body because I know now that some things in the world are worse than
others. That's why they have different sins, the sacrilege, the mortal sin, the venial sin. Then the masters and grown-up people in
general talk about the unforgivable sin, which is a great mystery.
No one knows what it is, and you wonder how you can know if
you've committed it if you don't know what it is. If I tell a priest
about Great Bladdered Emer and the pissing contest he might say

that's the unforgivable sin and kick me out of the confession box and I'll be disgraced all over Limerick and doomed to hell tormented forever by devils who have nothing else to do but stab me with hot pitchforks till I'm worn out.

I try to listen to Willie's confession when he goes in but all I can hear is a hissing from the priest and when Willie comes out he's crying.

It's my turn. The confession box is dark and there's a big crucifix hanging over my head. I can hear a boy mumbling his confession on the other side. I wonder if there's any use trying to talk to the Angel on the Seventh Step. I know he's not supposed to be hanging around confession boxes but I feel the light in my head and the voice is telling me, Fear not.

The panel slides back before my face and the priest says, Yes, my child?

Bless me, Father, for I have sinned. This is my First Confession.

Yes, my child, and what sins have you committed?

I told a lie. I hit my brother. I took a penny from my mother's purse. I said a curse.

Yes, my child. Anything else?

I, I listened to a story about Cuchulain and Emer.

Surely that's not a sin, my child. After all we are assured by certain writers that Cuchulain turned Catholic in his last moments as did his King, Conor MacNessa.

'Tis about Emer, Father, and how she married him.

How was that, my child?

She won him in a pissing contest.

There is heavy breathing. The priest has his hand over his mouth and he's making choking sounds and talking to himself, Mother o' God.

Who, who told you that story, my child?

Mikey Molloy, Father.

And where did he hear it?

He read it in a book, Father.

Ah, a book. Books can be dangerous for children, my child. Turn your mind from those silly stories and think of the lives of the saints. Think of St. Joseph, the Little Flower, the sweet and gentle St. Francis of Assisi, who loved the birds of the air and the beasts of the field. Will you do that, my child?

I will, Father.

Are there any other sins, my child?

No, Father.

For your penance say three Hail Marys, three Our Fathers, and say a special prayer for me.

I will. Father, was that the worst sin?

What do you mean?

Am I the worst of all the boys, Father?

No, my child, you have a long way to go. Now say an Act of Contrition and remember Our Lord watches you every minute. God bless you, my child.

First Communion day is the happiest day of your life because of The Collection and James Cagney at the Lyric Cinema. The night before I was so excited I couldn't sleep till dawn. I'd still be sleeping if my grandmother hadn't come banging at the door.

Get up! Get up! Get that child outa the bed. Happiest day of his life an' him snorin' above in the bed.

> E ven to say the words "expecting a baby" wasn't easy. A man I knew had to tell his mother his girlfriend was pregnant. His mother, who had been buying fruit, ran and got a big kitchen knife and plunged it into the melon in her basket. "That's what you've done to the Virgin Mary!" she cried. "That!" plunging the knife in again. "That!"
>
> —Nuala O'Faolain, *Are You Somebody? The Accidental Memoir of a Dublin Woman*

I ran to the kitchen. Take off that shirt, she said. I took off the shirt and she pushed me into a tin tub of icy cold water. My mother scrubbed me, my grandmother scrubbed me. I was raw, I was red.

They dried me. They dressed me in my black velvet First Communion suit with the white frilly shirt, the short pants, the white stockings, and black patent leather shoes. Around my arm they tied a white satin bow and on my lapel they pinned the Sacred Heart of Jesus, a picture of the Sacred Heart, with blood dripping from it, flames erupting all around it and on top a nasty-looking crown of thorns.

Come here till I comb your hair, said Grandma. Look at that mop, it won't lie down. You didn't get that hair from my side of the family. That's that North of Ireland hair you got from your father. That's the kind of hair you see on Presbyterians. If your mother had married a proper decent Limerickman you wouldn't have this standing up, North of Ireland, Presbyterian hair.

She spat twice on my head.

Grandma, will you please stop spitting on my head.

If you have anything to say, shut up. A little spit won't kill you. Come on, we'll be late for the Mass.

We ran to the church. My mother panted along behind with Michael in her arms. We arrived at the church just in time to see the last of the boys leaving the altar rail where the priest stood with the chalice and the host, glaring at me. Then he placed on my tongue the wafer, the body and blood of Jesus. At last, at last.

It's on my tongue. I draw it back.

It stuck.

I had God glued to the roof of my mouth. I could hear the master's voice, Don't let that host touch your teeth for if you bite God in two you'll roast in hell for eternity.

I tried to get God down with my tongue but the priest hissed at me, Stop that clucking and get back to your seat.

God was good. He melted and I swallowed Him and now, at last, I was a member of the True Church, an official sinner.

When the Mass ended there they were at the door of the church, my mother with Michael in her arms, my grandmother. They each hugged me to their bosoms. They each told me it was the happiest day of my life. They each cried all over my head and after my grandmother's contribution that morning my head was a swamp.

Mam, can I go now and make The Collection?

She said, After you have a little breakfast.

No, said Grandma. You're not making no collection till you've had a proper First Communion breakfast at my house. Come on.

We followed her. She banged pots and rattled pans and complained that the whole world expected her to be at their beck and call. I ate the egg, I ate the sausage, and when I reached for more sugar for my tea she slapped my hand away.

Go aisy with that sugar. It is a millionaire you think I am? An American? Is it bedecked in glitterin' jewelry you think I am? Smothered in fancy furs?

The food churned in my stomach. I gagged. I ran to her backyard and threw it all up. Out she came.

Look at what he did. Thrun up his First Communion breakfast. Thrun up the body and blood of Jesus. I have God in my backyard. What am I goin' to do? I'll take him to the Jesuits for they know the sins of the Pope himself.

She dragged me through the streets of Limerick. She told the neighbors and passing strangers about God in her backyard. She pushed me into the confession box.

In the name of the Father, the Son, the Holy Ghost. Bless me, Father, for I have sinned. It's a day since my last confession.

A day? And what sins have you committed in a day, my child?

I overslept. I nearly missed my First Communion. My grandmother said I have standing up, North of Ireland, Presbyterian hair. I threw up my First Communion breakfast. Now Grandma says she has God in her backyard and what should she do.

The priest is like the First Confession priest. He has the heavy breathing and the choking sounds.

Ah…ah…tell your grandmother to wash God away with a little water and for your penance say one Hail Mary and one Our Father. Say a prayer for me and God bless you, my child.

Grandma and Mam were waiting close to the confession box. Grandma said, Were you telling jokes to that priest in the confession box? If 'tis a thing I ever find out you were telling jokes to Jesuits I'll tear the bloody kidneys outa you. Now what did he say about God in me backyard?

He said wash Him away with a little water, Grandma.

Holy water or ordinary water?

He didn't say, Grandma.

Well, go back and ask him.

But, Grandma…

She pushed me back into the confessional.

Bless me, Father, for I have sinned, it's a minute since my last confession.

A minute! Are you the boy that was just here?

I am, Father.

What is it now?

My grandma says, Holy water or ordinary water?

Ordinary water, and tell your grandmother not to be bothering me again.

I told her, Ordinary water, Grandma, and he said don't be bothering him again.

Don't be bothering him again. That bloody ignorant bogtrotter.

I asked Mam, Can I go now and make The Collection? I want to see James Cagney.

Grandma said, You can forget about The Collection and James Cagney because you're not a proper Catholic the way you left God on the ground. Come on, go home.

Mam said, Wait a minute. That's my son. That's my son on his First Communion day. He's going to see James Cagney.

No, he's not.

Yes, he is.

Grandma said, Take him then to James Cagney and see if that will save his Presbyterian North of Ireland American soul. Go ahead.

She pulled her shawl around her and walked away.

Mam said, God, it's getting very late for The Collection and you'll never see James Cagney. We'll go to the Lyric Cinema and see if they'll let you in anyway in your First Communion suit.

We met Mikey Molloy on Barrington Street. He asked if I was going to the Lyric and I said I was trying. Trying? he said. You don't have money?

I was ashamed to say no but I had to and he said, That's all right. I'll get you in. I'll create a diversion.

What's a diversion?

I have the money to go and when I get in I'll pretend to have the fit and the ticket man will be out of his mind and you can slip in when I let out the big scream. I'll be watching the door and when I see you in I'll have a miraculous recovery. That's a diversion. That's what I do to get my brothers in all the time.

Mam said, Oh, I don't know about that, Mikey. Wouldn't that be a sin and surely you wouldn't want Frank to commit a sin on his First Communion day.

Mikey said if there was a sin it would be on his soul and he wasn't a proper Catholic anyway so it didn't matter. He let out his scream and I slipped in and sat next to Question Quigley and the ticket man, Frank Goggin, was so worried over Mikey he never noticed. It was a thrilling film but sad in the end because James Cagney was a public enemy and when they shot him they wrapped him in bandages and threw him in the door, shocking his poor old Irish mother, and that was the end of my First Communion day.

Frank McCourt was for many years a writing teacher at Stuyvesant High School in New York and performer with his brother Malachy in A Couple of Blaguards, *a musical review about their Irish youth. He is the author of the best-seller* Angela's Ashes: A Memoir, *from which this story was excerpted, and its sequel,* 'Tis. *He lives in New York City.*

SUSAN HUGHES

Mediterraneans of the North

Their talent for blarney with women
rivals that of Italians.

IT'S FOUR O'CLOCK ON A SATURDAY AFTERNOON IN JULY. THE sky is muted, shifting from blue to pewter above the ragged mountains and remote valleys of Connemara in County Galway on the west coast of Ireland, a place of great stillness and lonely bogs stretching as far as the eye can see, populated mostly by sheep, donkeys, and wild ponies. There are over 300 lakes here, "one," as the locals say, "for every day of the year."

The rental car is a maroon Fiat Uno. I'm listening to one of Ireland's two national radio stations for company, to a chat show where callers are talking about faerie rings they've seen while walking across the fields at night and such miracles as rosaries turning to gold. The moderator doesn't sound as skeptical as I'd expect him to be. One man calls and says he saw a vision of Christ in the glass of a pub door in Dublin, but stresses you have to approach the glass from a certain angle in order to see the face of God.

I've come to Connemara mainly to see old friends like Sean, the poet, and to escape the stress of urban life in Canada: the crowded subways with crabby people, the frenetic pace, the constant noise and fluorescent malls filled with canned music.

As I drive along the winding road from Galway City to Clifden,

I savor the sweet scent of turf smoke blowing in the window, and try to imagine how the primeval landscape of this rural backwater has shaped the lives of my friends; how it feels to be a lonely bachelor, living here perched on the edge of the twentieth century.

The road, the N59, is hazardous and full of potholes. Many people are driving down the center to avoid the gaps. Every summer a number of tourists is killed here on tortuous roads like this: narrow, two-laned, lined with hedges of fuchsia and honeysuckle or stone walls, and where sheep and cattle have the right-of-way. Signposts often point in the wrong direction, or, at a junction of two roads, to the middle of a field.

On my left a white horse chews grass and wildflowers by a lough; a rainbow arches above the horse's back, making it look like a scene from an old romantic painting. On the side of the road a man pushes a child in a wheelbarrow. The child, who is wearing an old-fashioned blue-and-white-striped jersey and wire-rimmed glasses, is laughing with such abandon that it makes me happy just to look at him.

In just about twenty-five minutes I should be in Clifden, my destination for the next few nights. The radio programme switches to one about Ireland's new law on blood-alcohol limits. One irate representative of a group of country "bachelors and spinsters" wants the law amended. He argues that country people will be condemned to a life of loneliness, if it isn't, since they'll have no chance to socialize or get together for a few jars of an evening. The group wants an exemption made, so people can drive in a two-mile radius from their home to the pub without fear of the Breathalyzer. When the announcer mentions the danger of the roads here and asks why they don't just take turns carpooling, letting the driver drink Ballygowan water, the man replies, "Ah, well it's the numbers, you see. We just don't have the numbers for that."

Such elliptical turns of phrase are one of the things that attract me to Ireland. When I first came here it was traditional music that drew me on. Groups like Planxty, the Chieftains, and Finbar and Eddy. I wanted to find the "Real Ireland," the areas that were like going back in time. I realize now that in addition to a relaxed attitude to life and a warm welcome, Ireland's main attraction is her people. In looking back on my stories of travel in Ireland, I see they're mostly about Irish people, their joie de vivre, hospitality, and curiosity about strangers—their engaging quality of being the "Mediterraneans of the North."

Like the Mediterranean peoples of Greece and Italy, the Irish will welcome tourists with open arms—like long-lost relatives. The old commonplace, that "a stranger in Ireland is just a friend you haven't met," still holds true. But the Mediterranean aspects of the Irish psyche are complex, and relate also to the sense of the holy from Catholicism, I think, a sense that the world is a mysterious place where anything can happen and very often does. Once on a launch to the Aran Islands, just off the coast of Galway, Leigh, an acquaintance of mine, watched as a boy enjoying the sea spray hitting his face laughed and exclaimed, "I think I'm going to have a revelation!" Celtic paganism is still a strong influence here, too; on Aran the islanders believe in a oneness of all people with the sea, which they see as the source of tears they shed in sorrow. Their belief is so strong that they won't go out to rescue a drowning fisherman, believing the sea has "taken him back."

Mediterranean-style hospitality is visible everywhere you go. You only have to stop someone for directions, and chances are you'll end up with an invitation for dinner, or in a detour to the pub. "Work," as one Dublin taxi driver said to me, "just gets in the way of social

The eternal is not elsewhere; it is not distant. There is nothing as near as the eternal. This is captured in a lovely Celtic phrase: "*Tá tír na n-óg ar chul an tí—tír álainn trina chéile*"—that is, "The land of eternal youth is behind the house, a beautiful land fluent within itself." The eternal world and the mortal world are not parallel, rather they are fused. The beautiful Gaelic phrase *fighte fuaighte*, "woven into and through each other," captures this.
—John O'Donohue, *Anam Cara: A Book of Celtic Wisdom*

life." Irishmen delight in giving help, with little thought of recompense. They want people to enjoy their stay in Ireland, and will frequently stop and ask you if everything's all right, or if you're having a good time.

Irishmen like the two Peters I met in the West who invited me to go shark fishing for a morning before I had to go back to Dublin. The morning passed peacefully on the Atlantic and we said our good-byes. When I had driven for about half an hour, and was slowing down to enter the village of Oughterard, one of the Peters, Peter Brady, was standing in the center of the road, his hand raised like a traffic warden's. I said I hadn't realized they'd been following me. "We thought you should have some lunch," Peter said. Over a smoked salmon sandwich, they announced they were following me back to Dublin, just to make sure I arrived safely.

Then, there's the actor Charlie Roberts I met at Neary's pub in Dublin. I was writing postcards and from across the bar heard a northside brogue call out, "Do you think you're James Joyce there, writing away?" After many stories over lunch about his days as a young rep actor rooming with Peter O'Toole and Richard Harris, Charlie invited me to the Gate Theatre that evening, where he was playing in *Pygmalion*. After the play he brought me backstage to meet the cast, and gave me a memoir of Dublin's literary community in the 1950s, inscribed, "A Neary's my God to Thee."

All of this talk of Irish spontaneity is bringing me far from Clifden, Sean the poet, and the darker side I've noticed in many Irishmen. Like their Italian counterparts, many of the men tend to live at home, where their mothers take care of them, cooking and doing their laundry, and in some cases, protecting them from femme fatales. Like the mother I saw at a pub in Castletownshend one evening. She came in four times looking for "her Michael." The villagers were laughing that he'd gone out with a tourist for coffee, and his mother was afraid he'd be carried off by an enchantress. Michael was thirty-five years old. Tied to the maternal hearth, many Irishmen tend to marry late in life, often not before forty. Add to that the prevailing trait of procrastination, the shortage of women (men outnumber women by four to one in the

West), and you can see why they still turn to traditions like matchmaking. Especially the shy "mountainy" men and women, who live in the hills, with their animals as their only companions. Playwright John B. Keane has written often about these lovelorn souls, whom he dubs "chastitutes."

Sean, the poet, is a good example of the loneliness and desperation many of these men face. I called him as soon as I arrived at my bed and breakfast in Clifden, and arranged to meet him at Mannion's pub that evening to hear about his writing and to catch up on his love life.

When I entered Mannion's around 8:30, the pub was beginning to fill up and smelled of stale beer, tobacco smoke, and the tang of the sea. Everyone was complaining about the heat wave, but I was wearing a sweater since it was cool, about seventy-five degrees. The bartender, said he was hoping

Long the poor cousin of Europe, Ireland in the 1990s has become an envied economic success story, leaping from the agrarian age to the information age in a few short years. Roughly 80 percent of the population lives in urban areas, the workforce is young and highly educated, and technology companies—both homegrown and foreign—are investing heavily. The land of farmers and bogs, while still here, has become increasingly a land of techies and microchips.

—JO'R, LH, and SO'R

for a thunderstorm, since there was no air to breathe and he couldn't sleep. "The flies are multiplying," he said, "and growing unwholesomely big. They'd knock the life out of you, if they hit you. They're twice as big as a ten-pence piece. It's desperate." Despite complaints of the heat, I noticed many people were wearing winter overcoats and tweed jackets.

The music was just beginning as Sean strolled in looking every inch the proud Lothario. He was wearing an elegant black jacket, a soft piece of gray and white tweed at his neck, brown workpants, and work boots. His clothes were fragrant with the perfume of the barn. It was his Saturday night outfit for summer, his best social season. When the tourists come to town, Irishmen tend to emerge like butterflies ready to meet each new swarm.

Sean is 6' 2", pushing forty, lives with his parents on a farm on the Sky Road, and has the dark-eyed Mediterranean good looks of many of the men here. Some people insist these dark looks show the influence of the Spanish soldiers who survived the wreck of the Armada off the coast here during Elizabeth I's reign, and who stayed on to marry Irishwomen. Sean's in a good mood, as he scans the room to see who's here. One of his poems is about to be published in Harvard's quarterly review.

Another in his long line of girlfriends had just left him. "My girl-friend's finally gone back to Germany," he said. "She just couldn't stand the long dark winter days. You have to remember fall starts in Ireland at the beginning of August, so it takes a very strong person to deal with the days cloaked in darkness. Some people just seem to lose their soul here. They can't take it. It takes incredible strength."

We talked about the rhythm of his days: working with the animals, tending the farm, five o'clock Mass, then home for supper and a bit of writing before heading back to the pub for some company. "Ah, but I might be married the next time you see me," he said. Raw emotion was in his eyes.

A long silence followed as we sipped our drinks. I thought about how Sean is one of the more lucky men I'd met here. Even though he had trouble sustaining a relationship, some of the men I'd met hadn't "courted" a woman in decades. Like the farmer I helped down in Clare. After I helped him load a runaway calf onto his truck in the hotel's parking lot, he started talking about what a fine-looking woman I was and how he wouldn't mind a Christmas wedding.

The band stopped for a break, and Davy MacNamara, the bodhran player, came over to say hello. Davy runs a successful café business in Clifden and drives two Saabs. He reminds me of the actor who played the saxophone in *The Commitments*; sandy-brown hair with gray streaks, tied back in a pony tail and lined skin that showed he wasn't as young as he thought. On the surface, he seems to stand apart from the mold of the lonely bachelor. But the competitiveness with which he dealt with Sean belied his swaggering exterior.

I noticed Sean looked uncomfortable in Davy's presence. When I asked him what was wrong, he whispered, "I don't like you talking to him. He's a yuppie. And I don't like the way he treats women. Don't you be talking to him."

When Sean excused himself to go to the bathroom, Davy moved in quickly and began to denigrate Sean, and other neighbours. "Sean's lazy," he said. "Just like all the people around here. No ambition. They can't be bothered working." Davy went on to brag about his business, and the many women he expected to visit him from various points of the globe that summer, and I began to think Sean was right about him.

When I mentioned Sean's writing, Davy laughed, "Writing! He's told you that, has he?" As Sean wandered back, Davy slapped the bar and asked, "Do you know what MacNamara means in English? Chieftains of the sea," he said as if he were the great Finn MacCool himself, and then he ambled back to his bodhran. I was happy he left.

This fairly typical scene of male braggadocio was repeated throughout my travels in Ireland. I've usually had a circle of men around me, all intrigued by the stranger who's come to town. It's very much like being pursued in Rome, but a gentler, less intrusive type of approach for the most part.

Irishmen will pay you fantastic compliments that only a half-wit would believe. They fancy themselves as impetuous romantics.

I think they're convinced that they should be worshipped in return. Whatever else you could say about them, one thing you can't accuse them of is excessive modesty. They love North American women because they seem free and independent. "No strings attached," is a phrase I often heard. In a country where divorce has just recently been made legal, the men seem suspicious of female motives, believing all Irishwomen want is to get married. "They're only after one thing," I heard, ironically, over and over again from the men.

The charm and conversational ability of Irishmen do make them wonderful companions, as long as you don't take them too seriously. But their conviviality masks a sadness just under the surface, a romantic yearning that you can hear in so much of Irish music.

Darker still is their quick temper and ability to take offence. They'll fight over who's going to buy you a drink, and who'll have your attention. "Listen now to me," they'll say. Proposals within minutes are not uncommon either. In Clare once at a dance, a man with eyebrows like question marks told me he'd decided to break off with his fiancée so he could marry me. "But she's my honey," said Padraic, a little Viking of a man with a flaming orange beard. I'd danced with Padraic only once that evening.

I've found Irishmen to be some of the most romantic men in the world. Most can quote poetry. Yeats is a favourite, especially "The Lake Isle of Inisfree." They'll promise you the "silver apples of the moon, the golden apples of the sun," as they gaze into your eyes and say you're the most beautiful woman they've ever met. And they do mean it, at that moment. One woman I met from California was so enraptured with the romantic tendencies of Irishmen, she dyed her hair black, since she'd heard they preferred dark hair to blondes.

As the evening wound down at Mannion's, the band was playing Paddy Kavanaugh's "Raglan Road," a bittersweet lyric about a dark femme fatale:

On Raglan Road on an Autumn Day,
I saw her first and knew.
That her dark hair would weave a snare
that I may one day rue.
I saw the danger, yet I walked
along the enchanted way
and I said let grief be a falling leaf
at the dawning of the day.

Sean stood beside me, sipping a glass of Guinness, listening to the lyrics and staring off into space. The laughter had died down, and a more reflective tone enveloped the bar.

He tightened his scarf, and led the way out as Mannion's closed for the night. "I find it hard to live out here on my own. It's beautiful, but seems to open me up and makes me rather raw," he said.

It was a scene that would be repeated countless times in the weeks, months, and years to come all over Ireland, as surely as the leaves would soon fall in the glens and a fresh wind bring in the winter gales. Waiting and watching, as if they're waiting for Godot, many Irish bachelors seem fated to be single. Some are lonely; some don't want commitment. They long to be free spirits. They're the last romantics, these Odysseuses without a Penelope.

When not tending her Old English sheepdog and three Burmese cats in Canada, Susan Hughes is living the country life in Ireland. Based in Toronto, Hughes is a special correspondent for the Irish Independent *and a freelance literary journalist and photographer. She travels widely with her husband, James, and over the past ten years her work has appeared in the* Globe and Mail, Irish Times, Financial Post, Ireland of the Welcomes, *and on CBC television. This story was excerpted from* Mediterraneans of the North, *a work in progress.*

J. P. DONLEAVY

✦ ✦ ✦

The Miracle of St. Bridget

Compose your prayers carefully.

Aʜ, ʙᴜᴛ ʟᴇᴛ ᴜs ꜰᴏʀ ᴛʜᴇ ᴅᴇʟᴀʏᴇᴅ ᴍᴏᴍᴇɴᴛ ɴᴏᴛ ʏᴇᴛ ᴀʟʟᴜᴅᴇ ᴛᴏ leaping leprechauns wearing their golden little boots and emerald jackets and tall orange hats and dancing their little dances on grassy mounds in the moonlight but instead focus on the saints. Now there is nowhere on earth where more praying goes on for favours to be granted from the above than on the isle of the shamrock. And using the intercession of these sainted holy folk, there'd be your long columns in the papers of Deo Gratias, and thanks be to Sancta Trinitas, St. Jude, St. Anthony, St. Christopher, and a list of the hallowed consecrated persons as long as your arm. And according to the publication promised, doing your miracles left, right, and centre. Now I know among you you'd have your sceptics. But by God there's one saint I'm telling you who for a fact didn't leave someone's prayer and fervent request unanswered. And it's astonishing that hardly do you ever see her name mentioned in the columns of thanksgiving. And I'm not talking about St. Clare or St. Martha but St. Bridget herself. Who long before she ever had anything to do with your sanctification and the Catholic religion, was more than rumoured to be the ancient pagan goddess of fertility.

Now you would, if not of the Roman Catholic persuasion, be forgiven if you were a might bit sceptical about the powers of these saints whose names are invoked up and down long lists in the newspapers. But let me tell you, you are making one hell of a big mistake. And plenty of the disasters and yearning in your life could be put right. For when he was still Blessed Oliver Plunkett, and not yet canonized as a saint, there was no end of requests this eminently blessed man was getting from all sides and for which he interceded. And weren't acknowledgments of thanks to him published one following the other in the columns of the better Irish papers, for an avalanche of favours received. And this Blessed man whose pre-served head in a tabernacle I visited in Drogheda, did much in sav-ing the idolatrous bacon of yours truly with miracles of a nature I won't go into now. And didn't the same Blessed Oliver, as he was then, do the same for all those to whom I recommended him. And in due course, following successful deliverance from ruinous mis-fortune, didn't he later become the patron saint of Sebastian Balfe Dangerfield, the notorious Ginger Man himself.

Now then. You Protestants, you Buddhists, you Jews, you Muslims, you Hindus, you Shakers, get ready. Here's a true story referring to an absolute miracle. The like of which and consider-ing the circumstances, is not often described in Ireland due to the religious devoutness of the people and due to the many celibate spiritual exercises in which the populace more normally indulges. And although this little tale might be considered by some to be somewhat bizarrely pagan in nature, if not a wee bit satanic or heretic, it is nevertheless religious enough in its sincerity. Nor is there the merest bit of exaggeration here about what happened and it is recounted just to show the power of the saints, and espe-cially your St. Bridget who comes out with flying colours.

Now there was this old, not to say ancient friend who some would, and many did, refer to as Mister Ireland himself. A well-built man of charm and intelligence from a prominent professional and farming family well reputed in their rural parish. And whom I had not met for this many a long year gone past. But whom I had remembered was reputed all over Dublin city as one of the great swordsmen of his time. And it was no surprise to anybody that with his ready smile and generally jovial nature, he was a great excitement for the women and they especially for him. And it would be no exaggeration to say that your Mark I and II, women, were they around at the time would have beat a path to his door ready to wait on him hand and foot, washing, drying, and mending his socks be they got as green from wearing as a shamrock. And wasn't it equally a fact that your man throughout his vigorous youth was obsessed ecstatic by any likely looking lass. Not unnatural enough you might say. Well now, much of your grunting and groaning of ecstasy has with the years gone past floated away like music out on the ether. And your man Mister Ireland himself was left a father of more children than he cared to count, and they were fully grown up now, and members in good standing of the Irish nation. And he himself was getting on a bit. Just that little extra long in the tooth, slightly greyer in the head, stiffer in the limbs. But, by God, still stiff where he'd more than occasionally continued to want to be. And his lust for the women wasn't fading in the least. Now when semi retirement time came from the stimulating occupation of breeding race horses, didn't he with his huge nest egg buy himself a little cottage in the far west where contentedly betimes he would go and where betimes there'd be a *hooley* or two and your singing and dancing in the town's local pubs. And where betimes too with Ireland's growing worldwide reputation for grand music there'd be coming along from foreign places a likely lass or two whom by a small kindness he might courteously inveigle to come back to the hospitality of his cottage to there be entertained in the cosy safe surroundings infused with your well-being and togetherness that comes from having a deep serious discussion about the Irish weather.

Now then. Where's the miracle in all that, you're asking. But I'd ignore the question and detour here to have take note all men edged a little bit past their prime. For your grey-headed Mister Ireland out in the pub most evenings would have to wait for the young lasses to choose their willing partners before they even deign give him a tumble. But such was your man's charm together with his patient persistence with more of your courteous kindness and assistance, that enough of the young ladies sought his jovial accommodating company. And there soon were one or two of the young ladies who became firm platonic friends. A fat lot of good that did him, you're saying. However, wasn't there one particular young attractive Germanic lady who more than anything else wanted to get married and have children. And she said to your totally and absolutely atheistic Mister Ireland that someone had told her of a St. Bridget to whom such a request of a husband and family might be made and her recent year or two of anguish be ended.

Now your Mister Ireland threw his head back with a burst of laughter, sure what saint had he ever beseeched could even tell him the month it was in the year never mind finding a husband for her. Nevertheless as she was about to return to Germany, he'd be more than happy to escort her up over the hill beyond to where there was known to be a St. Bridget's Well. And where, why not, you can write out your request on a scrap of paper and throw it into the waters and at least dream of your request being granted. And your man Mister Ireland, a pagan disbeliever from the age of his puberty, thought

"There are things on this island ye haven't heard the half of," Bridget warns. "We'd be a week talkin' if I was to tell ye's them all. But believe ye me, they make out they're very holy, but they're as low as the rat in the tide if ye ask me. Shur there was hardly a woman married in the last ten years didn't have the first child six months after. And those are the first ones ye see paradin' into Mass every mornin' of the week. It's enough to make ye sick!"

—Deborah Tall, *The Island of the White Cow: Memories of an Irish Island*

what the hell, here is a saint who was once a Celtic pagan goddess, while your young German girl was sending in her entreaty why not himself write out on a bit of paper his own petition and flick it into the water along with hers? At least to himself, and being that he was asking could he be delivered soon of a piece of arse, it would be a good old laugh and a miracle to boot.

Now a month went by and then two and finally a stormy autumn afternoon a letter came from Frankfurt, Germany, from your young lady which your Mister Ireland read with wide eyed amazement if not disbelief. Lo and behold didn't your Fraulein get picked up hitchhiking the day after the visit to the well and three weeks later got married to a prosperous engineer and wasn't she now sitting comfortable in a bijou residence in the best part of town and pregnant as she wrote. And didn't she say further words full of appreciation for St. Bridget and that she sincerely hoped he had also got what he had requested in his petition that he had tossed into the well. And didn't Mister Ireland sit reading with delight this letter in his cottage and as it was growing dark and the night brought with it greater gales lashing up against the coast and shaking the land, himself thought it the ideal time to sit down in front of the glowing turf fire and answer your German girl's letter. Sure on this very day wasn't it his birthday commemorating more years on this earth than he presently cared to count. In the cold wind and lashing rain he'd taken his usual six-mile hike up over the nearby mountain and had a raging appetite. And being a great wine connoisseur wasn't he cooking himself a bit of a gourmet dinner and he had cooling for himself outside on the doorstep a bottle of champagne to accompany the plate full of smoked salmon he had sliced and surrounded with choice bits of shelled lobster caught that day not more than 200 yards away down in the depths off the coast. A great thick slab of your best sirloin steak also awaited to be grilled over the fire. To be washed down with a grand booming burgundy decanted on the sideboard. To his previous platonic German lady he had in brackets already appended to his letter:

"Wish you were here to join me in my little lonely party. But meanwhile more power and praise be to St. Bridget, and it is well for you, and I still fervently hope the highly unlikely wish I want granted happens to me one of these days."

And for the sentiment that was in it, he had on his record player the great Irish tenor Frank Patterson singing "Abide with Me" and "Ave Maria." And he was really enjoying composing his communication in this musical atmosphere of piety. But let me tell you, before he fully answered and got to the last word of his letter expressing his delight with her developments and the bestowment upon her of the favour asked of St. Bridget, suddenly there was a ferocious thunderclap, the whole cottage shaking and the lights went out and Frank Patterson's singing stopped and the sitting room was plunged into darkness, as were the few lights that were usually visible in the town two miles away. He lit several candles around the room and continued to write his letter on the board over his knee, describing the wax blob which had just fallen on the paper as being from an ecclesiastic candle he'd bought specially to burn during dinner if he ever had the good luck to find another girl as pleasant as she had often been to cook for and have dinner with. Then he was interrupted in his reminiscing by what he thought were gusts of wind shaking the door. But then as he continued to listen, he realized the thumping was a knock. And he got up from the fireside from where he was writing his letter and went over to the door to open it, thinking aloud that bejesus God Almighty who'd be out on the highway and calling on me on a night the like of this.

Now remember, in the West and during a storm, Ireland is one hell of a wild and lonely place, and you wouldn't be outside having casual visitors on a night as the one raging outside where the salt from the sea spray breaking on the cliffs beyond was tasting on your lips. But forever generous and willing with his hospitality like anyone in the West would be, without caution he undid the latches and slowly opened the door as the gale and rain swept in. And by the faint light he could see nothing. Then came an almighty flash of lightning directly above in the sky which hit the steeple of an isolated small Protestant chapel down the road. And there revealed in the deluge coming down, as your man was straining, peering out from the door of the cottage, was a figure in a yellow sou'wester, with a shepherd's crook and a backpack on the back and stout walking boots on the feet and a foreign-sounding soft melodic voice.

"Forgive me sir for troubling you. I am lost. And I look for The Seaside Hotel I cannot find. I am apologising for disturbing you but perhaps you could direct me. I would be so grateful. I am Swedish."

"Come in, come in out of the rain, for God's sake, and don't be standing out there in the gales, thunder and lightning. Swedish or not."

"Thank you. But I do not wish to disturb you."

"Disturb me. Nonsense. Come in. And welcome."

Your grateful Swede, raindrops cascading down her exquisite face, smiled a relieved smile of thanks and hesitated no further over this unexpected invitation to enter into the dry warm fire-glow and candlelight of the cottage. Now we won't go too deeply into your man's age or that of the young Swedish girl. Suffice to say she was a slender blonde of medium height with soft lustrous grey-blue eyes. And he was certainly old enough not only to be her father but even old enough to give her the benefit of grand-fatherly protection should she need it. But also suffice to say that as your Swede stood there surveying a grinning Mister Ireland there was another lightning flash overhead and thunderclap that made it sound as if the roof of the cottage had just exploded off. And your man Mister Ireland opened his arms as the girl jumped forward in fear as the rumble of the thunder echoed back from the surrounding hillsides.

Well now, your man Mister Ireland, although he could believe his ears, he couldn't really believe his eyes, and was ruddy well de-lighted out of his mind at the golden-haired apparition he now re-leased from his protective arms. And he was grateful to have some company, however brief, on a stormy night, which even as he stood there thinking of the present wonderment, was increasing in fe-rocity. And while excusing himself to take a pee, he did in fact in the water closet, give himself a belt on the forehead with the heel of his hand to make sure this was still his own brain thinking in his old grey head on this the top end of this body. But sure enough, as luck was now rapidly having it and returned from the water closet, there she was removing from her shoulders the dripping wet backpack. And off came her hat. And then her sou'wester. Then her thick Aran Island sweater revealing two braided long golden locks of hair now hanging down her back nearly to her hips. Her hands and knuckles were red-blue with cold.

Now there was no trace of Man Fighter Mark I, II, or for the matter of that Mark III or IV in your young girl, as your man Mister Ireland led her across the room to the glowing turf fire. And as she smilingly stood there with the sudden whooshes of wind gusting up the chimney your man quick as a flash had in off the doorstep the bottle of champagne and with a ceremonial pop, filled and was handing your Swedish beauty a glass. Which she took gratefully enough, and, by God, downed in one delighted gulp. And then in the warmth she removed another sweater. Which left your man's mouth suddenly salivating with shock. For in the cerulean-blue cotton shirt she wore he could see the distinct outline upon her

Not only was there a bad connection, but the Irish pay phone was greedily swallowing my coins. During this expensive call to a female friend back in Galway, I managed to tell her that I was coming back to Galway soon, but I couldn't get a ride in Mayo. As the phone crackled with static, I spoke louder; "I can't get a ride in Mayo!" The damn phone went dead and I vigorously cursed the telecommunications in Ireland. That was until I was informed what "getting a ride" in Ireland meant. It did take some explaining to my female friend, but it ended up, as most things do in Ireland, with a laugh.

—Timothy K. Egan, "My Island, My Island…My @$*#%!"

chest of exactly the ideal of all breasts, the image of which he had ever had the temerity to conjure up in his dreams. And not that his own good Irish mother had ever deprived him. However, and notwithstanding, didn't your man Mister Ireland find he suddenly had a horn on him that would not only whip your Irish donkeys out of sandpits but would lever an African elephant up out of an

Irish bog. And, by God, so as not to inhospitably intimidate or alarm your poor Swedish stray just in out of the storm, your man had to sit down in a hurry. For over these past nearly three years of recent celibacy and to those ladies he was dying to fuck, he never once showed any of them anything but courtesy, kindness, and consideration. And thanking him for his flattery these same young women with equal courtesy, kindness, and consideration declined his invitations to bed.

Now then. The hotel your sweet young beauty was looking for was but a mere two miles away on the sea road, half of which by now was sure to be washed away by the ocean waves. But your man had his boots, a torch, and his own sou'wester and didn't he know a shortcut of only a quarter of a mile to the hostelry by footpath over the nearby hill. And so as your young lady had now caught her breath the temptation to tell a lie was desperate. But he did not yield. For it had long been his forthright honesty that the ladies had always come to love about him best. So despite the rain, lightning, and lashing gale he was without subterfuge about to offer to accompany her over the hill to her hotel. However at least he felt he deserved the pleasure of a little delay, and anyway your splendid Swede was already saying in her wonderful Elizabethan voice,

"I am, sir, from Uppsala. Where I study about moss and lichen in the university."

Well, the grin on your Mister Ireland's countenance stopped your Swede in her tracks, for it went from behind one ear to behind the other. And she wondered what she could have said to produce such radiant joy on this gentleman's face. And you won't believe this. But Mister Ireland had, tucked away right there in his library located in the corner of this room, some of the greatest scholarly tomes ever written about mosses and lichen. And not only that. There wasn't much to be known that he didn't know already about your bryophyte and the similar but unrelated lichen. And without saying a word he beckoned her over to his library shelves where were, as he pointed out, the six leather-bound volumes of the most brilliant authoritative texts ever written about mosses and lichens. And she too smiled from behind one ear to behind the other and then broke into an astonished delighted laughter. And let me tell you at that moment the minutes now didn't have any trouble flying by, nor was there any guilt in your man not setting out to hike through the storm to The Seaside Hotel. And as the two of them warmly stood there smiling into each other's eyes your young lady disclosed that she'd specialised in the study of the horn tooth moss. And now your man who knew everything about your species *Ceratoden purureus*, gave up worrying about how brief this encounter might be and even dared think of the possible endless hours of discussion to come. And for the first delicate time the name St. Bridget flashed like a lightning bolt across his mind. But just as it did, he dismissed it realizing that this was no time to be deluding himself thinking about the fertility miracles wrought by the Celtic deity.

But in your man now getting slightly apoplectic he did not forget to be the best of hosts and straightaway suggested that Katrina, as she was called, go immediately and help herself to a nice hot bath and warm herself up. While he whipped around a bit to put together a spot of supper they could have.

"O no. I could not. You have been far too kind already. I should now try to go find again my hotel."

"Sure after you've eaten, the storm may have let up and I'll lead you by the shortcut over the hill."

"I have already taken four glasses of your champagne."

"Actually you've had five and are welcome to more."

"Ooo la la. I did not know I had five. But you should not now have to cook for two. I must not please put you to so much trouble."

"This is Ireland where you wouldn't be worrying about a foolish thing like that. I'd be offended for you not to join me. And sure, since when was meeting a fellow botanist trouble? Besides it is my birthday."

"O how *underbar*, that is how we say wonderful in Swedish."

"Well, *underbar*, that's settled now. And now I am not too keen that you should be let go again out in this storm. And in that door there is another bedroom. And yours for the night. And let me assure you there is no need for there to be any compromising or any embarrassing proximity to be caused to anyone invited to stay."

"I stay for your birthday. Thank you so much. Now I go bath."

And despite her protestations over invading his privacy and taking up his time it was a whole hour later when she again presented herself bathed and fragrant in a sweater and skirt and ready to have another glass of champagne from the second storm-chilled bottle brought in from the front doorstep. For Katrina taught your man how to *skol*. And never did your man Mister Ireland pick up new Swedish words faster or ever see anyone so hungry or enjoy her food more. And gone in a thrice, washed away with the champagne, was every last bit of the smoked salmon and lobster. And the steak an inch and a half thick. Which she said she would have very rare and which she chewed down with gusto, admitting that she had only eaten an apple and an orange since the evening before.

"I am having such a lovely *underbar* time."

But now with the steamy baked spuds and a good heap of buttery spinach and gulps of her burgundy wasn't she now able to smilingly tell him between mouthfuls of her life up to date. The boyfriend who only eight months ago blew himself up with a stick of dynamite because she wouldn't marry him. And another whom she also wouldn't marry, now in a mental institution.

"I am a simple girl. I do not know what I do to men which I do not mean to do. It is why I come away and alone to Ireland."

"Ah now, with no shortage of simple men, you've come to the right place."

"Yes, I think so. I like to travel. Maybe I miss the skiing. Maybe too I miss the *bastu* and how one dives then in the cold sea. To collect moss specimens next year I go to visit the rain forests of Brazil."

"Now that's a great idea."

As they spoke and drank and spoke some more the storm still raged; the rain peppering the window panes and the wind slamming gusts at the cottage walls and tugging at, and a couple of times nearly lifting off, the thatch of the roof. But during this idyllic impromptu dinner party, they had become like old friends. And up and down he danced delighted attendance upon her, putting a hot water bottle shoved down between the sheets and placing a tome on the tropical lichens by her bedside. And now for the moment, and sure for the night that was in it, why not take the comfort nearest at hand and make herself entirely at home. Have a sup of brandy. And then a good sleep and after breakfast in the morning of pucks of rashers, sausages, eggs, and tea, he would in the brand-new day walk her to the hotel. Or for the matter of that, anywhere else she cared to go in this local kingdom come. And on the way show her some rare mosses and lichens to boot.

Enough said of any attempted enticement by your man, half sloshed. Katrina was only too delighted to accept the hospitality of a bed for the night. And after singing happy birthday in Swedish to him for the third time, and bowing and smiling to him, she moved her backpack into the spare bedroom. And here he was, your man Mister Ireland, well wined and dined, retiring, purring with near contentment to his bed. Recalling how, as she got up to retire to her chamber, she came over on tiptoe to peck him on each cheek and then one on the forehead. Now you would imagine with a storm still raging and such delectable company less than a few yards away, your Mister Ireland couldn't get himself to sleep in a hurry. And he lay listening to the lashing gale and the explosive thundering of the sea as it trapped air up the long caves extending inland from the bottom of the sea cliffs. Until he fell fast asleep. Deep in a dream of a heavenly angel winged lady in white diaphanous lacy veils hovering in the air over his bed. And didn't he suddenly wake up. And, by God, wasn't there coming a knocking at his bedroom door. And didn't the door open. And wasn't she herself Katrina standing there in a lacy nightgown.

"Please forgive me for disturbing you. I am sorry but I was frightened to sleep alone. Would you mind if I go in the bed with you?"

Now your man Mister Ireland, hospitable to the last and ready to do any kindness, swept open the covering of the bed, and Katrina like a dream descended in beside him between the sheets. As wasn't he, long before he went to sleep, hoping beyond hope that at the midnight high tide Katrina would be terrified by the ground shaking under the cottage with explosions of the seas in the caves that went in under the shore, and in thinking that the end of the world had come or at the very least an earthquake, would rush into his room in panic. Now every Irishman considering the highly religious nature of the country, has always been eternally grateful for any little taste of a piece of arse he can get. And might do a lot irreligious to get it. But your man Mister Ireland still had his principles of making no overtures to a woman without enthused reciprocation. And he lay still as total death itself beside her. But now, not that many minutes later, didn't Katrina's hand reach for that of Mister Ireland's. And take his fingers slowly and surely up, up, up, to place them upon her warm, silkily soft breast. By God, never mind the gales. Or the under-the-shore detonations. For soon the seas out in the ocean this night were nothing like the bedclothes that started to go up and down. With Mister Ireland having one of the most glorious nights of his entire life. And if he was less than a saint, he was at least betimes in the area of botany, a bit of a scholar. And appropriately enough it is by these two vocations that this isle became known as the Land of Saints and Scholars. And as he in the dawn's early light saw Katrina's startlingly stunning arse wagging its curvaceously white sparkling way to bring him his breakfast in bed, he was no longer the disbelieving pagan infidel of the day before. Thanks be to God the Big Himself of the Brogue Above and to St. Bridget for favours received.

> But now
> Don't all of you
> At once go
> Start praying to this
> Celtic deity
> And littering her well
> With wishes and requests.

J. P. Donleavy was born in New York City in 1926 and educated there. Following service in the U.S. Navy in World War II, he attended Trinity

College, Dublin, and remained in Ireland between 1946 and 1951, finally returning to live there permanently in 1969. Author of some fourteen books, including The Ginger Man, The Beastly Beatitudes of Balthazar B., *and* A Singular Man, *he is also a highly regarded painter. He makes his home on the shores of Lough Owel in County Westmeath. This story was excerpted from his book,* A Singular Country.

HEINRICH BÖLL

⋆ ⋆ ⋆

Thoughts on Irish Rain

Rain will never be the same
after you've been to Ireland.

THE RAIN HERE IS ABSOLUTE, MAGNIFICENT, AND FRIGHTENING. TO call this rain bad weather, is as inappropriate as to call scorching sunshine fine weather.

You can call this rain bad weather, but it is not. It is simply weather, and weather means rough weather. It reminds us forcibly that its element is water, falling water. And water is hard. During the war I once watched a burning aircraft going down on the Atlantic coast; the pilot landed it on the beach and fled from the exploding machine. Later I asked him why he hadn't landed the burning plane on the water, and he replied: "Because water is harder than sand."

I never believed him, but now I understood: water is hard.

And how much water can collect over 3,000 miles of ocean, water that rejoices in at last reaching people, houses, terra firma, after having fallen only into water, only into itself. How can rain enjoy always falling into water?

When the electric light goes out, when the first tongue of a puddle licks its way under the door, silent and smooth, gleaming in the firelight; when the toys which the children have left lying around, when corks and bits of wood suddenly start floating and are borne forward by the tongue, when the children come down-stairs, scared, and huddle in front of the fire (more surprised than scared, for they also sense the joy in this meeting of wind and rain and that this howling is a howl of delight), then we know we would not have been as worthy of the ark as Noah was....

Inlander's madness, to open the door to see what's up outside. Everything's up: the roof tiles, the roof gutters, even the house walls, do not inspire much confidence (for here they build tem-porarily, although, if they don't emigrate, they live forever in these temporary quarters—while in Europe they build for eternity without knowing whether the next generation will benefit from so much solidity).

It is a good thing always to have candles, the Bible, and a little whisky in the house, like sailors prepared for a storm; also a pack of cards, some tobacco, knitting needles and wool for the women; for the storm has a lot of breath, the rain holds a lot of water, and the night is long. Then when a second tongue of rain advances from the window and joins the first one, when the toys float slowly along the narrow tongue toward the window, it is a good thing to look up in the Bible whether the promise to send no more floods has really been given. It has been given: we can light the next can-dle, the next cigarette, shuffle the cards again, pour some more whisky, abandon ourselves to the drumming of the rain, the howl-ing of the wind, the click of the knitting needles. The promise has been given.

It was some time before we heard the knocking on the door— at first we had taken it for the banging of a loose bolt, then for the rattle of the storm, then we realized it was human hands, and the naïveté of the Continental mentality can be measured from the fact that I expressed the opinion it might be the man from the electric company. Almost as naïve as expecting the bailiff to appear on the high seas.

Quickly the door was opened, a dripping figure of a man pulled in, the door shut, and there he stood; with his cardboard suitcase sopping wet, water running out of his sleeves, his shoes, from his hat, it almost seemed as if water were running out of his eyes—this is how swimmers look after taking part in a lifesaving contest fully clothed; but such ambitions were foreign to this man: he had merely come from the bus stop, fifty paces through this rain, had mistaken our house for his hotel, and was by occupation a clerk in a law office in Dublin.

"D'you mean to say the bus is running in this weather?"

"Yes," he said, "it is, and only a bit behind schedule. But it was more of a swim than a drive…and you're sure this isn't a hotel?"

"Yes, but…."

He—Dermot was his name—turned out, when he was dry, to know his Bible, to be good card-player, a good storyteller, a good whisky-drinker; moreover, he showed us how to bring water quickly to the boil on a tripod in the fireplace, how to broil lamb chops on the same ancient tripod, how to toast bread on long forks, the purpose of which we had not yet discovered—and it was not till the small hours that he confessed to knowing a little German; he had been a prisoner-of-war in Germany, and he told our children something they will never forget, must never forget: how he buried the little gypsy children who had died during the evacuation of the Stuthof concentration camp; they were so small—he showed us—and he had dug graves in the frozen ground to bury them.

"But why did they have to die?" asked one of the children.

"Because they were gypsies."

"But that's no reason—you don't have to die because of that."

"No," said Dermot, "that's no reason, you don't have to die because of that."

We stood up: it was light now, and at that moment it became quiet outside. Wind and rain had gone away, the sun came up over the horizon, and a great rainbow arched over the sea; it was so

> I have just returned from my forty-seven days in Ireland. The only downside was that it rained for forty-three days. Plenty of time for reflection.
> —Anna Mullen, "Summer on Inis Meáin"

close we thought we could see it in substance—as thin as soap bubbles was the skin of the rainbow.

Corks and bits of wood were still bobbing about in the puddle when we went upstairs to the bedrooms.

German writer Heinrich Böll was born in Cologne in 1917. Conscripted into the German Army shortly before the outbreak of World War II, he served in France, the Soviet Union, Romania, and Hungary before being interned by both the French and the English. He is the author of numerous books including Irish Journal (Irisches Tagebuch *being the German title*) *from which this story was excerpted. In 1972 he was awarded the Nobel Prize for his contribution to a renewal of German literature. He died in 1985.*

JOHN BOLAND

A Begrudger's View

The new Ireland can apparently do no wrong,
but this writer begs to differ.

CULTURALLY SPEAKING, WE IRISH CAN DO NO WRONG, AND THAT'S official—the British and international media keep telling us so. I suppose it makes a change from all those centuries when we Irish could do no right, but nonetheless the extent of the praise puzzles some of us.

We think it's a bit over-the-top when English reviewers are so awed by Seamus Heaney that they can't write sensibly about him and when they exalt Roddy Doyle above the status of superb storyteller to that of profound novelist. We think they're being mesmerised by the myth of a new, vibrant Ireland that's being peddled assiduously by those of our own race who have an eye on the main chance.

That a new kind of Ireland did emerge in recent years is undeniable—an Ireland with a very large young population who weren't prepared to accept the pious platitudes of their elders, who had never experienced censorship, who didn't give two hoots about the clergy, who were contemptuous of their politicians, and who saw around them the same problems and possibilities that face any young person in any other country. The Ireland of De Valera was dead, simply because most young Irish people had never heard of him.

Old artistic divisions ceased to exist, too. We weren't just a literary country anymore. There was pop, there were movies, there was dance, there was whatever you wanted to do. A lot of energy went into these various areas, and the results were often pretty good, and people both in Ireland and elsewhere began to sit up and take notice. U2 was described as "the greatest rock band in the world" (by *Rolling Stone*, no less), *My Left Foot* ambled off with a couple of Oscars, and everyone was clutching their Roddy Doyle trilogy as they rushed to see *The Crying Game* and to listen to Van Morrison and Enya and the Cranberries, and suddenly it all started to get out of hand.

Suddenly, in fact, it seemed that somehow we were superior to everyone else, and an image of the Irish as drinking deep from some mysterious cultural well (to which no one else had access) began to be put around and packaged for foreign consumption.

And it worked. To the world, our pop music became somehow magically Celtic, our poetry danced with cadences that nobody else could manage, our novels exploded with exuberance, and our movies wiped the floor with their dreary British counterparts.

This image of Ireland as a breeding ground for extraordinary talent is puzzling because it bears no relation to any reality. We are producing just as much bad literature

The popularity of things Irish and Celtic certainly has a lot to do with nostalgia and cultural fads, but there is more to it than that. The Irish are now projecting prosperity more than their old trademark, gloom. As Mark Borden wrote in *Fortune* magazine: "Striding through the streets of Dublin these days is an entirely new species of Irishman and Irishwoman: educated, optimistic, and affluent—unaffected by the twin demons of poverty and despair that hounded their ancestors for the past several hundred years. 'They are the first Irish generation,' says historian J. J. Lee, 'that has never known defeat.'"

—JO'R, LH, and SO'R

and art and entertainment as we ever did and as any country does, and just as little good literature and art and entertainment, too. But for some reason it's been elevated to a status way beyond its merits. Indeed, a glance through the current catalogues from London publishers will demonstrate that you don't have to be any good to get published anymore, you merely have to be Irish.

You're not allowed to say that in Ireland these days. A nation famed for its begrudgers had become a nation of mindless enthusiasts: a land of hype and glory. Indeed, those who are brave (or foolish) enough to question what's going on are dismissed as being somehow un-Irish, perhaps even anti-Irish—if you're not with us, you're against us.

This is more than a little worrying, as it suggests a form of cultural fascism. And the debasement of standards that can present U2 as visionary artists rather than rock musicians and that can see *Riverdance* as anything more than a synthetic mélange of Broadway and bodhrans makes some of us feel very unsettled. If superlatives are being showered on the third-rate, what words are left for the first-rate? If Roddy Doyle is extraordinary, where does that leave James Joyce?

Perhaps Irish insecurity is to blame for all this. Perhaps our constant need to tell the world how great we are stems from centuries of oppression by our nearest neighbour. And perhaps we get a particular satisfaction when our nearest neighbour, riddled with postcolonial guilt, obliges us by agreeing that, yes, we really are great.

Some of us, though, will stick to our critical guns and will continue to point out that many of the Irish emperors being feted these days both at home and abroad are wearing very few clothes and are simply getting by on their Irish passport.

We won't be liked for it, because there's a cultural party going on in Ireland, and no one likes party poopers. We'll probably be spat on as begrudgers, but that's all right, because there's a certain intellectual rigour to begrudgery, and anyway—unlike *Riverdance*—it's a genuine part of what we are. Samuel Johnson acknowledged that fact more than two centuries ago when he observed that by never speaking well of each other the Irish were a very fair race. And

Jonathan Swift recognized it everywhere he went in Dublin when he spoke of "the daily spite of this unmannerly town."

Spite (if standards must be so called) at least suggests a point of view, and a vigorously held one, too. Better that than subservience to a myth.

John Boland is a poet and former columnist for the Irish Press *and* Irish Times *who now teaches journalism. He lives in Dún Laoghaire, County Dublin.*

✦ ✦ ✦

Walking the Kerry Way

A candle in a dark church
illumines family history.

I HADN'T SPENT MUCH TIME WITH MY BROTHER FRANK SINCE he was about twelve years old, back in 1973. That was the year I'd gotten engaged to a non-Catholic, and my parents wouldn't let me bring her home because "it would scandalize the children." I was nineteen and equally sure of myself, so I refused to come home without her.

I finally gave in seven years later, when my father's health was failing, and went home for a visit alone. After that, my parents also relented, and met my wife and three-year-old daughter for the first time. Our mutual stubbornness had cost us precious time together as a family, a loss made especially poignant by my father's death six months later.

My relationship with my younger brother and sisters took years to recover. By the time I came home after my long exile, Frank was away at college, and thereafter we'd met mainly at family holidays and reunions. Still, we'd found many common interests and a mutual admiration. Both of us were entrepreneurs—I in publishing, he in construction—and both of us had struggled with how to build a business with a heart, a business that served its employees as well as its customers. In many ways, our lives were mirror images, seven years apart.

But there was one big crack in the mirror, one gulf between us that we skirted politely (most of the time): while I had long ago left the church, Frank remained a committed Catholic. He had also retained an abiding love for Ireland, to which he had returned again and again with my father, mother, and sisters in the years when I was *persona non grata*. He and my father had gone for many a tramp around Killarney, the town where my father was born, and where my aunt still lives. Mangerton, Torc, and the McGillicuddy Reeks were more than names to Frank; hikes on the slopes of these mountains were the source of the richest memories of his childhood and young adulthood.

I envied Frank the time he'd spent in Ireland with my father, and I'd always wanted to spend more time there myself. When my mother suggested that Frank and I might want to walk part of the Kerry Way together (a higher altitude walking version of the Ring of Kerry), we both jumped at the chance. I had a week between a talk I was due to give in Rome and another in London. It was March—not the best time to visit Ireland—but Frank could get free, and with his eighth child on the way, it was now or never.

We set out from Killarney on a blustery day. Though neither of us had done much recent hiking, we had an ambitious itinerary, about eighteen miles a day for the next five days. We were planning on staying each night at bed & breakfasts along the way, but we still carried packs with plenty of extra clothes.

The first day took us through Killarney National Park, up around the back of Torc, then down across the road to Moll's Gap and into the Black Valley. The hike took more out of us than we expected, and we tottered the last few miles, grateful that our guest house was at the near end of "town" (a sprinkling of houses spread over the better part of a mile).

After a hearty dinner of local lamb chops, though, things began to look up, so when Frank confessed that it was his wife's birthday, and that he wanted to go a mile up the road to the valley's only public phone, outside the youth hostel and the church, to call her, I agreed to go along. It was pitch dark by then, and raining to boot. We managed to stick to the road, though, and eventually came to the phone. Unfortunately, Angelique was not at home. How about going in to say a rosary for her, he asked?

Now, I hadn't said the rosary for over twenty years, and wasn't sure I even remembered how the "Hail Mary" went, but I agreed.

The church was open, of course, its outer door swinging in the wind. In Ireland, at least in the back country, the church is never closed. There was no electricity, and only a single candle burning by the altar. The wind howled outside, the door banged open and shut.

We began to pray. Frank helped me recall the words; the memories I'd never lost. When we were small, the rosary, even more than dinner (where my mother never sat down till everyone else had eaten), was the time the family was all together. As we droned aloud through the decades, the joyful, the glorious, and the sorrowful mysteries, I remembered my father's passing.

He had had a heart attack. He knew himself to be a dead man, he said. He was met by Mary, St. Joseph, and surprisingly, the devil. He begged for more time to make his peace with his family, and his wish was granted. The doctors brought him back, and as he lay in the hospital, intubated and unable to speak, he was desperate to communicate with each of us, scrawling on a small white slate. He wanted to reply to my letter, he said.

I had written him a few weeks before, telling him that even though I had left the church, I had absorbed so much of him, his belief, his moral values, his desire to be good, and to do good. I didn't want him to think he had failed. His short, so poignant reply, written on a slate and soon erased, but burned forever in my memory: "God forgive me, a sinner." His apology for the long years we had not spent together: "I only wanted you to be with us in paradise." The desire for togetherness in a world to come had become a wedge between us.

As he recovered over the next few days, he was a different man. He had always embodied for me so much of the stern, dogmatic side of Catholicism. Now, in the face of death, all that was stripped away, and the inner core of spirituality was revealed. His passion for his God was the heart of his life. How could I have never seen it before? So many of us build a shell around who we really are; our inner world is as untouchable as the heart of an oyster, till forces greater than we are pry us apart. Now, all was exposed. "I never showed you the face of Christ when you were small," he told my brother James. Well, he showed it to us then. It's as if he'd been turned inside out, and all the love and spiritual longing that had been hidden by his shyness and his formality were shining out like the sun.

Three weeks later, the time he had asked for was up. He had another attack, and this time he went for good.

We had taken him back to Ireland to bury him. It was a magical day, early April but beautiful as only a spring day in Ireland can be beautiful, a day of radiance stolen from the gloom. The funeral mass in the cathedral was concelebrated by thirty or forty priests: his two brothers, his childhood friends, and many others come to honor the life of one of Killarney's dear sons now coming home for good. (He had himself studied for the priesthood before deciding to pursue family life instead; his brothers Frank and Seumas had become senior in two of Ireland's great orders of priests, the Franciscans and the Columbans.)

He was buried in a Franciscan robe. He had long been a member of "the little order of Saint Francis," a lay organization devoted to Franciscan ideals. We learned then of small penances he would do, like tying rough twine around his waist under his clothes. As if it were still the Middle Ages! I would have scoffed, but I'd seen the light shining through him when impending death had pried all his coverings away!

Afterwards, the four sons, Sean, James, Frank, and I, walked behind the hearse up the main street of the town. As the funeral procession passed, those walking in the opposite direction turned and took "the three steps of mercy," walking with the procession. The depths of Ireland's Catholic legacy was never so clear as when a group of loutish youths, who might have been a street gang anywhere else, bowed their heads and turned to take the three steps with us.

As we turned up the road to Aghadoe cemetery, a breeze blew, and the blossoms fell from the trees onto the coffin. If it had been a movie, I would have laughed. It's never that perfect! Except it was.

The cemetery, crowned with the ruins of a sixth century chapel, looks down on the lakes of Killarney. Ham-handed farmers (my father's schoolmates) helped us carry the coffin over rough ground to the family plot. Normally, after the service, we would have all left, and "the lads" would have filled in the grave. But we wanted a last farewell, so we sent the lads on their way, and Sean, James, Frank, and I filled in the grave.

Now, twenty-five years later, I was back in Ireland. My tiredness fell away. I was at the heart of my father's mystery, the place where he had turned his passionate heart to God, and the place where he had wrapped it round with rituals that had kept me from seeing its purity and its strength.

Somehow, Frank had seen through the ritual, had shared in it and sunk his roots to the same deep place. I was honored that he was opening the door for me as well. "Hail Mary, full of grace, the Lord is with thee..."

There are a thousand ways to God. Let us all honor the ways that others have found.

The next few days we wore our legs off, as the paths became wilder. The worst of it was the aptly named Lack Road, which our

---

Nature in Ireland in a certain sense functions as an eighth sacrament. The Irish sky and landscape speak to the soul of the nearness of the Creator to His creation. The starkness of a mountain, a sudden burst of light behind a cloud, the shimmering waters, all are signs which constantly beckon man to contemplate the "Lord of the Elements."

—Timothy O'Donnell, "Christendom in Ireland"

guidebook insisted had been used to drive cattle to market "within living memory." We couldn't see how you could drive a mountain goat herd across it now, as we picked our way down an impossibly steep slope. We understood why our aunt, who had worked in Kerry Mountain Rescue, had insisted we pack so many extra clothes. Turn an ankle out here, and you're many hours from help, with changeable weather bringing freezing rain at any moment. At one point, the trail, which had us up to our knees in mud at many a point, vanished beneath ten feet of water, only to reappear tantalizingly on the other side, with no apparent way across. Ireland is a wilder country than many people realize.

On the fourth day, we came round the crest of a hill and saw the ocean spread out below us. Thirty or forty miles back the other way, we could see the gleaming lakes of Killarney, and amazingly enough, the green below Aghadoe. We could see many of the passes we'd picked our way through over the last few days, the miles that had lent soreness to our feet.

Along the way, we had talked through much of the old pain of the lost years, we'd shared dreams of the present and the future, but as we went on, we'd mostly fallen into a friendly silence. The old magic of Ireland was driving our reflections inward, recreating in us the unique Irish temper—passion and wildness and boggy depths alternating with conviviality, and ending up in quietness— a mirror of the landscape and the changing weather.

Tim O'Reilly, senior partner and co-owner of Travelers' Tales, is the founder and CEO of O'Reilly & Associates, Inc. (www.oreilly.com), the most-respected name in computer book publishing. O'Reilly & Associates also runs a successful series of conferences on leading-edge technologies and manages online technical sites including www.perl.com and xml.com as part of the O'Reilly Network. Tim is an activist for open source software and internet standards, and is a board member of ActiveState and Collab.Net. He lives in Sebastopol, California.

CECIL WOODHAM-SMITH

The Root of the Troubles

The Troubles have been hundreds
of years in the making.

AT THE BEGINNING OF THE YEAR 1845, THE STATE OF IRELAND was, as it had been for nearly 700 years, a source of grave anxiety to England. Ireland had first been invaded in 1169; it was now 1845, yet she had been neither assimilated nor subdued. The country had been conquered not once but several times, the land had been confiscated and redistributed over and over again, the population had been brought to the verge of extinction—after Cromwell's conquest and settlement only some half million Irish survived—yet an Irish nation still existed, separate, numerous, and hostile.

Indeed, during the last few years it had seemed that Irish affairs were moving towards a new and alarming crisis.

On January 1, 1801, an event of enormous importance had taken place—the Act of Union between Ireland and England became operative. The two countries were made one, the economy of Ireland was assimilated into the economy of England, the Irish Parliament at Dublin disappeared and the Parliament at Westminster henceforward legislated for both countries. It was as if a marriage between England and Ireland had been celebrated, with the clauses of the Act of Union as the terms of the marriage settlement.

At first sight it seemed that Ireland had everything to gain. Free trade between Ireland and England meant that the discrimination hitherto practised by England against Irish industry would come to an end; united with English riches Ireland would gain the capital she desperately needed for development, while the hundred Irish Members who were to sit at Westminster would give Ireland, for the first time, a voice in imperial affairs. Further, an impression had been created that when the Union became law, Catholic emancipation would immediately follow. Catholics (and three-quarters of the population of Ireland were Catholics) would be assured of justice from the wide and unprejudiced views of the Imperial Parliament, and the laws which, amongst other restrictions, prevented Catholics from becoming Members of Parliament or judges or being appointed King's Counsel would be repealed.

The reality, however, was very different. The primary object of the Union was not to assist and improve Ireland but to bring her more completely into subjection.

Two years earlier, in 1798, the Irish had rebelled. England at that moment was in extreme danger, passing through the darkest days of her struggle with revolutionary France, and the rebels of '98 were assisted by French troops and with French money. The rebellion was put down with savagery, the strength of the army in Ireland was increased to 100,000 men, and the Union followed. England tightened her hold over Ireland; rebellious action, it was hoped, would henceforth become impossible.

The Union was bitterly opposed; contemporaries described it not as a marriage but as a "brutal rape," and Ireland was compared to an heiress whose chambermaid and trustees have been bribed, while she herself is dragged, protesting, to the altar. Nevertheless, after bribery on a scale such as history has seldom witnessed, and a generous distribution of places of profit and titles, "Union titles," the Act of Union became law.

As the years passed, however, no happiness resulted. The hope of English investment proved a delusion. Free trade between the two countries enabled England to use Ireland as a market for surplus English goods; Irish industry collapsed, unemployment was widespread, and Dublin, now that an Irish Parliament sat no longer in College Green, became a half-dead city. Above all, Catholic emancipation, expected to follow immediately on the Union, was only achieved, after a desperate struggle, in 1829.

Ireland besought a repeal of the Union, and by 1843 the strength of the demand was seriously disquieting to the British government. The Catholic peasantry was becoming organized, the commercial classes were being drawn in, substantial sums of money were being raised. All this was the work of one man, Daniel O'Connell, who gave up a brilliant career at the bar to devote his life to Ireland.

Adopted by a Catholic uncle living at Derrynane, County Kerry, a fluent speaker of the Irish language, with a magnificent voice and presence, a quick wit, a superb gift of invective, and a flamboyance his enemies called vulgarity, he was nicknamed "Swaggering Dan." Self-government, not separation from England, was O'Connell's aim; and he cherished a romantic admiration for Queen Victoria, "the darling little Queen." He had a lawyer's respect for the law, with a horror of armed rebellion which derived from his personal recollection of the hangings, torturings, and floggings that had followed the '98; his followers were pledged to obtain repeal only by legal and constitutional means.

Nevertheless, the Repeal movement was felt by the government to be menacing. From March 1843, O'Connell held huge mass meetings, "monster" meetings, demanding repeal, and tens of thousands, hundreds of thousands, flocked to hear him. At the historic hill of Tara, the ancient seat of Irish sovereignty in Meath, a quarter of a million persons gathered; and Sir Edward Sugden, Lord Chancellor of Ireland, wrote "The peaceable demeanour of the assembled multitudes is one of the most alarming symptoms." At forty monster meetings the only disturbance which could be discovered, after searching scrutiny by the government, was the accidental overturning of a gingerbread stall.

An Irish people united and controlled was an ominous spectacle, and the British government, seized with something near panic, began to prepare "as if in hourly expectation of civil war." Troops were hastily brought from England, barracks were fortified and provisioned to withstand a siege, justices of the peace who were repealers were dismissed, and in the courtyard of Dublin Castle a regiment of infantry was kept drawn up and under arms, in readiness to suppress a revolt.

In the autumn of 1843, O'Connell announced that a monster meeting, the greatest of all, would be held on Sunday, October 8, on the fields of Clontarf, near Dublin, where 800 years before the Irish hero, Brian Boru, had defeated the Norsemen and driven them into the sea. The government, convinced that a rising would follow, decided to "proclaim" the Clontarf meeting, that is, to forbid it, in a proclamation issued by the Lord Lieutenant. Later, O'Connell himself was to be arrested.

The subsequent conduct of the government was, as Greville wrote in his diary, "certainly most extraordinary." Instead of "proclaiming" the meeting at once, nothing was done until the eleventh hour, on the Saturday afternoon before the Sunday. Then the guns of the Pigeon House, the fort commanding Dublin Bay, were trained on Clontarf, warships entered Dublin Bay, and troops occupied the approaches to the meeting place when tens of thousands of people were massing. Had it not been for O'Connell's creed that "human blood is no cement for the temple of liberty" a massacre might have taken place; but O'Connell ordered the people to go home and, directed by his lieutenants, the vast multitude quietly dispersed. No monster meeting took place, no disturbance occurred.

Nevertheless, O'Connell was arrested a week later on a charge of trying to alter the constitution by force. Convicted by a "packed jury," a partisan jury on which no Catholic or repealer was allowed to sit, he was sent to prison. The verdict was reversed by the House of Lords on September 24, 1844, and he was released. But for the movement the psychological moment had passed: the iron of Repeal had cooled and O'Connell himself was a changed man, while in prison he had "lost his nerve." He was nearly seventy, and the strain of the monster meetings, followed by arrest, trial, and imprisonment, even though he had been treated with consideration in prison, had broken his health.

Constitutional methods having failed, as armed rebellion had previously failed, Ireland relapsed into helpless hostility. No outbreak took place in 1844, the year immediately preceding the famine, but the anxiety of the government continued to be acute, and on the eve of the famine, the government of Ireland was admittedly a military occupation, and the garrison of Ireland was larger than the garrison of India. "How do you govern it?" demanded Macaulay in the House of Commons on February 19, 1844. "Not by love but by fear...not by the confidence of the people in the laws and their attachment to the Constitution but by means of armed men and entrenched camps."

The hostility between England and Ireland, which six centuries had failed to extinguish, had its roots first of all in race. After the first invasions, the first conquests, the Irish hated the English with the hatred of the defeated and the dispossessed. Nevertheless, eventually the English and the Irish might have fused, as the English and the Scots, the English and the Welsh have, for practical purposes, fused, had it not been that in the sixteenth century racial animosity was disastrously strengthened by religious enmity.

The crucial event was the Reformation. The ideas of liberty which the English cherish and the history of their country's rise to greatness are bound up with Protestantism, while Ireland, alone among the countries of northern Europe, was scarcely touched by the Reformation. The gulf which resulted could never be bridged. In the political division of Europe which followed the Reformation, England and Ireland were on opposing sides. Henceforward, Irish aspirations could only be fulfilled, Irish faith could only flourish, through the defeat of England and the triumph of her enemies.

Freedom for Ireland meant Philip of Spain and the Inquisition in place of Elizabeth I, it meant James II instead of William III, it even meant, since misery and oppression make strange bedfellows, the victory of Napoleon.

So completely is the history of the one country the reverse of the history of the other that the very names which to an Englishman mean glory, victory, and prosperity to an Irishman spell degradation, misery, and ruin. In Ireland the name of Elizabeth I stands only for the horrors of her Irish conquest; in the defeat of the Armada, Ireland's hopes of independence went down; above all, with the name of William III and the glorious revolution of 1688, the very foundation of British liberties, the Catholic Irishman associates only the final subjugation of his country and the degradation and injustice of the penal laws. Freedom for the one meant slavery for the other; victory for the one meant defeat for the other; the good of the one was the evil of the other. Ireland, resentful and hostile, lying only a day's sail, in fine weather, from Britain's coasts, for centuries provided a refuge for enemy agents, a hatching-ground for enemy plots; her motto was "England's difficulty is Ireland's opportunity," and in every crisis of England's history she seized the moment of weakness to stab her enemy in the back. It is the explanation, if not the excuse, for the ferocity with which the English have treated Ireland.

Countries are either mothers or fathers, and engender the emotional bristle secretly reserved for either sire. Ireland has always been a woman, a womb, a cave, a cow, a Rosaleen, a sow, a bride, a harlot, and, of course, the gaunt Hag of Beard. Originally a land of woods and thickets, such as Orpheus had seen when prescribing the voyage of Jason, through a misted atmosphere. She is thought to have known invasion from the time when the Ice Age ended and the improving climate allowed deer to throng her dense forests.

These infiltrations have been told and fabricated by men and by mediums who described the violation of her body and soul.... Tacitus records how a Roman general gazed across the sea from Scotland and reckoned that a single legion could have subdued her. He was possibly mistaken, for despite the many other legions that tried to subdue her, Ireland was never fully taken, though most thoroughly dispossessed.

—Edna O'Brien, *Mother Ireland*

In the 1840s, after nearly 700 years of English domination, Irish poverty and Irish misery appalled the traveller. The Frenchman de Beaumont found in Ireland the extreme of human misery, worse than the negro in his chains; the German traveller Kohl wrote that no mode of life in Europe could seem pitiable after one had seen Ireland. He used, he said, to pity the poor Letts in Livonia: "Well, Heaven pardon my ignorance! Now I have seen Ireland, it seems to me that the poorest among the Letts, the Esthonians, and the Finlanders, lead a life of comparative comfort."

Exceptions were to be found in Ulster, particularly the northeast portion, which includes Belfast. Throughout the first half of the nineteenth century, while Dublin was decaying, Belfast was growing into a leading industrial town and port, and the linen manufacture in which Ulster was to lead the world was rapidly developing; Belfast was the headquarters and distributing centre, and flax-growing and weaving were carried on in the surrounding districts. A large part of Ulster differed from most of Ireland because it had been "planted." In the "plantation of Ulster," at the beginning of the seventeenth century, the original Irish owners of the soil had been driven out and mainly Scottish Protestants put in their place. The descendants of the plantation had not been dispossessed; they shared the religion of their rulers, had rights, seldom found elsewhere, relating to the occupation of land, and their standard of life, assisted by the rise of the linen industry, was somewhat higher than in the south and southwest.

Better conditions, however, were by no means universal in Ulster. Donegal, which then formed part of the province, was one of the poorest and most backward counties in Ireland and, nearer Belfast, in districts like the Fews, in County Armagh, the standard of living was as low as anywhere in the country.

"There never was," said the Duke of Wellington, a native of County Meath, "a country in which poverty existed to the extent it exists in Ireland." Housing conditions were wretched beyond words. The census of 1841 graded "houses" in Ireland into four classes; the fourth and lowest class consisted of windowless mud cabins of a single room, "...nearly half of the families of the rural population," reported the census commissioners, "...are living in the lowest state." In parts of the west of Ireland more than three-fifths of the "houses" were one-roomed, windowless mud cabins, and west of a line drawn from Londonderry to Cork the proportion was two-fifths.

Furniture was a luxury; the inhabitants of Tullahobagly, County Donegal, numbering about 9,000, had in 1837 only 10 beds, 93 chairs, and 243 stools among them. Pigs slept with their owners, manure heaps choked doors, sometimes even stood inside; the evicted and unemployed put roofs over ditches, burrowed into banks, existed in bog holes.

All this wretchedness and misery could, almost without exception, be traced to a single source—the system under which land had come to be occupied and owned in Ireland, a system produced by centuries of successive conquests, rebellions, confiscations, and punitive legislation.

In 1843, in the midst of the Repeal agitation, the British government, recognizing that the land question was at the root of Irish discontent, set up a Royal Commission "to inquire into the law and practice with regard to the occupation of land in Ireland." This commission, called the Devon Commission, after its chairman, the Earl of Devon, visited every part of Ireland, examined 1,100 witnesses, printed three huge volumes of evidence, and

> The particular misfortune of this country has been to fall into the hands of an upper class who are different from the masses in race, in custom and in religion and who nevertheless were invested with sovereign power, which they exercise under cover of the all-powerful protection of England... Consequently, therefore, two nations entirely distinct on the same soil. The one rich, civilized, happy; the other poor, half savage, and overwhelmed by all the miseries by which God can strike man.
>
> —Alexis de Tocqueville in Ireland (1835)

reported in February 1845, a few months before the outbreak of
the famine. Its secretary was an able and "improving" landlord, John
Pitt Kennedy, who had gained some celebrity as the author of a
pamphlet on the Irish question entitled "Instruct: Employ: Don't
Hang Them." It adds to the weight of its conclusions that the
Commission was a landlords' Commission; every member who sat
on it was a landowner, and O'Connell declared, "It is perfectly one-
sided, all landlords and no tenants."

The Report of the Devon Commission stated that the principal
cause of Irish misery was the bad relations between landlord and
tenant. Ireland was a conquered country, the Irish peasant a dispossessed man, his landlord an alien conqueror. There was no paternal-
ism, such as existed in England, no hereditary loyalty or feudal tie.
"Confiscation is their common title," said the Earl of Clare, the famous Tory Lord Chancellor, speaking of Irish landlords, "and from
the first settlements they have been hemmed in on every side by the
original inhabitants of the island, brooding over their discontent in
sullen indignation."

With some notable exceptions—whose names survive and are
regarded with affection in Ireland today—the successive owners of
the soil of Ireland regarded it merely as a source from which to extract as much money as possible, and since a hostile, backward
country is neither a safe nor an agreeable place in which to live,
from the first conquests the absentee landlord was common in
Ireland. The absentee evil was "a very great one" as early as 1377.
Rents were spent in England or on the Continent; in 1843 it was
estimated that £6,000,000 of rents were being remitted out of
Ireland, and Kohl, the German traveller, commented on the mansions of absentee landlords, standing "stately, silent, empty." Absentee
estates, however, were by no means always the worst managed, and
some, in particular the properties of great English territorial mag-
nates, for instance, the estates of the Duke of Devonshire, were
models. But too often owners visited property in Ireland only once
or twice in a lifetime, sometimes not at all; as Colonel Conolly, of
Kildare and Donegal, told a Select Committee of the House of
Lords in 1846, "Where the landlords have never seen their estates,

you can hardly suppose that their sympathies are very strong for sufferings they have never witnessed." Meanwhile, almost absolute power was left in the hands of an agent, whose ability was measured by the amount of money he could contrive to extract.

During the eighteenth century a new method of dealing with Irish property was adopted. Large tracts of land were let at a fixed rent to a single individual on a long lease, and he sublet as he chose. This "middleman system" produced misery: the landlord rid himself of responsibility and assured himself of a regular income, but the tenants were handed over to exploitation. Profit was the only motive, and contemporary observers denounce middlemen as "land sharks," "bloodsuckers," "the most oppressive species of tyrant that ever lent assistance to the destruction of a country." Moreover, the middlemen degraded the land because, as the slum landlord finds it more profitable to let out a house room by room, so they split farms into smaller and smaller holdings for the sake of increased rents.

Yet whether he held under a middleman, a resident, or an absentee landlord, the terms on which the Irish peasant occupied his land were harsh, and two provisions in particular, the two "monster grievances" of Ireland, deprived him of incentive and security.

First, any improvement he made to his holding became, when his lease expired or was terminated, the property of the landlord, without compensation. Second, he very seldom had any security of tenure; the majority of tenants in Ireland were tenants "at will," that is, the will of the landlord, who could turn them out whenever he chose.

Under a practice known as "tenant right," found mainly in Ulster, compensation for improvements was paid, and where the practice existed it was jealously guarded. "...It is one of the sacred rights of the county which cannot be touched with impunity," the agent for Lord Lurgan's property in County Armagh told the Devon Commission: "and if systematic efforts were made among the proprietors of Ulster to invade tenant right, I do not believe there is a force at the disposal of the Horse Guards (the War Office) sufficient to keep the peace of the province."

The Devon Commission stated that the superior prosperity and tranquillity of Ulster, compared with the rest of Ireland, were due to tenant right.

The annexation of improvements was made more inequitable by the bare state in which land was customarily let, so destitute of every aid to cultivation taken for granted in England or Scotland that it was often impossible for the tenant to work it until he had made "improvements" destined to enrich his landlord.

Even so, had the tenant possessed some degree of security, for instance held a reasonable lease, he might have been encouraged to exert himself. But leases were the exception not the rule, stated Lord Stanley, himself an Irish landowner, in the House of Lords on June 9, 1845, the eve of the famine. In many cases the landlord refused a lease because he had the tenant more completely under his control; in others, the tenant declined because recent legislation had so greatly increased the cost of the stamp on a lease that he could not find the necessary £10 or so.

In most cases, however, even a lease did not give security, owning to a deplorable and "very prevalent" Irish practice known as the "hanging gale"—"gale" being the term used for a periodical payment of rent. The

---

I was later to read about the Great Famine in James Charles Roy's *The Road Wet, The Wind Close*, in which he refers to the "massive starvation on the one hand and a multitude of fish on the other" and states that "one still hears the slur now and then that the peasants were too lazy to fish." The problem was not laziness, according to Roy, nor was it the lack of curraghs, but that the curraghs were too frail and too low in the water to allow nets: "The great runs of fish are all in deep water, several miles offshore, where nets are mandatory. Tricky weather and rough Atlantic waters sealed off the venture to any but the foolhardy, and so the people starved amidst the plenty."

—David W. McFadden,
An Innocent in Ireland

hanging gale allowed an incoming tenant to leave his rent in arrear, that is "hanging," for six, twelve, or fifteen months. Tenants were almost invariably without capital, land was let bare, frequently even a dwelling had to be erected, and it was useless for the landlord to look for his rent until at least one harvest had given the tenant a chance to gain something.

But, once the tenant owed rent, any security his lease might give vanished. Edward Wakefield, a well-known economist of the period, described the "hanging gale" as "one of the great levers of oppression...the lower classes are kept in a kind of perpetual bondage...this debt hangs over their heads...and keeps them in a continual state of anxiety and terror."

There were, of course, good landlords in Ireland, and on Lord Monteagle's estate at Mount Trenchard, the Duke of Leinster's at Carton, Mr. Guinness's at Stillorgan, Lord Bessborough's at Bessborough, to name only a few, farm buildings were erected by the landlord, cabins were tidy, and the people contented. In such cases a lease was often felt to be superfluous. A tenant of Lord Mountcashel's told the Devon Commission:"From the unbending integrity and honesty of Mr. Joy (the agent) we are considered as safe at will as under a lease. I have expended £500 without the scratch of a pen." He added, however:"But Lord Mountcashel may be gathered to his fathers and Mr. Joy may die, and another Pharaoh may arise who knew not Joseph."

Too often the powers given to the landlord, "the most powerful the law can create," were remorselessly used. "The dread of landlords was such that people trembled before them," recorded the writer of a manuscript in Donegal, just before the famine. "In Ireland alone," wrote John Stuart Mill, "the whole agricultural population can be evicted by the mere will of the landlord, either at the expiration of a lease or, in the far more common case of their having no lease, at six months' notice. In Ireland alone, the bulk of a population wholly dependent on the land cannot look forward to a single year's occupation of it."

In these circumstances industry and enterprise were extinguished and a peasantry created which was one of the most desti-

tute in Europe. "It would be impossible adequately to describe,"
stated the Devon Commission in its Report, "the privations which
they (the Irish labourer and his family) habitually and silently en-
dure...in many districts their only food is the potato, their only
beverage water...their cabins are seldom a protection against the
weather...a bed or a blanket is a rare luxury...and nearly in all their
pig and a manure heap constitute their only property." The
Commissioners could not "forbear expressing our strong sense of
the patient endurance which the labouring classes have exhibited
under sufferings greater, we believe, than the people of any other
country in Europe have to sustain."

Wretched though their condition might be, the pre-famine
Irish peasants were not gloomy. "Their natural condition," wrote
Sir Walter Scott during his visit to Ireland in 1825, "is turned towards gaiety and happiness," and the Census Commissioners noted
"the proverbial gaiety and lightheartedness of the peasant people."
Dancing was the universal diversion, and Lord George Hill,
who owned property in Donegal, has left an account of removing
a cabin with dancing and fiddling. "The custom on such
occasions is for the person who has the work to be done to hire
a fiddler, upon which engagement all the neighbours joyously as-
semble and carry in an incredibly short time the stones and timber upon their backs to the new site; men, women, and children
alternately dancing and working while daylight lasts, at the termination of which they adjourn to some dwelling where they
finish the night, often prolonging the dance to dawn of day."
Arthur Young, at the end of the eighteenth century, commented
on the fine physique of the average Irishman and the good looks
of Irishwomen, and even after the sufferings of the famine Nassau
Senior, the economist, revisiting Ireland, was "struck by the
beauty of the population."
The culture of the potato required little attention except at
springtime and harvest, and through the long winter nights the
people sat within their cabins, fiddling, talking, and telling stories.

Firing, in the shape of turf—peat cut from the bog and costing little or nothing—was plentiful.

"Few, if any, had any reason to complain of cold," records a manuscript, and poteen, illicit whiskey, was plentiful, too. Groups of neighbours gathered for dancing to the fiddle, indoors in the winter, in summer at the crossroads; wakes, with liberal potations of poteen, were social occasions; and crowds gaily travelled immense distances to attend markets, fairs, and, above all, races. "If there be a market to attend, a fair or a funeral, a horse race, a fight or a wedding, all else is neglected and forgotten," wrote George Nicholls, the leading English Poor Law expert, when reporting on the state of the Irish people.

As the main diversion of the women was talking, they disliked living in isolated houses. In schemes of land improvement the houses were separated, since in the old-style Irish settlement of cabins in clusters the women and the men spent too much time talking and quarrelling. The change was always unpopular.

In 1927 I was seven and was sent for health reasons to live on Bob Bothwell's thirteen-acre farm in the townland of Enagh about six miles south of Armagh. For a city lad from the mean streets it was rapture to be surrounded by the lovely countryside of trees and rivers and friendly people who were unfailingly kind and animals who were friendly too. The humble potato was still the staple diet of the countryside. For dinner, everyone sat down around the long kitchen table to eat six or seven spuds at a go: "Balls of Flour," not those despised soapy English efforts. Arguments would run high about the respective merits of King Edwards, Scotch Thistle, Kerr's Pinks, Skerries and more. Sometimes they were served with an egg floating in the middle of a creamy mash, sometimes beaten up with butter and scallions. Mostly they were served as is. But they were always washed down with good buttermilk.

—Leslie Gillespie,
"Balls of Flour"

Lord George Hill relates a story of an agent who observed to a tenant that he seemed to be doing much better now that he was living away from neighbours and could "attend to his farm instead of idling and gossiping." The man assured him that precisely the contrary was true, and "he could not stand it much longer on account of the expense, as he was obliged to keep a servant maid just to talk to his wife."

Good manners and hospitality were universal among the poorest Irish. "The neighbour or the stranger finds every man's door open, and to walk in without ceremony at meal time and to partake of his bowl of potatoes, is always sure to give pleasure to everyone of the house," wrote Sir John Carr, a Devonshire gentleman who toured Ireland soon after the Union; and twenty years later, Sir Walter Scott found "perpetual kindness in the Irish cabin; buttermilk, potatoes, a stool is offered, or a stone is rolled that your honour may sit down...and those that beg everywhere else seem desirous to exercise hospitality in their own houses."

A young lady named Elizabeth Ham came to Ballina, County Mayo, when her father, a British Army officer, was stationed there in connection with the disturbed state of the country, following the rebellion of 1798. She was astonished to find that she could roam the wild mountains without fear of molestation, while in England no girl could ramble in the woods and fields alone, even though at this time Irishmen who had taken a part in the rebellion were being hanged by the English on Ballina bridge. She would, she wrote, "have fearlessly trusted" the Irish peasantry "in any circumstances." The intelligence of the people surprised her. "I never met a solitary peasant in my rambles but I addressed him, and by this means got stores of legendary lore. One man I remember told me the subjects of most of Ossian's poems in his own version of English."

Returning to England after five years she was "greatly struck by the vulgarity of everyone." Driving from Holyhead in a chaise, "we happened to stop opposite a cottage and...asked for a glass of water. It was brought...and the woman asked for payment. An Irish woman would have considered it an insult to be offered such. The cottages were clean and neat and the country looked clean in comparison but the manners seemed far inferior."

Irish dignity, Irish hospitality, and the easy good manners which still charm the modern traveller have a historical explanation. Three times, at least, the native aristocracy was conquered and dispossessed; many fled from Ireland to exile in France or Spain, but many others remained, to be forced down by poverty and penal legislation to the economic level of the peasantry.

Until the famine, it was by no means uncommon for poor peasants in mud cabins to make wills bequeathing estates which had long ago been confiscated from their forefathers, and that figure of fun in Victorian days, the Irish beggar who claimed to be descended from kings, was very often speaking the truth. "I am descended from perhaps as good a family as any I address, though now destitute of means" runs a letter imploring assistance in the Distress papers.

There was, however, a darker and more sinister side to the Irish character. They are, said a land agent on the eve of the famine, "a very desperate people, with all this degree of courtesy, hospitality, and cleverness amongst them."

To understand the Irish of the nineteenth century and their blend of courage and evasiveness, tenacity and inertia, loyalty and double-dealing, it is necessary to go back to the Penal Laws.

The Penal Laws, dating from 1695, and not repealed in their entirety until Catholic emancipation in 1829, aimed at the destruction of Catholicism in Ireland by a series of ferocious enactments, provoked by Irish support of the Stuarts after the Protestant William of Orange was invited to ascend the English throne in 1688, and England faced the greatest Catholic power in Europe—France. At this critical moment the Catholic Irish took up arms in support of the Stuarts. James II's standard was raised in Ireland, and he, with an Irish Catholic army, was defeated on Irish soil, at the battle of the Boyne, near Drogheda, on July 1, 1690.

The threat to England had been alarming, and vengeance

followed. Irish intervention on behalf of the Stuarts was to be made impossible forever by reducing the Catholic Irish to helpless impotence. They were, in the words of a contemporary, to become "insignificant slaves, fit for nothing but to hew wood and draw water," and to achieve this object the Penal Laws were devised.

> All the penal laws of that unparalleled code of oppression…were manifestly the effects of national hatred and scorn towards a conquered people.
> —Rt. Hon. Edmund Burke,
> *The Works of the Rt. Hon.*
> *Edmund Burke*

In broad outline, they barred Catholics from the army and navy, the law, commerce, and from every civic activity. No Catholic could vote, hold any office under the Crown, or purchase land, and Catholic estates were dismembered by an enactment directing that at the death of a Catholic owner his land was to be divided among all his sons, unless the eldest became a Protestant, when he would inherit the whole. Education was made almost impossible, since Catholics might not attend schools, nor keep schools, nor send their children to be educated abroad. The practice of the Catholic faith was proscribed; informing was encouraged as "an honourable service" and priest-hunting treated as a sport. Such were the main provisions of the Penal Code, described by Edmund Burke as "a machine as well fitted for the oppression, impoverishment, and degradation of a people, and the debasement in them of human nature itself, as ever proceeded from the perverted ingenuity of man."

The material damage suffered through the Penal Laws was great; ruin was widespread, old families disappeared, and old estates were broken up; but the most disastrous effects were moral. The Penal Laws brought lawlessness, dissimulation, and revenge in their train, and the Irish character, above all the character of the peasantry, did become, in Burke's words, degraded and debased. The upper classes were able to leave the country and many middle-class merchants contrived, with guile, to survive, but the poor Catholic peasant bore the full hardship. His religion made him an outlaw; in the Irish House of Commons he was described as "the common enemy," and whatever was inflicted on him he must bear, for where could he look for redress? To his landlord? Almost invariably an alien conqueror. To the law? Not when every person connected with the law, from the jailer to the judge, was a Protestant who regarded him as "the common enemy."

In these conditions suspicion of the law, of the ministers of the law, and of all established authority "worked into the very nerves and blood of the Irish peasant," and, since the law did not give him justice, he set up his own law. The secret societies which have been the curse of Ireland became widespread during the Penal period, and a succession of underground associations, Oak Boys, White Boys, and Ribbon Men, gathering in bogs and lonely glens, flouted the law and dispensed a people's justice in the terrible form of revenge. The informer, the supplanter of an evicted tenant, the landlord's man, were punished with dreadful savagery, and since animals were wealth their unfortunate animals suffered, too. Cattle were "clifted," driven over the edge of a cliff, horses hamstrung, dogs clubbed to death, stables fired, and the animals within burned alive. Nor were lawlessness, cruelty, and revenge the only consequences. During the long Penal period, dissimulation became a moral necessity and evasion of the law the duty of every God-fearing Catholic. To worship according to his faith, the Catholic must attend illegal meetings; to protect his priest, he must be secret, cunning, and a concealer of the truth.

These were dangerous lessons for any government to compel its subjects to learn, and a dangerous habit of mind for any nation to acquire.

British writer, biographer, and historian Cecil Woodham-Smith was born in Tenby, Wales in 1896, and died in London, England in 1977. A leading authority of nineteenth century British history, Ms. Woodham-Smith began writing biographies in her forties. In 1950, her biography of Florence Nightingale won the James Tait Black Memorial Award. This story was excerpted from her book, The Great Hunger: Ireland 1845–1849.

PART TWO

SOME THINGS TO DO

ROBERT McGARVEY

A Windy Tale on Cape Clear

For a lesson in storytelling,
go to Cape Clear.

OUTSIDE THE OLD STONE HOUSE, A FORCE 10 WIND—A FURIOUS
gale upward of 60 miles per hour—battered Cape Clear Island, a tiny,
treeless speck of land 6 miles off Ireland's southern coast. Inside the
house Marion, a thirty-something Irish woman whom I had met
only moments before, reached over, grabbed my wrists, and yanked
with a power that rivaled the gale's, as she yelled, "Give it to me!"

"No," I bellowed back at her.

Marion screamed more loudly, "Give it to me!"

I could feel something coursing through my arms toward
Marion. Around me, there were other pairs of people—all tugging
on each other, screaming, and letting go at the start of the annual
Cape Clear Island Storytelling Workshop. In the background, as
Marion pulled my wrists, I heard the voice of our group leader,
storyteller Sheila Stewart, explaining why we were manhandling
each other: "You come to my workshop to be a better storyteller.
But you'll be that only when you're in touch with your inner self.
Let your inhibitions go!"

"Stories sparkle only when you put yourself in them," said
Sheila, who hails from a family of well-known Scottish performers

and has performed at the White House and guest-lectured on Scottish culture at Harvard. "For a story to work," she added, "you've got to let your *conyach* flow."

Conyach? Before gathering in this room none of us had known about *conyach*, but Sheila explained that mastering it would be our mission over the workshop's three days.

"When you leave here, you will be in touch with your *conyach*. It's a feeling inside," Sheila translated the word.

As I looked around, I saw faces filled with anxiety. There were sixteen of us, mainly Irish, English, and Scots, but including three other Americans. Most of us had traveled to Cape Clear—a journey that includes a two-hour drive from Cork to the wee town of Baltimore and a forty-five-minute ferry trip to the island—expecting to spend the weekend polishing stories that would wow an audience. Oh, we'd be able to do that, said Sheila, but only after we released our demons and embraced our individual *conyach*.

"Storytelling is not elocution," said Sheila, who went on to demand we hang our heads between our knees, shake our heads, and force out a primal sound: "*Wah! Wah!*" As I did this, I was suddenly overcome by a feeling of intense stupidity. Here I was, 6,000 miles from home, making infantile noises. But there was method behind the seeming madness.

"The head is for educational purposes," Sheila said. "Not for storytelling. You come to my workshop to learn to tell stories from your heart, with *conyach*, and that's when the words flow from your heart to your lips…and it is magical."

At last a break came, and a half dozen of us bolted through the door, to escape into the safety of the windstorm that raged outside on this three-mile-long island. Huddling next to a stone wall, I lit a cigarette. Another workshop participant came up and asked for a light. As he struggled to keep the flame going, I asked how he felt about the workshop.

"Zapped," he said.

"But," said a woman who also had come outside for a smoke, "isn't she a grand woman? It's not what I thought it would be, but…"

After a few minutes we drifted back into the room and took

our seats in the semicircle around the coal fire. That's when Sheila looked at me and commanded: "Sing the song, Bob."

Earlier she had passed out a traditional Scots ballad and told us our assignment was not just to memorize it but to learn to sing it with feeling, with our *conyach* at full tilt. But I don't sing in public, never have. I had merely glanced at the words, convinced that probably she'd ask only a few of us to sing, and I'd be able to hide. I'd even staked out a seat that was partially hidden behind a ladder leading up to a sleeping loft.

But my camouflage had failed.

"Sing it, Bob," said Sheila again. "Mix your soul with spirit and put this into voice. We can discover our *conyach* in songs. We can hear it."

I pulled the lyrics from my pocket, gulped, and stumbled through the words as though this was a poem I only vaguely comprehended:

> Faulse Faulse hae you
>   been to me
>   my love
> How often you've changed
>   your mind
> But since you've led your
>   love on
>   another fair maid
> I'm afraid you're no more
>   mine.

At the Kerry International Summer School, we hear poets and writers from across Ireland. A few days later, in unquestionably the strangest, yet most effective, poetry reading I've ever attended, we spend the evening in Kerry's Crag Cave in Castleisland. There, in a huge vaulted chamber where an ancient underground river once ran, we listen to poets read in Irish-Gaelic and English. It's a little difficult to concentrate on the poetry when it's in a strange language and you're surrounded by weirdly backlit stalagmites, but it works. And only in Ireland, I think, could it work so well. These poets, these writers, are so tied to the land, to the very soil of the place, that being a hundred feet under the soil is somehow effective and moving.

—Rick Wilber,
"An Irish Story"

I read without music in my voice, without much of anything, except a palpable fear that had surfaced as soon as she had called out my name.

When I finished, Sheila looked at me—was that pity?—and said, "That's interesting." She quickly moved on to other workshop attendees, and virtually all of them sang with more passion than I had mustered.

When the workshop closed for the day, I needed a drink, which meant a half-mile walk down the hill to Ciarán Danny Mike's. It was the only pub likely to be open that evening, according to Chuck Kruger, the workshop organizer and an American expat who has called Cape Clear home for six years. He holds the storytelling workshop (as well as a summertime storytelling festival) on Cape Clear, both because it's his home and "to help the local economy," which otherwise revolves around a little fishing, making Irish crafts, and farming. And, of course, there were the pubs.

But, added Chuck, "You never know when Ciarán Danny Mike's will be open. He keeps his own hours."

That, I had already discovered during my time on the island, is the Cape Clear style. The grocery store—with a sparse stock (canned goods, packaged soups, and packets of lunch meat) that's replenished only when the ferry arrives—is open a few hours a day. There was just one restaurant serving while I was there, and supper was a do-it-yourself affair, or perhaps a hot meal at Ciarán Danny Mike's or at one of the island's B & Bs.

But, absent prior arrangement, all of that was iffy on this rugged island where the 140 inhabitants are determined to do things their own way.

The cars proved the island's character. Cape Clear's few roads were jammed with rolling junk—rusted-out fifteen-year-old cars salvaged from the mainland and coaxed into delivering a little more service. And don't ask if the vehicles are registered.

I did not have to ask why residents need cars on so tiny an island, not as I descended the steep hill toward the pub. With each step down, I knew I'd be huffing and puffing on the trip back up.

The thought prompted me to accelerate toward the pub—a large, modern building that probably could accommodate the island's entire population. On this windy night, though, the crowd consisted of a half dozen locals, and the bartender greeted me as though I were an old-timer; "Hallo, what will you be drinking? 'Tis windy out tonight."

I ordered a Guinness, took a seat at the bar, and, when the drink came, downed the pint in a couple of swallows—but still my failure with the song fogged my brain. I ordered another pint and sipped this one more deliberately. Outside, the sun had set, and I knew that before me I had a half-mile, uphill walk on a mainly dirt road with no street lights.

N ed called for a pint, and when after a lot of *toascing* she put it on the counter, Ned said, "This pint isn't full."

"Ah," says she, "I left room on the top for your moustache."

—Eamon Kelly, *In My Father's Time*

I asked the barman for two Guinnesses to go, and when he delivered the plastic sack, he told me, "I won't charge you a deposit on the bottles. Just bring them back, aye?"

I hoisted the bag and wandered outside where, a few steps from the pub, I was plunged into darkness. Far up the hill I saw lights—that was my destination. I had booked a room in Kruger's Southernmost House in Ireland, the stone farmhouse that doubled as workshop site and accommodations.

"Take a torch if you go out at night," Kruger had told me, but I'd ignored his advice, and now my prayer was that my internal compass was working and I'd taken the right dirt road.

When I finally saw The Southernmost House, I nearly leaped for joy. I hurried inside, scavenged some mushroom soup from the kitchen's scant provisions, opened another Guinness, and, as I ate my dinner, chewed over that day's failure—and resolved that if I could stand up to the island's fierce winds and vicious hills, I could certainly handle this workshop.

And I did. In the days that followed, at Sheila's command, we chased more inner demons and also told brief stories—some funny, a few poignant, most deeply personal. One Irish woman talked about being chased for blocks by "a strange man" when she lived briefly in San Francisco.

"I ran for blocks," she said, "and when I turned around, he was gone. But I wouldn't live in America again. I wouldn't."

For my part, I told about several visits to Northern Ireland when it was a war zone, and how on the initial trip a young soldier with his finger on the trigger of an automatic rifle had asked me what I was doing in the north.

"On holiday," I'd said.

Where did I live?

"Los Angeles."

And then, as he stood there in a cold drizzle, he'd looked sadly at me and asked, "So why did you come here on holiday?"

"For the weather, of course," I'd answered. "I get so bored with sunshine at home."

With rain dribbling off his poncho, he'd turned angry and almost shouted, "Go on with you," as he shooed me through the border crossing.

With the stories, we all grew more comfortable in the workshop, and by the last day we were ready to tackle the pivotal exercise: we visualized our souls—mine looked oddly like a little pink ball—then mixed it with our spirits, and forcibly tugged the two of them out, propelling them into the air with a great shout.

"That's putting the *conyach* out," said Sheila. "Whatever you do from now on, you will do far better because now you'll know how always to tap into your *conyach*.

"In this workshop I've planted a seed. Your *conyach* will bloom. If you nurture it, within a few days or a month you'll have it working for you. It will happen. Your *conyach* will flourish."

With that, the workshop was over. And while many of us sighed with relief, I still couldn't shake my failure with that ballad.

I joined the rush to catch the ferry that would return me to my regular life, and when I took my spot on the boat, it was next to

Sheila. Abruptly we both found we had to labor to keep our footing, as the boat was bashed by high winds and tall waves. When an especially savage breaker slapped us, she turned to me and said, "I hate this wee boat. I really do. I'd never live on that island, not if I had to ride this ferry."

Something in me clicked and, suddenly I had the song lyrics on my lips. In a credible baritone, I bellowed, "Faulse! Faulse! Hae you been to me my love."

Sheila was as stunned as I was.

Again I sang: "Faulse! Faulse!"

She looked at me, laughed a deep laugh that came from her belly and slowly marched up her throat, and said: "You're brilliant! You've got some hidden talents. Just nurture that seed, Bob. You know," she added, "that is some voice you have."

I laughed. She laughed. Finally I had begun to comprehend what *conyach* is all about.

On one of his many trips to Ireland, California-based writer Robert McGarvey was asked by a taxi driver what brought him to the country so often. "The weather," said McGarvey. Replied the taxi driver, "You must be daft, man." When he's not in Ireland, McGarvey writes about technology for U.S. magazines and is the ombudsman for Porthole Cruise Magazine.

LARRY T. JORDAN

* * *

An Appointment with Doctor Caldwell

A wayward son returns to the links of his youth.

IT HAS BEEN SAID THAT IN A LAND WHERE BEAUTY, POETRY, conflict, and passionate belief in the individual are constantly intermingled, the Irish have found golf to be a ready expression of their character and flair for games. And although the Scots claim to have invented the game, it may be said that the Irish took it to their hearts and made music of it.

I was reminded of all this upon my recent visit to Ireland, a visit prompted at the urging of my family when my business failed. A couple of weeks playing golf in Ireland is what you need, they told me, plus, you've always wanted to play Portmarnock. And so, whimsically, freeing my mind of worries, off to my native land I flew to play some of the courses I walked as a boy, packing Doctor Caldwell's bag, his voice speaking to me now from beyond the grave: "Remember, boy, 'tis but a game, but the grandest of games. If you listen you may come to know yourself better. There's a value to that."

All true.

In the comforting half light of memory I recall my first addictive taste of the game. I was maybe all of twelve years old that long ago summer. While walking along a desolate Irish seashore it happened. The day was warm, the air heavy. The wind from the Irish Sea that usually howled along this spit of sandy beach was notably absent. The cry of wild birds filled the cloudless sky.

I heard the man's voice first. His language was not for the tender of ear. Then climbing up the sand dunes, I saw him. Dressed in a tweedy suit and even tweedier hat, steel rod in hand, he was flailing away at the waist-high reedy grass. In his brown brogues and plus fours he looked every inch the country squire.

I didn't know quite what to make of him. As I turned to leave, he saw me.

"You, boy!" he shouted, "Come help me find my bloody ball."

This was Doctor Caldwell, and I was later to become what he called, "My trusted caddie." What followed were years of richness and frustration toting his clubs.

There are more than 350 golf courses scattered around this small island, 38 of them around the north side of Dublin. Of all the courses few are blessed with the natural magnificence of Portmarnock, home course of my beloved Doctor Caldwell. It is a 7,103-yard, par-72 gem, which golfing legend Arnold Palmer once called, "One of the greatest courses in the world." Located ten miles north of Dublin's city center and within the fine sweep of coastline curving to an end at Howth Hill, the northern guardian of Dublin Bay.

Portmarnock is a long tongue of linksland between the Irish Sea and an inland tidal bay. It is thus almost enclosed by water, a private place where man is alone with the turf, the sea, the sky, and the challenge of the wind. And the light. Such a fickle thing: out of a sodden sky, a single beam bright as platinum slowly moves across the green land then suddenly scatters through the moist air with a warm glow. It rises from the earth towards the heavens. Then it's gone.

This is strong, seductive golfing country.

Like other links courses, Portmarnock often changes direction with two equally challenging nine holes finishing by the venerable white clubhouse. However, unlike other links courses here, the greens are always visible from the fairway even if the fairways are not always visible from the tee. God always holds one thing back.

Portmarnock's first hole, a 388-yard par-4, runs dangerously close by the sea and even now, after more than fifty years since I first stood here on this emerald expanse of memory, I could still see those errant tee shots disappear into the Irish Sea. I tried to rid my mind of the thought for fear that my first ball would also find its way to that same inhospitable place.

"Right you are, sir. Ready to play away are we?"

It was the voice of my caddie.

"Foley, sir. That's me. I like the 3-wood here, sir. Let the wind help us. We'll keep the ould driver in the bag for a while. All right?"

He was a small, portly man in a heavy sweater, tufts of gray hair peeking out from a cloth cap, a lighted cigarette hanging from his toothless mouth. I guessed him to be at least seventy. When he handed me my 3-wood I noticed his hands. Their huge size was somehow disproportionate to the rest of his small frame, rather like a poorly designed armchair.

After my tee ball landed safely in the middle of the fairway he

---

I had seen the old man ahead of me on the previous two holes and caught up with him on Portmarnock's twelfth. His swing had stiffened over the years, but he was still tall, his eyes still bright behind thick glasses, his hair a brilliant white beneath his cap. The first thing he said after he introduced himself was, "I am a Catholic priest."

It was no more surprising than seeing your tee shot settled in a deep pot bunker. Here on this classic links course that dates to 1894, where the wind sighs through the beach grasses and a group of men stands atop a dune watching the play below, I expected to encounter the embodiment of tradition.

"I might be the oldest playing member now," he said. "I played my first round here in 1934. I'm eighty-one years old."

—Larry Habegger,
"Links with Tradition"

took the club from my hand saying, "Well struck, sir. We'll have a mid-iron left to the green."

He walked ahead of me, suspiciously fragrant of fermentation. By the time we reached the third hole Mr. Foley had the measure of my game and myself. Clearly, he was not impressed with his findings. Ignoring my request for the yardage to the hole, he merely handed me a club and with the passion of a tent revivalist told me what to do.

"We'll need to be strong here now, sir. Steady head and give her a good whack. We'll need to be on the right-hand side of the flag here. Away you go."

At the fourth and fifth holes I played poorly, struggling to keep the ball in play, questioning the wisdom of my decision to come here. At the 585-yard, par-5 sixth, Mr. Foley handed me my driver. "You're ready for her now, sir, but weaken the left hand a touch. We don't want to be left."

When the wind is howling in your face this hole can be three woods for the best of golfers, yet the second shot can be as little as a 5-iron when the wind is at your back, as it was today. I watched in wonderment and disbelief as the wind took my tee ball high into the air, then let it slowly fall to earth to bounce and roll, finally coming to rest at what looked like a mile from the tee.

I had a tough time trying to restrain myself from an outburst of joy.

"We'll have a mid-iron left to the green, Mr. Foley," I said, with perhaps a touch too much pride and sudden confidence.

"Aye. We'll see," he replied, "but this old course has been here since 1893. She's broken the backs of many. We need to be mindful of that, sir."

I was resentful of this admonition yet said nothing. Like an old dog, I plodded along behind him hopeful of a word of praise. When we arrived at my ball Mr. Foley handed me a 5-wood.

"Leave her up there now, sir. Soft hands, if you don't mind. Give her a sweet kiss and she'll find her way sure enough."

If I'm ever to hit a pure shot, please let it be now, I nearly said aloud. I watched anxiously until my ball landed on the front edge of the green and rolled true, leaving me less than twenty feet from the hole and a rare and coveted attempt at an eagle. "Now, sir," Mr. Foley lectured, "let's not get greedy. Four is a good score here."

I lacked the courage to look Mr. Foley in the face when I three-putted for a par-5. At the par-3 seventh, I left my tee shot in the bunker, blasted out and over the green, then skulled my next shot back into the same bunker. Infuriated, I picked my ball from the sand and went to the next tee, where I promptly hit my tee ball less than a hundred yards.

This is not why I came here! My game was getting away from me. My grip tightening. My swing quickening. I wanted to beg for advice, but was fearful of the same impassive glazed look from a rumpled face. By the time we reached the ninth I considered quitting. I don't need to impress anyone, and that includes you, Mr. Foley, dammit. He was waiting for me at the tenth.

"We'll play on sir, will we?" He couldn't possibly know what I was thinking. Or could he?

I nodded and asked for my driver. He handed me a 3-iron and a new ball from my bag.

"I think maybe we're lookin' ahead, sir, for you have the game in you," Mr. Foley said. "You just need to let it out."

"Let it out?"

"Aye, sir. Let it out. You have too much on your mind, and that's not a good thing here, if you take my meaning, sir. Your business worries will be waiting when you go back to America. Just hold her loosely in your hands, let the breath out of you, and swing away, sir. The cares of tomorrow can wait 'til this day is done."

His thoughts keyed my own thoughts of Doctor Caldwell's words, spoken at this site so many years before: "If you listen you may come to know yourself better." I closed my eyes, took a deep breath, and tried to emulate the long, slow swing of Doctor Caldwell.

"Ah, well played, sir," said Mr. Foley.

With my club in hand, I strode toward the fairway, pretending not to notice when Mr. Foley tossed a small empty whiskey bottle into the trash container. So on we stepped on our back nine adventure. When we arrived at the fifteenth hole I was two over par for the back nine.

"I think you're hearin' the music now, sir, and a darlin' thing it is, if you take my meaning," said Mr. Foley, his smiling face a leathery monument to his share of good times.

For me at that moment, California seemed a lifetime away. On we trudged, Mr. Foley and I, soaking in the pleasure that comes from playing golf up to your best expectations, all the while oblivious of the jet-black clouds rolling in from the sea. Mr. Foley was no longer just my caddie. He was my companion.

When I told him of some of the personal problems in my life, including my failed business, he would merely listen, nodding his head and dragging on his cigarette.

"There's a drop in the mouth of the wind, sir, but we'll finish before it gets here," said Mr. Foley.

I didn't want this day to end. I wanted to tell him more, I wanted his companionship a while longer. Then, all too soon, we were at the eighteenth. When I told him that the last nine holes were the most enjoyable I'd ever played, he allowed himself the pleasure of a smile, and said from behind another cigarette, "Aye, sir." When I invited him to have dinner with me he declined, saying, "Ah, no sir. The missus, you know, she'll be waitin' for me. But I'll have a pint with you before you go, if you like."

Doctor Caldwell would have surely loved Mr. Foley.

Larry T. Jordan was born and reared in Dublin, where unlike some other Irish writers, he enjoyed a happy childhood devoid of angst and alcoholic bouts. After an eight-year stint as a ship's radio officer in the British Merchant Service he emigrated to the U.S. in 1960, settling in Los Angeles where he began his twenty-five-year newspaper career. A former associate editor of California Golf Magazine, *he is a lifetime member of the Golf Writers Association of America. Now retired and living in Redwood City, California, he counts the days till he can return to "the old country" once more.*

✦ ✦ ✦

In Killarney

*This is one town that knows
how to treat visitors.*

JUST BEHIND THE CONFIDENT, WELCOMING, FAÇADE OF KILLARNEY, there are fragments of its native history. The higgledy-piggledy lanes behind the main streets have not yet been prettified. Children play with the water in the gully. An old man gets carefully off his upright bike to check the racing results in a bookie's window.

In High Street there's a beautiful restored house—the Bricín craft shop and restaurant. When they were doing it up, they found in the ruin, letters home from America, from a son who emigrated in 1867, "P. S." the first letter ends, "We might be able to send you a little money in a few months but we were so bare for clothes." Farther along the street, Foley's Townhouse restaurant has Château Petrus, at £485, among its wines. It used to be the police station. Fenians were locked up in the space where the chefs now work. Up at the end of the town there's an unfinished memorial, put up by the Republican Graves Commission in 1972, which declares that it will not be unveiled until Ireland is free.

And, of course, there's the music. Within 100 yards of each other, on a Sunday night recently, two groups of traditional musicians, come into town from the hills and valleys around, were working up to serious sessions.

Mixed with that history, there's the history peculiar to Killarney. You can go walking, "guided by the family who guided for Queen Victoria." You can sit on benches and survey the views thought beautiful in her time. This or that stretch of the lakeshore is where her stag-hunting parties landed, or her entourage reclined at the picnics laid out by the servants. The scenery of the Killarney demesnes—the great canopies of trees, the mossy groves of fern and ilex and laurel, the heavy glossy parklands, the fleshy flowers of rhododendron, conjure a huge overfurnished Victorian parlour.

Like Luxor, or Venice, or Victoria Falls, Killarney's business is tourism. Its real self is not concealed by tourism; tourism is its real self. The boatmen who wait under the trees at Ross Castle, murmuring the prices of trips on the lake, might be dragomans beside their camels. The jarveys are Ireland's gondoliers.

The clop of brisk hooves is the special sound of Killarney. In the mornings, before motor traffic has built up, while thousands of fries are being cooked for visitors, just waking up, the horses and their carts—brakes, traps, jaunting-cars—come out into the quiet streets from wherever they've spent the night, and another ordinary day absorbs the exotic.

One hundred thirty years of serving visitors has made Killarney very good at the job. It is incomparably the best organized and the best value holiday resort in Ireland. Once it catered almost exclusively to Irish-Americans—an innocent type of people, it was thought, whom the sharks of Killarney took for every penny they could get. Not many Irish people, twenty-five years ago, would have cared to argue a price with a jarvey. But contemporary Killarney is not like that. It is smooth and good-tempered. The coaches are guided with helpful shouts as they back into the hotels to pick up that day's lot for the Ring of Kerry. Bicycles, jaunting-cars, German caravans, dogs, all weave in and out of the permanent, genial traffic jam.

People take it easy. There's no seaside to get to. The tyranny of the suntan is relaxed. There's just the idle day to get through, by this little stratagem or that, and deciding where to eat, and the pleasure of sleeping somewhere that isn't home.

At lunchtime, locals will tell you, there are 115 places you might eat in. In the evening, almost as many. So for an hour or so, before dinner, Killarney has something of a Mediterranean feel, packed with people strolling around window-shopping—no steel shutters here—and deciding where to have a meal. Town hotels do a four- or five-course dinner. You can have a whole lobster, and all the trimmings. Or have swordfish in the Italian place or deep-fried Camembert with red currants in Bricín, or, down the street, trout steamed in parchment, or chicken breast in a raspberry sauce out in West End House.

> In Ireland, shops actually close for lunch and in the evening. After cursing this seemingly unnatural practice, we learned to live with the constraint, instead of rushing after what we needed. The rhythm of days coming to an end and people going home to be with family began to erode our need for convenience and we began to look at the odd petrol stations with twenty-four-hour shops as foreign and inhuman.
>
> —Frank O'Reilly, "Across the Generations"

There's every level of food, from what people prepare themselves in the kitchens of hostels, through hamburgers and Chinese and vegetarian, to the grand cuisines at the top. Even the package people coming in for one night on a tour, are offered a menu with a touch of class.

The value for money in Killarney shows up other places in Ireland. If the Molly Darcy pub in Muckross, for example, can do an excellent toasted sandwich with fries and coleslaw for a few pounds, who can't everywhere else? Why do other Irish hotels not have the fine, starched bed linen of Foley's Townhouse, with its piles of embroidered pillows and ribbon-edged sheets? Where else besides Killarney do you get, as you did in the Randles Court Hotel last week, a sparkling—real—coal fire in a lounge on a grey, summer day, not for the heat, but to liven things up?

As for what to do between bed and board—they've been

working on that in Killarney for more than a century, too. A honeymoon couple from Dublin had hired bikes and cycled through the woods, and what they liked best, they said, was that they felt so safe. And they'd heard a great live band, the night before. They could have gone to Florida on the Hoover tickets they got for buying a washing machine but they figured they'd need £1,000 for that. As it was, they had £500 and could have five days of anything they fancied.

Tama, from San Francisco, liked the craft demonstrations in Muckross House. A family of wealthy, WASPish Americans who could vacation anywhere in the world were in Killarney for the golf. Two Basque musicians, playing archaic music on pieces of wood in the main street, were happy to be in an unpolluted landscape.

Some Swedish visitors preferred Killarney to anywhere else they'd been in Ireland because there's the buzz of crowds there—because there's entertainment pouring from the pubs. They don't particularly want unspoilt Ireland—they can get the unspoilt at home. As for Italians, they're already beginning to have the influence on Killarney that the Irish-Americans once did. People used to have dinner around 7:30 to 8. Now, the restaurants are busiest coming up to 10 P.M.

The Irish—and out in Gleneagle Hotel, 80 to 90 percent of the guests are Irish—are the visitors you don't notice. But this hotel thrives by providing very exactly what mainstream Ireland wants. Care Bears to mind the children. A crèche. A huge indoor swimming pool. Snooker tables and pitch 'n' putt. And after dinner, a family show which begins with magicians and goes on to a cabaret, with big stars like Joe Dolan. Then there's a Eurodisco. Then—at 1:30 in the morning—a singsong starts in the piano bar. Sometimes, the likes of Joe Dolan will drop in.

The Irish are the ones who are uneasy with stage-Irishness. But stage-Irishry can be handled: the captain of a water bus on the Iako sent the whole thing up in his commentary with considerable charm. The rain, he told us, was liquid sunshine. The brown colour of the lake water came from the Guinness in it. The young boatman was actually an old boatman come back from Tir na nOg.

Two swizzle sticks were oars from a leprechaun's boat. But this is just play; it's quite conscious of its own falsity. One of the jokes involved a leprechaun whose trousers fall down. And what turned out to be stamped on his bottom? Made in Taiwan.

In fact, stage-Irishness must be dying out, if only because the Continental tourists don't know about it, any more than they know songs like "How Can You Buy Killarney" or "The Old Jaunting Car." These new tourists seem to want a real Irish thing, but somewhat cleaned up, and on time. Elsewhere in rural Ireland, for example, there are penances the visitor must do before hearing live traditional music. It can't be arranged: it might or might not happen, and it certainly won't get going till late. In Killarney, the musicians are authentic; the ease of access to them is not.

The nearer you are to Killarney town, the blander things are. Even the folk park, which reproduces the old houses of the people—including the labourer's cottage—is much more tidy and odourless than real life ever was. Yet—in each of the

---

I approached the *jarvey* [horse cart driver] as nonchalantly as I could. The boatman who brought us up the lakes from Ross Castle to Lord Brandon's Cottage had scoffed when I asked about reliable "ponymen," who ply their trade in Killarney's Gap of Dunloe. Thus warned, I did not want to appear anxious about getting a ride for my mother and our daughters the seven miles back to Kate Kearney's Cottage.

"Are you taking passengers back with you?" I asked.

"How many are you?" he replied.

"Five girls and their grandmother."

After a long pause, "Eight pounds for the lady, and two pounds for the girls, nought for the infant."

Delighted, we packed his trap so full that there was no room for himself, so he walked beside his pony. The boatman, on the other hand, had charged us a "family rate" of fifty pounds.

—Frank O'Reilly, "Across the Generations"

"traditional" houses there is a girl or woman, to mind it, and to talk to visitors. And they are sharply real. It is a paradox, perhaps, that in a tourist place like Killarney, the local people remain their vivid selves because tourism is natural to them, whereas in places where tourism is occasional or new, the people handle themselves artificially.

So a bedrock thing about Killarney is its people. And above the busy little town, above the parklands, above the wooded flanks of the lakes, the land rears, up out of its domestication and wildness begins. An outfit called Tracks and Trails takes people trekking and rafting and exploring with archaeologists and geologists up here. In winter, they run adventure weekends, based on deer-watching and walking. But however many visitors go into the mountains they are still solitary and untouched. That's the other bedrock. On even the busiest evening, with the town bustling as maybe 100 coaches come in off the Ring of Kerry, the great ridge of lonely mountains is there at the edge of the eye.

This is what was offered to Queen Victoria—an interface, a place where the civilized and the savage seem each intensified, in proximity to each other. It was to experience that conjunction that travelers first took the steam railway to Killarney. Today, the holiday-makers forget all that. They just know that as visitors they're in the smooth hands of professionals. Shamrocks and leprechauns, madam? Certainly; step this way. But more likely, slip off the rain-jacket, settle down to a decent meal, and "A Woman's Heart" will be playing on tape.

Nuala O'Faolain has been a waitress, sales clerk, maid, university lecturer, TV producer, and, most recently, a columnist with The Irish Times. *She lives in Dublin and is the author of* Are You Somebody: The Accidental Memoir of a Dublin Woman, Almost There, *and* My Dream of You.

REBECCA SOLNIT

✦ ✦ ✦

Dean Swift's Dublin

*She visits the haunts of a man
whose work defines satire.*

I SET OFF FOR THE TOMB OF ONE OF THE MOST PUBLICLY UNSEN-
timental men in European history, Jonathan Swift, the Dean of St.
Patrick's Cathedral. Great currents of pale pedestrians in blues and
grays and browns washed down all the major avenues, damming up
at the traffic lights and swirling into each other wherever two streets
met. I poured with them across O'Connell Bridge, around the
bulge of Trinity College's white, many-pillared Palladian prow, up
Dame Street which acquired a few other names as it wavered along,
then southward, away from the Liffey, to another street of varying
names that delivered me to the front of the cathedral. Empty of
worshippers, if not of visitors and tombs, it seemed less like a church
than a museum of a church, clean and vacant, and the woman at the
door taking admission from every entrant confirmed its transformation. Both the hulking gold cathedrals in Dublin belong to the
Protestant Church of Ireland, as do many of the oldest and most
imposing churches throughout the Republic, though their congre-
gations constitute a tiny fraction of the population: the Republic of
Ireland is 95 percent Catholic. Church and state have never been
particularly separate here, and the north wall bore monuments to
soldiers of the "Burmah" campaign, of South African conflicts, and

of the First World War—signs that the old colony of Ireland was a launching ground for the rest of the British Empire.

Swift was a servant of the Church of England, and master of the cathedral. High above the south aisle, below a white bust of his heavy features and before the resting place of his remains, I found his famous epitaph inscribed on black marble, which Yeats translated from Swift's Latin thus:

> Swift has sailed into his
>   rest;
> Savage indignation there
> Cannot lacerate his breast.
> Imitate him if you dare,
> World-besotted traveler; he
> Served human liberty

—an inscription which anticipates the grave's status as a tourist landmark.

Another of the reasons to travel is to situate the past in its locale, to put a picture round the facts. The particulars of a battlefield, a poet's house, a monarch's throne often illuminate dusty events, making them immediate and imaginable in a way nothing else can, or undoing the imagined version with an unexpected scale or style. It is the texture of a life that is most often missing from accounts

It is a curious contradiction, not very often remembered by England, that for many generations the private soldiers of the British Army were largely Irish; the Irish have natural endowments for war, courage, daring, love of excitement and conflict; Macaulay described Ireland as "an inexhaustible nursery of the finest soldiers."

Poverty and lack of opportunity at home made the soldier's shilling a day, and the chance of foreign service, attractive to the Irishman; and the armies of which England is proud, the troops which broke the power of Napoleon in the Peninsula and defeated him at Waterloo, which fought on the scorching plains of India, stormed the heights of the Alma in the Crimean campaign, and planted the British flag in every quarter of the globe in a hundred forgotten engagements, were largely, indeed in many cases mainly, Irish.

—Cecil Woodham-Smith, *The Great Hunger: Ireland 1845–1849*

of the past: the size of a room, the height of a border-wall, the rock-iness of a landscape. For those stuffed full of the lore of a continent not our own, it's helpful to come and flesh it out once in a while with tangible places. I too was a tourist in Ireland, and I had come to look at relics of the past and literary sites, among other things. In the cathedral where Swift was dean from 1713 to his death in 1745, it's possible to picture a real man whose step covered a certain dis-tance on the stony floor, who entered here and mounted there to preach and looked out towards that river. But most of the terrain of Swift's life has been cleared away.

His St. Patrick's was situated on the lowest ground in Dublin and was surrounded by the slums that housed the city's poorest people; in narrow streets with names like Shit Street and Dunghill Court. Without sanitation or any system of waste removal at all, offal accumulated grotesquely, giving the place a stench politer eyes and noses than Swift's could hardly ignore. This filthy and often flooded little expanse was his kingdom. The dean himself once wrote sardonically of all this shit, "that these Heaps were laid there privately by British Fundaments, to make the world believe, that our Irish Vulgar do daily eat and drink." A great walker of the city, Swift was well acquainted with his poor neighbors and well loved for his charities and for his championing of their rights.

Literary historian Carole Fabricant points out that Swift's pre-occupation with cruelty and injustice, with dirt and shit, has its lit-eral ground here in the old neighborhood of St. Patrick's. Swift is usually portrayed as an English writer whose misanthropy, indig-nation, and preoccupation with the more repulsive aspects of the body were personal idiosyncrasies, or signs of mental disorder. Though he did go mad, his themes had grounds. In Fabricant's view, Swift's harsh antiromanticism was as rooted in his residence among the poor of Ireland as his friend Alexander Pope's man-nered poetry was the fruit of servants and English country-house living. Swift had an odd relationship to Ireland, once remarking, "I reckon no man truly miserable unless he be condemned to live in Ireland" and another time rejecting a return to London by saying, "I choose to be a freeman among slaves, rather than a slave among freemen." His grandparents had come over after Cromwell, and the question of whether he was English or Irish was and is answered according to desire and politics rather than any clearcut fact. It might be most accurate to say he was both. Born and raised in Ireland, he spent his young manhood in the literary and political coteries of England and the second half of his life back in his birthplace. He seems to have been something of an exile wherever he was, not wholly a member of either country, split between comfort and conscience.

Ireland has most often been defended by those who would emphasize its virtues and apologize for its failings; Swift took another approach entirely, harping on the ugliness of a denuded, overused landscape, of poverty and powerlessness, and tracing their source to the graceful powers of England. His most famous book, *Gulliver's Travels*, universalizes his spleen to become a critique of at least European man, but the less-known majority of his work dealt with the specifics of his own time and place—pamphlets and satires on the current political situation, poems mocking the elevated motifs and ideal landscapes of his peers' conventional poetry.

English literature itself sometimes seems to me a huge country house, a mansion to which the shanties and new wings of other English-language literatures are attached; perhaps they hold up the ancient hulk at their center. In this mansion, the principal rooms are occupied by the familiar furniture of epic and lyric poetry, of the novel, the side tables and cabinets of the essay. The books I used when I was an English major folded the Irish in as English literature, but the biggest, the most central, the most familiar pieces are almost always truly English, the results of an irreplaceable confidence and centrality. There's the dark throne of Milton, the banquet tables of Shakespeare, sonnets from Sidney to Shelley scattered everywhere like bouquets of flowers, and, huge and soft and inviting, the fat featherbeds of the English novel. Swift's work sits in a passageway, a hard chair with a view through the cracks in the walls. Joyce supplied his own furnishing for the house of English literature with Stephen Dedalus's comment that the "cracked lookingglass of a servant" could stand as "the symbol of Irish art," suggesting not only a subjugation but a fractured, unpredictable reflection. Then he went and built something new, with a monument to Dublin scattered within it.

Irish writers have punctuated English literature with works that seldom rest so easily on confidence and centrality, with works that reinvent and critique the dominant forms and place the viewers in unfamiliar positions. Irish masterpieces have taken apart the conventions not only of their genres, but of narrative, language, and tradition. *Gulliver's Travels* and *Ulysses* stand at either end of occupied Irish literature, both books of mockery, exile, and wandering, by one Irishman who chose exile in Dublin and another who chose exile out of it. *Tristam Shandy*, the first and in many respects the greatest experimental English novel, was published between 1759 and 1767 by Laurence Sterne, an Irish-born clergyman, and even the Brontës, so identified with the Yorkshire moors, were raised on their Irish father's wild Irish stories. They introduced a dark, violent strain to the complacent Victorian novel—a clutch of eels in the featherbed—and other surprises were subsequently delivered by Wilde, Joyce, Synge, Shaw, Beckett. A more intricate, sardonic, restless imagination seems to characterize the Irish works claimed by England, a sensibility more cognizant of the arbitrariness of literary form and all the opportunities of subverting it.

> If James Joyce is Our Father, then hallowed be his name. But his books should be read more, and his face should be taken off the money. Joyce was an anarchist and a rebel, an artist who swore the oath of the devil against the Irish past, I will not serve. We should not make him serve Ireland now, either its banjaxed tourist industry or its smug invented history of itself as a paradise of literary production. Neither, I think, should we serve that past ourselves, when modern Ireland is crying out loud to be celebrated, imagined and changed.
>
> —Joseph O'Connor, *The Secret World of the Irish Male*

In this century, a kind of literary geography has remapped the house of English literature. Jean Rhys's *Wide Sargasso Sea* imagined the Caribbean drama that preceded Charlotte Brontë's *Jane Eyre*, Edward Said has scrutinized the colonial rapacity that secured the stultifying calm of Jane Austen's *Mansfield Park*, whose idle gentry are living off unseen slave-plantation wealth. Early in the eighteenth century, Swift was already carrying on this cartographic operation, telling us what his gracious society looked like from behind, below, and outside. Humor itself can be a way of seeing double, of noticing the gap between how things are supposed to be and how they are, from the formal elements of logic and language to the hypocrisies of social and political life. Such an engine drives everything from a simple joke to an extended satire, from Swift's constant shift between lofty and vulgar styles in his poems to his *A Modest Proposal*, whose humor lies in its entertainment of cannibalism as a reasonable solution to Irish poverty and thereby makes apparent the well-established existence of cannibalism by other means. The most humorless are usually those who have most invested in the existing order, and humor has always been a pleasure, a tool, and a weapon of those who see the gap. The view from Dublin has often been tragic, and heroic, and sentimental, but it has sometimes been mordantly funny.

Rebecca Solnit is the author of several books, including River of Shadows: Eadweard Muybridge and the Technological Wild West, Hollow City: The Siege of San Francisco and the Crisis of American Urbanism, Wanderlust: A History of Walking, *and* A Book of Migrations: Some Passages in Ireland, *from which this story was excerpted. She lives in San Francisco.*

Climbing Croagh Patrick

Here's a worthy adventure for the pagan
and the devout alike.

IN THE MORNING THERE WAS A DULL INCESSANT DRIZZLE WHICH soon became soft rain. We sat having breakfast wondering if we should wait, if the weather would lift. Normally, the landlady told us, you could see Croagh Patrick in the distance from her kitchen window, but now you could see nothing. We drove into Westport and sat in a hotel lounge drinking coffee. I had spare shoes, but no real protection from the rain. My friends were in the same state.

Out at the foot of Croagh Patrick there were lines of cars parked and more making their way to the fields which were being used as car parks for the day. It seemed as though no one else had been worried about the rain. Some people had already been up the mountain and down again. As we bought our walking sticks I could see a line of people, like a small coloured stream winding up the mountain and disappearing into the mist.

This was where St. Patrick, according to legend, had come and fasted for forty days and forty nights in the fifth century. But it was thought that the tradition of climbing the *reek* was a much older, pagan ritual which had been incorporated into the Christian calendar. There was also talk that the climbing of the *reek* had once been accompanied by great festivities, but this had been ended by the clergy, and now the day was dedicated to penance and penance only.

William Makepeace Thackeray was in Westport on the last Sunday in July in 1842, and he ventured out to Murrisk, having heard that "the priests going up the mountain took care that there should be no sports nor dancing on that day." He disliked the idea of the pilgrimage: "it's too hard to think that in our day any priests of any religion should be found superintending such a hideous series of self-sacrifices as are, it appears, performed on this hill."

We set off in a spirit of self-sacrifice. At first it was easy, like mild hill walking. Some people were barefoot, but most wore shoes. The mist was wet and the ground was uneven and soggy, the staffs becoming more and more necessary as we climbed. Soon, we separated; my two friends went ahead, joining the others who seemed to be vanishing into the sky. The climb became more difficult, and the rain came down harder. I was passed by a travelling woman in bare feet being helped along by her two sons. They did not speak to each other, appearing intent on the climb, a look of furious concentration on their faces. Then the man who had taken our chair in the bar the previous evening passed me, also in bare feet. I had thought that the travellers were only here to make money selling staffs and running stalls, but a good number of them climbed the *reek* that day, as though it were a crucial part of their fierce Catholicism.

Thackeray did not climb the *reek*, but received a report from a friend who told him that the ascent "is a very steep and hard one...performed in the company of thousands of people who were making their way barefoot to the several 'stations' upon the hill." One hundred and forty-nine years later the stations are still there, and there are notices instructing pilgrims who arrive at the first station, for example, to walk "seven times around the mound of stones saying seven Our Fathers, seven Hail Marys, and one Creed."

Beyond the first station there was no visibility. I could see only a few yards ahead as the mountain became steeper. A rescue team climbed past me carrying an empty stretcher; there must have been an accident higher up. A few people were coming down; one man smiled as he passed and said that it would not be long before I reached the top.

Suddenly, there was a shout from behind me. At first I thought that someone had fallen, but when I turned I found that the thick fog had lifted and we could see Clew Bay clearly—all the little islands, grey and silver in the dark water, with the soup of mist hovering over them and then gathering and closing in once more. Everyone had turned to look at it, like a small revelation. Now, we turned and trudged on, the terrain becoming more and more difficult. A few times the mist cleared again, and filtered sunlight shone on the sea so that it seemed like solid metal below us, and then gradually the clouds would block our view once more.

Nothing had prepared me for the last part of the climb. The rise was sheer and there was nothing to hold on to. At every step I sank into a bank of large slippery stones. I moved slowly on my hands and knees in the wind and the driving rain. I stood back to let the stretcher pass, as the injured man was carried down.

Everybody concentrated on each step, and on making sure not to fall and knock other people over. We clambered forward. It was

> There is something terrifying, at least to me, in the mists that cover mountains—mists that hide you know not what; mists that cut a man off from the world and deny him the sight of the sky. To be lost on a mountain in mist is to experience all the horror of panic, for it seems to you that you might lose the path and go wandering vainly in circles answered only by a mocking laugh which seems to hide in all mountain mists. But I consoled myself by the thought that Croagh Patrick is a holy mountain from whose ravines and gullies all demons have been banished. Suddenly, right before me rose a white figure, and I looked up to a statue of St. Patrick.
>
> The saint, I discovered, stands there to hearten pilgrims, for the real climb begins behind him.
>
> —H. V. Morton,
> *In Search of Ireland* (1930)

impossible to see how close the summit was. At times progress seemed impossible; there was no foothold, and if you moved, you displaced rocks and stones, and there was still no foothold. Men and women walked down as best they could, pushing the staff into the ground ahead of them, letting it sink in between the stones, then sliding gingerly down. If they caught your eye, they smiled in encouragement. People kept telling you that you would reach the summit soon.

When I got there I was exhausted and exhilarated. Mass was being said, and everybody, including all the young people, were paying attention. Later, huge numbers went to confession and communion. I felt so well, so happy to have made it that I was half-tempted to tell all my sins to the priest and then receive communion. But I sat back, instead, and watched. People had not climbed the *reek* simply to keep fit; now, as they reached the top, I could see that they were serious about this pilgrimage, as they all blessed themselves and joined in the prayers, including teenagers and men and women in their twenties. Age did not appear to affect the intensity of devotion.

Why had Catholicism survived like this in Ireland? Why did the Reformation never work? Why does the Catholic faith seem to thrive here among the young as it does not elsewhere? The previous week I had gone to Maynooth, the Catholic seminary and university close to Dublin, founded in 1795, and I had spoken to a lecturer in the Old Irish Department, Muireann Ní Bhrollcháin, about how Christianity had come to Ireland.

We know very little about pre-Christian Ireland, she said. The Celts did not build temples, but tended to honour their gods in open spaces. We know that they believed in another world, but there seems to have been no conflict between them and the first Christians, who came in 431 and 432. There were no martyrs in the early Irish church. The two worlds appear to have worked together. Saint Colmcille, for example, died in 597, and a long poem lamenting his death was apparently written by a pagan poet.

The Roman system did not catch on in Ireland until the mid-twelfth century, she explained, and this is significant. Instead, Christianity was spread by abbots and monks who ran autonomous monasteries. There was no central authority; there were no dioceses until the twelfth century. Thus the monks, instead of going and spreading the word or doing battle against pagan druids, spent time copying out manuscripts, or writing down stories from pagan times, incorporating Christianity with what came before, making gods and goddesses into saints. Some monks went to live in remote places; others founded richly endowed monasteries where the abbots and monks were like lords and tenants, and power was passed from father to son. Rules and regulations varied from one monastery to another.

Ut Christiani, ita es Romani sitis.

If you would be good Christians, be good Romans.
—St. Patrick

We Irish, though dwelling at the far ends of the earth, are all disciples of St. Peter and St. Paul, neither heretic nor schismatic has ever been among us; but the Catholic Faith just as it was first delivered us by yourselves as successors to the apostles, is held by us unchanged.
—Letter of St. Columbanus to Pope Boniface IV, Sixth Century

Christianity, then, was never imposed on Ireland; Roman structures played no part in introducing the new religion. It grew slowly, and slowly the old set of beliefs faded. Christianity became the faith of the country over five or six centuries using the vernacular; it became a native religion. Having grown so organically, it was more difficult to change or dislodge.

Efforts were made to reform the Church in the ninth century, she said, but they had no effect. However, with the coming of the Vikings there were greater links between the east coast of Ireland and England, which was firmly under Roman control, and the possibility of restructuring the Irish Church increased once the Vikings in Dublin converted to Christianity. Between 1142 and the end of the century every monastery in Ireland was closed. The religious orders came in from Europe; they did not speak any Irish. It was the first and most significant invasion of Ireland, making the subsequent Norman and English invasions easier. It established structures in the society—parishes, dioceses, religious orders—which any invader would find useful. Ireland, which had been fully Christian, now became part of the Roman Church, but it did so much later than any other country in Europe.

It was still raining on the summit of Croagh Patrick. I assumed that people had also come here on an appointed summer's day in the time before Christianity. And I imagined that the pre-Christian rituals may have continued after its arrival. There seems to have been no battle between the rival religions, no year noted in chronicles when the big day on Croagh Patrick was turned over to the Christians. It is possible that both pagan and Christian rituals were carried on as part of the same thing, and then gradually the pagan disappeared.

I looked around. Another Mass had started and people were kneeling, while others queued for confession. The prayers were said with real seriousness, and when it came to the consecration people bowed their heads, ignoring the rain.

I set off down the mountain. By now the mist had cleared over the summit.

> We finally made it to the top. I really didn't care where we were, just that we were sitting down. There was a little white chapel there, and we all walked around it fifteen times, saying the Hail Mary since Croagh Patrick is a pilgrim mountain. Some people climb the mountain in bare feet! So, I decided to run around the chapel in bare feet.
>
> —Clare O'Reilly, age 13, "An Unwilling Pilgrim"

Around the islands in the bay, cloud was still melting and forming, and there were sudden darts of sunshine, as though the dawn were starting to break over the sea.

The first stretch on the way down was really hard. If anyone pushed against you, you would fall with nothing to hold on to. There had already been several injuries that day. You had to mind every step, use the staff for support and hope for the best. Once I was beyond the stones I knew I was past the worst. It was now the afternoon. The climb had taken about three and a half hours. There were still people coming up, but most were going down.

At the bottom of Croagh Patrick that day the Bishop of Clonfert, Dr. Joseph Cassidy, stood dressed in his Episcopal robes. He seemed part of what I had been thinking about—the Roman, the man in the official robes, civilized, from the diocese which did not exist until it was imposed from outside in the twelfth century. He was watching the pilgrims descend from their quasi-pagan encounter with rain and a holy mountain. He explained that he couldn't climb Croagh Patrick because of his bad heart. Instead, he waited there, greeting everyone warmly, being greeted in return. He smiled benignly at us all and spoke to anyone who approached him. He seemed pleased that the Church had so many pilgrims ready to climb Croagh Patrick, and happy to preside over the event.

Colm Tóibín is the author of several books and editor of another. His first novel, The South, *won the Irish Times Prize, and his second,* The Heather Blazing, *received the Encore Award. Both novels have been translated into several European languages and published in the USA. This story was excerpted from his book,* The Sign of the Cross: Travels in Catholic Europe. *He lives in Dublin.*

MICHAEL SEAN CAIN

* * *

The Reel Thing

Ireland's soul is in its music.

IT WAS THE MUSIC THAT DREW ME TO IRELAND: THE LILT AND WAIL of the fiddle, the bright laughter of the accordion, the windy purl of the flute. This was the music of my father's forebears: once it got ahold of me, a few years back, it never let go.

There's a power to this music that comes of its roots in the wild landscape of rural Ireland and in the deep recesses of the country's history. Most traditional tunes are of uncertain age and have no known composer. It's as if they have arisen out of the distant past as a birthright of the musicians who play them—yet there's nothing antiquated or musty about their haunting, driving energy.

My first real encounter with this phenomenon occurred in a series of New York City pubs. Before I stumbled upon them, I'd been playing rock and jazz on various instruments for years. Afterward, as some of my friends scratched their heads, I became a devoted student of Irish music. I put away my classical silver flute in favor of the wooden, Baroque-style instrument more common among Irish players. I took up the tin whistle. Eventually I formed a band and started playing in pubs myself.

What remained was to go to Ireland and hear the tunes played and sung in the places where they originated, by the people who have kept them alive down the centuries. I pictured myself at an intimate session in a dimly lit pub, welcomed into a charmed circle of timeless music.

I decided to make my pilgrimage in springtime, when the dark Irish winter was well past but before the onset of the tourist season. I would start off at a small festival in County Clare, and follow my ear.

Fleadh (pronounced "flah") is the Irish word for "festival." There are all sorts of *fleadhs* in Ireland throughout the year, most of them centered on music and dance. At the Fleadh Nua, in Ennis (the principal town of County Clare), I kick off my musical mystery tour with a glorious forty-eight hour immersion.

On my first afternoon in Ireland, I listen in on a crowded session (or *seisiún*—pronounced "*say*-shoon"—an informal gathering of musicians) at the pub in my hotel. Then I meander through the narrow streets of the town center, back and forth over the river Fergus, past the ruins of the Ennis Friary (founded in 1240), and finally up the hill to O'Connell Square, where a stage is set up on the back of a small flatbed truck. The clouds make way for warm sunshine (with which I'll be blessed for the next ten days), and the music, by a series of groups and solo players and singers, is bright and joyful. A troupe of young step dancers in colorfully embroidered costumes arrives and performs in the percusive, straight-armed Irish style on the street in front of the stage. Later, when a funeral procession rolls through the square, everyone is respectfully silent for a few minutes; then, at the all-clear from a policeman, the musicians break into a rousing set of hornpipes.

Up and down the streets, the sound of accordions, flutes, and fiddles pours from the doorways of pubs. In the evenings there are also concerts and dances. I hear the fabled Clare fiddler Paddy Canny, nearly eighty now, in suit and tie but with a farmer's sturdy build, easing through jigs and reels he's been playing since he was a boy. I hear famous players and discover others whose names are new to me. And on my first night, I go to the *ceili* ("*kay*-lee").

A *ceili* is an Irish party with music and set dancing—a bit like

American square dancing, only more complex and usually faster-paced. Inside the hall on a large octagonal dance floor, dozens of dancers, divided into sets of four couples each, swirl and step and swing through intricate patterns while accordionist P. J. Hernon's Swallow's Tail Ceili Band provides irresistible accompaniment. The dancers are working up a terrific high-spirited sweat: it won't be the last time on this trip that I will wish I knew the steps.

It's a long walk from the dance hall back to my hotel. I get there well after midnight, only to find a session in progress in the lobby. And another one in the pub. I've been in Ireland less than twenty-four hours. I'm in heaven.

We hadn't come out of the spell when the Kilfenora Jig was rising now with a heigh-ho-diddle-dee-idle-dee. They were *simply* brilliant, as the old man next to me said, putting the emphasis strangely on the first word not the second, and making me suddenly wonder whether Irish music was in fact simple or the incredible complex pattern of circles of sound that were still ringing in my ear.

—Niall Williams and Christine Breen, *The Pipes Are Calling: Our Jaunts Through Ireland*

Sunday afternoon, following a long, breathtaking drive through the wildflower-studded mountains of the Dingle Peninsula, I arrive at Dingle town, on a precipitous hillside facing Dingle Bay. The harbor area is clogged with tourists; fortunately they all choose to mingle within a few blocks of one another, so I have the rest of the town to poke around in peace.

Up the steep lanes, I find my way to Main Street and a quiet string of shops and hotels. A short walk along the road and I'm in the countryside, abruptly, climbing toward magnificent views over the bay to the Iveragh Peninsula. To the north looms Mount Brandon, the second-highest peak in Ireland; to the west is a scattered trove of archaeological sights. These things I will explore tomorrow. For tonight, I find what I'm after on Main Street, where a sign in the window of a pub called An Droichead Beag (The Small Bridge) announces that Séamus Begley and Stephen Cooney will be leading a session. Begley is a Dingle dairy farmer from a well-known musical family; his prowess on the button accordion and in *sean nós* (old-style) singing is widely admired. When he teamed up a few years ago with Cooney, an eclectic Irish-Australian guitarist, the duo became notorious.

The pub is a dark, atmospheric place with stone walls and low beamed ceilings, a fireplace, and two small bars. The musicians play in a corner by the front window, sitting on wooden benches built into the wall. When I arrive in the evening, savvy locals have staked out the best spots, but there's still room up close for a listener who doesn't mind getting jostled a bit.

As soon as Begley and Cooney begin to play, everyone seems to lift off the ground by a couple of feet. There's no space for dancing, but no one is standing still, either. Begley, a handsome, muscular man with a mad gleam in his eye, plays upbeat polkas and slides in the brisk, heavily accented west Kerry style. Cooney's sometimes manic rhythms drive him on. Yet when Begley stops to sing, an altogether different spirit seems to take control; he becomes an ethereal soul with a surprisingly reedy voice, singing Gaelic songs of love.

About half and hour into the session, a distinguished-looking gentleman enters the pub. Begley waves him over to a place on the bench, the newcomer takes out a tin whistle, and all the other musicians listen as he plays a slow air. The sad melody swoops and soars, wound about with ornamentation. Listeners lean in to hear, even as the din of conversation continues in the rest of the pub. When the white-haired whistler segues into a brisk reel, everyone is hopping again.

I ask a tall fellow standing beside me if he knows who the whistle player is. "Oh yeah," he says. "That's Sean Potts."

My jaw drops. Potts was one of the original members of the Chieftains, Ireland's most famous traditional ensemble. For years, I've been listening to his recordings—I can't believe I've caught him playing in a session.

It's often said that there is no star system among Irish musicians,

and now I can see this princi-
ple in action. Begley notices I
seem a bit awed at shaking
hands with the whistler.
"Here's the real VIP," he says,
introducing me to Bridie
Potts, Sean's wife. "Shake the
hand that rocks the cradle.
He's just a freakin' whistle
player."

Traditional music in the
city is a different creature
from the one that inhabits the
countryside. After my visits to
Ennis and Dingle, I move on
to Cork and Dublin, Ireland's
two largest cities. The musicians I encounter there are no
less accomplished than those
in more rural areas, but their
playing often has little sense
of regional style; at times it
seems disconnected from the
pastoral spirit that gave rise to
the tunes in the first place.

Not that I disliked the
cities or the music I heard
there. In Cork, once I got past
the hellish traffic and bewil-
dering one-way roads, I
found a pedestrian-friendly
downtown area full of eigh-
teenth- and nineteenth-
century buildings, broad
boulevards, attractive shops,

✳

Composer Sean O'Riarda's
influence on Irish tradi-
tional music and his tragic early
death have always haunted me.
Among other things, the group
of musicians who gathered
around him became known as
The Chieftains. I discovered that
his home in the West Cork
Gaeltacht hamlet of Coolea was
only twenty miles from our
holiday home in Killarney. Not
knowing where his grave was,
we settled on going to the
church where he prayed and
where his music still enriches
the worship. When we arrived, I
tried the first door I found.
Unlocked, it swung in to reveal
the sacristy, with vestments and
sacred gold vessels. Quickly
shutting the door, I smiled in-
wardly, thinking "Only in
Ireland!" Finding the proper entrance, we went in and discovered the church was named
after St. Teresa of Lisieux, whose
feast day it was. Kneeling to
pray, we lit candles and united
ourselves with the soul of Sean
whose music seemed to echo
off the walls, even decades after
his death.

—Frank O'Reilly, "Across the
Generations"

and surprisingly good restaurants. As for the music, after finding nothing but rock and blues on a Monday night, I tracked down three quality sessions on Tuesday.

In Dublin, too, I found ungodly traffic jams, but also a beautiful city with a profusion of music pubs. Nonetheless, when I left Dublin to head for Donegal, I was glad to be returning to the countryside, and to the west.

Donegal, the northernmost part of Ireland, is a realm of craggy ocean cliffs and high peat fields studded with rocks and overshadowed by scree-sided mountains. To a European of the Middle Ages, when St. Columba and his band of monks came here to set up places of worship, this was the remotest spot imaginable—the end of the earth.

Sometimes, in spite of the thriving towns along the coast, it still seems to be. In the interior, roads wind through mile after mile of high bogland where the black-faced sheep roam freely and even lounge on the pavement on sunny afternoons. At the shoreline the land drops down to the sea with a precipitous finality, leaving strips of beach here and there exposed to the lashings of tides and weather.

On the night of my arrival in Donegal, I stroll a beach near Ballyshannon with musician and scholar Caoimhin MacAoidh (pronounced "*kwee*-veen mac-*ee*"), a storehouse of knowledge about the music and folklore of the county. At nearly 10 P.M. in late May, the sun has just begun to set. It's low tide, and the broad strand below the Sand House Hotel is well populated with strollers, waders, Frisbee-players, and their dogs. Cars drive up and down the sand, and a truck tows a parasailer back and forth overhead.

MacAoidh points to the largest of the mountains up the coast. "The one with the big cliffs is Slieve League. The highest sea cliffs in Europe, they say. Con Cassidy"—a famous Donegal fiddle player—"lived at the foot of that one." He proceeds to single out peak after peak and name a noted fiddle player associated with each.

Near the dunes, beside the remains of a centuries-old stone lookout post built when the British occupiers of Ireland feared a

French invasion on this coast, a cluster of teenagers listens to American hip-hop from a boom box. "I wonder what Napoleon's friends would have thought of these fellows occupying their tower," MacAoidh says.

Up the road from Ballyshannon in Killybegs is the Sail Inn, a small and unassuming pub. Decoration is minimal here: what adorns the place is the people who crowd in, the friendliness of one and all, and the personality of Martin McGinley, part-owner and musician extraordinaire. McGinley is from Raphoe, a few miles to the northeast; after a decade in Belfast working for the BBC, he has returned to Donegal, bought the Sail Inn, and settled back down to the music.

McGinley is a robust man with a corolla of curly red-blond hair framing a round face. His voice, when he greets MacAoidh and welcomes me, has a nasal lilt like that of the uilleann pipes. He leads the session with a bonhomie that embraces not only all the players—and tonight, that includes me—but also all the listeners.

There are seven musicians altogether, but most of the playing is done by McGinley and MacAoidh and a guitarist and singer named Sean Con Johnny. These three have played together informally for years, and their enjoyment of one another is contagious. McGinley graciously invites me to start off sets of tunes on the flute, and when I do so he loses little time in joining in on the jig or reel and investing it with the Donegal fire he wields so masterfully. To play with him is what MacAoidh calls "a pure panic of brilliant music."

It is late by the time we leave the Sail Inn—through the rear exit, since the pub officially closed more than two hours ago. When we arrive back at MacAoidh's house, at around 3 A.M., he and I stand outside in the cool air while the memory of the night's music settles into the silence. Already the sky is beginning to grow light. And then I realize that I have just attended the session I came to Ireland to witness. The fact that I've actually played in it is a bonus I hadn't even begun to hope for.

From Donegal I make my way south again along the west coast. I visit Westport, County Mayo, where I stop in at Matt Molloy's, the music pub owned by the flute player of the Chieftains. From there I head through acacia groves and hillsides overgrown with rhododendrons into Galway and the remote wilds of Connemara, and then on to Doolin, County Clare.

A few decades ago, traditional music seemed on the verge of dying out in Ireland. No place in the country is more tied to its revival than O'Connor's, a modest Doolin pub made famous by a farmer and whistle player named Micho Russell. But revival has come at a price. This once-sleepy town is now mobbed in summer; O'Connor's has expanded, but still overflows with visitors. For all that, Doolin remains essentially a village in the middle of nowhere, and outside of the high season, O'Connor's is a fine place to hear music.

When I catch Martin and Maureen Connolly (on button accordion and fiddle) there on a Wednesday night in early June, the bar is indeed overrun with noisy and inattentive people. But the music is like an antidote to the chaos. After the supercharged playing of Donegal and the pyrotechnics of the players at Matt Molloy's, this return to the easygoing swing of Clare is like a plunge in a tranquil pool after a day spent shooting the rapids.

I spend a couple of days roaming the misty, rocky coast of Clare, then take a ferry to the island of Inisheer, which is basically a big limestone hill rising out of the sea. Its few hundred inhabitants live amid sheep, seabirds, medieval ruins, and an intricate grid of oddly delicate stone fences. There, the ghostly sound of a chorus of whistles prompts me to climb a wall into a schoolyard, where I discover a music lesson in progress in an open-fronted shed. I get out my own whistle and play a few tunes with the teacher, accompanied by a student on the bodhran (goatskin frame drum). When we finally get around to introductions, the teacher turns out to be Michael O'Halmhain, who took Sean Pott's slot in the Chieftains for a year or so after Potts left the band. I tell O'Halmhain about my chance meeting with Potts a few days earlier, and he doesn't seem surprised. He just smiles and nods.

After so many days traipsing about the west of Ireland, I find myself wondering: why did this music emerge from this place? Maureen Connolly's answer echoed what I heard from many. "It's the isolation, the quiet, the beauty of the country," she told me. "You should spend the winter here. It may be cool and damp, but when you step outside in the morning everything is so green. The birds are singing like crazy; if you take out an instrument and start to play, they go even crazier."

She wasn't the only person in Ireland to surprise me by waxing rhapsodic about the winters. The western part of the country depends on summer for an economic boost, but its soul is rejuvenated in the dormant season: the landscape empty, fog-shrouded, so that the old mysteries can re-gather. It's a land that has seen much hardship and deprivation, the heartbreak of families split by emigration, the sad sense among many that the best hope for a better life lay across the ocean. Those who stayed behind found comfort through the long nights of winter in the pub among friends, in a kitchen over tea, and in the sharing of some old treasures: a story, a song, a tune played on a flute or a fiddle.

> The careful listener will understand that music offers a glimpse of a reality behind appearances, where shapes shift and things are not what they seem. Music is a mirror of Ireland's outer form, the shrouding mist and quicksilver weather that make this place a strangely beautiful puzzle. The musicians reach through the fog, grasp a handful of the ungraspable, and give it form. From the darkness of chaos, they bring forth jewels of sound.
>
> Musicians are revered in Ireland, and to each listener their sound brings a different message, adding to what they already hold: drunks become drunker, the angry rage, the glad rejoice, and the generous move toward sainthood. The only instruments needed to partake in this mystery are a ready ear and a willing soul.
>
> —Andy Yale, "From Ireland with Music," *Islands*

"There used to be music in every house," an old stonecutter

named Kevin told me as I sipped tea in O'Connor's one morning. "It was all we had for amusement, sure."

On my last night in Ireland, I find myself at the Killarney Grand, a tourist bar in a tourist town. The place has ersatz stained glass, fake stone walls, and, at 8:30 on a Saturday night, some of the most genuine traditional music to be found in city or country.

Mick Mulcahy plays button accordion with an uncanny soulfulness and an obvious deep affection for the music. Tonight, in a corner by the fireplace, he's playing with his two talented daughters—twelve-year-old Michelle on harp, concertina, and fiddle, and fourteen-year-old Louise on flute, whistles, and pipes.

Mulcahy's love of the tunes gives him a sad look when he plays, but that seems only appropriate to the music, finally. For beneath even the liveliest jig there lurks an awareness of life's difficulties, of the often harsh conditions in which this culture was bred. When Mulcahy leans over between tunes and says to me, "Those were a couple of good old hornpipes—and these are some polkas from west Cork," there's a wistfulness in his tone, as if he is speaking of faraway friends he can visit only through the melodies.

At the end of the evening, I bid good night to Mulcahy and his family and walk through the rain to my hotel. Contemplating my return to the States, I don't feel as sad as I might.

Next morning, I hum all the way to the airport: a couple of good old reels I learned from Mick Mulcahy.

Michael Sean Cain, an editor at Travel & Leisure *magazine, plays flute and harmonica with the Irish-America trio Avoca. His travels as writer, musician, filmmaker, and actor have taken him to Ireland, England, Italy, Russia, Estonia, Mexico, and all over Canada and the United States.*

"The Reel Thing" is dedicated to the memory of Maureen Glynn Connolly, a fine and soulful musician as well as a teacher of note who did much to carry on the musical tradition of her father both in New York, where she was born, and in Ireland, where she died far too young.

JO BROYLES YOHAY

★ ★ ★

Renting a Piece of the Old Sod

Be careful—you may get addicted to it.

COWS WERE LOWING SOMEWHERE OUTSIDE. HALF-AWAKE, I LIFTED sleepy lids to the morning light and peered around the coverlet to the rose-embroidered canopy overhead. Across the room, curtains swayed in the breeze. Beyond the second-story window, open to welcome the moist air, lay a great salt lake—Lough Ine. The sea churned inaudibly beyond a cliff, and two gulls chased each other beneath low threatening clouds. I sank back into the pillows. There was no need to rush. My husband and I had resident status in this grand Irish house—for an entire week. We had needed a break. Frayed by a stretch of extra-hard work and the usual clatter of life in Manhattan, we craved the opposite: landscape wild and desolate, long walks beside pounding surf, vistas of shifting clouds and light, body contact with weather. We wanted books by the hearth, time to explore country lanes, days for our inner dust to settle.

A respite in the past, in other words. But where to go for a sojourn in the nineteenth century? The seacoast of Ireland flashed to mind. We pictured ourselves swathed in sweaters and sipping tea in front of peat fires or walking, shod in wellies, through sweet soft air on what the Irish poet Brian Coffey called "grass

181

green as no other green is green." Celtic magic was exactly what
we needed.

A week in one spot sounded right, and we already knew the va-
cation-rental experience was for us. Of course, it also feels grand
to be pampered by hotel staff. But at a hotel you are ineluctably a
guest, a visitor. With a rented house you can freely indulge in the
pleasures of domesticity. You inhabit not just the rooms but the
landscape as well. We decided to rent.

Choosing a house abroad does hold some risk. We would have
to take a place sight unseen—and pay the entire rental fee, plus
security deposit, up front. How could we insure against disappointment?

A fervent researcher, I rolled up my sleeves and set to work. I
listed our specifications: my architect husband wanted a venerable
house, strong on character, restored with love and respect, tastefully
furnished. It could be either rustic or elaborate—that didn't matter. But some things, for me, were non-negotiable: isolation, fabulous stretches of horizon, proximity to the sea, a dramatic setting
in nature. I answered some ads and started calling agents.

Faxes flew and phones jangled. The Irish Tourist Board sent its
Self-Catering Guide of holiday rentals, with short descriptions and
microscopic color photos of dozens of houses. We laughed when
someone sent a brochure showing a fine castle to be had for a mere
$37,000 a week.

One piece of news sounded ominous. Some agents had
dropped Irish listings because, as one said, "the standard of quality
expected by Americans is difficult to find." Carpets tended to be
worn, wallpaper peeling. There are wonderful rentals, they assured
me, but I had to be careful.

If we wanted high style or perfect plaster walls, clearly we should
visit some other country. But we weren't high-gloss customers; in
fact, we like bumpy walls. However, we still wanted plenty of hot
water and central heat. Prudence led us to search for an agent who
had set foot on the exact piece of old sod offered.

Gradually we narrowed the field to several houses from Dublin-
based Elegant Ireland, and one—Regency House—a renegade

from a New York agent who hadn't actually seen the property. "Alert" signs flashed. But the profile, designed to capture my heart, read: "...isolated Regency manse, on the edge of a 400-acre lough, built in 1825 as a fishing lodge...Living room offers views on three sides...island in lake's center with castle ruins...rowboat...working farm attached...fresh milk delivered daily."

The conservatory in one photo cinched it. We imagined ourselves there sipping coffee on a rainy morning. The die was cast—along with a small bag of money and the commitment of precious vacation days.

Six weeks later we flew into Shannon airport, rented an Opel, and headed south toward Skibbereen in the glow of dawn. Road signs in both English and Gaelic guided us past greener-than-green slopes sprinkled with white cottages, sheep, and occasional roofless ruins. As we got closer to the house our anticipation mounted.

In the final few miles the narrow road twisted between pine-covered hills and pastures outlined in stone. Around the last bend we saw Lough Ine—a salt lake linked to the Atlantic by a small channel. Hills purple with heather rose out of the water on three sides. On the fourth, Regency House (we recognized it from the photos) sat in a clearing, the lawn sweeping down to the shore. The road ended at our gate—an excellent portent. At the door, Mary Burke, the caretaker from the neighboring farm, waited with the key. Scarcely daring to breathe, I stepped into the entry hall.

I swallowed hard. A stag's head hung on the wall—not my idea of coexistence with wildlife. Its glass eyes peered down from unfortunate faux-embossed wallpaper. The green carpet on the stairs was worn and patched carelessly. My heart sank. I remembered the agents' warnings.

Bravely—wondering for a moment where the nearest hotel might be—I walked on through double doors into the living room. Majestic floor-to-ceiling windows merged the indoors with the outdoors where battered old trees stood in the hedgerows, framing the unbroken view of the still lake. This was more like it. I could see our own pebble beach, blue rowboat waiting for a voyage, rough lawns and flowerbeds-gone-wild rising behind the house to a fine rock wall and an orchard beyond. I flashed a thumbs-up sign to my husband.

I was hooked and I knew it, even before turning back to the stone fireplace, before wandering through the dining room to the conservatory with its immense 100-year-old grapevine, heavy with fruit. Upstairs we found the four-poster-with-a-view; outside, a mermaid on a stone fountain. I would simply have to slip through the entry hall with eyes shut, I decided.

Like much of Ireland, Regency House was old, in a splendid state of dilapidation with a sweet melancholy air—mercifully out of sync with the modern world. We were grateful there was no television set, equally happy with the up-to-date kitchen and huge hot-water tank.

Declaring Regency House our own, we stashed our clothes in an antique chest of drawers, then headed out on the three-mile drive to Skibbereen to stock the larder. Three-story buildings painted a rainbow of colors lined the narrow streets like strings of Celtic jewels: the bright-blue Atlantic Fish Market, the lavender Kitchen Garden, the red Windmill Tavern. We spent an hour trying on waxed coats that are essential for a stay in Ireland, and later bought heavy sweaters hand-knit in the patterns of seafaring families—the designs traditionally varied for identification of sons and husbands drowned at sea.

Our schedule evolved easily. I got up early to say good morning to the cows, then sat for a while by the lake, watching the tide come in and the birds careen overhead. After breakfast in the conservatory we scouted the edges of the lake on foot or by rowboat, then took off for sightseeing and lunch in places with names like Goleen, Crookhaven, Glengarriff. Late afternoon was the time for warming toes by the fire or napping on the overstuffed sofa. Sometimes we had dinner at the house, other times at a nearby restaurant.

We got the landscape we had come for—and the weather. The chameleonlike Irish climate alternately drenched the countryside in shadow, sun, and rain. Moist headwinds gusted past the tops of great stratified cliffs that dropped into the ocean, where clouds of flying spray broke over half-submerged cave entrances. Along narrow lanes we happened on aging churches and dark-gray granite ruins. The 2,500-year-old Staigue Fort, isolated at the head of a desolate valley, rose out of a misty field of sheep and boulders.

One rainy afternoon, warmed by our sweaters and waxed coats, we climbed over a stile and hiked through a pasture to see a prehistoric ring of stone. Fifteen hulking monoliths looked as if they had sprouted from the earth. In the distance a farmer and his dog moved a herd of sheep from one mountainside to the next. We watched in silence—imagining ourselves arm-in-arm with the druids—before heading back toward Lough Ine, grateful to be going home.

The house gave us the chance for both camaraderie and privacy. At lunchtime we often found a small-town pub for fresh-caught salmon, coarse brown bread, a creamy glass of Guinness, and a friendly helping of musical brogues. Evenings at Regency House, we sprawled by the fire and resurrected the pleasures of reading aloud: an

Suddenly, the land ended, fell away in a rush and scream of biting wind and brittle sunshine. All sound was swallowed in the sight. Black rock simply ceased in space, dropping straight down 700 feet to white foam and blue-black sea. The wind howled with such force that spray from the water below shot another hundred or so feet into the air above our heads. I don't know how long we stood there, Matthew and I, a few feet apart, yet totally oblivious of one another. Then I abruptly became conscious that Matthew had spoken.

"What?" I asked, stepping closer to hear him over the keen of the wind.

He turned to me, his eyes afire, holding something I'd sensed in him as he had spoken about the Cliffs of Moher the night we met. The wind whipped his hair around his head like a halo as he said, "It's the most beautiful and relentless thing I've ever seen."

—James Villers, Jr., "On the Cliffs of Moher"

autobiography of a fisherman on nearby Great Blasket Island, Synge's *Riders to the Sea*, Yeats's poetry.

The convenience of a hotel was occasionally missed. Our coin-operated telephone ate change at an alarming rate. With no desk clerk to instruct me in the use of charge cards, I had to spend twenty minutes studying obtuse instructions in the phone book. Unable to figure out the furnace one unexpectedly cold night, we shivered until morning, when we went for the caretaker Mary's help.

By the end of the week, even though we had cooked for ourselves, washed our own pots, made our bed—or not, as we wished—we felt restored. The green carpet had long since faded into the background, in the same way that chipped woodwork back home soon becomes invisible.

We had watched the lake change a thousand times, seen how the light cast its spell on the water. We learned which plot of grass the cows liked best in the morning and which they preferred in the afternoon. We became companions to the cormorants.

Driving away from Regency House on our last morning felt like leaving a friend behind. That fresh and timeless corner of County Cork had become ours in a way that a hotel room could never be. Today, if I stop and think what time it is in Ireland, I can still tell you which side of the yard the cows are grazing on—and that, as the poet said, makes all the difference.

Once she recognized that wanderlust was a part of her spirit, New York writer Jo Broyles Yohay began feeding her need for adventure. With the support of her family, she regularly troops off in search of the exotic. Her preferences run toward old-growth rain forest, developing world street life, remote villages, and hot country roads clogged with donkey carts and stray dogs.

✦ ✦ ✦

The Fox Hunt

The pleasures of the hunt are many.

IT WAS A QUARTER TO ELEVEN, A SATURDAY MORNING, AND THE meet was at the hotel. Along the driveway and in the parking area, horses ranging in style from potential steeple-chaser to probable cart-horse were being backed out of their boxes. On the lawn in front of the handsome old building, hounds packed expectantly around the huntsman. Mounted members of the field circled the master just as eagerly.

There was that familiar atmosphere of "tuning up"—girths tightened, leathers adjusted, hats squared, gloves drawn on—which produces in me a mild state of panic under the best of circumstances. And these were not the best of circumstances. For here was I, a faint-hearted fox hunter, waiting in the yard of an Irish hotel for the strange horse who was to carry me over strange country with a strange hunt.

Nearby, a stable boy introduced two cheerful men and a pretty blonde to their mounts. They drew a rather chubby chestnut called Honey, a sober-looking grey named Daphne, and Polly, a sedate brown mare. On their heels, however, came a fidgety bay, prancing in dainty arcs away from the lad doing up the girth.

The bay's name was Javelin, and he was for me.

Javelin was tacked up in the modest minimum of gear: a flat saddle and a snaffle bridle.

"Has he any peculiarities I should know about?" I suspiciously asked the boy who shouldered him into the mounting block.

"None in this world," he assured me, running down the offside stirrup leather with a resounding slap. "He's a proper racehorse. Keep him well to the front and he'll soon settle down."

Bracing, these words, like rain down the coat collar.

Gingerly I mounted; silently I introduced myself to my proper horse—"Underbitted horse, meet overmounted rider." Then I trotted gamely off to join Honey, Daphne, Polly, and fifty or so other hunters waiting for the signal from the master's horn.

Months before, when I first admitted to friends that I planned to hunt in Ireland, advice was freely offered. Indeed, it was pressed on me. "Lean back and push your feet forward over a drop fence. Take the bank and ditch from a standstill. Hold the mane. And remember, if little children on their ponies can do it, so can you."

It sounded quite simple. Once in Ireland, arranging to hunt had been simple too. Fixture cards for several local packs were posted in the lobby of the hotel. The hotel itself could provide a mount. In my off-the-peg fawn britches and black coat, plain black boots,

Fox hunting is not a leisure sport in Ireland. It is a way of life. With an abundance of fox in a farming community, hunting is viewed as a service to the farmers, particularly during lambing season. And the hunt relies on the farmers to permit the use of their land. On the day of the meet, the townspeople follow the hunt by car and "foot followers" track the fox and hounds' progression. Known formerly as a wall builder, our guide, Kid Farragher, is one of a group of locals who follow the hunt and replace the stones knocked loose from the twelfth-century walls. But he is also an expert fox finder.

—Joanne Meszoly, "On the Hunt with The Kid"

white stock, and velvet cap, I was—if not superbly turned out—at least inconspicuous.

Now all I had to do was keep my seat on Javelin and I would be hunting in Ireland.

The master touched his horn, the huntsman flicked his whip, and we were away at the hounds' jog down the driveway.

A few moments trotting on a hard road brought us to an open gate at which we turned in. The master greeted the farmer who stood there, unaccountably smiling, as half-a-hundred horses entered his field. We were upon the first covert, a yellow-flowering furze thicket into which hounds dove willingly.

It was a good day for scent; it had rained during the night and was still cloudy. Almost immediately, hounds opened. Javelin stiffened. I stiffened, and the practical short course in Irish hunting was underway.

My snatchings at the snaffle notwithstanding, Javelin carried us well up in the first flight as the field strung out.

The first obstacle was a drop of about three feet off a ha-ha into a sea of mud. The approach was a six-foot-wide gap in a thorn hedge. Everyone made for this at once. I dug my toes into Javelin's ticklish sides to keep the stirrups from being pulled from my feet. I couldn't be sure when it would be my turn to lean back and push my feet forward as it seemed to depend on the resistance of the horse in front and the strength of the horse behind. In fact, when the time came, I forgot to do either, but I clung to the mane and all was well.

Once away, the streaming hounds led us over varied, hilly country, with stone walls and drops that made me feel like Alice down the rabbit hole. We encountered rails in water which required a take-off downstream, a landing upstream, and a long gallop midstream under arches of holly. I rode this distance with my face in Javelin's neck and one stirrup flapping.

Mercifully, as we gained the field, hounds checked.

"You're going well," remarked a kindly lady I had splashed rather thoroughly under the holly. "God grant I continue," I thought prayerfully, regaining the stirrup.

On again, this time in bank and ditch country. Now I discovered the nice variety in this class of obstacle: plain banks, banks with one ditch, banks with a ditch each side. High banks and low banks. Narrow ditches and ditches so wide those little children on their ponies go down one side and up the other. In general and in combination, banks and ditches are the sort of "attractive nuisance" which really ought to be fenced off.

Javelin hadn't heard about taking them from a standstill. We approached my first bank and ditch at the speed of light. "Steady does it," cautioned a well-contained gentleman as we shot by. There was a breathtaking spring to the top of the bank, a hairsbreadth of a pause, a smooth curve out over the ditch, a sigh on landing.

The meadows grew larger, but there were plenty of banks and ditches. They turned from mountains to molehills as Javelin dealt with them. My proper racehorse was hardly lathered; I felt surprisingly fit myself. I would have been proud—if I hadn't remembered in time what pride goeth before.

Then topping a rise, there was a cry of "tallyho" and a rider pointed his velvet cap almost straight ahead. Some distance away, on an upward slope which rose behind an old stone wall, a fox streaked towards the woods at the crown. He was as big as a hound. Behind him drove the pack.

I had time for just one good look at what seemed a hunt print come to life—the fox and hounds on the bright green hill, the pink-coated huntsman galloping on, the master hard pressed by the field. Then I focused on the fairish bank coming up. Javelin and I were in distinguished company…the huntsman was over, the master landed safely, a stone wall of a grey-haired gentleman on a grey horse made it. It was not 'til Javelin was airborne off the bank that I saw the variation this one offered; a sheepwire fence pegged in halfway down the far side, angled out like a fireman's landing net. With an inflight recalculation, Javelin cleared it too. Shouts of "'ware wire" diverted the rest of the field.

Only a few strides away the same sheepwire fencing presented itself again. Here it was rigidly upright in front of a lower bank. The huntsman, his heart with the hounds, flew wire and bank effortlessly. The master followed. The gray-haired gentleman gave his horse a good run at it, yelled "do or die," and—his horse having hooked the wire—crashed over the bank. The rider was up in an instant; the dazed horse gained his feet more slowly. There was no damage to either and they were at least on the right side of the fence.

Having checked the girth and brushed his derby, the gentleman gallantly trampled the remains of the wire fence into a springy wicket which Javelin and I gratefully trotted over.

Now the field was ahead of us, the order reversed. Javelin was coming back to his snaffle quite handily when we caught up with the hunt on the hill. Hounds had lost in the woods, and to my unabashed relief, the master was calling it a day. Even if I came a cropper next time out, this time at least I had survived the banks, coped with the drops, stuck in the saddle, and would soon be restored to my next of kin.

When we reached the road, a lucky few found horse boxes waiting. The rest of us pointed our tired horses towards the hotel for a quiet ride at a slow pace. It was thirty or forty minutes before we turned up the long driveway again, now very cool in the shade.

I was met in the stableyard by the lad who'd helped me aboard almost four hours earlier. "How did he go for you, ma'am?" he asked. "Like a bomb," I assured him.

In the hotel lounge, a number of other veterans of the day were already sunk in flowered armchairs drawn up to the fire. They made a place for me and ordered my tea with theirs. It may have been the sherry we had while waiting, or simply a ravenous appetite, but surely no sandwiches were ever so delicious, no scones so buttery, no tea so restorative as those after my first Irish hunt.

Drinks followed tea. We spun out the early evening around the hearth, and story topped story. "Do you remember the time...Were you out the day..." Finally I told about Javelin and the sheepwire.

I may have angled that landing net out from the bank a bit wider. Perhaps I suggested that Javelin cleared the upstanding fence before it was demolished rather than after. And did I say that the grey-haired gentleman was dead to the world for a full five minutes when he failed to make it?

A little luck and a lot of horse had made me quite the dashing hunter after all.

Maryalicia Post, a travel writer, came to Ireland on holiday in 1967 and never got around to going home. Now home is Dublin. Previously she lived in Virginia, USA, where she was a member of the Warrenton Hunt.

✦ ✦ ✦

Wisdom in the Feet

Irish dance—is it simple or complex?

IT WAS EIGHT O'CLOCK ON A THURSDAY MORNING IN ENNIS, County Clare. *Ceili* music was playing on the radio, Chris and I, still clad in our pajamas, were dancing, hop two three, around the kitchen. Our heads jigging up and down, flashing past the window and round again, we were mad Irish clockwork figures, characters of the May morning spinning and wheeling and housing away to the fiddles, pipes, and whistles of the Tulla Ceili Band.

We were mad for dancing.

Every Thursday evening at nine o'clock for three months of the winter we had gathered down at the school with four or five other couples to learn Irish folk dancing, "set dancing." Beside us were the Normoyles, the Reidys, the McMahons, the Cotters, and our great friends the Hartys. Our dancing master was Noel Conway. He taught us, with patience and bemusement, the Clare Set (also known as the Caledonian Set), in much the same way it has been taught and danced in the west of Ireland for a hundred years. Most of the Irish, particularly those reared in the west, have at one time or another danced a set. In country pubs or in wedding halls and in kitchens around the country, set dancing is still a great pastime.

The Clare Set is composed of six figures: three reels, followed by a jig, another reel, and a hornpipe. Four couples make up a set: They stand in a square and dance in a circle, and if that isn't confusing enough, one couple is "tops," another "tails," and the other two are both known as sides. In olden days, the tops were the couple standing at the kitchen dresser, and opposite them were the tails, standing with their backs to the hearth. The best dancer always won the place of honor at the hearth and when he rose from his seat to dance a set, the host would say to him, "You're for the flag." His dancing, drumming feet, then, keep time on the flagstone before the hearth. His "battering" could be heard throughout the house.

It is unclear from the annals of history when Irish folk dancing began. In fact, in eleventh-century, pre-Norman Ireland, when Irish was the only language, there doesn't appear to have been any word for dancing. The word *leimneach*, its primary meaning being leaping, was used to translate the Latin word *saltare*, to dance, in describing Salome's dance before Herod. But most historians discount the assumption that because no Irish word exists for the activity of dancing that the activity itself was unknown in ancient Ireland.

The Normans introduced "round" dancing in Ireland around the twelfth century, and later, dancing inside "The Pale" (the area in and around mid-sixteenth-century Dublin) was extremely tame in comparison to dancing done "beyond the Pale." The dance names themselves indicate what an exciting amusement was the folk dancing of the pre-Anglo-Irish countryside. "The sword dance," "A dance of ranks with change of music," and "The long dance with the sporting of young maidens" are just a few examples.

The word "*ceili*" in some parts of Ireland means a gathering of neighbors in the evening. In Clare this is known as "making a *cuaird*," or a visit; no musical entertainment or dancing is implied. So using a word "*ceili*" to describe organized dancing is, in fact, a misnomer, but the borrowing of the word is justified by the qualities of sociability and friendliness that are inherent in the *ceilis* of today.

Ironically, the first organized *ceili* was held on October 30, 1897, in London.

The long-awaited night of our own Ceili Mór had been Friday, January 27, at half past eight in Cois na Habna, in Ennis. It was arranged that we would meet the other members of "our set" there, Brendan and Geraldine, Noel and Moira, and Liz and her nondancing husband, Aidan. Michael and Gerry were coming with us but at the last minute Gerry had to stay home with a sick child. That left Michael without his partner. But as the saying goes, "*Is olc an gaoith na seadann le duine eigan,*" or "It's an ill wind that blows nobody good." Michael and Liz teamed up and the Kilmihil set was completed.

Cois na Habna is a wooden decagonal-shaped building ideally suited for *ceilis.* In keeping with the philosophy of Comhaltas Ceoltoiri na hEirinn, the organization of Irish traditional musicians and a body dedicated to the preservation of Irish music and dance, all functions held within Cois na Habna must be strictly involved with the traditional aspects of Irish culture. And on that night, the national chairman of Comhaltas Ceoltoiri na hEirinn, Labhrás O Murchú, came from Dublin to participate in the grand occasion of an evening's meal and a *ceili* dance.

Chris and I were very keyed-up for the night. We had practiced in our kitchen for hours, with little Deirdre sounding the steps with us, "hop two, three, and a two two three, and a three two three, and four two three..." We had danced down at the school with the rest of our set, and we had danced over at the Hartys'. We had even shown Mary Breen, our neighbor, our steps one day out on the road when a group of us went walking one Sunday afternoon. She giggled and said, "Oh ye have it, Niall, so you do," and she danced part of a reel herself, lilting the tune and wheeling me around and around on a boreen in Kiltumper.

The air was filled with the quick lively sounds of fiddles. The Kilmihil set met over near the front doors while twenty-five or so other sets established themselves around the room. One of the band members announced that the first set would be a Clare Set and the dancing began. But were we ready? Was the Kilmihil set assembled? No, we weren't. There was a moment of panic when Noel shouted, "Where's my wife? Where is Moira?" But it was too late for a search party, the set had begun. We had rehearsed this so often that when the music began, the dance took over and our feet flew away to the rhythm of the reel. We were holding hands and advancing and retreating in the opening steps of the first figure. Chris and I and Brendan and Geraldine were declared tops and tails and in a flash, we were off halfway around the "house," and advancing and retreating. Fortunately, just then, Chris whispered to me the crucial reminder "own place," which meant that we were to dance a measure in our own place before another advance and retreat and halfway around the house to "their place" before coming home again.

In unison the room bellowed with the excited sounds of 250 people in shared activity. The tops and tails and the sides joined together in one loud burst of exuberance. It was as if we were all members of a team in a contest and our team was winning. All around the room, the tops, tails, and sides of each and every set advanced to the center of their squares and retreated. Smiles abounded.

I have to say that we were beside ourselves with joy. Pure joy.

Niall Williams was born and raised in Dublin. He has an M.A. in American Literature from University College Dublin and a Certificate in Farming from the Irish Agricultural Advisory Board. Christine Breen was born in New Jersey and grew up in Westchester County, New York. She is a graduate of Boston College and has an M.A. in Irish Literature from U.C.D., where she was studying when she met Niall. They were married in 1981, and they worked in publishing in New York before deciding to become small farmers. They live now in the cottage in which Christine's grandfather was born near the village of Kilmihil in County Clare. Their books include O Come Ye Back to Ireland, When Summer's in the Meadow, *and* The Pipes Are Calling: Our Jaunts Through Ireland, *from which this story was excerpted.*

CAROL McCABE

★ ★ ★

To the Great Blasket

Off Ireland's Dingle Peninsula,
the author pays homage
to her literary heroes.

I AM HERE TO FIND SOME TRACE OF EIBHLÍS O'SULLIVAN, WHOM I know only through the letters she wrote a half century ago from this island. This is her family's house; its walls are still intact. The home she shared with her husband is among those ruined stone cottages huddled against the slope like sheep in a storm. The door of this surviving house isn't locked. It opens to a room littered with fishermen's junk: a scrap of net, a couple of floats, hanks of line hanging from the rafters.

"My dear there is no place like home," Eibhlís wrote to a friend in 1931, when she was a twenty-year-old beauty with wild black curls and a flashing smile. "The very day I'll have to leave it won't be a pleasant day for me. I think my dear heart will break that day."

I wonder, did she visit the Great Blasket later, after the islanders all left?

After a week of fog, wind, and rain, this island off Ireland's southwest coast is green under the morning sun. The dirt path I've climbed from the boat landing is slippery, and so steep I had to stop not even halfway to catch my breath. But up here at the top of the abandoned village, I'm among landmarks that were familiar before I ever laid eyes on them.

There, for instance, is the house that Tomás O'Crohan, Eibhlís's father-in-law, built with his own hands. "It isn't a large house," he wrote in his book *The Islandman*, "but, all the same, if King George were to spend a month's holiday in it, it isn't from the ugliness of the house that he would take his death."

His house was roofed with felt, Tomás wrote. Now his house is roofed with nothing but the sky above, and green grass is its floor. Beyond its tumbling stone walls, I can see the White Strand, the long, lovely beach where the women gathered fresh sand to spread on their floors.

Today the Blasket islanders, their children, and grandchildren are themselves scattered like grains of sand, from Irish mainland villages to American cities. Their island is home only to flocks of storm petrels, guillemots, and razorbills—and Manx shearwaters that come screeching in at about one in the morning, a fisherman has told me, making a hair-lifting sound like a coven of witches cackling.

I slide to a seat on the damp grass and watch a pair of rabbits, the inheritors of the land, bouncing through a patch of eyebright and self-heal. The mainland at Dunquin is three miles to the east. I'm perched on the western edge of Europe, on ground important to Ireland's history.

Thirty-six years after the last few families left the Great Blasket, the Irish Parliament passed legislation to make the island a national historic park. Issues concerning land purchase have been in the courts for years, however, and in 1998, the Irish High Court ruled in favor of a group of private owners resisting purchase by eminent domain. But no matter what the future of the park, a spokesman for those owners told me, visitors will continue to be welcome on the island.

In good weather, ferries cross from Dunquin several times a day, leaving passengers time to explore the home of a remarkable brood who, as the poet David Quin wrote, "kept their boats high on the waves and their roofs low to the ground/and were grateful for seals when God withheld pigs."

The prettiest town in all of County Kerry, Dingle is built

around a busy fishing harbor. It is no hardship to stay here for a few days, waiting for the skies to clear and for the water to calm enough to cross to the Great Blasket.

One morning I travel through fog that has overrun the coast road from Dingle to Dunquin. Gray stone walls have gone a damp lavender, and water drips steadily from the wild roadside fuchsia blossoms the Irish call "God's tears." The whiteout erases the sea below and camouflages the perils of cliff-hanger shoulders and tight switchbacks ahead.

The "Open" sign at Máirín Daly's Dunquin Pottery offers relief from the road. Shopkeepers here often have more than one string to their bow; Miss Daly's pottery shares a roof with her bookstore and coffee shop. The women in the kitchen are speaking Irish, but the boss slips into English as she offers me a choice of empty tables.

"Not many tourists out today, and who can blame them?" she asks. "Jesus, Mary, and Joseph, who can blame them? It's not likely you'll have much company today."

But Daly herself is fine company. She serves me fragrant chowder and thick-cut brown bread, then points out a gallery of photographs. "There's Robert Mitchum, that one's Trevor Howard, and she's Sarah Miles, of course." The photos are film stills from *Ryan's Daughter*, which was shot here in 1969.

Along another wall, Daly has displayed a personal collection of books. The titles are familiar: These are the books that have brought me to the Kerry coast. Here are first editions of *Peig,* the autobiography of Peig Sayers, and her later book, *An Old Woman's Reflections.* Two books are by Tomás O'Crohan. Others include Maurice O'Sullivan's *Twenty Years A-Growing,* Mícheál O'Guiheen's *A Pity Youth Does Not Last,* Seán O'Crohan's *A Day in Our Life.* And I find my favorite, *Letters from the Great Blasket.*

That modest book includes selections from the letters that Eibhlís O'Sullivan wrote to a Londoner named George Chambers, beginning in 1931, soon after Chambers visited the Great Blasket, and ending twenty years later.

Altogether, almost forty published books have come from the

Great Blasket, whose population never rose above 176, and there
are memoirs and diaries still in manuscript form, as well as
recorded oral histories. Many of the books were written by the
islanders, but some were written by scholars and other outsiders,
John Millington Synge and Dylan Thomas among them, who
were attracted to the folklore and the pure Irish language. The result is a unique body of literature about life in a turn-of-the-
century Irish fishing village.

"Have you been to the Blasket Centre yet?" Daly asks, after I
say a reluctant no to rhubarb pie. "It's just along the road."

In fact, the Blasket Centre is the reason I'm out in the morning
fog. And a few minutes after leaving Dunquin Pottery, I'm there.

The interpretive center, built with some of the money that has
been poured into Ireland since the country joined the European
Union, opened in 1993. It's a low, starkly modern building of stone
and glass that fits snugly into a field overlooking Blasket Sound and
the island. Inside are offices and a research library, exhibition
wings, a restaurant, and a small theater, where a video includes the
islanders' story in their own words.

Early fears that the center would bring to the area only
"coachloads of befuddled grannies," with no idea of what the
Blaskets were all about, have been assuaged, says Micháel de
Mórdha, the director. Most of the center's visitors know the
Blasket story, for *Peig* was assigned reading for Irish schoolchildren
for many years.

The history books note that the Great Blasket is the largest
group of seven islands, and the only one that was continuously inhabited into the twentieth century. There's written record that
people were living there in 1597, but it's unlikely they were the
first. The remains of an Iron Age fort encrust the northwest end
of the island. And because excavations on the nearby Irish mainland have revealed a settlement predating 6000 B.C., it could be
that the Great Blasket, with its defensible position and freshwater
springs, was settled about the same time.

I look out the windows of the center and see the rough bulk of
the Great Blasket looming through a scrim of fog. Old Tomás

O'Crohan, born on the island in 1856, saw it as "a crag in the midst of the great sea." As for spells of bad weather, he wrote,

"Again and again, the blown surf drives right over [the crag] before the violence of the wind, so that you daren't put your head out any more than a rabbit that crouches in his burrow...."

For many years fast-changing weather and rough water isolated the island from the passage of time. It was almost a medieval existence there, I'm told, the island needing to be almost entirely self-sufficient. There were no police, and there was no crime, but there was an island "king." The Great Blasket had no hospital, no doctor or nurse, no resident priest, no church, and in the final years, no school.

The islanders raised their own food, gathered seaweed to fertilize their fields, and, until none was left, cut turf to warm their cottages. They shared their labor and its rewards, fishing for mackerel and lobster from *naomhóga*, the buoyant and biddable three- and four-man boats they built of lattice covered with tarred canvas.

There is a lack of physical barriers at many Irish sites that are either decaying or precariously close to a cliff's edge. Nor are there signs to warn of doom. While I was at these sites, I could imagine how they would look if Americans had at them: huge warnings quoting the laws I would break if I got too close, plus a high fence with, perhaps, some barbed wire. At the western tip of the Dingle Peninsula, we hiked out to greet the ocean. I have an adventurous spirit, yet I actually had to stop and sit down to ground myself. I realized the path had shrunk down to a sheep-sized path, with a drop-off of about 300 feet. As I sat there, taking in the view of the Blasket Islands, I wondered if sheep ever fell off. As I walked back to the car, I chatted with an Englishman, who confirmed that, indeed, sheep are dropping into the oceans around Ireland at a regular rate.

—Margaret Lynn McLean, "Insights on Ireland"

It all ended in 1953, when the government sent boats to evacuate the islands.

"We had to leave," Seán Guiheen says. "It had gone down so much. All that was left was old people and the crews of two *naomhóga*."

Seán and his brother, Muiris, are among the last half-dozen surviving Blasket islanders. These old men are national treasures (even if the government has yet to dub them that), carrying old knowledge into the new high-tech, fast-track Ireland of the EU.

The bachelor brothers occupy their usual chairs, pulled up to their frugal fire of peat briquettes. Both are as lean as a poor mackerel season; they wear flat tweed caps and woolen sweaters against the damp of their cottage. Seán, who is eighty-six years old, sits at the left, a Silk Cut cigarette held rather elegantly between fingers roughened by hard work and salt water. Muiris, who has played the role of younger brother for eighty years, is at the right.

Muiris defers to Seán, never disagrees but occasionally interjects a piece of information. Micháel de Mórdha, who is a neighbor and has known the Guiheens all his life, translates their low, rhythmic Irish speech.

Seán and Muiris have lived alone since the death, at age eighty-eight, of their mother, whose father was king of the island. He was, the brothers agree, "just like anybody else. You'd never know to meet him that he was the king."

Forty-five years on, Seán and Muiris have clear memories of the evacuation of the Great Blasket. On November 17, 1953, "a boat was sent out from Dingle with two people from the Irish Land Commission," Seán recalls. The name of the boat was the *Lawrence O'Toole*; a man named Dan O'Brien was there to collect the islanders' signatures accepting transfer to the mainland.

As he moves swiftly from Irish to English, de Mórdha ticks off some of the factors that brought the end to island life: the replacement of barter by cash, the decline of fishing, and, most crucial, emigration of the young and the strong.

"It was the young girls, especially, who went first," de Mórdha says. "There were few prospects for marriage on the island, and visitors brought stories of a better life across the Blasket Sound."

And like young people all over Ireland at the time, the youth of the Great Blasket were going to America. "One or two were leaving every house," Seán recalls.

(In 1942 Eibhlís O'Sullivan had written to Chambers: "Everyone is quite tired of the wind and rain and would prefer to be in any other place but here." She was by then married to Tomás O'Crohan's son, Seán, and the mother of a small child. "Visitors…would never believe the misfortune on this Island no…comfort, no road to success, no fishing.…")

An event that occurred at the end of 1946 made the islanders face the inevitable. On Christmas Eve, Seán O Cearna, one of the island's last young men, was stricken with an agonizing headache. The island's radiotelephone wasn't working, and rough seas prevented the few able-bodied men from rowing to the mainland for help. The young man died; an autopsy showed the cause was meningitis.

"The death of Seán O Cearna was the straw that broke the camel's back," de Mórdha says, as Muiris stirs the peat fire. "The people said, 'Oh, my God, you know we're not able to live here any more. We're not able to deal with a crisis, because there aren't enough men to row the boats.'"

Just months later the Great Blasket was again isolated by a storm that lasted for days. De Mórdha recounts the story: "This prompted the islanders to send a famous telegram to Eamon de Valera, then the prime minister." The message read: "DE VALERA DUBLIN= STORMBOUND DISTRESS SEND FOOD NOTHING TO EAT—BLASKETS."

De Valera sent a boatload of food, reportedly tucked in a few spirits, and appointed a commission to devise long-term help for the island.

"The government, after listening to the people themselves, decided that the only option was to resettle them on the mainland," de Mórdha says.

Resettlement was a solution for other dwindling Irish islands, too. John Sayles's 1993 film, *The Secret of Roan Inish*, tells a story of one such island, abandoned but not forgotten. The story is fiction, but the life it depicts is not.

On the Great Blasket only twenty-one people remained by November 1953. Houses had been built or bought for them in Dunquin; the cottage beside the coast road was new when the Guiheens were handed its key. They have grown old here, living contentedly without electricity, plumbing, central heat, or a telephone.

Seán has been mulling one additional comfort, however. He says his bed feels cold as his bones grow older. "I think it might be good to have a woman," he says, his eyes taking my measurements as de Mórdha translates. "To warm up the bed, you know."

It has been ten years since the old men set foot on the island, and they're not likely to go again.

"Do you miss it?" I ask.

"Everything was hard there," Seán says. "There was no comfort like here. The sun would not shine in the houses in the winter. From January to March was bad. Then the wives and mothers would worry when the men were out fishing on a cold, dark night. Sometimes we'd have to wait until the sea calmed before we could come in. The *naomhóga* though were very adept."

"Yes, they could go where no other boats could go," says Muiris.

"They were our horses and our carriages." Seán says. There were good things about that life, he concedes: "There were no rats and no foxes. You could leave the henhouse open, and there was no need ever to lock a door."

"The clean air, the water…" Muiris looks up from where he sits, his hands folded in his lap. The room is quiet but for the somber tick of a clock.

"We were happy there," Seán says, "but, of course, we didn't know any other place then."

Still, doesn't he sometimes miss the island?

"Not at all. Whenever I want to, I can go right outside the house and look at it."

The Great Blasket lies beyond the Guiheens' field like a ship at anchor, like a piece of the past floating just out of reach.

On the shore of the Great Blasket a few days later, I climb the banks of Gullies and walk to the fields beyond the village. Gray stone walls seam the slope, dividing the land into family patches. They had names for all the fields: the new field, the old field, the sandy field, the short field, the field between two paths. The lowest one, just above the long white beach, must be a strand's edge field.

In summer, Muiris had told me, there would be great dances just over the strand. The island's musicians would also gather beneath low cottage roofs on some of those long dark winter nights. And always, there were stories told around the turf fires.

Peig Sayers was the most famous island storyteller. Her memory was stuffed full of stories—legends and myths and local tales, peopled with fairies, invisible fiddlers, priests and drunkards, heroes and strongmen. In Peig's stories, hands reached from the sea bottom to snatch unwary

The light was fading when we came upon a ruined stone house with sheep grazing outside. The roof and windows were gone, had been gone for decades. The grass was low and clipped, a bright shade of green; a stream gurgled beside the road. More ruined homes dotted the land across the stream, abandoned because of famine, emigration, the passing of generations, who knew? One time they had been full of life, full of men and women and children working through all the emotions of their existence. Now they were tended by sheep nibbling at grass sprouting from ruined walls. We drove on along the stream that became a river, following its silvery lead through the loamy fields toward the sea and Donegal town, to find a hearth, a hot meal, and a quiet place to spend the night.
—Larry Habegger, "The Road to Donegal Town"

swimmers; letters from castaways floated ashore in bottles. Secrets were told, and lost men found. To one collector alone, Peig passed on 375 tales and 40 songs.

"Big Peig," who was born on the mainland, entered into an arranged marriage at eighteen. She had never seen her husband, Peats, an islander, until they married, and had never been to Great Blasket until he took her home.

"Isn't this a queer place?" she asked a neighbor woman soon after she arrived. "How is it that the cows don't fall over the edge of the cliffs? Is the island all as high as this? I'm shivering in my skin with dread when I look down on the blue sea running right underneath me."

Although her life there was tragic, Peig grew to love the island where she lived for fifty years and gave birth to ten children. Four died of illnesses before the age of nine. Another, Tomás, was killed as a young man when he fell from a cliff where he had been gathering fuel for the fire. ("The poor fellow was pulling a bush of heather when it gave way with him and he fell over the cliff top," Peig wrote. "He fell on his back pitching from rock to rock, each rock hundreds of feet above the sea until he crashed down at the bottom of the ravine. And may God save the hearers!")

The beauty of nature was her solace in sorrow. Peig wrote of walking in fields after the death of her fourth child: "I sat on the bank above the beach where I had a splendid view all around me." She watched the seabirds, then, "I turned my gaze to the south—towards Iveragh and Dingle Bay…The whole bay was as calm as new milk. With little silver spray shimmering on its surface…"

She let the calm envelop her until, "A sigh welled up from my heart and I said aloud: "God! Isn't it an odd person indeed who would be troubled in mind with so much beauty around him and all of it the work of the Creator's hand?"

Like Peig, I feel the island's calm wrapping me like a shawl. The shush of the waves over sand and rocks, the cries of the seabirds, and the puttering of an unseen boat are the sounds I hear, but I can imagine another—the slow falling of stones. Stone by stone, the cottages are returning to earth.

One that's still standing firm is Peig's house at the top of the village. Slate-roofed with concrete walls, it was one of several new dwellings built in the early 1900s by the Congested Districts Board (a strange name for a body that created public works on a three-mile-plus island with 160 people).

In Dingle I had come across a scene from Peig Sayers's earlier life. Dingle can still be recognized as the remote rural town it was when Peig was a girl, especially in the old pubs like Foxy John Moriarty's or J. Curran's. Foxy John's is a combination pub and hardware store, whose windows display weed killer, bike locks, and bathroom scales. ("He'll sell you rat pizen on one side and a pint on the other," a cab driver said, "and I hope he never gets 'em mixed up.")

On the afternoon that I stepped into J. Curran's public house I felt that it had changed little since Peig worked there late in the last century. Sacks of Irish potatoes, cabbages, and carrots leaned against counters. "You can pick out your spuds and your lumps of coal while you drink your pint," explained a fellow who sported sideburns as gray and woolly as a Kerry sheep.

The bar runs down one side of the room, its stools occupied by men who seemed to know each other very well. I asked how long the pub had been there.

"Oh, a couple of hundred years at least," Mary Curran said as she pulled a slow pint. "There used to be more business in the days when the farmers came around back for sacks of feed. Now, of course, it's much slower. We don't suit the youth," Curran added. "Well, you have to take it as it comes, don't you?"

Out on the Great Blasket, surrounded by memories of people who took it as it came, I turn back toward the harbor. A heavy gale is on the way, and the boats must return to Dingle before it arrives. I'm lucky to have had this time on the island.

"The life would have been the same on almost any island along this coast," the boatman tells me. "What makes the Great Blasket different was the books they wrote."

Tomás O'Crohan would have been pleased. "One day there will

be none left in the Blasket of all I have mentioned in this book," he wrote in *The Islandman*, "and none to remember them. I am thankful to God, who has given me the chance to preserve from forgetfulness those days that I have seen with my own eyes and…when I am gone men will know what life was like in my time and the neighbours that lived with me."

Carol McCabe has no Irish forebears; her surname was a wedding gift. She never visited Ireland before 1996. Still, she says, "Ireland has become the place I'm drawn to as if it were home. Each time I return, whether to the North or the Republic, I cross new fields, learn more music, meet new books and new friends. No other place, except perhaps Australia, ever seemed to enfold me so quickly and completely."

Soon after her Blasket story was first published, McCabe received a letter that began, "My name is Niamh and Eibhlis was my mother." The daughter of Eibhlis O'Sullivan lives now in Tralee and is a member of the Blasket Foundation, working towards National Historic Park status for the island. Sadly, a subsequent letter from Niamh brought the news of the death of "national treasure" Sean Guiheen.

A Fish Story

Angling in Ireland is a real treat,
but you may need to sharpen
your storytelling skills.

IT WAS THE MOST SLENDER OF VOLUMES—NO MORE THAN FIFTEEN pages in all—yet enough to feed the imagination with visions of peat fires and mist-layered mountains, crisp linen and fine wine and, not incongruously, fish.

Just flicking through "Great Fishing Houses of Ireland," a modest booklet available from the Irish Tourist Board, seemed to achieve precisely what some cunning marketing mind intended: a gossamer of wistful fantasy around stately looking places with names like Ballyvolane and Ballynahinch, Mount Juliet and Delphi Lodge, Newport House and Black Water Lodge. But, most of all, the booklet seemed to evoke the possibility of fulfilling several ambitions for someone who had not visited Ireland for decades, never fished for salmon and most of all, had no Spartan hankering for cold showers and dawn risings.

Of the twenty-one houses listed, I sought three that met various criteria: comfort without ostentation, fishing on both lough and river, and no need to invest in expensive new gear.

I ruled out accommodations on some of Ireland's most renowned salmon rivers, like the Moy and the Blackwater, simply because I wanted smaller rivers that I could fish from the bank using single-handed gear. And I was looking for places within easy striking distance of my chosen landfall in Ireland: the leprechaun-sized airport at Knock in the west, which is reached from Stansted Airport near London in an hour. After much poring over of maps and guides, I chose Newport House, Ballynahinch Castle, and Delphi Lodge.

What I hadn't reckoned on in my planning were two irritants. One was utterly minor—midges—and one obsessively major. As in parts of Scotland, Norway, and elsewhere, commercial salmon farming in the estuaries of western Ireland had in recent years all but wiped out sea trout and salmon runs, a matter not just of deep ecological concern but also of local contention, locking fisheries like Delphi, Ballynahinch, and Newport into lawsuits with both the fish farmers and the government. In a way, it is a classic contest between farmers—and government—citing the need for industries in these remote areas, and the concerns of fishery owners over an equally important source of revenue and jobs, touring anglers.

> While angling opportunities vary depending upon the area, the Irish fishing season generally runs from February through September. The best time to fish for spring salmon is from February through April, for grilse starting in June, and for sea trout from August onward (though recently, due to sea lice, the trout runs have begun earlier). For more information, including a free copy of "The Great Fishing Houses of Ireland," contact the Irish Tourist Board: www.ireland.travel.ie.
>
> —JO'R, LH, and SO'R

But there was no such ambiguity about accommodations: each of the houses offered variations on the themes I was looking for—from the wonderful art of Newport to the vast communal dinner table at Delphi, where food and wine flow as smoothly as a tall tale from an angler's tongue.

The early June afternoon was already well advanced by the time

I reached Newport House, dominating the estuary of the Newport River in County Mayo. Kieran J. Thompson, the proprietor, is a former oil company executive who had been a regular visitor to the ivy-clad, eighteenth-century manor house, once the seat of a scion of the rebellious O'Donnell clans expelled from Donegal in the seventeenth century. When it came up for sale in 1985, Mr. Thompson took early retirement, he said, and bought it, finding a home not just for paying guests but also for some of the rugs, prints, and furniture he had accumulated during his years in the Middle East.

A large painting of Col. Sir Hugh O'Donnell, who died in 1760, by the Irish portraitist Hugh Douglas-Hamilton dominates the dining room, just one of a series of public rooms that range from an elegant drawing room to a down-to-earth Irish-style bar. The dining room has tables for forty, who can choose from a menu that might include home-smoked salmon, Clew Bay oysters, and fresh steamed flounder. The wine list, too, is a product of Mr. Thompson's collecting. Experts assured me later that the prices were relatively reasonable.

But the idea was not just to enjoy good food, fine wine, and late-night chatter in the red-leather club chairs on the lounge. Mr. Thompson's son, also Kieran, was assigned as my gillie, or guide, for a couple of hours on the Newport River, a short stretch linking Lough Beltra to the sea. There, the challenges became apparent.

There had not been enough rain (when is the weather ever perfect for anglers?) so the river was too low for a good run of grilse, as salmon are called when they return to their home rivers to spawn after their first winter at sea. Coupled with that, Kieran explained, fish farming had decimated runs that once yielded catches of a couple of salmon and ten sea trout a day. He could remember taking twenty-seven sea trout—a migratory version of brown trout—in a single day. But, in a story repeated throughout the trip, he said the fish farms had changed all that.

The pens holding the farmed fish, he said, had proved a breeding ground for infestations of sea lice. These tiny crustaceans were once found only in a very small number of wild fish fresh in from the sea. But the pens multiply them to epidemic proportions, attacking the gills and fins of wild fish as they head out to sea. That in turn disrupts the migration cycle, forcing fish to turn around to seek fresh water, where the lice fall off but where there is little food.

The problem is far more acute for sea trout, which linger in the estuaries where the pens are situated, while salmon head swiftly out to sea. Still, both species have been affected.

Unlike wild fish, those in pens can be treated in a chemical bath or given food with lice medication.

As Kieran and I cast our way down the Newport River, we saw nothing beyond a few brown trout rising to the surface, but nary a salmon or a sea trout—tribute either to the veracity of this story of ecological decline, or to my ineptitude as a tyro salmon fisher. The next day, Beltra Lough yielded much the same result, although we met up with an English couple who had taken an eleven-and-a-half-pound wild salmon a couple of days before.

Fortunately, then, fishing is not the exclusive charm of lakes like Beltra. In these parts of western Ireland, with mighty hills rising from the loughs and estuaries and the kind of silences that city-dwellers forget exists, just being there eases the soul. And, should other appetites intrude, there's always the Kelly Kettle, part of the legend of Irish lough fishing.

This portable object looks like a small milk churn, but, in fact is built from two skins of metal around a central flue. A fire of kindling is drawn up the flue with the ferocity of a volcano, heating the water around it in no time. Combine that with the clear, peaty water of the lough and the result is a distinctive cup of tea to accompany a packed lunch. After several hours of casting, that came as a pleasure. But still, my fishing log recorded no catches that day, save a small, lonesome brown trout, which was returned to the water.

A two-hour drive south through Westport and Leenane, across peat bog uplands and wild moors, brought me to Ballynahinch Castle in County Galway, and a different kind of comfort. The rambling, crenellated, early nineteenth-century pile dominated the Ballynahinch River and has known various owners, including Maharaja Jam Sahib of Nawanagar, a renowned cricket player and flyfisher. In recent years, it has been owned by a largely American syndicate.

Of the three places on my itinerary, Ballynahinch had more of a hotel feel than the others. It was the only one to offer television in the rooms. It seemed to cater to American and other tourist groups as well as to anglers. While its public rooms were comfortable, they did not have the quiet, salonlike elegance of Newport. The view from the dining room (and from my room), however, was a breathtaking stretch of the Ballynahinch River, and, before dinner, I followed a manicured trail along the river and through dense forest, watching the stream slide silently by, dark, mysterious, and enticing.

By now, a peril of this venture was emerging: there was just too much to eat—from copious cooked breakfasts to hearty packed lunches to elaborate evening meals. Ballynahinch offered a four-course dinner featuring, among other things, pickled local salmon and honey-roasted duck, but I settled for a seafood medley and an Alsatian gewürztraminer from an expansive wine list.

And another hazard was becoming apparent: the way things were, with the water low and the fish stocks depleted, it was turning into a fishing trip where the only fish were those on the menu. Michael van Mourik, a gillie of Dutch descent with an Irish brogue, did his best to reverse the trend on the Ballynahinch. He bade me cast across fast runs and down from high banks into a deep, dark stretch of water called the Dentist's Pool. He chose the fly and pointed out where to cast, offering praise for the few on target and a diplomatic silence for those gone astray.

"It's a good spot for salmon, just off the boulder, do you see," he'd say. Or "Did you see that one?" when a sea trout shot out of the water like a submarine-launched missile.

Sadly, though, the fish I caught only seemed to underline the problem: one was a skinny sea trout that should have been feeding at sea but had, the gillie said, been driven back into the fresh water by the sea-lice contamination. The other was a smolt—a young salmon heading to sea for the first time after two years in fresh water—that for the same reason had also got trapped in the fresh water, where it would most certainly die.

From Ballynahinch, the drive to Delphi Lodge took less than an hour, and I was beginning to feel I would never see a salmon, let alone catch one. That changed only marginally at Delphi: I saw one—a beautiful, spring salmon, head-and-tailing in the water not ten yards from the drifting boat I took with a Swiss guest, Urs Liebundgut. We were spending a final hour after settling in there in Finlough, the smaller of the two lakes that form the fishery along with the Bundorragha River. It weighed, probably, eight pounds and, with its disdain for the artificial flies I placed across its path, would probably grow to be a few pounds more.

Peter Mantle, Delphi's owner, bought the lodge—an elegantly relaxed 1830s country house built for the Marquis of Sligo—in 1985 when its sea trout runs were legend. Initially, the twelve-bedroom house catered prin-

---

I had arrived in Ballyduff with the fly fishing version of a cannon, the sort of rod many California guides would scoff at as being too big to have any feel or finesse. When the men of Ballyduff heard what I planned to use—a nine-and-a-half foot graphite rod rated for a seven-weight line—they laughed and elbowed each other. They then explained that, with my rod, it was necessary to work way too hard—false casting again and again to get the flies upriver so they could drift with the current. Real salmon fishermen, they explained, use a two-handled, eighteen-foot rod. "Isn't nearly as flashy," one man confided, "but you catch more fish this way, since most of the fish here on the Blackwater are in the water and not in the air." I, of course, set out the next morning to prove them wrong. I didn't catch a thing, but my false casting sure looked fine.

—Lee Gotshall-Maxon,
"Gone Fishing"

cipally to anglers, but around 1990, when fish farming took root, catches dropped off dramatically. Since then, Mr. Mantle had opened the lodge more to nonangling visitors, while also beginning a program to raise hatchery fish from the river system's genetic stock and releasing 50,000 tagged smolts a year in the hope that some will return as grilse. And he has been at the forefront of legal battles with the commercial fish farmers and the government, aiming in part to force fish farms to control sea lice and lie fallow during key periods of the wild fishes' life cycles.

Of course, there is another side to the story. The Irish government and the fish farms say the salmon-farming industry creates jobs in an otherwise depressed area. The duel has borne some results: in 1998, 1,060 salmon were caught at Delphi, a record for Mr. Mantle's fourteen years there, and in May 1999, 110 multiwintered spring salmon were caught and mostly released—another record. He ascribed those figures to the success of his stocking program—many of the fish had originated as smolts in his hatchery—and negotiations with the farms to reduce sea-lice infestations.

But the statistics miss a point: in these parts, you earn a salmon. Only the fortunate few luck into a fish. Under lodge rules, the only fish that may be kept are salmon tagged as returning hatchery fish. All sea trout and wild salmon must be released.

Forget those stories of fanatical fishermen rising before dawn and fishing nonstop until dark. Cooked breakfast started only at a leisurely 9 A.M. and the gillies picked up their clients at 10. The various fishing areas—two loughs and sections of the river—are rotated every half day, so a break for lunchtime soup and sandwich fits nicely. By 6, most guests are back in the library and the adjacent lounge with a drink in hand. There's no formal bar—only a well-stocked trolley with a book to sign on an honor system.

All that leads up to what is probably the most distinctive social feature of Delphi Lodge: dinner round a long common table that, in the manner of ambassadorial entertainment, can seat up to twenty-six for a meal of the same standard as the other two lodges, with an ample selection of wine. Here, too, the five-course dinner was laid before what is usually an international clientele. During my brief stay, I encountered French, German, Swiss, English, and South African guests, and some of them had caught fish.

With time running out, I desperately wanted to join the select few who had boated or landed a salmon or sea trout. Sandy Walker, the gillie, tried hard. Together, we plied the Doolough—the bigger of the two lakes. The technique is to cast out fifteen yards of line and retrieve the artificial flies attached to the leader in the hope that a salmon will go for it. (Salmon do not feed during their spawning runs and no one really knows why they take an artificial fly.) I cast and cast, catching only tiny brown trout. We tried the river, casting from rocky stances into swift, cascading runs. But my fishing log recoded zero for salmon or sea trout, unlike a German guest who not only caught a spring salmon but videotaped it for posterity before releasing it. Ultimately, it didn't seem to matter that much. The majestic hills, the water lapping against the wooden boat induced a delightful sense of well-being. That, at least, is what I told myself as I headed—fishless—for Knock airport.

Alan Cowell is a correspondent in the London bureau of The New York Times.

PART THREE

GOING YOUR OWN WAY

GRETCHEN FLETCHER

★ ★ ★

Mollie and Eddie

The elderly have a special place
in the Irish heart.

WE WERE IN ENNIS, COUNTY CLARE, TAPING A SEGMENT ABOUT
the west coast for a video my husband was producing called
Discover Ireland. In this scene the script called for a model to be sitting at the hotel reception desk. Traveling without actors, we
looked around the lobby to see whom we could use. The manager
of the hotel suggested Eddie.

Eddie was sitting in the lobby with apparently nothing else to do.
He looked as if he had been sent by Central Casting. His smooth
pink complexion and white hair were set off by a rough wool tweed
jacket with suede patches on the elbows. He willingly, proudly, sat
at the reception desk while Jaf shot over his tweed shoulder.

Later we needed a fire in the lobby fireplace to set the right
mood for another scene. The manager came to our rescue again.
"Paddy will set a fire for you…Paddy! Light a fire in the lobby
fireplace…Paddy helps out with things like that in return for
meals. He was living at the old folks home before he came here."
That was nice, we thought, letting a poor old soul have a warm
place to hang around along with a square meal every day.

Now we needed some people to sit around Paddy's fire. Would
the ladies who were reading in the lobby mind being in the

219

scene? No, they would be delighted. Jaf taped the scene, and then Mollie appeared.

Mollie was Eddie's wife, Eddie of the tweed jacket and white hair. Why hadn't she been asked to be in the scene? Why, she was there at the hotel every day, and some of these ladies only came occasionally. Her pink satin skin, which matched her husband's was flushed with anger; her pink scalp glowed in the bare spaces between her tight corkscrew curls. We soothed her hurt pride by saying there would be another scene, and if she and Eddie were still staying at the hotel, perhaps we could use them.

"Oh, sure and ye shall be seein us every day, ye shall."

And sure enough, there they were every day in the same corner of the lobby, Eddie and Mollie, with a tray of toast and tea before them in the morning and another one in the evening. Never anything else on the tray, just tea and toast and little pots and plates of cream, sugar, butter, and jam.

On the other side of the room from them, in an antique chair, always sat an antique gentleman, his feet stretched out in front of him, in more of a reclining than a sitting position, enjoying a deep eight hours sleep with his mouth wide open.

Who were these people? And why did they seem to occupy their respective chairs all day? Other guests started their days with breakfast in the dining room, then disappeared for a whole day of sightseeing, shopping, or golf, to return in the evening for dinner. But these people, Eddie and Mollie, the antique chair man, and the cluster of ladies reading around the fire, seemed to be there all day. None of the other guests noticed this, of course, for they assumed that during the day these people were out of the hotel as they were. But since we were videotaping around the hotel off and on throughout the day, we began to notice that they never left.

One evening on our way to the dining room we asked Mollie and Eddie if they were going in to dinner. "Oh, no, ye see. We enjoy our tea and toast. We only eat dinner every other day."

"Where do you live?" we asked.

Vaguely, "Just behind the 'otel. Down the road a wee bit."

We began to notice that the antique man was spending more

and more of his days with his eyes open and mouth closed, watching us videotape. When he began to ask us questions, we struck up a conversation with him. It took only one pint of Guinness from the Poets Corner Pub to encourage him to tell us his life's story.

Jim had emigrated in the '20s, as had so many of his countrymen, to New York. He told us proudly that he had worked on the construction of the Empire State Building. In later years, he became very ill and underwent open-heart surgery. When he recovered enough to leave the hospital, President Reagan sent him a letter on White House stationery congratulating him and wishing him well. With the letter folded into a small square in his worn wallet, he returned to his native County Clare to live out the rest of his days. He had a bed-and-breakfast room down the road, but he spent much of his time in the lobby of the hotel cheered by both the fire of the hearth and the warmth of human activity.

We began to piece the separate stories together and to suspect the hotel manager of some great kindness. We even began to suspect that his kindness went beyond trays of tea and toast, an occasional meal, and a chair to sleep in.

When videotaping the rooms and suites, we had been told that we couldn't enter one wing of the hotel

---

In Buncrana we stayed with friends above a shop on Main Street. They had a five-month-old girl, their first, who voraciously sucked down milk, slept soundly, and loved to go out on the town where friends gathered in pubs and shared conversation, humor, and gossip.

In Dunfanaghy we visited a red-haired, eighty-four-year-old beauty who for twenty-five years ran a café on the square at the harbor. As we were saying goodbye after a long cup of tea I was shocked by a similarity I saw between the eighty-four-year-old with the failing body and the five-month-old we'd just left— two ends of the spectrum with a similar quality of serenity. I thought I was seeing both of them at once.

—Larry Habegger, "The Road to Donegal Town"

because it was closed for refurbishing. Could it be? No, surely not. This was a five-star hotel, after all, not an old folks home. But these guests were always clean and respectably dressed; they even added a genteel charm to the ivy-covered hotel furnished with antiques.

When we asked the manager if he was doing what we thought he was, he just smiled. He wouldn't admit it, of course, but we were sure we were witnessing the kind of unselfish act we saw so many Irish people perform.

After we'd spent a week in the hotel, our cast of characters had come to seem like old friends. On our last day, as we were checking out, Mollie told us that she wanted to see us before we left. Getting our equipment and luggage into our two small rental cars took so much time that we almost forgot to seek her out in her accustomed place in the lobby. In their same corner, on their same sofa, in front of their same tea tray, sat Mollie and Eddie, all pink smiles.

"We wanted ye to have this to remember us by," she said, holding out a small wrapped package on top of an unwrapped purse calendar. The calendar had a scene of Ireland to illustrate each month.

I unwrapped the box to find a tiny china teacup and saucer covered with lilies of the valley. Inside the cup was printed the word May. This was August. Was there some significance?

"She took it from her set of cups for every month of the year," Eddie explained. "She thought ye'd like that one."

Now when I think of Mollie and Eddie, I see them in their room (at the hotel?) with a set of eleven tiny cups and saucers parading across a shelf...cups that say January to April and June to December.

Gretchen Fletcher's personal essays and travel articles appear frequently in national magazines and newspapers, and her poems have appeared in literary journals and anthologies. She is the scriptwriter for travel videos her husband produces, and she leads workshops in poetry and the personal essay for Florida Center for the Book, an affiliate of the Library of Congress.

✦ ✦ ✦

Under the Light of Vega

A naturalist ponders starlight and
monastic creativity in Ireland.

IRELAND SITS WELL UP ON THE SHOULDER OF THE GLOBE. IN THESE latitudes in midsummer the sun sets late. There is still a hint of twilight in the northern sky when our publican in Ventry blinks the lights in the pub, the signal that it is half past eleven o'clock and time for ordering last pints. I have had enough drink. In the amber glow of Irish ale and good conversation I strike off up the *bothareen* toward home.

By the time I reach the high road and emerge from the dark hedgerows of bramble and fuchsia, the stars are appearing one by one. It is a Van Gogh sort of sky, splashed with gaudy swirls and streamers of starlight. Not long ago a scholar analyzed Van Gogh's paintings of the night sky and found that they were more "realistic" than anyone had supposed; apparently it is possible to recognize in the paintings the patterns of certain constellations. Perhaps. But Van Gogh saw something in the night sky that is not to be found on any other star map I have seen. He saw the stars as vortices of color, and not as white dots. Van Gogh's stars are huge multihued cyclones that pull us up by the hair and empty us out of the Earth like water from a broken vessel, as are the stars that shine above me tonight. Look, *now*, at Antares, low above Valentia Island, exploding like a Roman candle, outlandishly red. Or there, above Mount Eagle, golden Arcturus, waving like an oriflamme. Or near the zenith, scintillant Vega, like a smoke hole in the tent of the sky, aswirl with blue and silver light. I go all giddy. It is no wonder Van Gogh went mad. A glance at a sky like this one is enough to unhinge any reason. Once these stars have spilled their color on tonight's black canvas, there's no putting it back. We are splotched and splattered with it and go blubbering about, wildly shaking our heads, like madmen or village idiots.

I sit on a grassy bank at the side of the "road of the fairies" to wait and watch. Smoky Vega smolders at the zenith. The star's name is derived from the Arabic *Al Nasr al Waki*, "the swooping eagle." And, indeed, Vega appears to swoop, to plummet luminously, exactly as Van Gogh painted it. It dives toward me, straight down from the roof of the sky. It is twenty-seven light-years away, 160 trillion miles, but I swear that if I reached out my arm I could touch it. What the Arabs did not know is that the name they gave the star is more than poetry, more than metaphor. Vega *does* dive toward us, in a literal sense; or rather we dive toward Vega. The star is very near to that place in the sky called the solar apex. It is the place among the constellations toward which the sun's motion among the stars of the galaxy is carrying us. The sun is flying toward Vega, and we go with it. We are falling toward Vega at twelve miles per second, spiraling down onto that blue star out of the black backdrop of the universe. We will be there in half a million years.

Up the smoke hole, down the drain! The stars are more than we bargained for. They are thermonuclear furnaces, incandescent with the heat of vanished matter, globes a million miles in diameter, or 10 million, or 100 million, voluptuous presences. Give Van Gogh this—he saw the stars for what they are, undisguised by distance. Some people say that Van Gogh's stars, those vertiginous volcanoes of color, were a product of his madness. Perhaps it was the other way around.

This is the world I love best—the world lit by starlight. There are a few dozen electric lights burning in the parish below me, and

I can make out another dozen or so lights on the Iveragh Peninsula across Dingle Bay, including the resolute beacon of the Valentia Harbour lighthouse. My immediate environment—the grassy bank, the hedge of honeysuckle and fuchsia, the wild irises and foxgloves massed in the ditch—is illuminated solely by the light of stars. Vega, at the zenith, is a thousand times less bright than the full moon, 50 million times less bright than the sun. But multiply Vega's faint light by the 10,000 stars of the summer Milky Way, and it is illumination enough.

In the bardic schools of ancient Ireland, the young poets-in-training, having been set in the evening a theme for composition, retired each one to his private cell, a cell furnished with nothing more than a bed and perhaps a peg on which to hang a cloak, and—most importantly—without windows, there to compose the requisite rhymes, taking care to observe the designated rules as to syllables, quartans, concord, correspondence. termination, and union, in *total darkness*, throughout the remainder of the night and all the next day, undistracted by the least ray of the sun, until

We continued for an hour or so as the path wound between lichen-covered boulders and shallow pools. There was no sound beside our steady breathing and the bleating of sheep. We had started our walk with neither of us talking much, except for an occasional comment on the splendor before us. This beauty, the quiet, and the exercise had quieted our minds. We were no longer tourists in a rush to see everything. We were in the present, enjoying just where we were. We began to talk. Not of jobs, family, or home. Instead we talked of our dreams, our goals, and what we really expected of our lives. We held hands. We stopped and hugged before turning around. Quietly tears fell down my cheeks. My husband asked, "What's wrong?" "Nothing," I replied. These weren't tears of sadness, but rather blissful tears.

—Laura Strehlau,
"Irish Pleasures"

the following evening at an appointed time when a light was brought in and the poem written down. An eighteenth-century account of the bardic schools by the Marquis of Claricarde asserts that the discipline of darkness was imposed so that the young poets might avoid the "Distractions which Light and the variety of Objects represented thereby commonly occasions," and in darkness "more fully focus the Faculties of the Soul" upon the subject at hand. From the Marquis's language one might suppose that the soul has a light of its own, that it glows with a self-luminosity, like the owls or the Blackwater Valley, and that the soul's crepuscular light is drowned out by the light of day. Certainly poets, like mystics, have traditionally been creatures of the night. The world of daylight is a world of impenetrable surfaces, resplendent, metallic, adamantine. In starlight, surfaces are transparent, like the flesh of a hand held to a bright light, and the soul sees into objects and beyond. But there is a danger in starlight—the danger of infinite dilution. There is a danger that the soul will leak away like water into loose soil, or be dispersed like breath in wind. Could that be why the poets of the bardic schools shut themselves up in *total* darkness to compose their verses, without the light of a single star? The light of one star is enough to prick night's dark skin, and the enclosing sphere of the sky goes pop like a balloon, and we fall out of ourselves, upward toward Vega, at twelve miles per second, into Infinity.

I lie back on this grassy bank and the light of 10,000 stars enters my eyes in sufficient quantity to enable my brain to form images of the stars. Ten thousand subtle but distinct wavelets of energy enter my eyes at slightly different angles from out of the depths of space, and by some miracle my eyes and brain sort it all out, put each star in its proper place, recognize the familiar patterns of the constellations, construct a Milky Way, and open my soul to a universe whose length and breadth exceed my wildest imagining. Starlight falls upon me like a gentle rain. It blows across me like a furious wind. I am soaked and shaken.

And there is more. Out of the minuscule quantities of starlight that reach the earth, astronomers, with the proper instrumentation, can deduce the sizes, distances, densities, and compositions of the stars. The astronomers take those grains of starlight and with a grating or a prism spread them out into spectra and recognize in the patterns of color (or the absence of color) the telltale radiations of the very same elements out of which the Earth is made—hydrogen, oxygen, calcium, iron, and so on. Vega's substance is the same substance as the iris in the ditch! It is an astonishing revelation of the relatedness of everything that exists. The stellar spectra of the astronomers are another wrap of a wound-up universe, a universe as compact as a hazelnut in the palm of my hand.

Julian of Norwich asked: *What is the use of praying if God does not answer?* In starlight, God answers. Starlight blows through my body like wind through the hedge. My atoms ebb and flow in a cosmic tide of radiation. Vega surges into luminescence and electrons do handsprings in the cortex of my brain. Planets are gathered in Vega's dusty brim; I am warmed by their gentle heat. If you sip the sea but once, said the Zen master, you will know the taste of all the oceans of the world. Tonight I sipped 10,000 stars. I have tasted the universe.

Chet Raymo is Professor of Physics and Astronomy at Stonehill College, Massachusetts. A teacher, naturalist, and science columnist for The Boston Globe, *he is the author of the highly praised* The Soul of the Night, *the best-selling* 365 Starry Nights, *and several other books, including* Honey from Stone: A Naturalist's Search for God, *from which this piece was excerpted.*

KATHARINE SCHERMAN

* * *

Skellig Dreams

On an exposed rock off the coast of Kerry,
ancient Ireland was dreamed
by saints and scholars.

MIST LAY OVER THE NORTH ATLANTIC NEAR BRAY HEAD, County Kerry, in the southwest of Ireland, a remnant of the rainstorm that had flattened the water a few minutes before. The wind had driven it off and now it lay to the south, a dark cushion of cloud hiding the horizon. Near shore the ocean was flat under the thinning fog. In the north the great massif of Brandon Mountain hulked over Dingle Peninsula, its unseen summits wrapped, as they always were even on the fairest days, in moving clouds. Over the ocean the sun broke through and the water began to shine. It looked like a lake.

The boat picked us up at the bridge over Portmagee Channel between Valencia Island and the mainland of the Iveragh Peninsula. It was a thirty-two-foot fishing boat fitted out to take a dozen or so passengers on short expeditions, with benches along the sides in the stern and a cabin forward.

For a short way beyond the bridge the channel was protected; green fields rose to mild rocky heights. But when we passed Horse Island on the left we were out of the lee. The wind off the open ocean hit us, and waves came from every direction as conflicting tides and currents crossed at the meeting place of inlet and ocean.

The water that had been a gray monotone from afar was a surge of flying white spray and thick green whirlpools in the wake of the breakers. Our solid little boat was picked up and tossed like an empty snail shell. For a few minutes we wallowed, making no headway at all. The motor took hold and we slowly crawled out of the riptide. The open ocean was no better. Near shore the waves were short and choppy. Out in the swell they were relentless, rhythmic combers far bigger than our boat. We would climb a steep green hill and poise at the top, shuddering, the screw out of water. Our pilot cut the motor so we wouldn't dive to the bottom, and we careened down the other side, sometimes sideways or backwards, to pitch and rock uncontrollably in the trough. There was barely time to gun the motor to meet the next wave, which wasn't always directly in front but might be coming at us from the side, roughened by the gusty west wind.

We couldn't see where we were going nor where we had come from. Everywhere we looked there was only water—above us, beside us, before us, behind us, at every pitch but level. Out of the corners of our eyes we glimpsed unconcerned birds, kittiwakes playing with the wind and puffins beating low across the wave tops. Sometimes there was a seal, head high, staring curiously before submerging in its element, while we unqualified humans clung to the rails, numb to the water breaking over us, one identifiable thought in our minds (beyond the unvoiced fear that this was our last journey)—"We have to come back the same way!"

Sometimes a big bird, all white but for black wing tips, rose out of the water near us and climbed in stately flight to circle the boat before disappearing beyond the waves: a gannet. We hardly noticed that this was becoming more frequent, until we were surrounded, the gannets hovering over the boat like gulls, wheeling in our wake, swooping close as if to see what we were and what we had with us. Unlike gulls they did not utter a sound. Their scrutiny seemed like an inspection by spirits: the gods of the bird world come down to see if we were worthy. Suddenly dead ahead appeared a tall rock of spires and castellated walls, covered with gannets, perching, nesting, landing, taking off, diving. It was the island of Little Skellig, inhabited entirely and only by gannets, 20,000 nesting pairs of them, the second largest colony in the world, their home for possibly the past 1,000 years. As we came under the island's sheltering peak, the boat steadied enough so we could see, a mile or so beyond, the sharp dark triangle of Great Skellig, also called Skellig Michael, 714 feet high, which had been home to a few of Ireland's wandering monks even longer ago.

They had come across the same eight and a half miles of ocean in their curraghs, wooden-frame, hide-covered boats that bobbed lightly as thistledown over the waves. On the last part of the journey, between the two rocks, the water was no less rough, but they must have felt a somewhat startled elation as did we at seeing their destination. The sun was so bright now that we could not look at the sea, and the shadowed island was a formidable silhouette without detail, piercing the light sky. As we neared we could see waves breaking, scattering their spray far up on bare and shining rock. We looked in wonder at the vertical slab of the wall, thinking of those ancient voyagers.

> ※
>
> An incredible, impossible, mad place...I tell you the thing does not belong to any world that you and I have lived in and worked in.
>
> —George Bernard Shaw, describing Great Skellig to a friend (1910)

No harbor was visible until all at once we came around a corner and were in it, a small straight-walled inlet protected on three sides from open ocean. A cement dock was built into one corner and a paved walkway cut from the sheer rock led out of sight away from it. Before the walkway was built no one could have climbed from here. We learned that hand-hewn steps made by the monks ascended from another landing place on the north side, a triangular cove open to the sea, where today boats can land possibly four days in a year. But for several hundred years they had brought their little vessels into that exposed corner, where they had to haul them up on the sharp rocks above reach of the waves. They came with the few supplies they could carry in their curraghs, to an island open at every point to wind and rain, where only small hardy plants can take root in rock crevices and no animals but seabirds and rabbits can find sanctuary in weather-eroded fissures in the sheer walls.

The monks did not come here to escape. They left their quiet lives within the sheltering walls of their monasteries to set forth with hope over the savage ocean, ill equipped, unworldly, caring not what hardships they would meet at the end of the voyage. They came for love.

Today the narrow road from the harbor ascends part way up, curling around Skellig Michael's perpendicular south side, to end at a lighthouse on the southwestern tip, below West Peak, the taller of the rock's twin peaks. About halfway along the road the stairway of the monks appears, rising uncompromisingly straight up toward the rounded dome of the eastern peak: 600 steps crudely cut in the rock face, of differing widths and not always level. Their tools must have been other rocks, and they must have worked fast. Summer off the coast of southwestern Ireland is notably cool and rainy, but winter is almost insupportable. Never does the wind cease long enough for the ocean's turbulent swell to subside. Winter gales drive the waves 30 feet up on the lee side of the island, and up to 200 on the south, where the full force of the North Atlantic hits. Nowhere on the rock is there so much as a cave for refuge, nor is there a level place anywhere near sea level that is wide enough for building. If they came in April, when the storms diminish, they had to complete their stairway to the island's only practicable terrace, 550 feet up, and build their houses all within the four spring and summer months of comparative calm. Because when September came, with its equinoctial tempests, the monks could neither live there without shelter or could they depart.

The flight of steps is not continuous. The slope moderates here and there, and a precarious layer of soil has had a chance to form. In these places, a few yards wide, the steps cease and we walk over pillows of sea pink and big soft clumps of sea campion, those hardy colonizers whose roots twine together in tangled mats, catching their own dead foliage and making of it their own soil. The monks took advantage of a few of these slanting terraces, erecting stone crosses where those who came later could stop and worship, or just catch their breath and look at the birds. One of these monuments is still there, a pitted stone worn almost shapeless by time and weather, rising stark out of the flowers at the threshold of the cliff, the sea fierce beyond it.

A few steps beyond the cross, lichens and mosses have invaded a section of rock already eroded by wind and rain, and the spongy surface is honeycombed with puffin burrows. The stubby, black-and-white birds fly straight at their holes in a businesslike manner, unconcerned with human nearness, dozens of shining little fish hanging in their triangular orange beaks for the young hiding in the moist darkness.

These oases give token that in summer, at least, the monks would not have gone hungry. Besides the puffins, which are easy to get at, the cliffs are home to hundreds of other nesting seabirds: kittiwakes, fulmars, razorbills, and guillemots lay their eggs and raise their young in clefts and on ledges high above the sea. The monks could have kept a few goats, the only domestic animal un-fussy enough about its diet to live on the rock's scanty pickings. Some of the plants are edible, such as scurvy grass, a low-growing succulent whose thick heart-shaped leaves contain vitamin C; and the anchorites could have grown a few herbs. In the sixth century, when it is probable that the first voyagers arrived, the climate was warmer than it is today. There could not have been much more soil, because there simply is no place for it; everything slips down-ward, and only in a few places can a plant take root for long enough to provide its own continuing habitat. But the summers then were not quite so short nor the winters so unkind. Fish and the few birds, such as gulls, that wintered over, would have seen them through the cruelest months.

The last few yards of the climb are in a tunnel under a retain-ing wall, built in modern times to protect the monastery site from the depredations of burrowing rabbits. These animals, relative newcomers, have no predators on the island and they are increasing uncontrollably. Their digging has endangered the lighthouse road, part of which is roofed against the resultant rock falls, and it is undermining the foundations of the ancient buildings, a feat that the attrition of fourteen centuries of wind and rain have not sufficed to accomplish.

We climb upward through dripping darkness. Behind us is the fearsome voyage and the slow ascent up the lonely rock scourged by Atlantic storms, habitable only by birds and seals. Ahead of us, as we come out of the tunnel into the mild sunlight, is a living fragment of the sixth century. We have walked back in time, out of our own mundane earth into the world of the Irish saints and their pagan Celtic ancestors.

The pitch of Skellig Michael at this place, between 550 to 600 feet above the ocean, levels off in a series of narrow, uneven terraces before it mounts the last steep 50 feet of the eastern peak, out of sight on the rounded hillside. Six little beehive-shaped stone huts, a slightly larger stone oratory with a barrel-vault roof, and the roofless walls of a small church are clustered here at varying levels, some nestled close against the swell of the hill, some poised at the very edge, only a low dry-stone wall between them and the breathtaking cliff. Between them are winding walks lined with flat stones. A widening of the central walk into a miniature plaza is occupied by leaning tombstones, their inscriptions obliterated. In its own green square beyond them is a stele, probably originally a cross, its crosspiece two blunted knobs, the weathered carving on its face blending with lichens to form a design of geometric abstractions. It stands alone, tall as a man and somewhat resembling one, as if an anchorite had been forgotten there and still stands lost in contemplation of Little Skellig rising out of the sea, framed by the curving walls of two beehive huts.

The buildings and walls are constructed of flat stones, without mortar. From the sides of the round huts project stone corbels, which probably supported sod roofs. Each one has a hole in the top, originally closed off by a rock slab. As living quarters they offer small latitude. The highest, which is thought to have had two stories, is sixteen feet, the lowest is about nine, the walls from three to six feet thick, and the square interior floor space hardly big enough for a man to lie down in. They have no windows and the doors are only about four feet high and two wide. They must have been cold in winter and damp all year round. But the people who dared the ocean waves to find their peace on this rock had no interest in comfort. On the contrary, their disregard for the everyday usages of ease was the very core of their spiritual vitality. Austerity not only pleased them, it was necessary to them.

And the rough life had compensations. Asceticism gave an intensified response to the smell of flowers, the texture of stone, the feel of rain or sun or wind, the flight of birds. When they came out of their dark cells, their spirits must have lifted to heights rarefied beyond our experience. The ground they knelt on was of springy moss with flowers growing in it. Beyond the low stone walls the sea was blue, lavender, silver, and green in broad uneven patches, and it appeared from this height flat as a pond. The morning clouds looked like white Skelligs, and the penitents could almost talk to the fulmars and puffins flying to feed their rockbound young. As they watched the sunrise, a curtain of rain might fly over the sea from the west, bright steel with the sun's low rays on it, to pass overhead in a few minutes leaving a rainbow and the clover-like scent of wet sea pink. In such a setting the simple prayers to God might have been tinged with almost pagan pantheism.

It is not known positively when the first voyagers arrived, nor who they were. Tradition attributes the founding of the monastic village to one St. Finian. Three eminent holy men of this name, teachers and founders of monasteries, lived in the sixth century. The style of the building goes back to this period and beyond: to the pre-Christian dwellings on which the first Christian structures were modeled. Although the earliest churches and dwellings were usually built of wood or of wickerwork daubed with mud, on Skellig Michael the builders would have had to use the only material at hand. According to the annals, the settlement survived at least four attacks by Norse raiders in the ninth century. The monks evidently turned the other cheek, because in the tenth century one of Skellig Michael's holy hermits, says tradition, converted Olaf

Tryggvesson, the fierce Viking who became Norway's first, and combatively, Christian ruler. The last monks left in the twelfth century, when life had grown soft, to settle in the village of Ballinskelligs, nearby on the mainland coast.

Through all the years the name of only one monk has survived. That is Etgall, an anchorite who was apparently living there alone when Vikings arrived in 823 looking for treasure. The poor little island monastery, which could barely support six or seven ascetics, would hardly have run to the silver chalices and jewel-studded shrines that provided the freebooters such easy pickings in the mainland monasteries. In anger, or perhaps in hopes of getting a ransom, the raiders took Etgall, who died while their prisoner, say the annals, of starvation. The implication is clear: the stark rigors of Skellig Michael held no dangers for Etgall, but when he could no longer hear the cries of seabirds and the crash of waves, or taste the salty wind of his island retreat, he grieved until death rescued him.

In no other connection is Etgall mentioned. He was not a saint whose feast day is on the calendar; history

This union of charity between Ireland and the Holy Roman Church has remained inviolable and unbreakable down all the centuries. You Irish Catholics have kept and loved the unity and peace of the Catholic Church, treasuring it above all earthly treasure. Your people have spread this love for the Catholic Church everywhere they went, in every century of your history. This has been done by the earliest monks and the missionaries of Europe's Dark Ages, by the refugees from persecution, by the exiles and by the missionaries—men and women—of the last century and this one…. I am living a moment of intense emotion. As I stand here, in the company of so many hundreds of thousands of Irish men and women, I am thinking of how many times, across how many centuries, the Eucharist has been celebrated in this land.

—Pope John Paul II on his visit to Ireland, September 1979

records no heathens converted by him, no miracles performed, no poetry written, no manuscripts illuminated. He might have done all these things. Ireland's legion of holy men and women, the luminous quality of whose piety, learning, and imagination inspirited the Western world for more than 600 years, were most of them anonymous. Even many of the saints whose names still shine over the dimness of the centuries are probably composite personalities. Legend has blurred their outlines until they have become as large and brightly unreal as the pagan heroes they superseded.

Yet their accomplishments were very real. The intricate art of their illuminated manuscripts is still as brilliant as when it was first set to parchment. Their poetry makes the heart sing today. Greek and Roman literature and lore, as well as the authentic voice of their own Celtic ancestors transcribed by them from oral tradition, are ours to study now because these cloistered monks reached into a receding past, rescued the vanishing knowledge, and gave it back to the world. In a darkened and barbaric Europe, Irish priests and scholars kept alive the light that had burned for Greek philosophers, Roman colonizers, early Christian martyrs. By the time dawn came to Europe again with the early Renaissance, Ireland's day was over. The Norse raiders and the Anglo-Norman conquerors between them extinguished that bright torch.

Though Ireland owed the extraordinary literary, artistic, and scholarly flowering of this age to these inspired clerics, they were only secondarily artists and poets, teachers and missionaries. Their first purpose was the same that brought them to Skellig Michael: to achieve a state of grace.

It is hard for us today to understand the rationale behind this imperative yearning of the early Christian mind. What made them take their little open boats out into the Atlantic, to the Faeroes, to Iceland, possibly to America, looking for a land that had been promised in a vision? What made them starve themselves and live without sleep until the world around them was full of strangeness and the wind in the leaves became the wing-beats of angels? Why did they leave their comfortable monasteries to wander friendless and defenseless in the lands of barbarians?

Maybe we can find out by looking into the past, where their roots were, and examining the subsequent world that they themselves created. For however enigmatic are their motivations to us, it is clear that the Irish saints made something new on earth. That was what we had felt when we stepped back in time high on Skellig Michael. The little monastic village was part of a world that came out of a dream. Let us look at the people who dreamed it.

Katharine Scherman has authored various books, including The Birth of France, The Long White Night, *and* The Flowering of Ireland, *from which this story was excerpted. Her interests range from rock climbing to ornithology to chamber music. A seasoned traveler, Ms. Scherman prefers to explore areas accessible only by foot, horseback, or dogsled.*

KENT E. ST. JOHN

* * *

Captain River Yank

An American discovers water therapy.

THE WATERS OF THE SHANNON RIVER SEEMED AS MUDDLED AS MY life had become. The failure of my business, marriage, and life skills clung like bad breath. In such times many a man has looked to the sea as a way of redemption, or at least an escape. I was no different, a new chance to be a master of my fate—a Captain. Did I posses any qualities to be a Captain—a steady mind, confidence, a navigator? I badly needed to find out. With no certification or skills needed by any navy anywhere, I turned to my trusty travel agent. The only option left open to a man of my ilk was a self-cruise down Ireland's River Shannon. At the very least I had taken a quick path to captain of a vessel. The guarantee of a boat and instructions were secured with the drop of my last piece of plastic...sure it is St. Brendan started with far less.

With a jet-lagged journey by bus, driven by a man with arms the size of Popeye's, I arrived at my craft's berth. The center of the Isle, Athlone, a spot where many wars have been staged. It was here I was to begin my battle for self-worth. It seemed only fair that Athlone has always been known as a strategic fording place, a place where the sculptures called Sheela na Gigs are on exhibit. The nude female sculptures with their legs splayed are said to ward off the evil eye. I considered myself a prime test case for that legend. After a quick pint at Sean's Bar it was time to report for my instructional cruise. When I boarded my boat it was with amazement that this grand vessel was to be under my command, my responsibility. What had I gotten myself into?

The panic and doubts grabbed my very soul. Apparently my instructor, Michael, had seen that look before. With a firm grip he helped me board my vessel for my shakedown cruise. In a soft voice he briefed me about my new command and the river. In no time at all I was speaking like a long-time captain. Words such as portside, stern, and galley were becoming a part of my vocabulary. Soon it was time to head back to the marina to drop Michael on shore. It was the moment to stow my gear aboard and head out on my own. By way of a smile and a nod, he assured me I was now ready to handle any surprises the River Shannon might deliver. With new confidence, it was time to ship out and face the tests to come. As the marina faded from view I was about fail my first! Entering the first lock, I tied up. Wrong strategy. The water level dropped and the ropes tightened. My boat started to lean heavily to one side. With the speed of a banshee, the lock keeper swung an axe and cut the lines. "My god, boy, what the hell were you thinking?" he screamed. I yelled out apologies sprinkled with confessions of my inadequacies, and a smile spread across his face. "A Yank?" he asked. That seemed to explain everything. Shamefaced, I continued down the river with the self-doubt that had become my constant companion.

The scenery passed by unnoticed by me. The weather darkened as much as my mood. Just making it to the next village became a chore and burden. After docking I fled my boat and headed to a pub. It seemed time to jump ship, just one more failure chalked up. After a few fortifying Guinness pints and plenty of advice from fellow cruisers, it was time to return to the now seemingly very large boat. I awoke the next morning determined to maintain the semblance of a captain. Following the instructions, I started the loud diesel engine for its warm-up. As fellow boaters scrambled to their decks the realization of another failed test became apparent. Never warm up your craft at 6 A.M. in port! From the looks surrounding me it seemed a hanging from the yardarm was in my future. As confessions of my inadequacies again came pouring out, a hush came over the mob. In a quiet voice, the owner of the best-looking craft asked if I was the "Yank."

"The Yank?" I asked. "What Yank?"

"Why the one trying to tie his boots."

"Tie his boots?"

"Yes…the one on a quest." It was then that the skipper explained that because of my mistake at the first lock, word had been passed down the Shannon that an American should be watched and cared for. The lock keeper apparently thought that anyone foolish enough to tie up while the water level dropped was bound to run into trouble. With a grin, Sean (the kindly skipper) sent one of his children back to his boat for something I should have. It turned out to be an American yachting flag. As I planted the flag on the bow, it brought a sense of pride long ago surrendered. I became a man on a quest, look-

In no other island I've visited has a river played so large a role as the Shannon—two successive roles, actually, both of them rising naturally out of Irish geography. During the early Middle Ages the Shannon was Ireland's great highway, a natural thoroughfare down the middle of the island that opened the central plain not only to local water traffic but, bloodily, to Viking raiders, who brought their longships right up the river's estuary to loot and burn as far north as Ulster. Later, when the English had invaded to stay, the Shannon served as a barrier between Connaught, Ireland's wild west, and the three milder, wealthier provinces—Ulster, Leinster, and Munster—where the newcomers concentrated. In the endless tumult of Anglo-Irish history the river was a wall that sometimes protected the English against the Irish and sometimes provided the natives with a shield to hold off their attackers.

—Tony Gibbs,
"Riding the River," *Islands*

ing to "tie his boots." Over breakfast, Sean gently counseled me on the ways of cruising. The number one rule, he explained, "was to let the river flow as it chose." The simple message struck like lightning. Accept and learn, navigate *with* not against. I stopped trying to control.

Setting under way later that morning, I was being carried, not forced. The river had become my guide. The waterhens, curlews, and swans became my focus, not the fuel gauge. Fishermen on the banks waved, and children ran alongside. Daily the waters of the Shannon seemed to clear and soon I felt a part of it.

The river hadn't changed its course, I had. The water was guiding me to the round towers, paths, and villages. The evenings spent fireside became a time to share stories of life on the river, an ageless pastime. With the sounds of *Sean Nos* drifting through the woody and warm pubs, friendships grew nightly. By virtue of Sean's flag, the nickname of River Yank clung to me like the early morning mist on the river.

By the time I entered Lough Derg I truly felt blessed by the many spirits that weave their way through Ireland. The time soon came to head upriver against the Shannon's currents. Anxiety again reared its cursed head, but Sunday stop at Banagher's Vine and Pub for a weekly gathering proved to me that some of the luck of the Irish had rubbed off. At the door stood a smiling Sean. With a booming voice, Captain River Yank was greeted.

Kent E. St. John is a contributing editor for Transitions Abroad *magazine and* GoNomad.com *as well as a staff writer and public relations manager for* Places *magazine. He is currently at work on his first book,* Be Our Guest, *tales of press trips.*

JOHN McLAUGHLIN

Land of High Spirits

A high-octane mixture still fuels
many an Irishman.

IT BEGAN WITH A BOTTLE. TWENTY-FIVE YEARS AGO WAS THE FIRST time I saw it, shaken out of the doze induced by a turf fire and the deep burr of men's conversation. It was time to be away, son, and as my father and cousin Paddy did their leave-taking, rising to fill every inch of the tiny cottage, I saw the bottle pass silently from one to the other. I remember the contented half-smile that accompanied Dad all the way back to our lodging, the bottle rolling gently under the car seat as we careened along the narrow, moon-lit roads.

Back it went with us on the Dublin-to-Liverpool ferry, lodged under the spare tire of the sky-blue Ford Cortina, thence to be ex-humed and reburied in the coal shed at the back of the house. Every so often, I would pick away the coals just to gaze at it, but that was as far as I got. In my eight-year-old mind, the dark ori-gins of that bottle conjured visions of explosions and sirens and a pair of smoldering sandals, my sandals, landing softly in the next county. "Drink from it?" I would have said if pressed. "Drink from it yourself."

Dad never drank the stuff either, but shortly before the next trip back, the bottle would disappear, to be replaced by another on our return. The bottle lived in the coal shed through my childhood like an Irish rebel yell amid the clipped suburban propriety of Little England. Logical? Not a bit of it. Just a small, lovely act of defiance.

And then, two years ago, rummaging in the shed, now a storeroom, I came across the bottle buried away at the back. "Ah," said my mother with a smile of recognition, "that will be Dad's *poitín*."

Seán O'Faoláin wrote that the imagination of the Irish was infused with a sense of the Otherworld. And that may be one reason for the endurance of Ireland's moonshine, pronounced "pot-CHEEN" ("little pot") and fondly dubbed *mountain dew* in song and story. *Poitín* making is an underground art, often literally so. And in the popular mind it also seems to survive in some middle ground between the darkness and the light.

So *poitín*'s trail is littered with Gothic tales of doom. "Sure, half the asylums of the West of Ireland useta be filled with men who drank too much *poitín*," a Kerryman told me once with grim disapproval. "There's no secret to why it continues. You can buy it for half of nothing, and it'll blow your head off."

But then for every warning about "the original gut rot," for every grim tale of broken men, you'll find a fella who swears on "the good stuff." A publican in County Clare told me how he ran it down from Mayo, from a still sunk under a cowshed. "Jaysus!" he screamed into my ear of his smuggling days, discretion abandoned under cover of the raucous fun of a couple of blazing fiddles and a bodhran drum. "Jaysus, the crack was mighty."

Of course, the Kerryman took as much delight in his tale of destruction as the smuggler did in his soaring defiance of the law. And that says something else, and not just about *poitín*. In the poor West and the ravaged North of Ireland, which is *poitín*'s heartland, life has always had an element of struggle. But there is nothing like an extraordinary tale, laced with wit and derring-do, to shoot lightning through the darkness. And that is one thing that *poitín* has always offered.

On a fine summer day in Connemara, the sun softens the edges of the rock and strikes glimmers off the water, transforming this barren landscape of lake and mountain and bog into a kind of Eden. The sky bustles with clouds, as if the ghosts of the West have been let loose to wander overhead, but nothing much moves at ground level. And why should it? The notion of idleness as some kind of curse never quite took off out here. Indeed, the merest hint of a work ethic is likely to elicit cries of "Call a physician" and "Get that man a whiskey." In the West, as Yeats so happily put it, "peace comes dropping slow."

At the cattle market in Maam Cross, toward the eastern end of Connemara, a couple of farmers lean against a stone wall under the shade of an elm, discoursing gently on the price of beef and pulling earnestly on their pipes as if this were a feat of almost Olympian exertion. A BMW roars past, whisking a couple of Dublin swells westward toward Clifden, where a holiday home lies waiting above a long silver strand. In its wake, a fleet of Dutch caravans rumbles along purposefully, pale faces twisting like reeds behind the windscreens to take in the immensity of their surroundings. Just as suddenly, they are gone in a clatter of camera shutters, leaving the slow silence behind them. The two farmers smile to themselves, as if to say, "Well, there's nothing like a drop of sun to get a fella movin'." Irony is not unknown in these parts.

But there's a knowing resignation in those smiles, too. For this

---

Many of the Irish place names in Connemara, the Galway Gaeltacht, and other areas of the West may have disappeared without the efforts of author and cartographer Tim Robinson, who retired in 1999 from his work as a map maker. He was the last of a dying breed who drew maps in manuscript form with pen and ink, and he recorded countless original Irish names which had been Anglicized over the years. He is the author of seminal works on the West, including *Stones of Aran: Pilgrimage; Stones of Aran: Labyrinth;* and *Setting Foot on the Shores of Connemara & Other Writings.*

—JO'R, LH, and SO'R

is Connemara in her party dress. When the days begin to shorten, the Dubliners will pack up their shiny roadster and roar east again to the snug safety of the city, and the Dutch will take tidy ship for home. But the farmers will remain as winter edges in, to set their faces once more against the rain.

Connaught, of which Connemara is part, is Ireland's poorest province, dramatic, unforgiving, its landscape the perfect metaphor for the life. From summer's end, the rocky land will slowly rope in the sky until it seems close enough to wrap around, like a chill gray cloak. The dark looks of the Connemara natives are shaped by the rain, not the sun. Much of the land is unfarmable. And if fishing provides a good living for some along the coast, it has never been enough in this country of large families. Emigration has decanted the youth from this region for centuries, but in the last twenty years entire swaths of countryside have been drained dry. The West is dying people say.

Well, that may be so. But there's a quiet endurance to the people here that over centuries has helped them survive the ravages of famine, the "civilizing" influence of the British, and the winter harshness of this place. More than just survive—this area is as close to the old Gaelic Ireland as still exists. The language persists, though the British managed to eradicate it in more prosperous climes, and the old folk beliefs still hold—there are roads that go untraveled at night in Connemara because they are known to be haunted. And just as redolent of the old ways, *poitín* making thrives, primed by a defiant reluctance to accept the law's definition of right and wrong.

For more than 300 years—ever since the British had the outrageous gall to slap a tax on liquor in the mid-1600s—the Irish moonshiner has waged relentless war on the authorities, and with such panache that *poitín* is still an accepted fact of life in the West. Indeed, to hear the locals tell it, the area is awash with the stuff, hidden in stone walls and scarecrows' pockets, in hollowed-out gateposts and sunken lobster pots. More than just ingenuity, though, *poitín* offers an echo of life out here before the English came along with their book of rules and the narrow materialism of empire. In the underground life of the *poitín* maker—hounded by the police, thundered at from the pulpit, reviled by the pure of heart—there is the irreverent, pagan breath of the Gaels.

The road west from Maam Cross carves through sun-dappled avenues of fuchsia, twining between glass lakes and green mountains combed smooth by a giant hand. From time to time, the road bursts out of this labyrinth into open bog land, and it's a surprise suddenly to see people here: a man on an ancient bike inching doggedly across the brown plain; a father and his young son stacking logs of turf in small pyramids to dry, framed against the sky like a frieze, bent double for eternity.

By the time I reach Ballyconneely, on the Atlantic's lip, the sun is dropping toward six o'clock, turning the waves the silver of fish scales, flooding with light the front room of the big parish priest. Father Ben Corrigan is one of those strapping religious specimens modeled on the early apostles. He has a booming laugh, the arms of a laborer, and a ready hand with the Jameson that is a throwback to less heathen times.

He talks of the emigration, how Boston is "a great neighbor to this part of the world" and how "every household would have some over there." He looks out to-

We needed to get out of the isolation of Ballyconneely so we were on the short drive to Clifden when we encountered what the Irish so appropriately call "lashing rain." The world was black except for our headlights. Rain blew so heavily the wipers couldn't keep up and we could barely see the narrow road. We were certain we were going to be killed when a car sped toward us, lights blazing. It roared past, followed by another, and our car shuddered with the wind. By the time we got to Clifden we'd encountered a dozen cars, all driving as if pursued by Satan himself. How people avoid dying on these lanes in weather like this explains the expression, "luck of the Irish."

—Larry Habegger, "Travels in Connemara"

ward the Atlantic as if the missing generations had simply walked into the water one day and might walk back out of it any minute. "I should do loads of marriages now," he says. "In fact, I do very few."

Ben insists that "the fella to talk to about *poitín* is Padraig" the fisherman, and so we drive out toward his harbor-side cottage. Stone houses ruined in the eviction years rear up like shipwrecks against the evening sky, and we catch the occasional glimpse of a shimmering empty beach. Kids here must realize early the inevitability of leaving. But in the cramped neon corners of Boston and New York, the beauty of this place must stay with them long years after. Padraig it is, a weather-ravaged face with eyes youthful with good humor, who tells me the old way of making *poitín* as his dark, beautiful daughter offers tea and gentle reminders of the methodology. How the barley would be steeped in water until it began to bud and then laid out to dry. How water and yeast and hops would be added to make the wash. And how, after twelve days' fermenting, the wash would be distilled twice through the coiled copper tube called the worm to make the *crathur*. "Ah, well, he'd have plenty of company then," says the fisherman of the *poitín* maker. "Of course, I never drank too much of it myself."

One time he did, though, out fishing with Liam when their motor failed, and so to keep themselves warm they worked their way through a bottle. "But it was the really good stuff," Padraig says. "I didn't feel that awful terrible the next morning like I would with a whiskey now."

Ben has a funeral to say, and we take our leave. As I leave the village, the sun dying gloriously behind it in a burnt orange flare, I'm forced to stop on the tiny road to allow the mourners to pass. I count 200 cars before I lose interest, almost all occupied by couples fifty and older, or by mature bachelors safe in their own company and destined to stay there. I count five adults under forty.

Oughterard, the guidebooks tell you, is in Connemara, but spiritually it is in another world. The river Owenriff ripples gently through the town, lined with beech trees and bearing salmon to Lough Corrib. The town itself is a quiet conservatory of green,

like the last oasis before the desert. Suitably enough, this town on
the edge of the wilderness is the center of the *gardai*'s anti-*poitín*
operation in Connemara.

In the last quarter of the year especially, four-man raiding parties swoop south on the distillers in the hope of landing a big
Christmas run. They find plenty of wash—the sheer bulk of the
fifty- to sixty-gallon barrels, hidden up to twelve at a time, makes
them difficult to hide. But *poitín* is more elusive, especially since
the miracle of gas eliminated the telltale smoke of a turf fire. Last
year, the guards here made eighteen seizures, bagging 2,600 gallons
of wash and just $9\frac{1}{2}$ gallons of *poitín*. This year, they are already
ahead: one raid alone netted 20 gallons of *poitín*.

"Hangover," Big Jim Begley reads aloud. "Blindness, insanity,
murder, death. Well, it might not be that bad," the country copper
admits of the perils of *poitín*. "But you get the idea." The veteran
guard and *poitín* raider pores over his archives with the nervous intensity of a butterfly collector. On this day, Jim is more nervous
than usual. There's a music festival in town, and some of the lads
are already a few pints ahead of the game. Every ten minutes or so
he will make his excuses and then return to sling some young buck
into a cell for the duration. "You haven't come on the best night,"
he says.

Poitín's probably as plentiful now as it was twenty years ago," he
admits, "even though the fine for possession has gone up to £1,000.
But nobody transports it anymore. And there used to be much more
hidden in houses. Now it's mostly hidden in commonage. The she-
been owners will bring it into the house at night, and the clients
will knock at the window, and it'll be passed out to them."

Jim's main problem is that "to get a conviction, we have to get
a sample" for analysis. He recalls a raid: "I rushed up to the door,
but the fella had it locked. So I ran round the back. I could see him
through the window as close as I am to you. He had a bottle in either hand pouring it down the sink, and it was coming out the
drain below, but I had nothing to soak it up with.

"And so there we were," he adds ruefully, "looking at each other
with only the pane of glass between us, himself just smiling a little."

Jim seems to feel the same ambivalence toward his longtime an-
tagonist as the country judges do. He can't remember anyone
being fined to the full extent, let alone jailed, for *poitín* making.
And he talks with relish of a man who blatantly tossed a bottle of
the stuff over a stone wall and then claimed successfully in court
that he'd never seen it before. The arm movement was just him
"throwing away a snort from his nose; he got a big laugh in court,
all right." Another time, a woman surprised on a country road
"raised a terrible row when we tried to get her to hand over the
poitín—sure, she had three bottles hidden in her bosom clear as day,
but we couldn't get them off her."

The very landscape here seems pitched against the guards. As
they set out toward the hidden still, every bobbing head on the
crest of a hill becomes a lookout, every cow in the middle of the
road a delaying tactic. They often turn up little more than a
warm patch of ground. Nor do they get many calls from a concerned public.

"No matter how big an enemy you have," says Jim, "it's seen as
a Judas thing, and traditionally here if you tell on anybody, you'll
never get any luck." But tip-offs do come, invariably from a desperate wife or mother, sick at heart over *poitín*'s effect on a loved
one. Jim has bagged *poitín* as high as 120 proof: "A couple of rock-
ets of that stuff'd be lethal."

Why do they still make it? For tradition, partly. For the money,
too. Jim figures four barrels of wash would make twenty-five
gallons of *poitín*, and at five pounds a bottle that's a tidy sum around
Christmas. "But it's also kind of a challenge," he says. "Like with
the salmon. There are people out here who don't do much of anything, but they'll set a net in the river and risk getting caught. The
laziest man in Connemara still has to chance it now and again."

The British knew what they were about when, centuries ago,
they dispossessed the rebellious Irish of their rich farmland and
hounded them westward "to hell or Connaught." That part of
Connemara stretching southwest from Oughterard is a shattered
plain of granite, treeless, wind blasted, a landscape of purest
despair.

As I drive one day from gentle Oughterard into that beautiful, barren rock-scape, it is as if Connemara has chosen its most theatrically gloomy colors in ironic welcome. Through Screeb and Beladangan, the very names a burst of scorn, the rain skitters down from gray-black skies, ruffling the gray water of rock pools, painting whatever grass there is a flat monochrome. You won't last long here, lad, is the message.

Jim had described Lettermullan, an island itself and as far south as you can go without climbing into a boat, as one gigantic still. For years, the church bell would ring out in warning at the approach of the guards.

No bells sound on my arrival, but the locals still see me coming from a mile away. Around lunchtime I stop for a pint. The pub stands alone in the plain of rock, over the unearthly quiet of a still lake, but inside it is packed with dark countrymen in worn jackets, conversing animatedly in Irish. I get talking with Colm, a big truck driver just back from a stint in England.

For thirty minutes we chat—he polite and watchful, I in my most practiced circumlocutory manner—about the fishing, the tourists who drift in over the summer, the old curragh boats that are used only for racing now, maneuvering delicately toward the real object. But no sooner is the word re-

My first exposure to Irish sectarianism and its surprising relation to drink came when I was tending bar in San Francisco in my twenties. I worked with a Catholic Irish American named Jim who would bellow at any customer who ordered Bushmills Irish whiskey, "What do you want with that Protestant whiskey?!" and encourage them to order Jameson. At the time I couldn't fathom why it would make a difference; only later did I realize that Bushmills was distilled in Northern Ireland and Jameson in County Cork in the far south. Jim was just trying to support the old community.

—Larry Habegger,
"An Irish Diaspora"

leased than he steps subtly away from it—and me—and is back conversing intensely in Irish, no doubt laughing at the idiot presumption of this blow-in-here. As I finish my pint, I have to agree with him.

Cormac MacConnell lives with his four kids in a small house between the wilderness of the bog and the settlement of Barna. And though he might not thank me for saying so, I can think of no more telling illustration of landscape as character. For Cormac has one foot, his kicking foot, in the garrulous, urbane world of Galway, where he plies a good living as a writer. The other is firmly planted in the bog, where he plies very little of anything but lives the slow life of the West with a gleam in each flinty eye. It is Cormac, whippet thin, with a beard the condition of Lear's in his wilder moments, who tells me how the guards "carry sledges with them on a raid to break up the barrels, which are the most difficult things for the *poitín* maker to replace.

"But they leave the staves intact, and the boys just hammer them in again," Cormac says. "There's a gorgeous tokenism about it all. It's necessary they raid, and it's necessary they catch a few. It contributes to the whole system."

It is Cormac, too, taking another in a string of cigarettes, who gives me the best explanation for *poitín*'s endurance. "It's too easy to dismiss it as cheap firewater," he says. "It's too easy to look at it as a commercial product. *Poitín*-type legal spirits have been marketed in the past, but they just sit there on the top shelf of the bar. They might taste better, but why would you ever buy them? Once you rob *poitín* of its illegality, you rob it of its bouquet.

"What it is, is not for sale," he goes on. "There is a dark side to it. But it's also part of people's whole definition of themselves as Irish. It's about not going to the factory on a Monday because the salmon are running or not turning up for a week because there's a *fleadh* (fair). And it says something about the character of people in the West. This should be a dark, morose society, a broken people. Instead, there are more laughs per acre than anywhere. The day that people here start going to work happy at six in the morning, all to buy a bigger car, that's the day *poitín* making will stop."

Nothing much has changed in the northern town where my family lived for generations. The border post is still just a couple of guards in a porta-cabin, in contrast with the Orwellian fortresses going up at busier crossings. The road runs into town through the same undulating patchwork of farmland. And the police station in the center—still looks more like a hiding place than a civic asset.

This is not Connemara. The land here is excellent, for one thing, as impossibly green as it is supposed to be and pleasantly soft on the eye. But here too emigration is high, spurred by the closure of the old linen mills and by army and police harassment. The British mandate may have ended in the South, but in Tyrone it continues, as does resistance, whether in violent form or more passively in a resolute dedication to beating the system.

The random artificiality of the border, dissecting farms and traversed by so many uncharted paths it is unpoliceable, makes this great smuggling country. As for *poitín*, Tyrone and neighboring Donegal have been major centers of production for centuries. Nothing much has changed there, either.

As Terry, the local publican, says, patiently drawing the first pint of Guinness: "Ah, there's plenty of it around. A few have given up making it because it's a little hot for them now. The police and army are raiding all the time for guns. But people around here have been generations cheating the establishment. That doesn't just disappear." (Terry's name, and some others remaining, have been changed.)

He sets up the pint and reaches up to a bottle on the top shelf of the bar. Sure enough, it is a bottle of the legalized sham *poitín*, labeled POTCHEEN for all those dupes in the export markets of the world. "Did you ever try a drop of this?" he says, placing a glass in front of me and depositing inside it a finger of the clear liquid.

Resigned, I take a sip, rolling it a little inside my mouth. There is nothing, no taste at all, just a faint texture of oil. I send it to the back of my throat and, I'm sure of it still, swallow. It doesn't move.

I swallow again. It is still there. A small fire begins to spread from my tonsils to the back of my tongue until for one panicky moment my whole throat seems aflame. A glug of Guinness douses it. "That's the real stuff," says Terry needlessly, grinning from ear to ear. "Sure, ye don't think anybody'd drink the legal stuff, do ye."

From that point on, I stumble on *poitín* at every turn. The town is still abuzz with the tale of Donegan, nabbed the week before after advertising *poitín*, complete with his home phone number, in an English newspaper. They found 12 bottles in his house, but Donegan is a schemer, and he let his wife take the rap, figuring correctly that she would get only a fine. Already he's back in business. The police, with a warrant only for the house, had missed 450 bottles stacked neatly in the caravan behind.

I hear glowing reports of *poitín*'s effect on ailing newborn lambs or as an embrocation for greyhounds or as a winter warmer mixed with hot water and sugar. Stephen, the local bank manager, tells me how years ago the kids walking barefoot to school would be given a shot for warmth, and how Bishop Farren—"who was as good as reared on the stuff himself"—reacted by making it a reserved sin to touch, taste, or handle *poitín*. That meant it could be confessed only to the bishop, a fair disincentive that required some ingenuity to get around. "The boys went over to the next diocese," Stephen says. "They came back drunk as lords but free from sin."

And with bottles appearing out of nowhere, I sample enough to know that Terry's stuff was indeed on the rough side. Martin the shopkeeper slips me a draft from a vodka bottle, a Christmas gift from a farmer up in the hills, that goes down smooth as a good grappa.

Finding a talkative *poitín* maker is more difficult, though. They're "a different breed altogether," Terry tells me. "The police have been trying to catch your man Hegarty smuggling for years now. I remember a policeman asking him, 'D'ye have a hundred sheep?' and Hegarty said, 'Well, now, a hundred's an awful lot of counting.' Sure, they wouldn't tell you anything."

Finally, though, late one evening the call comes, and I head out of the town into the half-light, making countless sharp, climbing turns until I reach a cottage high above the valley. The headlights of the car light up a rutted farmyard, sheep skittering away in the glare. Milk churns for the *poitín* and a big barrel for the wash lie around by an outhouse well off the road. The sheep offer the only affront to the silence. This is *poitín* country.

Brian is there in the back room, a squat, merry man in his stockinged feet, with his wife, Deirdre, beside him. "A lock of old men taught me how to do it," he says quietly. "It's passed down from father to son here. They all love to think of themselves as the *poitín* maker, and each one thinks he's better than the other. I use five pounds of oat flakes for a forty-five-gallon drum of water. And then four stone of sugar, four pounds of yeast, two dozen apples, and four pounds of treacle. I'd let it sit for twelve days and then strain it into a creamery can and run it through twice.

"Ah, no," he says, laughing, "if you ran it through three times, it'd blow the head off ye. Sure, ye'd have no customers left."

The *poitín* they make in these parts is powerful enough, all the same. "There was a fella up near here making a delivery of hay," says Brian, with the wry beginnings of a smile, "and he stopped to ask a young lad for a drink of water, and he gave him *poitín*. Sure, he couldn't get down from his load. They had to lift him off it." Deirdre says, laughing: "Daddy would buy *poitín* for the arthritis, but he'd drink it before he had the chance to rub it in. He'd go to bed sucking his wrist," hoping the vapors would have an effect. "It's lucky it wasn't his ankle," says Brian.

Brian's considered approach to the law is one of sunny disregard. He has, you might say, its measure. He used to make *poitín* in the house, and the odor of the wash would almost knock you down fifty yards away, but still he was never raided. "If you make too much of it, they'll shut you down straightaway. Otherwise they turn a blind eye. Sure, they'd be cutting off their own supply if they didn't. In fact, if the police in town hear the customs people are coming down on a raid, they pass the word to you somehow."

The British army is less predictable. "There was one night," Brian says, "we hadn't been in with the still two seconds before they were on us. And when they saw the creamery cans—and there are a lot of bombs packed in creamery cans up here—well, they thought they'd found a bomb factory. So they're very nervous, and they want to know what's in the cans. And we're there with our hands up saying it's only *poitín*. Anyway, this one soldier takes off the lid of the can, very gentle like, and he looks inside. 'Holy shit,' he says, 'It's the Waltons.'"

Next day I cross the border again into the South, taking the lonely, unapproved road that snakes over the hills into Pettigo. As the car climbs, the lushness of the valley fades into thin grassland and bog, slivers of still water gleaming amid stark outcroppings of rock. The few houses are built far off the road, as if in bloody-minded rejection of all human concourse. This area has the feel, and the reputation, of bandit country. And that same morning the guards will find four Kalashnikov rifles just outside Pettigo, wrapped carefully in plastic and hidden in a ditch as if they were bottles of *poitín*.

"I knew nothing in the world there was anything

Poteen, still known as a "drop of the crittur" in the 1920s, was for hard drinking only. An abiding memory is of one field of potatoes stricken with the blight, or dreaded Colorado Beetle, with blackened leaves along the drills and Bob plodding up and down pumping gallons of blue-green copper-sulfate solution from a tank on his back. In retrospect, I'm amazed that this Famine aspect was still present in the early twentieth century. But of course, that time was a saga of unending tragedy and disaster: the famines of the late nineteenth were followed by the Great War and the Titanic, followed by more hunger and depression, followed by more war, which was arguably the human condition. And in Ulster, sadly the spectacle was of sectarian conflict, where the only unifying feature was a drop of the crittur and Balls of Flour potatoes.

—Leslie Gillespie,
"Balls of Flour"

going on there, and I never made *poitín* in my life," said Jim Flynn of Doonadoba, Ballycastle, accused of making *poitín* after a still and burner were found in a derelict house on his land. "The old still I saw would not be worth a pound. I think the thing would not have worked as far as I could see, and I said to the guard that I would not like to drink whiskey out of this thing."

Judge Brennan said to the defendant that he was inclined to believe him but added, "You would not be fooling me, would you?"

The defendant replied: "I would not sit here, a man of my age, swearing for the sake of a few hundred pounds. We have not long to live for that kind of crack."

When the judge said he was dismissing the charges against the defendant, Superintendent Deacy remarked, "It was a brilliant defense anyway."

In the steaming summer chaos of Manhatten, that article from *The Western People* reads like a dispatch from another world, where the lineaments may be the same but the proportions are happily different. I have that as a gentile reminder of the landscape of *poitín*. And I have the bottle again, the liquid inside as clear as nitro, the proof of its quality the tiny beads that rise to the top when it is shaken. Just having it here is a joy. In the grit and clamor of the city, it is a heady breath of the wild. But drink it down? You must be kidding. Sure, it'd blow your head off.

John McLaughlin wrote this story for Men's Journal.

J U D Y   W E L L S

* * *

The Sheela-na-gigs

A sacred site resides within the female.

ON THE BACK CORNER OF MAEVE'S SACRED SITES FLYER WAS A curious little female figure, all smiling head and limbs in a most unlikely yogic posture. Her legs seem to be jutting directly out of her head. Her arms, also jutting out of her head, reach under her legs and hold wide an enormous vulva. Her face bears enormous eyes and a happy, self-satisfied smile.

I found Maeve's explanation of this icon on her flyer: "Day 7. Dublin. After breakfast in our hotel, we take the coast road to Dublin and the National Museum to view the sheela-na-gigs, ancient stone carvings depicting the Hag holding open her gaping vulva, inviting us to the death passage, from whence we came to where we return." An echo arose from my Catholic childhood: "Remember, man, that thou art dust and to dust thou shalt return." Then the priest would put a cross of ashes on our foreheads. These sheelas certainly put a new twist on things!

Dan Flynn, the co-leader of our tour, had an itinerary which mentioned nothing of the sheelas. The last image on his flyer is a round tower, a huge stone phallus rising in the sky built by Irish monks. This image seemed to verify my sister Nancy's hunch that Dan's was a "butch tour." By the time we got to Ireland, my sisters and I were getting used to the idea of the sheela. Before our tour, we had seen one of her sisters in the Hunt Museum in Limerick, a headless sheela with a deep, smooth hollow between her legs. We had even been practicing saying, "gaping vulva," among ourselves, but I bet more than a few teeth dropped when Maeve stood up on the bus in her MTV jacket and black boots on Day 1 of our tour and, in that marvelous, self-confident manner which puts all native-born Americans to shame, announced we were about to stop and view a sheela-na-gig holding open her enormous gaping vulva.

While I was wondering what the uptight Easterners were thinking of our Maeve, Michael, the bus driver, thought it fitting at that moment to talk about Padraig—St. Patrick. He told the ancient sun worshippers of Ireland, "My way is better," said Michael, but he didn't end their symbolism. The Celtic cross incorporates the sun. Maeve didn't miss a beat and commented that the sheela was an amazing figure, considering how sexually repressed the Irish are. I suppose we could have had a mini-battle between the vulva and the cross right there, but Michael broke in to say "our little darlin', the sheela," didn't seem too well lately. He had been by to see her, and she was doing rather poorly.

Michael pulled up the bus in front of our first Irish ruin in Kilinaboy, County Clare, an ancient church covered with green vines. There, tucked over an arch was the sheela, and Michael was right. Her genitals were chipped away, and little remained of the famed gaping vulva. Maeve was outraged; she had friends who passed by just weeks before, and all was well with the sheela. She would report it to the National Museum in Dublin, and that's just what she did when many days later we arrived in the capital city.

Amidst a chaos of reconstruction, our group was ushered into a side exhibition room in the National Museum, and there, lying on little metal gurneys, were two stone sheelas, pried from their prior homes in churches and castles and now living in the museum basement. These sheelas, however, did not bear the sly smile of our comic Mona Lisa sheela on Maeve's flyer. One sister looked almost African with her long neck and elegant, stylized face. She had two small high breasts over prominent ribs, giving her a four-breasted look. The middle finger of her left hand delicately pointed to a small vulval opening. The second sheela was more corpselike and bore a thick-lipped Aztec grimace. Her rib lines slanted downward toward a large, prominent vulva.

While Maeve held up the stone sheelas for us to photograph, a serious young woman from the museum explained to us that the sheelas were twelfth-century medieval figures used to warn people of the evils of lust at their festivals and during their travels. J. J., our perky goddess scholar in her seventies, muttered fiercely against that theory and the fact that we had been handed brown packets of paper information instead of access to ten or twelve more sheelas in the basement.

We had photos of two more sheelas in our packets: two ugly little corpses, one with tiny sagging tits, huge ribs, and nine holes below her waist, and one with hollow socket eyes. No more pictures but pages of bibliography, and now on viewing it, I keep remembering Virginia Woolf studying the subject WOMEN in the British Museum, all studies done by men, and wonder how she would have reacted to this entry: "Sheela-na-gig discovered by Major Trevelyon," E.C.R. Armstrong, 1911–1912. I can just see the bumbling guy in *Fawlty Towers* as the major encountering his first gaping vulva. My Lord! What a mess! Or how about: Feehan, J. and Cunningham, G., 1978, "An Undescribed Exhibitionist Figure from Co. Laois." Was this pudendum so awful they couldn't even describe it? "The Divine Hag of the Pagan Celts" in *The Witch Figure*, Ross, A., 1973, seems more promising, but my personal favorite is "Heads and Tails of Stone," Siggins, A., 1990. That person must have seen the sly smile on the comic sheela.

Who are these sheela hunters? For that matter, who are these sheelas? In the Hunt Museum in Limerick, an effusive Irish woman in an odd white knitted dress gave us a handout: "SHEELA-NA-GIGS: This monument is similar to other examples presently on display in the Coptic Museum in Cairo and found throughout North Africa. It represents a second and third century Christian sect who used sexual ritual as an integral part of their religious celebrations, hence the female.... (The rest of this sentence is whited out.) Monks of this Coptic sect came to Ireland about the third and fourth centuries and founded monasteries, especially one at Naas, Co Kildare." So, are the sheelas really Coptic-Christian figures? Medieval Christian figures? Pagan-Celtic Hags? Pre-Celtic Goddesses? Do they fertilize the barren or the land, ward off the evil eye, admonish against lust or entice us to it? And once again, who are these sheela hunters?

I unwittingly became one the day our sacred sites group sailed to Skellig Michael, the ancient mountain top jutting from the ocean off the west coast of Ireland. I started up the 600 stone steps straight up the cliff with Jane, our Amazon, a triathlon athlete, but soon she was only a small turquoise spot high above me in the mists. I finally arrived at the ancient monastery atop, breathless, my heart pounding, marveling that I was now viewing what I had so long imagined in my mind's eye: those ancient stone beehive huts built by

---

I ducked through an arch and stood eye to eye with eight elongated figures etched in high relief on a stone wall. For these carvings White Island is almost famous. Unknown to tourists, that is, but renowned among archeologists and historians.

I'd read that scholars still pondered these figures. Are they pagan, or early Christian, or a bit of both? To me, reluctant product of Catholic education, some of the carvings surely seemed ecclesiastic. One, complete with crosier and soutane, looked to be a bishop. St. Patrick, maybe.

Another's hands rested on spreading thighs. No bishop here. She looked like a sheela-na-gig, pagan symbol of female fertility. But sheelas found elsewhere in Ireland are generally much more graphic than this bashful Fermanagh one. Her smile, in its own way as enigmatic as Mona Lisa's, disclosed little.

—Peter O'Neill, "Lough Erne"

sixth-century monks who came here to be as close to God as they could imagine.

I passed by one beehive in wonder, then another, and then another, and did a complete double-take. There, sitting in the doorway of the third stone beehive was Jane in her pale-blue shorts and royal-blue jacket, with her wild curly hair, doing a complete sheela-na-gig: her arms holding her legs widespread, her eyes bulging, and her mouth in a hideous grimace.

Electricity hit my brain, and I had a thousand impressions all at once: laughter first, but then the startling recognition of the archetype, the very human image of a beautiful woman, suddenly grotesque in a flash, and then beautiful again. In that instant, stone had become flesh. And I felt completely that the sheelas were very ancient images of great power. No wimpy woman would assume that posture. She was powerful, she was funny, she was lusty, she was fierce, she was scary. She gave birth in that posture and she took life. And there she was, sheela, the Irish Kali, sitting in the house of monks, mocking their celibacy, reclaiming their beehive as Queen.

And then she was Jane again, laughing, the posture over. I asked her to do it again for a photo, which she did, but the charge was lost. The sheela archetype slid once again into stones scattered over Ireland and Britain, and now in museums, safe from the hands of curio seekers and hacking moralists, but not from the hands of censors.

Judy Wells is a Berkeley poet, academic counselor at St. Mary's College, Moraga, California, and great-granddaughter of Irish immigrant Edward Rodgers (McRory) of Gortin, County Tyrone. Her latest poetry collection, Everything Irish, *explores her Irish-American identity through a comic look at her work with adult students at St. Mary's College.*

* * *

My Own

In which the author finds blood to be thicker
than the Atlantic is wide.

TURF WAS BURNING IN THE FIREPLACE, AND I TOOK MY PINT OF Guinness and pulled a chair to the fire. The owner of the pub sat talking to an elderly villager. Now they turned their attention to me.

"So, it's a holiday you're on, is it?" Mr. O'Mara asked.

"Well, I'm here to see someone, Peg Vaughn."

"Sure and what would you be wanting of Peg?"

"My grandmother came from here," I said abruptly.

"What was her name?"

"Mary Ann Naughton Harrington."

"Ah, sure, wouldn't Peg be related through the Naughtons," he said to the old man.

The villager agreed. "Didn't I know your grandmother's youngest brother, Martin," he said. Not a question; a statement. "That would be your great uncle. My oldest brother was in his wake."

And the link was joined again. Someone brought me another stout, and we talked about my great aunts and uncles and their children, and how the family had gotten on in the States.

Then O'Mara said, "One of your second cousins lives up the street. Why don't you go to see him tonight."

"Well, I don't know. I just wanted to have a pint and a good night's sleep for the morning."

"Sure, why don't you. He and his wife'd be glad to see you. A terrible thing has happened to them." He lowered his voice. "Their house just burned down."

"Oh, my God," I gasped. I was sure now I didn't want to see people I didn't even know who had recently lost their home.

O'Mara pressed on. "You really should go up there. They lost their son, Neil, the Lord have mercy on him. He was killed in the fire."

The pubkeeper blessed himself and explained how the boy, just sixteen years old, had died of smoke inhalation in the bathroom.

I felt saddened by the tragedy, but I knew, in my American mind, that it would be inappropriate to call on them in this time of mourning.

But Old Man O'Mara persisted. "So, why don't you go up there now. Spend some time with them."

"No, I don't think so," I said feebly.

The old villager looked at

I met the prototype of my female relatives in the landlady at a Limerick B & B shortly after arriving in Ireland. Despite exhaustion, I couldn't wait to begin adventuring. The guidebook advised just that— ignore jet lag, adapt to the new time, go to bed early and rise in an Irish frame of mind the next morning. "You'll do no such thing," a no-nonsense voice interrupted my thoughts. I looked up to see the landlady's ample frame blocking the doorway. "Go up to your room and nap for a couple of hours before you set foot outside. All the Americans from off the plane stay here and I know what I'm talking about." Too tired to protest, but convinced I wouldn't be able to rest, I staggered upstairs, sank onto the bed and fell fast asleep. Waking refreshed a few hours later, I laughed. The landlady had been right. Now who did she resemble more—Aunt Kitty or Mom?
—Veronica Deasy, "Bound to the Emerald Isle"

me oddly, and I saw the blood rise in O'Mara's face. He slammed his glass down on the bar in front of him. "Man, that's your cousin. And his child just died. Now you go up there and pay your respects."

I could hear my own father scolding me through O'Mara's voice. I drained my glass and made for the door. "Yeah, I'll go up there now," I called over my shoulder, determined to go back to the B & B and forget I'd ever come to this place.

"I'll take you," O'Mara said.

I saw him put on his coat, and I knew I was trapped.

He drove me to the door of the house that the family was renting from a shopkeeper. Their own home had been about two miles out of town.

I was trembling as I got out of the car and O'Mara patted me on the back. "Sure, won't they be glad to see you."

What would I say? I asked myself as I knocked.

A woman of about thirty-five answered the door. Her eyes were red and puffy with grief. "Can I help you?" she asked.

"My name is Jonathan Harrington." I searched desperately for words as the woman stood staring at me. "I…my grandmother was Mary Ann Naughton."

She opened the door wider. "You favor the Naughtons," she said, looking closely at me. "Come in." And she led me inside.

In the parlor, her mother sat weeping and her husband, Pat Naughton, shook my hand. "You're welcome, Jonathan. Thanks so much for coming."

His wife disappeared into the kitchen and returned with a platter of tea, brown bread, butter and jam which she set before me.

I felt at that moment as if I had come home after a long absence and they accepted my presence as natural—hardly unusual at all.

"At first," the boy's mother said, "there were lots of people coming. Everyone loved Neil. But now things have quieted down. We get lonesome. It's so nice to have you here."

Suddenly, I realized that to them I wasn't some distant relation whom they barely knew. It was as if I had stepped out for just a moment and come back in, not that I had been gone for an entire generation.

They told me more about their son—how he loved little children. They showed me family pictures and pointed out that in every picture he was holding or playing with a little child.

I grieved with them that night, and wept with them, and prayed for the soul of Neil Naughton as if he were my own.

He was.

Jonathan Harrington has published two mystery novels set in Ireland: The Death of Cousin Rose *and* The Second Sorrowful Mystery. *He lives in New York City, but travels to Ireland frequently to gather material for the mystery series. Much of his research is conducted in pubs.*

JANINE JONES

Tea with Mr. Curtain

*It can get a little weird
out in the country.*

A MOVING TRAIN FORGING ITS WAY THROUGH A SPINNING WORLD,
seen as still from the window. My forehead pressed against the
glass, I sat, unmoving, as I often do when heading for a destination
and don't have to work on the way. One region blurred into the
next so subtly that the difference between them might have been
a mere act of imagination.

I had caught a train in Dublin, late morning. A luminous, blustery day, and I was heading for Tipperary, little more than a
melodic phrase in my mind, and a flash-image of land ever green.

Why was I going to Tipperary, not one book to guide my trip?
No friend to welcome me, or enemy to avoid? What had I sought
to discover in a place I'd decided upon on the strength of a picture? How the melody unfolds? Or had I been charmed by the
idea of stretches of undulating green deluding me into thinking
that life, unlike trips, goes on forever? I couldn't have been going
for the novena. I only learned that it would take place days after
my arrival. And no one in his right mind travels to Tipperary for
a shopping spree.

In *Overcoming Tourism*, Hakim Bey raises the following question: "Of all the three archaic reasons for travel—call them 'war,' 'trade,' and 'pilgrimage,' which one gave rise to tourism?"

Bey believes that many would argue that pilgrimage did, because the pilgrim and the tourist resemble one another in so many respects. The pilgrim and his contemporary counterpart, the tourist, both go "there" to *see*. Both are keen on collecting souvenirs, and must take "time off" from their daily lives to undertake their journeys, the goals of which, for sacred and secular globe-trotters alike, are nonmaterial.

Nonessential traits aside, "The pilgrim," Bey notes, "undergoes a shift of consciousness which is real for him. He goes to a site of pilgrimage to receive a blessing. The tourist, by contrast, travels to some far away place, he dubs 'exotic' to see a difference.

"And so," concludes Bey, "Pilgrimage is a form of initiation, and initiation is an opening to other forms of cognition.... We need a model of cognition that emphasizes the 'magic' of reciprocity, [a model which illuminates what just might be a structural truth of the world]; namely, that 'to *give* attention is to *receive* attention, as if the universe in some mysterious way responds to our cognition with an influx of effortless grace.'"

The need for such a model is urgent; for Difference, a finite *commodity*, consumed at an exponential rate by tourist-consumers and the accommodations which serve them, is being swallowed alive. Before long, Difference will have become a lost category. Of course, we can always fabricate Difference in our idea factories, and distribute It on virtual playgrounds across the globe. But it is the extinction of a precious, abstract *natural* kind which threatens to leave us inconsolably distressed.

That being said, much of Ireland remains such that a tourist who is looking for *a difference* can find one there, if he has a mind to.

Where I wandered—in the region of Tipperary—difference was immediately perceptible: villages didn't spread out little by little until they disappeared into countryside. Nor did countryside gradually give way to villages. Villages, like Skellig, were just there, existing in the middle of it all, as though having sprung up through the richness of the soil.

The cab driver (a local man) who picked me up at the train station in Tipperary asked me how I had found the small, pink-colored house that was to be my home for the next three weeks, since he had such a hard time locating it himself.

I had hit upon my dwelling in a listing put out by the Irish Bureau of Commerce, at the time not knowing what I came to learn years later from a guidebook on Ireland: Northern Tipperary is a long way from the beaten tourist track and for good reason: its fertile fields are fascinating to farmers only.

But for the traveler who is intrepid with respect to experiencing shifts of consciousness, the farming community of Tipperary may provide precisely that space where giving attention is receiving attention for a few unforgettable moments.

The cab driver eventually found my house (which sat far back off the road, hiding behind trees and bushes), and entered it with me to give it a thorough checking over.

First, he went upstairs to make sure the hot water worked. "You'll want a hot bath after your trip," he said, or something to that effect. Then he checked the gas and the electricity.

Before leaving he questioned me to make sure I really wanted to stay in the house by myself. "You'll be staying here alone, will you, Miss. Are you sure?"

Sure I was sure.

"What a great girl you are!" (Throughout my visit a consensus would form around that opinion, leaving me to suspect that the Irish use of the word "great" must be far less discriminating than my own.)

The driver handed me his card before he left, telling me that should I have any problem, any problem at all....

I took the card, gratefully, knowing I could use it if necessary, without a moment's hesitation. One must always reflect on the meaning of such a gesture in cities like New York or Los Angeles, not to mention Paris, where sex is almost certainly in the offing.

When the driver left I decided to check out the real essentials of the house—food. The nearest village was a thirty-minute walk, one way. I didn't mind walking. Don't go to Ireland if you mind walking. But I was hungry, and thirsty, right then and there.

I opened the cabinets in the kitchen—a large rectangular room with a long, wooden table flanked by benches on either side—and searched. I found tea. And tea. And more tea.

Apparently tea was the thing to have (my visit with neighbors and people I would meet in various regions would confirm that). So I found some matches, lit the stove, and put the water on to boil. Tea there was. Tea it would be.

While waiting for the kettle to sing, I decided to take a look around. The house, owned by an English couple, was neither built nor maintained for tourists such as myself. I was glad of that.

The bedroom upstairs housed walls of books. I ran my fingers across their used spines till one struck my fancy—Charlotte Brontë's *Villette*. I grabbed it, and brought it downstairs to the sitting room. It was then I noticed that the fireplace had been prepared with turf to make a fire. My neighbors, whose houses could not be seen from mine, had been expecting me.

I barely had time to fathom that thought when I heard rattling outside the sitting-room window. There on the path leading to the house, an elderly gentleman with hair like dandelion fluff, coasted on a black bike similar to the kind commonly seen in Holland. Not only were my neighbors expecting me, they knew I was there! I lit the turf, and it did burn.

What else did these people know about me?

I felt rather excited to receive my first guest, though I had nothing to offer him, other than tea and a chat by the fireside. I rushed to turn off the kettle, which was screaming now, walked outside calmly (like someone used to receiving visitors) before my guest had time to reach the front door, and greeted the spindly gentleman, whose name will not be disclosed. I call him Mr. Curtain when I have a need to call him something.

Mr. Curtain entered my new home, without shaking my hand, which I extended to him with the utmost sincerity. He looked rather dazed. His milky-blue eyes wobbled in his head, his frail limbs shook as he walked. He had seemed much heartier on the bike, and may well have been, since *it,* rather than he, was charged with carrying his weight.

I showed Mr. Curtain to the sitting room, and offered him the rocking chair, placed at a comfortable distance from the fire. It's the chair I would have chosen for myself had I been alone. Mr. Curtain sat down and rocked.

I sat across from Mr. Curtain, in an armchair, balancing my behind on its edge, leaning forward. Something had given me the impression Mr. Curtain was hard of hearing. Perhaps because his jittery eyes quizzed my lips, as though trying to make out the words bubbling off them. But whatever I said to Mr. Curtain went unanswered. Quite naturally, no conversation ensued.

I sat back and relaxed. Mr. Curtain seemed happy enough. I certainly was. The fire, the house, the meadow, which could be seen through a window facing me—I certainly was happy.

Then Mr. Curtain started mumbling something. "What's that you say, Mr. Curtain?" I said scooting forward. He paid me no mind. Just kept talking to himself. I sat back, smiled. He could understand my smile, maybe.

Then Mr. Curtain did something which might be called, let's just say *different,* for lack of a better word (I must confess that every time I tell this story people wonder at me rather than at him).

Mr. Curtain unzipped his pants and took out his penis. It was a rubbery, limp-looking thing. It appeared as though very little life remained in it, as though it were no longer real. It was the kind of thing that made you sorry that people do grow old.

Old that penis may have been. Still it was dear to Mr. Curtain. He fondled it and pulled on it, rocking gently in the chair, perhaps to the rhythm he used to jerk off. His eyes were on my face as he carried on. Confusion clouded them. Maybe I was supposed to do something, and he couldn't figure out why I wouldn't get on with it.

Yes, I am supposed to do something, I thought, but it's not what you might have in mind, Mr. Curtain. "Mr. Curtain, care for a cup of tea?" I offered.

He didn't answer. I told him I'd be right back, and returned with a tray, a full teapot, two cups, and two saucers. I set the tray down on the table, which separated me from my determined suitor, and poured for him. Then for me.

But when I tried to hand Mr. Curtain the cup, he didn't reach for it, though I sincerely offered it, just as I had offered my hand before he crossed my threshold.

With his left hand Mr. Curtain held on to the arm of the rocking chair. With his right, he continued to clutch his penis, as though it were his heart.

"Well, that's okay, Mr. Curtain," I told him. "If you want to stroke yourself and rock yourself you go right ahead. No one will die in the process."

Actually, I didn't say that. But my attitude did. I took my tea, sat back again, and had a good drink. I finished off the pot by myself, and felt my stomach fit to burst.

Only one thing disturbed me about Mr. Curtain. His penis never budged an inch. Ungrateful member, it neither grew longer, nor wider. If his penis was his heart, then it was a heart to make him suffer.

What you need is a transplant, Mr. Curtain, I thought nodding my head to the rhythm of his rocking.

Then again Mr. Curtain betrayed no disappointment. At one moment, he rose and left. Just like that, forgetting even to zip his pants, let alone take his leave in a conventional, well-mannered fashion.

I wondered: Did Mr. Curtain do this kind of thing often, or did he think that me being a foreigner, I might work some magic on his incurious genitals? Perhaps an American woman might be

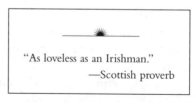

"As loveless as an Irishman."
—Scottish proverb

bold enough to kiss them awake, Mr. Curtain? Is that what the devil whispered in your ear the night they told you a certain woman, traveling alone, would be coming from the U S of A?

Sorry, Mr. Curtain, wish I could have obliged you. Truly I do. Unfortunately, I don't have that much love in me for my fellow man.

The next day, after a restful sleep, I met my neighbors, the very

ones who had prepared the turf in my hearth. The family included
a mother, a father, and two girls. I spoke mainly to the mother
(over a pot of tea). She stayed all day in her large house, alone,
while her children got on with their school activities and her husband attended to his farm. At least, that's the way she described the
situation, with a reconciled sigh and a faraway look, as though gazing at the past, and from that vantage point, viewing a future that
might have been.

Her face brightened when she asked me about myself: *A student, traveling. All alone!* She called me a great girl, and I could see
her wishing—though no envy spoiled the warmth in her eyes—
that she too were what she called a great girl.

Towards the end of my visit we got on to the subject of Mr.
Curtain (my neighbor, of course, referred to him by his real name).
I began: "An old man on a bike visited me yesterday. He's quite—"

"Oh yes, that would be Mr.—" my neighbor said, any tension
that had remained in her face melting away. "He's a lovely, old gentleman, the likes of which you won't find these days. You can pay
him a visit without phoning first. He'll listen to what you have to
say with both ears on you, rather than grudgingly lending you his
left while tuning his right in to the television set. I think I can
speak for everyone when I say that we could none of us do without Mr. Curtain. He opens up to you, shows you his heart, listens
to your own when you feel it failing. I often wonder what we'll
do when Mr. Curtain is no more."

My neighbor sighed as if to say, "But then everything passes, and
you gather your strength for a new season, should you live to en-
dure it."

"Mr. Curtain is very lovely indeed," I mumbled, really talking
to myself, my eyebrows probably elevated to a level equal to my
bafflement.

"What did you say?" my neighbor asked.

"I said Mr. Curtain is lovely indeed. Just as you described him."

"With no offense intended, I beg to disagree," my neighbor
said, her voice trilled with laughter. "Neither my words nor anyone's could describe him. But I'm telling you. It won't be long be-

fore the likes of Mr. Curtain aren't to be found anywhere. You'll be talking about Mr. Curtain one day and people will think you're describing some Golden Age-myth instead of God's own truth."

"No offense taken," I said, and smiled.

I left that farmhouse in a mental daze. My head felt light, giddy, but my thoughts had attained a degree of crystal-sharp lucidity commonly associated, in my body, with the absorption of about a glass and a half of red wine.

I had thought Mr. Curtain slightly eccentric, taking liberties most men only reach for in their dreams. But if eccentric, Mr. Curtain must have saved his eccentricities for my especial benefit, or for others like me. People passing through. Strangers. Foreigners, who surely wouldn't give him away. Curious birds likely never to return.

Obviously, Mr. Curtain had no inkling of how easily tourists, like myself, gossip about all kinds of things with people they barely know. (What could he have known about me?!)

Tourists can be wizards at hiding behind veils of constructed innocence. This allows them to do and say as they please, guilt-free. And call it curiosity. Then they move on, having satisfied their lust for a novel situation.

Eventually, tourists go home. They pack up their bags, return to their families and friends, and develop pictures (their own, personal evidence of all things seen), often unaware that, like an organ grafted onto a foreign body, they may have acted as a catalyst for the transformation of an entire community.

"Go ahead, Mr. Curtain. Jerk off till your heart's content and the cows come home, moo moo moo. No one will die in the process." That had been my blessing to him. And yet, no less than a day later I could have intentionally, but oh so innocently, planted delectable bits of information in the mind of one woman…(you can all imagine how telling such a story, whose details had ripened from a good night's sleep, makes the mouth water). That info-byte would have meant Mr. Curtain's demise.

Me and my careless tongue, we had been on the brink of revealing what most likely would have been perceived as a deadly sin. We narrowly escaped closing Mr. Curtain's curtain, which would have closed a sacred curtain on the entire community, a community which had truly acted as a host to me.

Fortunately, paying attention to someone who had openly marveled at me, I bit my tongue in time. Nothing was lost, much was gained. Though no camera could ever capture them, I'll never forget those instants in which I realized how swift and unfeeling a killing can be.

Mr. Curtain has not to worry now. Except for the readers of this story, no one knows his secret but myself, and they don't know his precise whereabouts (there's far more to Tipperary than meets the eye). What's more, readers, you don't even know Mr. Curtain's name. For all you know, I made him up, notwithstanding truth's being stranger than fiction.

I have one last word, and this for Mr. Curtain. Should you decide to continue clutching your heart with such passion, I only pray that it may rise and shine to keep you warm. God be with you and your neighbors, who think the world of you. Indeed, for whom your frail, old bones comprise a part of the structure that holds their world together.

Janine Jones grew up a military brat. So there is no place she really calls home, except where she happens to be living. She received a Ph.D. in philosophy from UCLA; lived, on and off, for ten years in France, and traveled throughout Europe. She is now living in Brooklyn, New York, where she makes a virtual living working for a global company located in Emeryville, California. She contributed "Surviving the City of Angels" to Travelers' Tales's Danger!

THOMAS FLANAGAN

★ ★ ★

The Long Memories of Mayo

*During a 1979 visit to Ireland, the author traces the events
of 1798, which were the subject of his acclaimed novel,*
The Year of the French.

"THE FRENCHMAN LANDED THERE," THE FISHERMAN SAID, NOD-
ding his head toward a break in the black rocks of the strand;
square, capable head, dark hair flecked with iron gray, knitted cap.
"He set his foot upon a great stone that was there, and he stepped
ashore from that stone." A pity the stone is not still there to be
seen, I said. "It can be seen on the road to Killala," he said, outside
the pub on the hill. "That pub is called the Kerryman now, but it
was once called the General Humbert, in honor of the
Frenchman."

Kilcummin is a small fishing village on the northern coast of
Mayo, between Rathlackan and Killala. A boreen of small, whitewashed houses leads down to a low seawall and a rocky shingle.
Beyond the shingle, Killala Bay stretches toward the distant
Atlantic. Small flags hung from the windows; the green, white, and
orange tricolor of the Republic and papal flags of white and gold
flourished in welcome to the Catholic primate of Ireland,
Cardinal O'Fiaich, who was visiting an old friend, the parish priest
in Rathlackan. The flags seemed homely rather than grandiose,
like bits of bunting at a country fete.

This had been a Mayo August, days of low, heavy gray clouds, mists shrouding the tops of distant hills, soft, insistent rain. In the narrow, twisting streets of the market towns—Castlebar, Swinford—dour shops and pubs faced one another. Then, without warning, the weather would turn around. Hills, fields, and houses would be bathed in clear, delicate light, and above them, an immense sky of pale blue. Suddenly, the illusion of Mayo's vastness was revived: its dark green lakes, Lough Mask, Lough Conn, Lough Carra, the ribbon of road that threaded its way across endless red bogs toward the Belmullet Peninsula, the scarred cliffs that faced the ocean beyond Downpatrick Head.

It had been such a day on August 23, 1798, when three frigates dropped anchor outside Kilcummin, bringing to Mayo 5,000 firelocks with which to arm local rebels and 1,100 French troops under the command of General Joseph Humbert, thirty-one years old, an illiterate dealer in the skins of rabbits and goats, flung upward by the revolution, hero of La Vendée, a master of irregular warfare.

"When was the stone taken up to the pub?" I asked the fisherman. "It was taken up at the time," he said. "Humbert stepped ashore, and when he was on dry land, the stone was taken up." A very old man, well into his eighties, had been standing close to us. "It was not taken up at the time," he said. Introductions were made. His hand was gnarled and dry. Ridges worked upon it by decades of labor and salt weather creased its surfaces. "My mother's father saw the stone taken up from the strand and carried off by cart. It was too huge to be carried off in the one piece, so they shattered it lengthwise and put the parts back together again outside the General Humbert."

Then the stone had played its part in the centenary commemoration of the rebellion, in 1898. Nationalist politicians, crammed uncomfortably into frock coats, had made speeches in Ballina and Killala; sidecars had taken them to visit the strand. But for a century before that, the folk imagination had been at work upon the insurrection. Hidden, shadowed, it had gathered legends to itself, village by village along the line of march of an extraordinary campaign of an ill-sorted army—French regulars, seasoned and cynical veterans of Italy and the Rhine, a ragbag multitude of Gaelic-speaking peasants equipped with unfamiliar weapons and pikes hammered out on crossroads forges.

They defeated yeomen and militia at Killala and Ballina, seized the market and coastal towns of Mayo, smashed a British army upon the meadows and grassy slopes outside Castlebar. From Castlebar, they cut a scythe-shaped gash across the island, fighting their way eastward across Sligo and Leitrim, then swerving southward along cool, reed-fringed Lough Allen, across the small, humpbacked bridge at Drumshanbo and down into the Midlands, where disaster awaited them.

To catch the insurgents, the main British forces, under the command of the viceroy, Lord Cornwallis, had been spreading a net across Ireland, northward from the Shannon, mightiest of the Irish rivers. Cornwallis had lost a continent once; he did not propose to lose this island of bogs and rain, purple mountains and wide, lush pasturelands. At the small, wretched Longford hamlet of Ballinamuck—the Place of the Pig—he closed the net. The French were permitted to surrender and were brought down to Dublin to await repatriation. But the Irish were cut down in their hundreds, skewered upon lance and bayonet in a red bog beyond the battlefield. Of the survivors, some were hanged from the gable ends of cabins in the village, and others were taken off to be hanged elsewhere, at leisure.

Ballinamuck was fought on the eighth of September, sixteen days after the French landing. The Mayo rebellion was a moment of time in the history of Europe, a cheap gamble lost by

> But this is the last ditch fight that every Irishman loves; he has been found with every forlorn hope for the last 1,000 years. As the tragic Gael once cried out:
>
> > When the Kings of Eternal Evil
> > Darken the Hills about,
> > Our part—is with broken sabre
> > To rise—on the last Redoubt.
> >   —John P. McEnery

the French Directory, but it was to loom immense in the imagination of western Ireland—*bliadhain na bhFranncach*, the Year of
the French.

The stone upon which General Humbert may or may not have
stepped lies among long, pale grasses to the left of the door into
the Kerryman. It had indeed been split in two, and the pieces then
mortared together. Propped behind it, against a wall, is a naïve,
rain-gentled painting on wood. Three ships at anchor, a road
choked with French soldiers resplendent in uniforms and sashes, a
mass of rebels in jackets of rain-colored frieze, pikes and scythes
slung over their shoulders. Perhaps it had once been the tavern
sign. An elderly farmer on his way in saw me standing by the
stone. "They were grand fellows in those days," he said, "to carry a
stone the weight of that from the strand up to here, in a cart drawn
by the one donkey." They were, I agreed.

In the pub, I had a whiskey with a local schoolmaster and a
friend of mine, a bookseller in Ballina. At the far end of the bar,
three small-farmers stood before their pints of Guinness, avoiding
our conversation with the careful, instinctive courtesy of Mayo.
For a thirty-acre farmer, a round of pints with friends is a serious
social and financial occasion. A pint is as much ritual as drink,
pulled slowly, allowed to settle, pulled again, until there is a white
collar, thick as cream, and beneath it stout dark as bog water. They
will let the tall shells stand before them on time-blackened oak
counters, studying them, before making an approach. The farmers
had north Mayo faces, broad and hard-boned, the eyes dark brown
or blue, clear and cold as the sea.

"You will still find a few of the old families here and there," the
schoolmaster said, "but most of them are gone." His voice was soft,
neutral. In the pubs of rural Ireland, matters of any delicacy are discussed in low tones; it is a bad country for the hard of hearing. By
"the old families" he meant, in mild euphemism, what had been in
1798, and for another century would remain, the ruling class.
Settled upon the soil by Cromwell or by earlier English plantations, tied together by their loyalty to the British Crown, by their

Protestantism, by shared traditions, often by bloodlines and marriages, the landlords had been the absolute masters of Mayo and of most of western Ireland.

The Kilcummin peasants who had marched against Killala with their pikes had been in rebellion less against the Crown, a distant abstraction, than against the old families, secure behind their walls of dressed stone, plantations of larch, oak, willow, screening graceful manor houses from winds off the wintry Atlantic. Many of the manor houses stand derelict now, and many others were destroyed in the civil war of the 1920s. Works of architecture are seals set upon a land, seals of power, authority, sovereignty. And Ireland is a land in which atavistic tribal loyalties and hatreds run centuries deep, beneath grass, bog, limestone, corroding foundations, sending tendrils into mortar....

On a day of clear, intense light, I walked with my friend Sean White, the Irish writer, along the road that runs to Easky on the Sligo side of Killala Bay. We were in search of the O'Dowd Stones, as the locals call them, which stand beside a tumulus, near the water's edge, at Enniscrone.

In fact, they are pillar stones, erected by the people who constructed the magnificent prehistoric passage graves of the coastal mountains. But during the Celtic centuries, when this was O'Dowd land, a legend linked the stones to the ruling family. One of the O'Dowds seized a mermaid's mantle—her shroud, as it was called by the Killala man who first told me the story—and thus doomed her to a life on land. They had seven children. But one day she found the shroud where he had hidden it. She led her children to the water, with O'Dowd pursuing her, and before she slipped back to her home, she changed them to stones. There they stand to this day, the Children of the Sea. It is one of those stories of the seal-people that resonate within some deep chamber of the imagination.

We never found the stones. Sean consulted his half-inch map, and we set off across tall-grassed fields divided by stone walls and fences of barbed wire. In each field, we made our way past herds of the small black cattle of the West, patient cows and suspicious bullocks. At last I abandoned the search to Sean and settled myself on a low hill.

North Mayo lay stretched before me across the bay—the tower and the church spire at Killala, the Asahi chimneys, and three lovely abbeys like shattered pearls, Rosserk, Moyne, Rathfran. In rural Ireland, such ruins are always called abbeys, to the irritation of archaeologists. Two of these are in fact friaries, founded in the fifteenth century for the Observantine Franciscans. Rathfran, the third, was founded in 1274 as a Dominican priory and was partially rebuilt in the fifteenth century. The dates are important, for they connote the final flowering of a culture.

The fifteenth was a splendid century for Ireland, in part because the English were involved in their own turmoils and left the island to its own devices. West of the Shannon, and especially in Mayo, the Gaelic lords and those Norman lords who had become more Irish than the Irish themselves reshaped a civilization, developed a rich and haunting vernacular literature, built or refashioned abbeys, priories, castles, wed by the felicity of architects to the soft, rolling hills and cloud-shadowed lakes. The names of the founding lords, Gaelic or Norman—Jordan, O'Malley, Bourke, O'Conner— are still common as blackberries in Mayo, but now they are the names of farmers and shopkeepers; all of them may be found in the lists of those convicted of rebellion in 1798.

The world that had shaped those abbeys was destroyed in the two centuries that followed by Elizabethan adventurers and Cromwellian troopers. Their present silence is heavy with the fullness of that destruction, which brought to an end the existence of an autonomous Irish culture. After Cromwell, all of Ireland, even Mayo in the remote West, was governed by a caste differing from the native population in language, in religion, even, indeed, in its notion of what constituted a culture.

To visit Rosserk, one of the three abbeys, you walk down a narrow road called in local tradition, although not upon the maps, *bother na sop*, the road of straw. It is a part of the legendary history of the Year of the French, for the rebels moved along it by night, out of Killala, for their attack upon Ballina. You walk then across fields, tall grasses after rain wet against ankles, and Rosserk lies un-roofed out beside the water.

Pass through the carved west doorway and walk through the ruined chancel to the elaborately carved double piscina. The sky stretches above your head. In the late eighteenth century, romantic lovers of the past would sketch such abbeys as Ros-serk, placing before them, to indicate scale, wandering peasants, figures of pastoral.

Killala, like many towns of the West, is a lost, defeated village of pubs and mean shops and houses crowded together, pale-painted gable walls streaked by salt wind and fre-quent rain. Its name is known to most Irishmen dimly, if at all, be-cause of the hours of that August day that brought three French ships into its bay. But like every town in Ireland, it has had its own life in history, the decades and the generations tumbled together.

> The sound of the departing guests' car dwindles toward lights lying scattered in the bog, on black slopes already in deep shadow, while on the beach and over the sea it is still light; the dome of darkness moves slowly toward the horizon, then closes the last chink in the vault, but it is still not quite dark, while in the Urals it is already getting light. Europe is only as wide as a short summer night.
> —Heinrich Böll, *Irish Journal*

I sat with some locals at a table in the Cruiskeen Lawn, listen-ing to stories of endless Victorian litigations by which certain farmers had been impoverished and certain solicitors enriched. Of a celebrated conflict of authority between the great nineteenth-century Catholic prelate Archbishop MacHale and his successor, which had come to a head in an unseemly squabble between rival priests in the green outside the Killala church. Of a certain con-temporary politician of whom it was remembered, not to his ser-vice, that a complaint made by his father had been the occasion of the Black and Tans entering north Mayo in 1921. Tea and biscuits were followed by tumblers of malt liquor.

The weather had broken, and a fine mist of rain drifted against the windows, but inside the Cruiskeen Lawn we were held safe and dry by the blanket of Irish conversation, easy and well-shaped anecdote laced with a tart yet forgiving malice. The talk would veer away from present and from recent past, back to that August day in 1798. We were all of us trying to imagine ourselves into the passions and motives of those peasant soldiers who had marched upon Killala, of those thousands of rebels who had joined the army after the capture of Ballina and the great victory of Castlebar. They had not been moved, surely, by the abstract nationalism expressed in ballads composed for the centenary ("Remember the gallant old West, boys...") and in the centenary statues of pike-clutching patriots. But we were separated from them by a river of time bridged only by half-forgotten legends, stories handed down within families....

An Irish-American sent me a question. His grandmother had always told him that she came from Borneysop, near Rosserk Abbey, but he could never find it on a map. By the time Humbert attacked Ballina, he had more than a thousand recruits, men from Rathreagh and Rathlackan and Coolcarney and Doonfeeny. He moved his army by night, along the narrow road that ran southward past Rosserk. Men and women stood by cabin doors, listening in the moonless dark to the sounds of an army, feet, hooves, creak of leather, wheels strained upon the rutted path. Then they lighted torches of hay and straw, flaring against the darkness. In the 1930s an old woman remembered, for the folklorist Richard Hayes, a grandfather's story: "There was one Myles Ford living here then, and he brought the straw mattress he had for a bed and lighted it to a great blaze to show them the way. And up to the day he died,

The people are thus inclined; religious, frank, amorous, sufferable of infinite paines, verie glorious, manie sorcerers, excellent horsemen, delighted with wars, great almsgivers, passing in hospitalitie.

—*Holinshed's Chronicles* (1586)

and he lived to an old man, he was known by no other name than Mylie French."

Borneysop: "*bother na sop*," the road of straw.

Along 150 miles of road, the legends linger of the Year of the French, fading away decade by decade in this place, swelling and coloring themselves in others. The English and the French kept careful records, filed in their ministries of war, but the annals of the Irish are legends, folktales, wisps of song wedded to a hill, a road, the foundation stones of a vanished cabin.

The Crown forces, in their headlong retreat, did not pause until they had reached Foxford, ten miles to the south. They left behind them the town of Ballina, the hinge upon which Humbert would swing Mayo open.

The Ballina Humbert captured must have looked much as it does in Bartlett's delicately tinted early Victorian engraving— long, four-arched bridges spanning the Moy, church spires in the distance, the tall, narrow houses of merchants and the thatched cabins of artisans crowding the riverbanks, shawled women gossiping, baskets balanced on their heads, fishermen in flat-bottomed boats, and in the distance a splendid early Victorian mountain, conical and cloud-capped. By Bartlett's day, the rising had faded a generation into the past, and the West lay open to the sketchbooks of lovers of the picturesque—mud-daubed cabins and elegant manor houses, a few market towns, bogs stretching toward ranges of distant hills.

The streets of Ballina are still narrow and twisting and are crowded now with the cars of farmers. The window of Michael Keohane's bookshop was decorated with copies of *The Year of the French*, a handsome seventeenth-century map of Mayo, a 1798 pike head, black, brittle, pitted by age and corrosion. A zealous nationalist came in to show me other souvenirs, a contemporary account of the rising, a proclamation issued from Dublin Castle. Others came too—farmers, several Catholic priests, small tradesmen, a Protestant clergyman, and a dignified, quiet retired schoolmaster who is descended from one of the rebel leaders, a young farmer named Ferdy O'Donnell. He had been a natural leader of men, a reluctant but staunch rebel. At the very end of the rising, he led the Killala men in a desperate, hopeless fight against the British. His bayoneted body was found in a potato field....

The English expected Humbert to attack Castlebar along the coach road, through Foxford. Instead, he took his men by night along a herdsman's path, through desolate and difficult terrain, and at eight in the morning flung them upon a superior British army. He smashed the British, driving them across the battlefield and then through Castlebar. They fled, leaving all behind them, their wounded, their munitions, their flags, and retreated thirty miles southward, to Tuam, where they awaited Lord Cornwallis.

The rebels came to Humbert in groups of 20 or 50 or 100, under the command of local leaders, and at Castlebar, several hundred militiamen from the Midlands deserted to their ranks. We know the names of many of them because informers later made copious depositions or because songs in Gaelic lingered for a century. But we do not know what they looked like or what they thought. Their leaders, most of them, were peasants or farmers, but the man chosen to serve as president of "the Republic of Connaught" came not from a farmhouse or a cabin but from one of the great estates of Mayo, Moore Hall.

Moore Hall was still a new house when John Moore rode out from it, down the winding carriageway and through Ballintubber and then northward to Castlebar and his death. The date of its founding, 1791, is incised upon a stone high above the portico, and beneath it is the Moore motto, *Fortis cadere cedere non potest* (The strong man may fall, but he is unable to yield). The house sits upon a slight hill overlooking the cool green waters of Lough Carra.

George Moore, its founder, belonged to the old Catholic gentry and came to manhood in an Ireland shackled by penal laws imposed upon those of his creed. He left Ireland for Spain, made his fortune in vineyards and shipping at Alicante, and then, when Catholics were once again permitted to purchase land, returned to Mayo and built Moore Hall. He had two sons, John, the rebel leader, and

George, a cool, scholarly man who spent years laboring on a history of the French Revolution that was left unfinished at his death.

George's son, George Henry, was a dashing figure in Victorian Ireland, a handsome, clever, extroverted man, a breeder of horses and courter of women, a Home Rule patriot, perhaps a Fenian conspirator. And he, in turn, had two sons. The older was George Moore the novelist, author of *Esther Waters*—an outrageous man, wit, jester, dandy, a bit of a genius. His brother, Maurice, inherited the father's serious side. He joined the British Army and became colonel of the Connaught Rangers, the regiment that drew the impoverished farm boys of Mayo and Galway to serve the Empire on distant shores. The Boer War sickened him, however, and in particular, the herding of Dutch farmers and their families into compounds for which the English coined the term "concentration camps"—a bland, neutral term. He left the army and returned to Mayo to manage the estate for his brother. In 1921, Maurice was elected a senator in the new Irish Free State. In retaliation, the irreconcilable Irish Republican Army burned the great house. Nothing survived the flames save for a portrait of the old founder in the court dress of Madrid, and some priest's vestments he had brought back from Spain.

Moore Hall is now a gutted shell, a Piranesi ruin with blind windows staring upon the lake. A visitor may climb the grass-covered steps to the yawning doorway, beyond which lie the blackened bricks of what was once an elaborately frescoed drawing room. Or walk along the woodland paths to Carnicaun, where George the historian lies in the family burial vault. (A different fate awaited John, his rebel brother.) The ravaged building haunts me; we know its present appearance, and old photographs disclose its confident solidity in the Victorian high noon. But only the imagination can recreate its first existence or the sentiments that drew John Moore away to cast his lot with an army of desperate peasants.

When I visited Moore Hall in August, 1979, a young hawk flew down and perched upon the portico, then moved to a low tree branch. It was astonishingly tame and allowed us to walk within a few feet of it, staring at us with lidless eyes. Someone had tamed it, we agreed, but who, and where, and why?

From Castlebar, Humbert moved eastward, across Mayo, across Sligo, across Leitrim, to within a few miles of the Ulster border. Then, at Manor Hamilton, he turned to the Midlands, cutting himself off from the coast. As the rebel army moved, it drew recruits, knots of men who had assembled at crossroads, farm boys with scythes who had slipped away from hillside cabins. But the Mayo men, who remained its core of strength, peasants who had never been beyond their own baronies, were waging a war that had Mayo as its true terrain. They were moving now into an unfamiliar land.

The land is older by far than its history. At Creevykeel, in the Truskmores, stands a court cairn built in the third millennium before Christ, an open court with a large burial chamber and two smaller ones. It was already ancient when the Celts first came to Ireland, and they peopled it with the gods and heroes of their mythology.

We stood with our backs to the cairn and looked northward, past the fishing village of Mullaghmore, toward Donegal Bay. Before us, dominating the low fields, was a Victorian mock-Gothic castle, towers and false turrets. Its owner, Lord Louis Mountbatten, was in residence there that August afternoon. He had eleven days left to live. In Ulster, across the neighboring border, the plans for his assassination had already been made. The castle of Classiebawn stood firm and confident facing its estuaries, stolid in its English confidence that history is but the vanished past, harmless and picturesque in its real or its contrived ruins. Ireland knows history in different terms, a quaking bog.

Thackeray, who visited Mayo in 1842, was the quintessential Victorian tourist, with an alert eye for Irish poverty and drollness of manner, grandeur of natural setting, the well-tended demesnes of the great landlords. "Remote as the spot is," he says, speaking of the western coast, "Westport is only two days' journey from

London now, and lies in a country far more strange to most travelers than France or Germany can be."

Westport House itself, of which Thackeray does not speak, is as lovely today as it was when Bishop Pococke, his indefatigable predecessor, visited it in the preceding century. It was built by Richard Cassels, the great German architect, with alterations by James Wyatt, a master of the gracefully ornamental, and is the residence of the branch of the Browne family that in time achieved the marquessate of Sligo.

The Brownes were the greatest of the ruling families of Mayo in the eighteenth century, prolific, powerful, and tenacious. "I am the first Englishman that in the memory of man settled himself to dwell in the country of Mayo," their founder wrote in 1585. Their great mansion has a nine-bayed façade and eagles with outspread wings at the cornices. Walking through the main apartments ("on no condition will visitors wearing stiletto heels be admitted"), one is filled with a sense of absolute power over the countryside that Westport House once exerted. In Wyatt's magnificent dining room, ornamented and filigreed in the Italian manner, the table is set with Colonel John Browne's silver dinner service, goblets of Waterford glass, Worcester china. On the sideboard are candelabra, "one presented to Second Marquess of Sligo when Governor of Jamaica by the liberated slaves, and the other by the people of Westport on his return with a hundred local names upon it," and "a unique bowl of bog oak, the inside of beaten silver."

One begins to have a sense of why Mayo went into rebellion, the country folk swarming down from the tumbled hills to seize the town and occupy Westport House. After the surrender, they paid a terrible price for it. Dennis Browne, the high sheriff, scourged treason out of Mayo, and his name passed into folklore as that of an ogre. His portrait by Reynolds hangs in Westport House, a smooth-faced man with mild eyes and soft, inoffensive lips. After the scourging, Mayo settled back into its old ways. The rebellion, it was agreed, had accomplished nothing and had left behind it only a confused legend of resistance.

At Westport House, each year now the brocades seem a bit

more faded, the Chinese wallpaper a bit more dim, temples and pagodas and horsemen with parasols. Belowstairs are tearooms serving scones to the public; shops selling Aran jumpers, posters, souvenirs; an amusement arcade; a shop that does portraits "while-u-wait"; a "kiddy karr arena"; another shop that will sell you your very own heraldic shield with your name in Gaelic lettering.

The great famine of the 1840s hit Mayo savagely. In July of 1847, 200 of the starving of Erris made their way to the workhouse of Ballina but were turned away for lack of room. The lucky ones shipped out of Killala and Westport to America and Newfoundland. Of the 278 who were herded aboard the bark *Elizabeth and Sarah* at Killala, 42 died on board of starvation and thirst. The poorhouse at Westport, which from a distance had seemed to Thackeray so like a Gothic castle, was filled to overflowing. The Marquess of Sligo was deeply distressed by the suffering beyond his walls, but there was little he could do, and at last he was forced to evict peasants. It was all the government's fault, he complained in an indignant letter to *The Times*: the Soup Kitchen Act had been poorly administered.

The village of Straid was as hard hit as most, a cluster of cabins on the Castlebar—Foxford road, beside the ruins of a thirteenth-century friary. The peasants were swept away by their landlord and perished on the roads or made their way to a workhouse. One family, the Davitts, reached Lancashire, where the son, Michael, took work in a factory, losing an arm at the age of eleven. In the 1860s, he joined the Fenian Brotherhood, an abortive revolutionary conspiracy that took its inspiration from the '98 rebels, was arrested and endured seven years of ill-treatment in an English prison. In 1879, in the middle of another famine, he returned to Mayo with a fierce, hard determination to destroy landlordism.

Newport, north of Westport on Clew Bay, sent its men to the uprising and then sank back into obscurity. One wet, windy night, I sat with the scholar Kevin Sullivan in a fishermen's pub.

On a map of the distant Midlands, we traced the route Humbert and the rebels had taken southward through Leitrim, down the shore of Lough Allen, and into Longford. And then the movements toward them of Cornwallis's armies. The lines converged upon Ballinamuck. Trophies line the wall above the bar, salmon and sea trout.

Behind us, on a hill dominating the river, was Newport House, once a gentleman's residence but now a hotel. Anglers from England patronize it, ruddy-faced men in rough, long-cherished tweeds. In late afternoon, they spread their catch upon the floor of the entrance hall; eyes glassy as marbles and iridescent scales. The scenery is magnificent, the fishermen would agree over coffee in the tall, graceful drawing room. The locals are more affable than those in France, and they speak English. Let the dead bury the dead, one of them said to me in the bar one night. Several friends of his, retired army officers, had settled quite happily in Mayo, and Lord Mountbatten had a place somewhere up the coast. A fascinating country, his friend said; are there any reliable histories?

If history can be read iconographically, then the past and present of Mayo can be read in Castlebar. Not in the town center, crowded and ugly, eighteenth- and nineteenth-century buildings wedged together in narrow streets, their fronts remodeled into shops selling the cheap wares of London and Dublin. Nor yet on the roads leading out to the farms, where the cabins, wretched and picturesque, have been replaced with modern bungalows vying against one another in awkwardness.

But walk down Castle Street to the mall, and the past lies waiting, a wide, spacious square of well-tended grass. The pillared and porticoed courthouse and the buildings facing it are comely and well proportioned. Outside the dark, trim Protestant church stands the handsome statue of a handsome soldier, Major General O'Malley, C. B., twice wounded at Waterloo, commander for many years of the Connaught Rangers. His body lies in Murrisk Abbey near Clew Bay, founded by his family for the Augustinian canons in the fifteenth century. The O'Malleys were one of those Gaelic families who had accepted the new order imposed by Elizabeth and Cromwell, by William and the Georges.

Across the road is a modern tomb that bears this legend: "*Fortis cadere cedere non potest*. Pray for the soul of John Moore of Ashbrooke and Moore Hall, County Mayo. Who gave his life for Ireland in the Rising of 1798. Born Alicante, Spain, 1763. Died a prisoner awaiting transportation in the city of Waterford, 6-12-99."

They face each other in death, two shards of Ireland's broken mosaic. Another fragment, the Imperial Hotel, stands on the far side of the mall.

In Irish towns of any size, there usually was an Imperial Hotel. Often, as in Ballina, the name has been changed, but not always, not in Sligo, for example, nor here in Castlebar. They are Victorian in design and by their name suggest the high Victorian confidence that Ireland would remain in perpetuity a part of the British Empire. All that has changed.

The Ireland of the Anglo-Irish is now one with that of the old Gaelic lords. The gentry survive here and there, but their estates have dwindled to the very edges of their walls, the taxes are heavy, and at last they move away. With the establishment of the Irish Free State, political power passed to the descendants of the '98 pikemen, but the economic defeat had been worked before that, by events that began in Mayo.

Child of the famine diaspora, mutilated veteran of the child-labor mills, Fenian rebel, convict, Michael Davitt returned to a Mayo once again threatened with evictions and emigration. In Dublin, he had been welcomed by the Fenian organization as hero and martyr, but he was done with romantic rebellions of that kind. His years in prison had hardened in him a conviction that the enemy was the landlord system itself, and he had worked out a plan of campaign. In April of 1879, he organized a meeting of tenant farmers in a Mayo town so poor that it was called Irishtown, and he followed it with others. Then, in August, at the Imperial Hotel in Castlebar, the Land League was founded.

Its method, as Conor and Máire Cruise O'Brien have written, was "to select estates especially notorious for rack-renting and eviction; concentrate public attention on those estates by means of mass meetings; and then, by pressure of social ostracism and refusal of services, render life as difficult as possible for the landlord (if resident) or his agent, and especially for 'grabbers'—those who rented land from which the previous tenants had been evicted, and which the Land League had placed under ban." In the Land War, which followed, one Mayo gentleman, Captain Boycott, unwillingly donated his name to the language. By then the war had run its course, it had "transformed the conditions of land tenure in Ireland and cracked the entire basis of the Cromwellian settlement."

A yellowed photograph has captured the Castlebar meeting—the Royal Irish Constabulary, mounted, armed, and caped; a great mass of people filling the roads to the mall, shawled women, and men in dark jackets. There is a portrait of Davitt in the hotel, a slight, plain-featured man, bearded, with dark eyes set deep in his narrow skull. He sits at an angle to the painter to draw attention away from the empty sleeve. In the hotel bar, shouldered by boisterous farmers who owed their land to Davitt, I raised a glass to his memory.

For the better part of a century, the '98 rebellion had no visible memorial. The rebels were honored only in legends and in songs whose singing carried with it the excitement of complicity. This has appropriateness. When the civilization that had created the abbeys and friaries was shattered, the visual arts, and above all the art of architecture, passed into the keeping of the new order, whose Palladian mansions rose up as an assertion in stone and ornate plasterwork of their authority and their social master. And the arts of the conquered people became the arts of the voice—the tale, the oration, the song.

Perhaps this is one reason why visitors leave Ireland praising the speech of the Irish, why the art of conversation has not quite died away. A country pub in Ireland is likely to be a naked barn of a room, with uncomfortable chairs and stools, plastic tabletops ringed and grimed by the stains of last night's pints and bottles. But if a voice, near closing time, is raised in song, the room will be transformed, a melody intricate in its simplicity moving through the fog of cigarette and pipe smoke.

The statues began to appear at the centenary, after the triumph of the Land War, crude and naïve. You can follow them, from Ballina to the one at Collooney in Sligo and south into Longford. The one in the village of Knock is typical: "To the memory of Captains Richard Jordan and James O'Malley, who offered up their lives on the altar of their country in the year 1798. Also Geofferey Cunniff and Tom Flatley, who paid the penalty of devotion to Ireland. May their actions tend to stimulate us to do something to throw off the yoke of the stranger."

There is one at Ballinamuck, of course, the figure of a pikeman, and the local pub is called The Pikeman.

A British officer made a hasty sketch of Ballinamuck, two hills with a road running between them. The disposition of the Crown forces is carefully indicated, and that of the French and the rebels. Beyond the battlefield, he noted, lay "deep black bog." It was into this bog that the Mayo men, and the Longford men who had joined them, were pushed back and then slaughtered. The map, of course, makes no reference to this.

A few days after this battle, Maria Edgeworth, the novelist, visited the scene. The bodies lay strewn on the bog. The hedges were thick with blackberries, and soldiers were gathering them, in their tall helmets. Several years ago, I went there with my friend Seamus Heaney, the poet. For Seamus, bogs are deep, mythic repositories of the past, but he also has a great practical knowledge of them. The contours of the "deep black bog" had changed in a century and a half, but with his help, I worked out what must then have been its shape. The hedges were again heavy with blackberries. We broke off branches and carried them with us to Dublin. We had little to say to each other about the bog at Ballinamuck. He had said it already, writing of a different rebellion in '98:

> Terraced thousands died,
> shaking scythes at cannon.

> The hillside blushed,
>   soaked in our broken wave.
> They buried us without shroud
>   or coffin
> And in August the barley grew
>   out of the grave.

This August, I returned to Ballinamuck with an American poet, Louis Simpson. We walked past the pub and the statue of the pikeman and climbed one of the two hills marked on the British officer's map. I pointed to the positions of the two armies and to the bog that lies beyond them. "There is always something sad about lost causes," Louis said. We spoke casually about other defeated acres, Culloden Moor, Flodden Field. Their names had no resonance for me.

Here, where the Mayo men had fallen, I was remembering Mayo. Perhaps some of them did, too, but more likely they knew only terror and despair as they faced the long thorns of bayonets, the downward-slashing sabers of the dragoons. Far more privileged than they, and with time to kill, I remembered the slender arches of Rosserk Abbey, the present quiet of the road of stray, the deep blue of the ocean beyond Kilcummin Strand.

In the last four decades of his life, Thomas Flanagan considered Ireland his second spiritual home. He was a Professor of English at Columbia University, the University of California, Berkeley, and the State University of New York. He received honorary doctoral degrees from Amherst College and the National University of Ireland. He was the author of three novels about Ireland: The Year of the French, The Tenants of Time, *and* The End of the Hunt. *He died in March, 2002.*

Cycling to Dún Aengus

Irish time is not measured by the clock.

AN OLD WOMAN STEPPED OUT OF A BRICK HOUSE. SHE UNFURLED a gray rug over a whitewashed rock wall, then beat it with a hefty stick. Before her, toward the jagged Atlantic shore, thin shadows of ambling men wobbled in dusk light. These actions unfolded as though in slow motion, as though each passing minute was weighed down by a spell.

"I think we've entered Irish time," said Robyn as she shifted gears and veered ahead.

It was July. Having landed at Shannon airport earlier that day, the two of us had peddled our bicycles over a dozen miles along the sunny coast of County Clare. Robyn, the artist, appreciated settings conducive to letting her mind wander. But she had never seen the likes of western Ireland before.

"It's as though," she surmised while gazing at boats bobbing in Liscannor Bay, "we could spend the whole day watching this harbor, and nothing would happen." Her voice trailed away; her gaze gained distance.

"Would that disappoint you?" I asked.

"Never," she replied. "That's the attraction of this place."

Years before, while growing up in County Wicklow on the

east coast of Ireland, I had learned the strange magic of Irish time. Perhaps it came from the long shadows of summer (Liscannor Bay is just shy of fifty-three degrees latitude) or from the lack of anxiety the Irish felt about their future. Perhaps this altered sense of time had been ingrained into the island's collective unconscious by its people's patience through a history of painful famine, Viking raids, and colonial disdain. For although you may say that the clocks of Connemara and of Clare beat to the same cadence as other clocks on earth, I disagree. Irish time differs. It is like a tweed fabric whose subtle textures appear only when looked at askance.

Robyn stopped her bicycle. She began to talk with a farmer who herded cattle along the narrow road. She then stopped again to sniff wayside flowers and fresh cut grass. When I pulled over beside her to adjust a brake cable, a housewife—out walking to the butcher shop—stopped to advise me about tomorrow's weather. Having seen red clouds over the bay, she foretold morning sunshine.

"That's only for the mornin', mind," she added, placing a caveat on her forecast. "There's no tellin' about the afternoon."

In Ireland, even predicting weather required a special regard for time.

Near the end of our first day of bicycling, we stopped at a pub in the town of Lahinch. As I sat on an outside terrace, sipping a pint of stout and facing the rocky coast, Robyn wrinkled her nose toward me, then pointed her eyebrows to the left. There, three tourists sat close by.

One large American spoke. "Let's drink up and pay," he said. "We still have a lot to see."

The man sounded rushed. He had calculated how much daylight they had left and wanted to chase vistas and viewpoints as though they were running errands in a shopping mall. Given his fixed annual lump of vacation, he wanted to fill it with motion. To him, time was a cone into which he scooped measures of activity.

Seated across the table, his bearded partner had assumed more compliance with the land. His voice, thick and sedate, blasted the notion of rushing around. "Castles, fortresses, viewing points—all in time. Let's finish our drinks peacefully. Enjoy where we are."

As he spoke these words, Robyn's eyes locked on mine. They sizzled with understanding. We both smiled. Already, a tacit understanding about Ireland had grown between us, an awareness highlighted by these men's disagreement. The tone and content of their voices outlined the shape of a lesson we had learned earlier that day: that land and time have their own relationship. That to impart urgency on a location where it does not fit is to invite a troubled journey.

We got back on our mountain bikes and left the quibbling travelers. I feared that the anxious one might spend his whole vacation trying to see a land whose greatest gifts are invisible.

The next day we rode farther up the coast, then loaded our bicycles onto a small ferry boat. The wrinkles on the kind captain's face had been sculpted by years of rough weather. As Atlantic spray pelted our faces and the boat chugged out of the harbor, the captain lit up his Peterson's pipe. The boat then bobbed toward Inis Mór, one of the three Aran Islands that lay off the weather-shattered coast of County Clare.

To an Irishman, a bicycle is a straightforward matter: one speed, one color (black), a sturdy frame, and a set of coaster brakes. In the countryside, the Irish glide along on their bikes in a dignified manner, upright, tweeds in place, never showing the slightest signs of being winded. I was put to shame on several occasions during a two-week cycling trip through the hilly North and West Country when I, a reasonably fit young American woman astride a modern twelve-speed touring model (albeit laden with packs and gear) was joined and then surpassed on long uphill grades by hardy old men who were my grandfather's age. They seemed to pedal effortlessly on their banged-up one-speeds, never missing a beat of conversation, no matter how steep the lane. They inevitably asked me to join them at the nearest pub once we'd cleared the crest of the hill.

—Julie Sell,
"The Tour of Ireland"

On arrival on Inis Mór, we rode our bicycles away from the quiet harbor. We moved toward Dún Aengus, an ancient stone semicircle encompassing eleven acres of wind-lashed land. This stone monument is perched atop cliffs that rise for over 200 feet out of the Atlantic. There, we dropped our bicycles in a lush green field and paced to the cliff edge beneath a mackerel sky. Though the purpose of Dún Aengus is unknown, it is thought to have been a focus for druidic rituals. As we lay on stomachs at the precipice edge and watched ocean waves crack against cliffs below, we tried to imagine attending such rituals. We did this until our minds quit their ceaseless buzz of analysis and appreciated the place simply for what it was: desolation in the language of landscape. We rested at the ancient fort—fashioned long ago by megalithic architects—and watched gulls soar above. Surrounded by raucous seabirds, sheer cliffs, and lichen-covered boulders, we winced in howling gales and spread our arms across hard soil. We were, as Robyn had noticed, in Irish time. It seemed such a patient place.

Eventually, mesmerized and relaxed, we rose and rode our bicycles away. Yet our journey to Dún Aengus did not leave us. To this day, the moments spent bicycling in Ireland and the hours spent at those ruins on Inis Mór repay us. Though far from Ireland, whenever I become frustrated with life's pace, I consciously slow down to remember the journey to the stone semicircle of Dún Aengus. In doing so I remember those who—for spiritual reasons—patiently and methodically spent years constructing a ritual center on a desolate, awesome landscape. I recall the woman by the roadside who formed her personal weather forecast not because she ignored the television weather report, but because she enjoyed looking at the sky for herself. These people knew, intuitively, that as their appreciation for space expanded, their regard for time slowed down. By remembering this I grow aware—again—that there are larger considerations to life besides paying the phone bill.

For the two of us, traveling with open minds and flexible schedules, this trip through western Ireland was a journey to view the world in a unique way. Dún Aengus turned out to be a mentor as much as a ruin. The perspective it illuminated about time and space was a reward, a gift for slowing down to appreciate Ireland's countryside at its own pace.

Tom Mullen has spent the past ten years working as a water resources consultant while living in Europe, Africa, the Middle East, Asia, and Latin America. As a boy he spent seven years growing up in the village of Delgany in County Wicklow, Ireland. He occasionally returns to Ireland to refresh his perspective on life.

BRIAN MOORE

✦ ✦ ✦

Going Home

Where is the talisman that unlocks
the mystery of your life?

A FEW YEARS AGO ON HOLIDAY IN THE WEST OF IRELAND I CAME
upon a field which faced a small strand and, beyond it, the Atlantic
Ocean. Ahead of me five cows raised their heads and stared at the
intruder. And then behind the cows I saw a few stone crosses, irregular, askew as though they had been thrown there in a game of
pitch-and-toss. This was not a field but a graveyard. I walked
among the graves and came to a path which led to the sandy shore
below. There, at the edge of this humble burial ground, was a
headstone unlike the others, a rectangular slab of white marble laid
flat on the ground:

BULMER HOBSON
1883–1969

I stared at this name, the name of a man I had never known, yet
familiar to me as a member of my family. I had heard it spoken
again and again by my father in our house in Clifton Street in
Belfast and by my uncle, Eoin MacNeill, when during school holidays I spent summers in his house in Dublin. For my uncle and
my father, Bulmer Hobson was both a friend and in some sense a
saint. A Quaker, he, like my uncle, devoted much of his life to the

cause of Irish independence, becoming in the early years of this century an exemplary patriot whose nonviolent beliefs made our tribal animosities seem brutal and mean. That his body lay here in this small Connemara field, facing the ocean under a simple marker, was somehow emblematic of his life.

Proust says of our past: "It is a labor in vain to try to recapture it: all the efforts of our intellect are useless. The past is hidden somewhere outside its own domain in some material object which we never suspected. And it depends on chance whether or not we come upon it before we die."

I believe now that the "material object" was, for me, that gravestone in Connemara, a part of Ireland which I had never known in my youth. And as I stood staring at Bulmer Hobson's name, my past as a child and adolescent in Belfast surges up, vivid and importunate, bringing back a life which ended forever when I sailed to North Africa on a British troopship in the autumn of 1943.

There are those who choose to leave home vowing never to return and those who, forced to leave for eco-

---

A friend of mine, a priest in Connemara, was going to build a parking lot outside his church. There was a ruin nearby that had been vacated for fifty or sixty years. He went to the man whose family had lived there long ago and asked the man to give him the stones for the foundation. The man refused. The priest asked why, and the man said, "*Céard a dhéanfadh anamacha mo mhuinitíre ansin?*"—that is, "What would the souls of my ancestors do then?" The implication was that even in this ruin long since vacated, the souls of those who had once lived there still had a particular affinity and attachment to this place. The life and passion of a person have an imprint on the ether of a place. Love does not remain within the heart, it flows out to build secret tabernacles in a landscape.

—John O'Donohue, *Anam Cara: A Book of Celtic Wisdom*

nomic reasons, remain in thrall to a dream of the land they left behind. And then there are those stateless wanderers who, finding the larger world into which they have stumbled vast, varied, and exciting, become confused in their loyalties and lose their sense of home.

I am one of those wanderers. After the wartime years in North Africa and Italy, I worked in Poland for the United Nations, then emigrated to Canada, where I became a citizen before moving on to New York, and at last to California, where I have spent the greater part of my life.

And yet in all the years I have lived in North America I have never felt that it is my home. Annually, in pilgrimage, I go back to Paris and the French countryside and to London, the city which first welcomed me as a writer. And if I think of reemigrating it is to France or England, not to the place where I was born.

For I know that I cannot go back. Of course, over the years I have made many return visits to my native Belfast. But Belfast, its configuration changed by the great air raids of the blitz, its inner city covered with a carapace of flyovers, its new notoriety as a theater of violence, armed patrols, and hovering helicopters, seems another city, a distant relative to the Belfast which in a graveyard in Connemara filled my mind with a jumbled kaleidoscope of images fond, frightening, surprising, and sad.

—My pet canary is singing in its cage above my father's head as he sits reading *The Irish News* in the breakfast room of our house in Belfast—

—A shrill electric bell summons me to Latin class in the damp, hateful corridors of St. Malachy's College. I have forgotten the declension and hear the swish of a rattan cane as I hold out my hand for punishment—

—In Fortstewart, where we spent our summer holidays, I have been all day on the sands, building an elaborate sand sculpture in hopes of winning the Cadbury contest first prize, a box of chocolates—

—Alexandra Park, where, a seven-year-old, I walk beside my

sister's pram holding the hand of my nurse, Nellie Ritchie, who at that time I secretly believe to be my real mother—

—I hear the terrified squeal of a pig dragged out into the yard for butchery on my uncle's farm in Donegal—

—I stand with my brothers and sisters singing a ludicrous Marian hymn in St. Patrick's Church at evening devotions:

> O Virgin pure, O spotless maid,
> We sinners send our prayers to thee,
> Remind thy Son that He has paid
> The price of our iniquity—

—I hear martial music, as a regimental band of the British Army marches out from the military barracks behind our house. I see the shining brass instruments, the drummers in tiger-skin aprons, the regimental mascot, a large horned goat. Behind that imperial panoply long lines of poor recruits are marched through the streets of our native city to board ship for India, a journey from which many will never return—

—Inattentive and bored, I kneel at the Mass amid the stench of unwashed bodies in our parish church, where 80 percent of the female parishioners have no money to buy overcoats or hats and instead wear black woolen shawls which cover head and shoulders, marking them as "Shawlies," the poorest of the poor—

—We, properly dressed in our middle-class school uniforms sitting in a crosstown bus, move through the poor streets of Shankill and the Falls, where children without shoes play on the cobbled pavements—

—The front gates of the Mater Infirmorum Hospital, where my father, a surgeon, is medical superintendent. As he drives out of those gates, a man so poor and desperate that he will court minor bodily injury to be given a bed and food for a few days steps in front of my father's car—

—An evening curfew is announced following Orange parades and the clashes which invariably follow them. The curfew, my father says, is less to prevent riots than to stop the looting of shops by both Catholic and Protestant poor—

—Older now, I sit in silent teenage rebellion as I hear my elders talk complacently of the "Irish Free State" and the difference between the Fianna Fail and Fine Gael parties who compete to govern it. Can't they see that this Catholic theocratic "grocer's republic" is narrow-minded, repressive, and no real alternative to the miseries and injustices of Protestant Ulster?—

—Unbeknownst to my parents I stand on Royal Avenue hawking copies of a broadsheet called *The Socialist Appeal*, although I have refused to join the Trotskyite party which publishes it. Belfast and my childhood have made me suspicious of faiths, allegiances, certainties. It is time to leave home—

The kaleidoscope blurs. The images disappear. The past is buried until, in Connemara, the sight of Bulmer Hobson's grave brings back those faces, those scenes, those sounds and smells which now live only in my memory. And in that moment I know that when I die I would like to come home at last to be buried here in this quiet place among the grazing cows.

Brian Moore, the author of nineteen novels, died in 1999 at the age of seventy-seven. This essay, the last piece he wrote, was originally commissioned by Granta.

PART FOUR

IN THE SHADOWS

SCOTT ANDERSON

* * *

Making a Killing

*The cost of peace is high
in Northern Ireland.*

I FIRST CAME TO NORTHERN IRELAND IN 1986 AND HAVE RE-
turned regularly ever since. Like all who come to write about The
Troubles, I initially focused on the exotic. I struggled through the
conflict's complicated math—the myriad paramilitary groups that
had formed, splintered, disappeared, only to reappear under new
acronyms—and listened to long lectures on why it was or wasn't a
religious war. I heard many an expert explanation of how it was
impossible to understand the present situation without first studying the signal event—in 1969 or 1690 or 1169, depending on the
lecturer—that had set the whole bloody chain of events in motion.

Yet beneath all the layers of history and mythology were hints
of a darker, more cynical explanation. In the underground economy operated by the paramilitaries was the suggestion that the war
had mutated into something quite different from its origins.

But exploring this shadow world was no easy task. Belfast, I
quickly discovered, is a very small and incestuous place, where the
killers of one side often have links—school, marriage, prison—to
those on the other. Because of this web of communal entangle-
ment, because both haven and danger might come from any direction, the city is a perfect repository for secrets—and no secrets

are more jealously guarded than those concerning the paramilitary mafias. Due to the time and persistence I put in, though, some of those involved warmed up to me. The confidences started small— the true motive behind a recent assassination, for example, or where the gunmen bought many of their assault rifles (gun marts in central Florida)—but they steadily deepened. I was undergoing a peculiar baptism, I realized, and one that carried a price: with each further step into the shadow world, with each new secret I shared, I was being held that much more accountable by the hard men. This became bluntly clear to me on a spring night in 1988, when I was taken to a heavily fortified row house just off the Falls Road to meet a man whom I will call Martin, a senior commander in the Provisional IRA.

"Do you know what the most dangerous thing to possess in Northern Ireland is?" Martin asked me. "Knowledge. People run into trouble here for knowing things they're not supposed to... What you are looking into, the money aspects, no one in Belfast talks about—it's a death sentence. If you ever identify me in any way, I will be destroyed. If that happens, you will be destroyed. That is not a threat; it's simply a new fact in your life."

Although Sinn Fein, the political wing of IRA, finally was permitted to join the Northern Ireland Assembly as part of the peace settlement in 1999, this story sheds light on why the peace was so hard to come by, and why it remains so fragile.

—JO'R, LH, and SO'R

Well into the night, Martin and I discussed the financial underpinnings of the Republican war machine. He described the IRA's fund-raising empire, how it had begun in the west Belfast ghettos and slowly extended to the city center, to the entire province, spread out to embrace legitimate businesses in London and Dublin and hidden bank accounts in Switzerland.

"We are fighting a war here," Martin said. "To wage that war, we will raise funds in any way available to us. People can call that gangsterism—and certainly you can say some of the other (para-military) groups have fallen into that—but that is not true with us. All of the money we raise goes back into the war effort."

After that meeting with Martin, I crossed a certain threshold, accepted—not as a brother, certainly; more as a trustworthy gad-fly—by hard men on both the Republican and Loyalist sides. Over the years, these men have allowed me glimpses into the Belfast un-derworld, and I've come to see that this landscape is not a sideshow to the war but the war's true playing field, the place where deals are struck and execution orders drawn. Of the five people I've per-sonally known who have been murdered in Belfast, only one has been the victim of old-fashioned sectarian politics; all the others have been killed by tripping up on the paramilitary money trail.

"My name is Raymond McCord. I want you to use my real name because, if they kill me, I'd like people to know why."

We were meeting last autumn in a cramped office in downtown Belfast, and Raymond was scared, the fear registering as a dull stare of his blue eyes. A burly, thirty-eight-year-old Protestant from the Rathcoole ghetto of north Belfast, he had a problem with the UDA, the largest and most ruthless Loyalist formation. More specifically, he had a problem with some cadres on the lowest rung of the paramilitary power structure—the punishment squads. As a result, there was no one in Belfast just then who had a shorter life expectancy than Raymond McCord.

The squads were borne out of the early days of The Troubles, when the paramilitary seized control of the ghettos. Along with taking over the neighborhood economy, gunmen on both sides instituted a perverse brand of "informal justice" to preserve the in-tegrity of their "popular struggle." Those deemed guilty of engag-ing in "antisocial behavior" were punished, and punished severely: execution for drug dealers and violent freelance criminals, beatings and kneecappings for juvenile delinquents and auto thieves. As the war economy expanded and ever more Volunteers were needed to run the drinking clubs and protection rackets, the more menial law-and-order chores were farmed out to paramilitary wanna-bes, usually neighborhood kids too young or untrustworthy for full-fledged membership.

From the paramilitary leaders' standpoint, the punishment squads have been a tremendous boon: powerful instruments for maintaining order and fear in the ghettos without putting important operatives at risk, reliable purveyors of violence against businessmen who fall behind in their war-chest donations, training schools for future warriors. And the squads have performed with zeal, killing dozens of people and kneecapping at least 1,500 more. No longer content with mere beatings or shootings, they have graduated to more sophisticated forms of cruelty and introduced a whole new glossary of terms to the local language. There is the "fifty-fifty" (the victim is forced to touch his toes while a bullet is fired into his spine)/ "breeze-blocking" (the methodical shattering of bones by dropping flagstones or cinder blocks on joints); and the "six-pack" (shots to the knees, ankles, and elbows). Through long experience, the squads now know how to maximize suffering: injuries can be heightened by forcing a shooting victim to lie on concrete, and the most efficient way to destroy an elbow is by bringing the hand toward the shoulder and firing into the bend. The punishments are now often "scheduled," the offender told to come to a certain alley at teatime, say, where the squad will be waiting to administer to him. It is advisable to show up.

For Raymond McCord, the trouble started over a personal argument with a member of one of the UDA's Rathcoole squads. It got worse when, working as a bouncer at a neighborhood bar, he had the temerity to eject several unruly squad members. "So that's what marked me. All of a sudden, I'm an enemy of the Loyalist cause. In the eyes of the UDA command—because they are listening to these guys—I'm a traitor and have to be punished."

In September 1991, a UDA man cornered Raymond's sixteen-year-old son and beat him senseless. Two months later, shots were fired at Raymond as he walked along his street. The climax came in February 1992, when he was ambushed in a pub by more than a dozen squad members. Dragged into a side alley, Raymond was kicked and beaten to the edge of unconsciousness, then breeze-blocked.

"They were climbing up on top of this wall to get more of a drop, then heaving the stones down, aiming at my joints. I passed out, but I was later told that a couple of the guys went back into the pub, had a pint, then came back and started dropping on me again."

Incredibly, Raymond escaped with little more than a broken arm and shattered legs. While recovering in the hospital, he made a fateful decision.

"These guys say they're patriots defending the Loyalist cause, but they're just a bunch of fuckin' thugs, a mafia. So I thought, 'Someone's got to stand up to them or this is going to go on forever.' There was just no way I was going to sit back and wait for them to come back on me."

Raymond went to the police and pressed charges against five of his assailants. It was a remarkable act; for years, both the local police and British authorities had tried to go after the punishment squads. Virtually without exception, the victims refused to talk, knowing their next punishment would be death.

Raymond's novel decision changed his life dramatically. His neighborhood friends, most of whom he'd known since childhood, suddenly avoided all contact. There were constant death threats, carloads of squad members parked outside his house. His goal became to simply stay alive until his attackers could be brought to trial; after that, he would have to leave Belfast and probably never return. In that pursuit, he wasn't getting much help from the authorities.

"You know, they (the security forces) are always on the telly—'fight back against the terrorists, don't give in'—but when someone does stand up, they just don't want to know you. I've been on them for months trying to find out what plans they have for me when this (trial) is over, and they just keep stalling and passing me on to someone else. It's like they don't understand: if I don't get out of here, I'm a dead man."

The next day, I brought up Raymond's story with a man I will call Jackie, an upper-level officer in the UDA. Loyalist hard men have always had the reputation of operating more as traditional mafiosi—self-interested, the vast majority of money raised for the cause disappearing into their pockets—than their Republican counterparts. It is a reputation fortified by their appearance. Whereas IRA men tend to be austere and understated, favoring blue jeans and imitation leather jackets, Loyalist chieftains have a fondness for gold jewelry, musk-scented cologne, and seventies-era bouffant hairstyles. When I'd first met Jackie in 1988, he'd been only a UDA capo with one thin gold necklace; now, five years and several promotions later, the jewelry around his neck had multiplied and spread to his fingers, and his permed hair was dyed an intriguing blend of metallic hues. He didn't seem pleased when I asked about Raymond McCord.

> The greatest curse of Ireland has not been English invasions or English misgovernment; it has been the exaggeration of Irish virtues—our stubbornness, conservatism, enormous arrogance, our power of resistance, our capacity for taking punishment, our laughter, endurance, fatalism, devotion to the past, all taken to the point where every human quality can become a vice instead of a virtue.
>
> —Seán O'Faoláin, *The Irish: A Character Study*

"I'm not all that familiar with his story—I'm not up in that area much—but I understand he's been touting (informing) to the authorities. Turned in some of his own mates, from what I understand."

When I told Raymond's version of events, Jackie nodded knowingly.

"Well, you see, that's exactly my point. If he had a problem with some of the (punishment squad) lads, he should have taken the matter up with the UDA commander in his district. Touting to the police, we can't tolerate that. The situation here requires we maintain a certain level of civic discipline."

I asked if, in this case, "discipline" meant execution.

Jackie shrugged. "We've got a war on here, a war where our very cultural identity is at stake. We don't have time to fuck around with people like Raymond McCord."

On one cold, drizzling night, a friend—I will call him Seamus—took me on a tour of the Republican drinking clubs along the Falls Road. I'd known Seamus, a gregarious and charming man in his early forties, for several years. Born and raised in the Catholic ghettos of west Belfast, he had, by all appearances, escaped that world to become a successful businessman, a family man with several teenage children.

After a while, the drinking clubs blended together. It was more than the cigarette smoke and beer-soaked carpeting, or that all the customers seemed to sport fading blue tattoos on their forearms. The clubs shared a restless energy, as if everyone were waiting for something to happen that was long overdue, a sensation reinforced by the clubs' exteriors—floodlights and closed-circuit cameras, steel mesh over the windows to thwart sniper fire and grenade attacks.

Leaving one club, Seamus stopped on the sidewalk to gaze down the Falls Road. Clouds were tumbling over the western headlands, and from somewhere overhead came the steady thump of British Army surveillance helicopters. The unchanging pitch meant the helicopter was hovering in place over some corner of the city that interested its crew. Seamus stared in one direction, then the other. "A lot of life played out on this road," he said. "A lot of British soldiers, a lot of innocent Catholics. The Loyalists used to come by at closing time to pick out someone to do. Right here"—he pointed to the short stretch of asphalt before us—"I can remember eight men dying."

The section of the Falls we stood on had earned the nickname Murder Mile for the scores of people killed there over the years.

That night it was quiet. Cast in the yellow glow of high-intensity street lamps, it looked much like any other working-class commercial street after hours: garbage-strewn vacant lots, shuttered shops, deteriorating row houses.

"It's different now," he said. "Everything's different."

Returning to Seamus's car, we left the Falls and headed for a trendy discotheque in an affluent neighborhood where the bouncers wore tuxedos and the patrons were in suits and party dresses. The discotheque owner, a man I will call Kenneth, seemed pleased to see us—overjoyed, in fact. He greeted Seamus with a hearty handshake, threw an arm around my shoulder like we were old friends, and led us to a prime table overlooking the dance floor. When he rushed off, on his way to the bar to order us complimentary drinks, Seamus whispered to me:

"This club is under the protection of the Provisional IRA. You wouldn't know it now, but Kenneth was very resistant about signing on at first—simply didn't see the need for security. So then he got bombed a couple of times. Now he loves to see me come around."

In addition to the other truths about his life—prosperous businessman, devoted father—my friend Seamus is a powerful functionary in the shadow economy of Belfast, a portfolio manager in the IRA's underworld business empire. He sees no contradiction in this. He is an Irish patriot, and the money raised goes to further the "armed struggle."

He is also, in a perverse sort of way, a peacemaker. The reason the drinking clubs along the Falls Road are so quiet, why Murder Mile is not living up to its reputation these days, is that the paramilitary godfathers have established co-prosperity spheres that require the violence to be controlled and outwardly directed, a policy implemented by men like Seamus. Even Kenneth is probably grateful on one level; now firmly under Seamus's protective wing, he won't be leaned on or bombed by another paramilitary organization.

This is not to suggest that the hard men are performing a valuable civic function, or even that they are motivated by the patriotic causes they claim to represent. Although even its most bitter enemies concede that the Provisional IRA funnels most of its money back into the war machine, that rationalization is rarely attached to the other paramilitary formations. Members of the Official IRA, the Provisionals' chief rival in the Republican movement, are commonly regarded as self-aggrandizing gangsters. Until they were shut down by the Provisionals in a Belfastian version of "The Night of the Long Knives," the young thugs of the Irish National Liberation Army (INLA) were peddling drugs and slaughtering each other in turf wars. On the Protestant side, it's generally understood that only a tiny fraction of the millions the UDA and the Ulster Volunteer Force (UVF) raise through their business fronts, tax frauds, and shakedowns ever reaches the Loyalist war chest.

"How did the Japanese take to Ireland?"

"They loved it from the start—the sense of openness and freedom, the wide open spaces, the ease with which they could fish or play golf. They were surprised at the lack of discipline. When their first general manager was leaving, and there was a party to mark it, he was asked, 'What's your most important memory?' and he said, 'How people who are so nice and lovely individually can be so disagreeable collectively.'"

—Desmond Fennell,
A Connacht Journey

The slide into outright gangsterism began—not coincidentally—with the first big influx of British money in the early 1980s. As part of the ambitious campaign to remake Belfast, huge tracts of the west-side ghettos were slated for demolition, and large companies—their insurance underwritten by the British government—were energetically wooed back to the bombed-out city center. For the hard men, these were the golden years. The protection rackets were refined and expanded across the city. Cashing in on the construction boom, the paramilitaries repackaged themselves as labor brokers with a decidedly hard-sell approach: hire our crews and the job will get done without pilferage or strikes, or hire your own crews and buy them bulletproof vests.

No one was immune from the squeeze of the hard men, not even the British civil servants sent to Belfast to oversee the redevelopment projects. One night I was introduced to a man I will call Trevor, a former manager for the Northern Ireland Housing Executive, the principal government agency in charge of public housing. In the mid-1980s, Trevor was assigned to an urbanrenewal project on the lower Shankill Road, an area under the control of the Loyalist UDA.

"The intimidation started the moment I got there," Trevor explained. "My second day on the job, (local UDA commander John) McClatchey sends a couple of lads up to the office to invite me over for tea. When I get there, McClatchey is holding this teletext and he starts telling me all about myself, where I'd gone to school, where my brothers and sisters worked, everything. Then he says, 'You take care of us, we'll take care of you.' Well, I understood what that meant."

As soon as construction began, the UDA placed the job site under the protection of its "security service" and assumed total control of the operation. Work crews were handpicked from among a pool of idle UDA foot soldiers, and a nice nest egg was set up for the local UDA command with the addition of two or three ghost workers to the payroll. All went peacefully until Trevor's supervisor decided to rock the boat.

"He gets the brilliant idea of standing up to McClatchey by taking the ghosts off the (employment) rolls. When the pay packets didn't come in, McClatchey sends his second-in-command round to the office. He walks in, starts up a chainsaw, and, without a word, saws a desk right in half. He then puts the saw up to the neck of one of my coworkers and very calmly asks. 'Where are those other pay packets?' So the ghosts went back on the payroll."

Soon the hard men advanced to the next stage of crime syndicalism—collusion. In the 1980s, the chieftains of the various factions, while still publicly committed to one another's annihilation, came to a series of very private understandings: recognition of one another's free enterprise zones, joint administration of the rackets, even "integrated" crews of Loyalists and Republicans working side by side at construction sites. It gave rise to one of the great ironies of The Troubles: the death toll declined steadily as the commanders realized that their old ways—tit-for-tat murders, city-center bombings, attacks on one another's drinking clubs—were simply bad for business.

But the networks of collusion produced ugly side effects; it suddenly became very difficult to tell who was killing whom whenever the underground peace broke down and a paramilitary leader was assassinated. In the mid-1980s a number of Belfast commanders of the Loyalist UVF began turning up dead, and each time, a Republican faction came forward to claim "credit" for the hits. The story swirling through the underground, however, was that the murders had actually been carried out by thuggish elements in the UDA—the UVF's brethren in the Loyalist camp—with logistical support from the IRA and other Republican groups. The bloodletting had little to do with politics; it was simply a gangland turf war over control of the Belfast protection rackets. By the time the feud was over, the UVF had been decimated, the UDA disgraced, and the paramilitaries, scrambling to save face, announcing that the era of collusion had ended.

In the wake of the scandal, the British stepped up the activities of the antiracketeering police unit, C13, a special task force devoted to cracking the paramilitaries by going after their hidden bank assets, cooked business books, and dummy corporations. The newly reconstituted war on crime got under way with great fanfare. With regularity, C13 proclaimed victory after victory against the underworld, the shutting down of illegal drinking clubs, whole wagonfuls of arrests. Left unsaid in the press releases was that those arrested were primarily paramilitary grunts or "ordinary decent criminals," rarely the hard men. Nevertheless, in the early 1990s the British claimed to be on the verge of crushing the "gangsters," just as they had been on the verge of crushing the "terrorists" for more than two decades.

This was not a view shared by a middle-aged man—I will call him Richard—whom I met last summer. For days I had discreetly searched for a businessman willing to talk about the current state of Belfast's protection rackets. Only Richard, the owner of a retail business with about ten employees, had agreed. When he ushered me into his private office in downtown Belfast, Richard was gracious, offered me cigarettes and coffee, but continued to stare at me with a haunted, vaguely sad expression, as if he would have much preferred I simply leave.

"I can tell you from direct experience that everything the (C13) authorities say is fantasy," he told me. "The situation isn't better; it's far worse. Used to be the paras would send someone around the shop, hit me up for forty, fifty quid—say it was for the prisoners' welfare fund or the war orphan fund or some damned thing. Today, it is a mafia, as professional a mafia as any you will find in the world. Today they have accountants who come in, look over your books, decide what you can pay, and bill you accordingly. You get a phone call: 'We've put you down for an annual donation of £4,500, payable in quarterly installments; we'll send a lad around tomorrow to collect the first installment.' And when the lad shows up I have the money waiting right here. If I didn't my shop would be blown up, or I would be killed, or my workers would be shot—maybe all three."

When I mentioned the British government's claim of great progress in breaking the rackets, that they've persuaded a number of businessmen to step forward and identify their tormentors, Richard laughed.

"An absolute bluff. Where are these businessmen? Where are the trials that are putting the big (racketeer) men behind bars? They don't exist. I've known three men here in Belfast who refused to pay (protection). They're dead now. I've known several men who have gone to C13, and C13 has told them, 'Work with us, we'll set up a sting, and we'll do it in a way they'll never trace it back to you.' I mean, these (C13) idiots think they're dealing with punters, have absolutely no concept of the stranglehold the paras have going here. If any of those businessmen had agreed (to cooperate on a sting), they'd have been dead before suppertime."

I asked whether, as the paramilitaries claimed, collusion had ended. Richard laughed again. "Let me put it this way. A while back, I was paying out £8,000 a year, £4,000 to the (Provisional) IRA, £4,000 to the UDA. One day I get a call from the IRA saying they're raising my annual contribution to £4,300. A few days later, the UDA calls: 'We're raising you to £4,300.' What does that tell you? They're all the same: IRA, UDA, UVF, INLA, they're all just ribs running off the same spine."

Before I left, Richard showed me the loaded rifle he kept in a closet just behind his desk. He handled it gingerly, seeming both awed and frightened by the feel of it in his hands.

"I'll tell you this," he said. "If the politicians sit down tomorrow and end this thing, nothing will change. The paras are into it for the money now. If peace comes tomorrow, that's when you'll see what this is really all about—and that's when the real troubles start."

Today, it is only natural that people have again started to talk of peace in Northern Ireland. The December 1995 agreement between Ireland and Britain was designed to let formal talks with Sinn Fein begin, an overture the Loyalist paramilitaries have vowed to sabotage. Their point was underscored by a whole new wave of random killings of Catholics as well as a bungled attempt to smuggle in a gigantic cache of explosives and Kalashnikov rifles. This confluence—greater intimations of peace accompanied by greater violence—has made Belfast more schizophrenic than ever. In the city center, the patina of normal life is zealously maintained, as if by appearing to be just one more midsize European city it can be made so. There are Pizza Huts and Burger Kings, and the pedestrian arcades are crowded with shoppers at all hours. Whenever The Troubles intrude on this pacific scene, the authorities immediately adopt a policy of aggressive normality; even before the smoke at a bomb site clears, it seems, legions of masons, glaziers, and scaffolders swarm in to perform instant cosmetic surgery on the scars.

In the ghettos, by contrast, nothing much has changed. Raymond McCord continues to get death threats. The Loyalist paramilitaries, shattered and disgraced by the mob war of the late 1980s, outwitted and isolated by Gerry Adams's peace initiative, have roared back to life. For many in the UDA, the fact that it was their men who walked into the Rising Sun in Greysteel and gunned down unarmed civilians is a point of pride; it proves they are, once again, a fighting force to be reckoned with. For many in the IRA, Thomas Begley's devastating bomb on the Shankill Road is a welcome symbol, a reminder that they have not tired, that they will not be appeased.

When I asked Jackie, the UDA man, what the future holds, he was upbeat.

"People have been coming back to the organization in droves. It's like the (bombing on) Shankill Road and (former British prime minister) Major's dealing with the IRA was a wake-up call: 'Look, we're being sold down the river and we're all just sittin' here takin' it.' The entire community seems more united, more committed than it's been in years."

What Jackie left unsaid is that the recent events have also enabled the UDA to momentarily shed its gangster image in the Protestant community and reapply the patriotic cloak to its underworld fund-raising tactics. For Jackie and the other Belfast hard men, all news—the massacre of innocents, the suggestion of peace—is good news, for it is all convertible into reasons to keep fighting, to keep raising money for the cause.

Talking with Jackie reminded me of a conversation I'd had with Martin, the IRA commander, a few months earlier, before the October slaughter, before the renaissance of the Loyalist paramilitaries. We'd been discussing the IRA's financial outlook, and Martin had admitted that money was very tight just then. He blamed the situation on the worldwide recession but was confident that once the international economy improved, so would the IRA's war capabilities.

He was almost certainly right. Today, the IRA brings in nearly $10 million a year from the shadow economy. As the antiracketeering specialists in C13 have concentrated on closing their drinking clubs and business fronts, the Provisionals have diversified their operations into a bewildering array of money-generating schemes, everything from the penny-ante selling of contraband cigarette lighters on Belfast streets, to video- and computer-game piracy, to smuggling bovine antibiotics into Europe from cut-rate labs in Brazil. According to police, they've also expanded into the counterfeit designer-jean business and have a lucrative sideline with antiques stolen in the Irish Republic and resold at antiques fairs in the British Midlands. The IRA has truly become the world's first multinational guerrilla conglomerate.

And it has increasingly become a legal conglomerate, beyond the reach of C13 or any police force to dismantle. A cooperative of some 300 taxis on the Falls Road that are owned and operated by the Provisionals in west Belfast grosses approximately $1 million a year, a sum reported to and taxed by the British government. Whatever "dirty" money raised from the Belfast protection and extortion rackets that is not needed for immediate operating expenses is smuggled into the Irish Republic, laundered through one of an estimated three dozen IRA-owned pubs around Dublin, then deposited in legal bank accounts.

All of which means the Provisionals no longer have to live the hand-to-mouth existence of most guerrilla groups; through prudent financial planning and entrepreneurial acumen, they have achieved long-term fiscal security, a solid base of assets and investments to draw on—the estimates range to as much as $60 million—an endowment fund for the waging of future war.

"Fact is," Martin said, "a lot of our money now is coming from legitimate sources and there's no way the Brits can touch it. So now they can't bleed us to death and they can't starve us to death. That's why we're going to win."

But perhaps they have already won. As long as the British remain and the Northern Ireland issue stays unsolved, the IRA and its paramilitary brethren have not only a rationale for existence but a financial fount that keeps the underground economy flourishing and keeps them clothed, fed, and armed. If the British ever leave, the hard men lose not only that subsidy but also their incentive for working together to uphold the underground nonaggression pact; they will then have to go beyond slaughtering the innocent to prove their patriotism, and start killing one another in earnest in the long-anticipated final battle for primacy in Northern Ireland. In a certain grotesque fashion, then, the British pursuit of an "economic solution" has actually brought a measure of peace. And defying the old maxim that war destroys economies, this war has created one, rock-solid so long as the British stay and the flow of blood is kept to a steady trickle.

At the end of our meeting, I posed an idea to Martin. If it were really the intention of the IRA to hasten a British departure from Northern Ireland, I said, perhaps there was a better way than renewing the "armed struggle"—or even sending out peace feelers. Perhaps the most effective tactic would be for the IRA to buy some airtime in London and thank the British taxpayers for their twenty-five years of financial largesse. Could anything sicken the British more? Martin was greatly amused by the idea.

"It will always be IRA policy that the British have to leave Northern Ireland." He smiled. "But maybe it's better they don't leave just yet."

Scott Anderson is the author of The Man Who Tried to Save the World: The Dangerous Life and Mysterious Disappearance of Fred Cuny, The 4 O'Clock Murders, *coauthor of* War Zones: Voices from the World's Killing Grounds, *and a recipient of the Pope Foundation Award for investigative journalism.*

* * *

The Chill of Autumn Charity

It isn't easy being human.

THE CHILD HAD A SMALL ROUND DIRTY FACE AND BRIGHT HOPE-
ful eyes. He had only one opening line as he hung around the car
park.

"It'll be Hallowe'en soon," he would say as if he were delivering some joyful news. It was a bit like some terrible Hollywood
frenetic saying "Hi folks, it's party time."

Most people looked at it all glumly. They knew it was going to
be Hallowe'en soon, they had seen pumpkins in the shops and
witches and masks and nuts and grapes and games, and their own
children wanted all of them all the time. They didn't want to be
reminded of it all by someone who looked as if he had been sent
over by Central Casting to play the role of Urchin.

He had his hands in his pockets, not out in any kind of request.
His jumper was not the kind you *could* shoot straws through, it
looked more as if someone had. He had canvas shoes on that had
once been white and had laces. He looked six, but he might have
been eight. He looked as if he should have been at school, but he
might have had a day off.

He wasn't a bit disappointed with the lack of response to his reminder of festivals to come. You felt he had been used to people

323

being downbeat about marvelous things like Hallowe'en and all it implied. "Don't talk to me about Hallowe'en," said a woman struggling with shopping and trying to open the boot of her car at the same time. "And stay away from my car will you. I've had quite enough already without having to meet someone like you at the end of the day."

He was remarkably philosophical about this and moved politely a few steps away so that she didn't need to fear his turning into a mini-vandal.

"It'll be here any day now," he said full of optimism.

"It will," she said grimly. But her voice had lost its edge. So far he hadn't scraped the side of her car with a penknife, whined at her for money, or called her any abusive names.

"I don't have any change," she said in a softer tone.

"Ah, that doesn't matter," he said.

It was a civilized exchange in a way, but she couldn't let it go. "You should be at school instead of out here in the cold," she said. "You'll grow up knowing nothing." He nodded as if it were only too possible. She drove away disturbed by him, looking back at him in her driving mirror.

A man with a weaving kind of a walk came in to the car park and fortunately directed himself at the passenger seat of a car. He had some considerable difficulty with the key.

"Will I open it for you, Mister?" the boy said.

"Are you out of your mind? Don't touch it," said the man, who seemed to have sobered up very fast at the thought.

"It'll be Hallowe'en soon," the boy said.

"Call it by its proper name, it's All Hallows' Eve," said the drunk, who still couldn't open the door.

"It's what?"

"Say it, say it, nobody can speak the language any more. Say it, boy, for God's sake." He was getting purple in the face and the child moved back. The wife of the drunk, stern and righteous and without the air of someone who was going to be much fun for the evening, arrived.

"Aren't you in the car yet? God almighty it's a male nurse

'round the clock that you need, and what are you roaring at that *gurrier* for, drawing him on us?" Tight-lipped and resentful at the hand which had been dealt to her in life she swept past, not giving the child the chance to remind her of upcoming celebrations.

A priest gave him tenpence and told him not to be out begging. "I wasn't begging, Father. I was only saying it would soon be…"

"I know but it's the same thing."

He looked at the tenpence thoughtfully. "I suppose it is in a way, Father."

A young mother with a toddler came into his view. He addressed his remarks to the small boy in the blue leggings. He told him of the nearness of the big day. The mother lifted her baby up into her arms. "He doesn't talk much," she said.

"Ah no, I suppose he wouldn't much," the boy consoled her in case she was feeling anxious about this.

"If I give you fivepence will you go away?" she said. He seemed nonplussed.

"Go away where?" he asked.

"Just away until I put Aidan into his car seat."

"All right," he said and started to walk off.

"Here," she said and gave him the coin.

"Thank you," he said.

"And go home like a good boy and don't be annoying people," she said.

"I wasn't annoying people."

"No, but you know what I mean."

He did. He went to the edge of the car park until they had gone.

In half an hour he had got tenpence from a priest, fivepence from a young mother, a lecture from a drunk, an apology for not having change from a busy shopper. He had been told that he was begging, that he was annoying people, that he was to move out so that he couldn't damage the cars, that he was a *gurrier*, and also to go away.

Nobody had shared his enthusiasm about Hallowe'en. Even if they had given him money to help him buy some of its essentials.

There was charity in that car park, but it had a chilly autumn feel about it.

Born in Dalkey, a village outside Dublin, Maeve Binchy is a novelist, short story writer, playwright, and journalist who has worked as a columnist and editor for the Irish Times. *She is the author of many best-selling books, including* Circle of Friends *and* Tara Road. *She lives in Dalkey with her husband, Gordon Snell.*

✦ ✦ ✦

Annie and the Bishop

They were dancing the oldest jig in the world.

JUST BEFORE YOU TURN OFF THE MAIN ROAD TOWARDS
Mullaghmore interpretative centre, now one of the most symbolic
sites in Ireland, there is a ruined old church in Kilnaboy that is, in
its way, yet more powerfully symbolic. Roofless and open to the elements, it has yet survived the centuries and its grey, hand-cut
stones embody the unadorned endurance of the Irish Catholic
church, its gravity and its ascetic beauty. Just over the doorway,
though, is a sheela-na-gig, a grotesquely sexual and sternly obscene
figure of a woman exposing herself. The same monks who prayed
and fasted here placed this figure of terrifying womanhood at the
centre of their church, a reminder, perhaps, of the flesh they had to
fear and shun.

Annie Murphy is the Irish Catholic church's sheela-na-gig
made flesh, an avenging spirit risen up from the dark of the celibate mind to haunt and to terrify, to embody all those dangerous
thoughts subdued by prayer and fasting. She is their worst nightmare come true, a figure from the mediaeval witch-hunters' man-
uals: wild and indiscreet, loose-tongued and lusty. She has written
a book [*Forbidden Fruit*] about her love affair with a bishop, a book
that is full not just of sex, but of the body itself, of beard rash and

327

high blood pressure, of colitis and groin infections, of cancers and amputations. Of all the ills and sins that flesh is heir to.

In Irish folklore, the priest's mistress is a figure of almost supernatural evil. One old Gaelic proverb tells of "three who will never see the light of Paradise":

> *The angel of pride,*
> *The unbaptised child,*
> *And a priest's concubine.*

The angel of pride is Satan. The priest's concubine (*ceile shagairt*) is associated with him. So, too, is the buried child, the forgotten child, the child interred at night in unconsecrated ground. For some true believers, *no doubt*, Annie Murphy and her son, her long-buried child, will still be associated with the satanic. Her book will be not just an act of personal betrayal, but an act of sacrilege.

Both of these roles—sheela-na-gig to terrify the Irish church, and desecrator of the faithful's ideas of the sacred—are ones which Annie Murphy is happy to play in her book. They are, after all, starring roles, big parts in a drama that has been played for centuries. To describe making love in the bishop's palace in Killarney, to describe distracting the bishop while he is saying Mass, to mention his cross and ring in the context of furtive coupling, is to be one of the two main players, not in the kitchen tragedy of Annie and Eamonn, but in the grand opera of the clash of eternal forces. It is to play Body to his Soul, avenging angel to his tarnished saint, world, flesh, and devil to his Father, Son, and Holy Ghost. It is a lot more glorious than to be poor, wounded Annie.

Yet the real story, the story that comes through so painfully in her book once you get used to the strange circumstances of this love affair, is ineffably ordinary. Take away the one sensational aspect of the story—that the man involved is a Catholic bishop, sworn to celibacy and preaching a strict code of sexual morality—and what you are left with is a story that life has told over and over, until it is blue in the face.

A younger, more vulnerable woman meets an older, more powerful man. He dazzles her with his power, his confidence, his com-

mand of the world. They fall in love and begin a sexual relationship. He promises her nothing, but he doesn't need to, for hurt and
abused as she is, she is more than capable of making him into a
promise to herself. She gives him pleasure, excitement, and adora-
tion. He gives her the first two but probably not the third. She
thinks of the future, he thinks of the present, floating on the delusion that he can have the best of all worlds. He makes her pregnant. The baby forces choices on her, choices which, because he is
a man and a powerful one, he doesn't believe he has to make. He
behaves badly, hypocritically, politically. It ends in tears: first hers,
then, after many years, his.

Take away the thrill of discovering that bishops as a class are no
better than many other men, and what remains is the fact that they
are no worse. Little would have to change in Annie Murphy's
book if Eamonn Casey were a prominent politician, or a judge, or
just an ordinary married man indulging in a passionate but
doomed side-affair which he will shake off when it becomes too
threatening to his marriage and his settled place in the world.
Desecration lies in the treacherous, abusive things that people do
to each other, not in the fact that they are done in a bishop's palace
rather than a bedsit.

We were promised some shocking revelations: that the affair
lasted longer than was previously believed and continued after the
birth of their son, Peter, that it was conducted for a period in a car
parked in a gravel pit in Dublin; that they slept together again in a
New York hotel in 1991. But given the initial premise—that an
Irish bishop had an affair and a child—and the inevitable decep-
tions and moral contortions that flow from it, these are not shocking at all. They come with the territory, and the territory is a well-
worn ground of deceit and double-dealing, a landscape that is
there whether bishops choose to tread on it or not.

What is actually much more striking in Annie Murphy's story
is the shock of the familiar. The view from the bishop's bed is a
new angle on the sumptuousness and luxury of life at the top of
the clerical ladder. There is nothing shocking in the notion that
some bishops live in palaces, eat like kings, and behave like

princelings, that they are often waited-on, flattered, and pampered. But this is seldom described, because outsiders do not get close enough to do so. Annie Murphy is one outsider who did, who became privy to a world whose sensual delights may exclude sex but include the best of food and drink, the finest places to live, the swankiest cars, clothes brought straight from Harrods. She is a privileged reporter, and the value of her testimony lies at least as much in its description of things that are taken for granted by the faithful, as of things that will shock and horrify them.

If there is an extraordinary dimension to this story of ordinary things, it is not the clash of sacred and secular, but the clash of Ireland and Irish-America. Annie Murphy's family could have been invented by Eugene O'Neill, such is its archetypal drama of lace-curtain Irish respectability riddled with alcoholism, subdued violence, and the hard bitterness of exile. John Steinbeck looked at the Irish-Americans and said that they "do have a despairing gaiety, but they also have a dour and brooding ghost that rides on their shoulders and peers in on their thoughts." Annie Murphy embodies both the despairing gaiety and the brooding ghost, with a view of the world that is often wildly comic and often haunted by nameless forebodings.

Her love for Eamonn Casey seems inextricable from her love for Ireland, an exile's love of the dream homeland. She is in love with the place as much as with the man. The sea, the mountains, the flowers are characters in her love affair. She brings to that affair both the illusory longing and the driven ambition of Irish-America, both the rosy view of Ireland and the all-American drive to make the world conform to her view of it.

In many ways, Eamonn Casey is as typically Irish as she is Irish-American. Energetic, garrulous, at home with the world, but also full of evasions and denials. In certain ways, she is more ambitious than he is, for she wants the world to change, wants a clerical princeling to come down off his throne and take charge of her messy life, while he wants things to be the same only more so. He wants everything he has and something else as well—the joy of sex, maybe the comfort of being loved rather than adored. He just has to make room in his busy life for another pleasure. She has to re-invent the world, make it conform to her desires. It is a clash of mother country and restless exile as much as it is a clash of Mother Church and restless desire.

As in a Greek play, the clash of these incompatible but ineluctable forces can produce only tragedy. The directness which the Irish learned in America cannot communicate with the evasions of life at home. The elaborate cathedral of airy self-justifications which he builds on the restless foundations of his desire is demolished by her impatience. The ambition of her desire, the vision of a future in which she and Eamonn and Peter will live happily ever after, is thwarted by his ability to live with all his contradictions in a never-ending present rather than have to face the hard choices for the future.

The tragedy, strangely, is at its sharpest when the story is most comic. The awful events—the abandonment of a son and the humiliation of an important public man—are awful only because there

"Have you thought of what you are going to be?" [the nun] asked with a certain coyness. Almost flirtatious was she. Oh, to please her and wind one's way into her hard heart and be invited to do little favours for her, like carrying her books, or opening or closing a window or cleaning the blackboards, oh, oh, to be her slave!

"A nun," I said, quicker and more soulfully than I had ever said aught. The thought of a vocation danced before me; like a banner, the word waved and with it the vision of a young postulant with a see-through veil, one foot in the world and the other sinking deeper and deeper into the mists of spirituality, towards the "never to be forgotten day" when one would take final vows and be cut off from the world outside, from family, from pleasure, from men, from earthly love, from buses and shops and cafeterias, from life.

—Edna O'Brien, *Mother Ireland*

is a glimmer that things might have been otherwise. What is most wretched about the abandonment of Peter is that there are times when there is another sort of abandonment, times when Annie and Eamonn seem to have abandoned themselves to a kind of exuberant madness in which their laughter mingled into one wild cascade.

There are episodes in their story during which the absurdity of their situation is funny instead of sordid, during which they seem to have been able to stand back and look at themselves and collapse in a helpless laughter.

That kind of removal from oneself, that release into a zone where nothing matters, is what lovers call love and saints call a state of grace. Though the faithful may think it blasphemous, it is nevertheless possible that in those moments of wild laughter, Eamonn Casey and Annie Murphy were in love and in a state of grace at the same time.

If that is so, then it is also possible that the real sacrilege in relation to Annie Murphy's story would be not to allow for those moments when the sacred and the secular, the soul and the body, the monk and the sheela-na-gig, sex and holiness, were, however fleetingly, one and the same thing. Because the story is so public, so symbolic, it is easy to overlook this precious intimacy at its core, the sacred humanity without which there would be no tragedy.

Tragedies are supposed to teach us something, and what is to be learned from the tragedy of these hurt people is that a world which insists on neat divisions between the holy and the unholy, between men and women, between courage and hypocrisy, is one which creates tragedies.

Brecht replied to the adage "unhappy the land that has no heroes" with the correction "unhappy the land that needs heroes." Equally, unhappy the Church that needs heroes, that is so threatened and terrified by the revelation that within its upper ranks there exist ordinary human desires and ordinary human hypocrisies. All Annie Murphy has really done is to state the obvious. That she can gain so much notice from doing so is the fault of those who have denied the obvious for too long.

William Butler Yeats stated the obvious more elegantly many years ago in a poem called "Crazy Jane Talks with the Bishop":

A woman can be proud and stiff
When on love intent;
But Love has pitched his mansion in
The place of excrement;
For nothing can be sole or whole
That has not been rent.

Whether the bishop listened to Crazy Jane or not, Yeats does not tell us. It would be nice to think, though, that some bishops might listen to the strange, abandoned laughter of Annie Murphy and Eamonn Casey before they became hateful and afraid.

Fintan O'Toole has written extensively on politics, theater, and current affairs and is a columnist and drama critic for The Irish Times. *In 1993 he received the AT Cross Award for Supreme Contribution to Irish Journalism.* Black Hole, Green Card: The Disappearance of Ireland, *from which this piece was excerpted, is a follow-up to his acclaimed book,* A Mass for Jesse James: A Journey Through 1980s Ireland. *He is also the author of two collections of essays entitled* The Lie of the Land: Irish Identities *and* Shakespeare Is Hard but So Is Life.

The Unsettled People

*The Tinkers, better known as travellers, exist at
the boundaries of the Irish mind.*

When I was a child I remember going hawking the houses
one day with my mother. It was freezing cold and people kept
banging the doors in our faces. If anyone gave something they
wouldn't speak to us: we weren't real people to them.

The door of the chapel was always open so we went in and my
mother lit a candle. As she was down on her knees praying with
the child in her arms, I looked at the statue of Our Lady with the
Child Jesus in a sort of a shawl. I looked at my mother and I wondered why people should be treated like this and I said to myself,
"I'll make a better life when I grow up—I won't have to beg, I
won't have to be pitiful-looking to get charity just to survive."

Well, I wonder sometimes did I make a better life. I never really wanted anything for myself but I wanted things for the children, a warm place for them in the winter and a clean bed and
enough food. My older children got no education, they lost out
on everything because we were hunted from place to place. Young
people are completely lost today if they can't read or write, they
can't manage computers or anything and their traditional way of
life is gone.

My two youngest children got a better chance: they started

school at the right age with the settled children and they're getting on great. I'd like to be able to afford to send them to college. But they will still always be travellers. I would like all the travelling children to have self-confidence and to grow up proud of what they are because they are very special people with their own traditions and their own way of life. But the way they've been treated and discriminated against, they grow up ashamed of their own parents.

It used to be that the one time you heard about travellers was when they did wrong; nothing about us was ever taught in schools and when children came by our camp they would just run by—they were afeared of the travellers. Even today some people are afeared to come near us and chat with us—it's a fear of the unknown.

But the last few years have been a great point in the travellers' history. When I first started speaking it was very hard to get other travellers to speak as well or to take my place the day I wouldn't get out but now there are loads of travellers well able and willing to speak up for themselves. Our own group, Mincéir Misli, is working for travellers' rights and we have help from settled people and priests and nuns who want us to help ourselves—not to be doing things for us—and that's another great change. And today the newspapers and the radio and television are very fair to us.

We are a different people. There'll always be travellers who want to keep going when they see the summer and they feel lonely. If I'm in the one camp now I'll sort of get tired and I'll move the trailer up about thirty yards and I'll feel that I'm after shifting. We shouldn't be bullied to settle down. I would love a house in the wintertime, but I'd like to be free to go off if I took it into my head maybe to go to Belfast for a couple of months. We are a different people but what we want most of all is a better understanding with the settled people: that we should understand them and that they should understand us—the travelling people.

Nan Joyce, born into poverty, grew into a proud and independent spokesperson for her people, the travelers. She played a key role in the campaign for travellers' rights and has became a prominent and articulate voice among those who have demanded justice for the travelling people. Her book, Traveller: An Autobiography by Nan Joyce, *from which this story was excerpted, was reissued in 2000 under the title* My Life on the Road.

MARTIN DILLON

The Last Confession

He's damned if he does, damned if he doesn't.

THE MOST HARROWING ROLE OF A PRIEST IS TO PERFORM THE
Last Rites for a dying person, and watch life ebb away. During the
course of conflict in Ireland, priests have often been at the scene of
tragedies, ministering to the injured and dying. Everyone remem-
bers the television images of Father Edward Daly waving a hand-
kerchief as one of the Bloody Sunday victims was being carried
across a Derry street as paratroopers continued to fire into the
Bogside. His was a brave, selfless act, performed in the midst of danger, yet other events in priestly life have been more shocking and
have never made the headlines. Priests have been summoned to a
lonely hillside or a derelict house to hear the last confession of
someone condemned to die by the IRA. The reason why this had
remained a guarded secret is because of the dilemmas it presents for
the Catholic Church in Ireland, and the risks it poses for individual priests, should they break an imposed silence. Few priests are
prepared to discuss that side of the conflict, first because what
passes between priest and penitent in the confessional must be kept
secret, and second, they know that even priests are not immune to
bullets. Some in the Catholic Church feel that if a priest who had
been in such a situation were to compromise the executioners, the
IRA would no longer allow their victims a last confession.

Two priests spoke to me about their experiences in this shad-
owy world of religion and violence, and their experiences highlighted the acute problems facing all those summoned to perform
the Last Rites or hear a final confession. To protect them, and at
their request, I will change their names. They did not, at any time
during their discussions with me, violate the secrecy of the confessional, or act in any way to compromise their priestly vows.

Father Pat is a sprightly curate in his early seventies with a dis-
arming smile and sharp features creased with lines that convey a
troubled soul. The weekly queue outside his confessional implies
that he is popular with sinners, and understanding of sin. He is a
priest of the old school, who believes that the faithful need the
sacraments of confession and the Eucharist to keep them on the
straight and narrow. He has watched what he describes as the
"modern disease" of occasional visits to church and a commitment to materialism, and he has also observed that young people
have lost respect for all authority, and are easily trapped in a spiral
of violence.

"The paramilitaries control the kids in this area," he declared.
"The paramilitaries have usurped God. They declare that they've
the power of life and death. How can someone like me tell them
that this is a falsehood? In reality, it is hard to argue otherwise.
People have stormed out of the church during some of my ser-
mons when I condemned the IRA. What sort of message does that
send out to the young?"

Father Pat's face was drawn in anguish when he described what
he called the "crude justification" of violence. "Seemingly intelligent people have said to me that war can be just. They don't see
the real destructive character of violence and how it dehumanizes
everyone. How they can see God in that is beyond me. They trot
out these old clichés about fighting injustice, and I tell them you
can do that effectively without killing the innocent. I ask them
why they abdicate responsibility for intellect, and why they cannot
see that the voice of reason has a more plaintive and persuasive
sound than that of anger."

As he talked, he drew heavily on his pipe. "You see, I am not blind to the power of the IRA argument, particularly when delivered in a moral and political vacuum. Attitudes to religion are changing while society itself is not moving on politically. Put the decline in moral standards against the decline in political standards, and you've a dangerous cocktail. I condemn all violence from wherever it arises. When the British government acts in a fashion which implies there is a dirty war and killing is justifiable, my crusade is weak. That's been one of the problems throughout the conflict...neither the paramilitaries nor the military hold the high moral ground. When agencies of the state act in a fashion which flouts the basic principles of justice, the chasm opens wider. Sometimes I feel torn between two warring factions—the IRA and elements of the state who act like paramilitaries. And, there's that old gut tribal instinct that draws you towards the Republican argument and the history of injustice under British rule. God, you have to get hold of that one, like the dentist, and tear it out before the rest becomes infected." He paused. Then he said, "IRA men go to confession, you know."

———————✳———————

It was, after all, another Irishman, Jonathan Swift, who invented, in *Gulliver's Travels*, the idea of a flying island, Laputa. Ireland is now a sort of flying island hovering between a number of different contexts, often flying blind with no one too sure of how the controls work anymore. It touches down now in the Bronx, now in Bonn, now in Britain, seeking connections with a set of overlapping places, but always taking off again into its own outer spaces.

—Fintan O'Toole,
Black Hole, Green Card:
The Disappearance of Ireland

I nodded as he looked at me, expecting disbelief. "Of course, I cannot reveal anything that has happened in the confessional, but can you imagine what is in my head?"

I remained silent, knowing that it was not a question to which he required an answer.

"The minds of people prepared to kill and justify it to themselves are tortured minds, almost detached from the soul. I don't mean the soul is not there, but the connection is damaged. I alone can't repair it. I can only restate the Christian message about love, forgiveness, and the sin of killing. The leaders of society must embrace those principles so that society's own damaged soul can be repaired and gradually the souls of the tortured minds."

Again he paused, then began quietly, almost whispering, to address the main subject of my interview. "I was sitting in here late one evening…just reading…and the doorbell rang. I hadn't scheduled any appointments though I always allowed for the fact that there might be an emergency. I opened the front door, and there was a young man there with the collar of his coat pulled up in an attempt to hide his face. He was about eighteen. He was clearly agitated, if not embarrassed. I said, 'Come in, Michael,' because it was cold outside, and I was wearing my pyjamas, slippers, and an old pullover. As soon as I mentioned his name he backed away. 'It's nothin' t' do with me, Father,' he told me. 'You're wanted.'"

Father Pat was handed a piece of paper containing an address.

"Instinctively, I knew this wasn't a normal request, and I mentally prepared myself for the worst. I knew Michael was in the Provisionals, so maybe one of their people was injured. As I walked towards the particular street, I tried to convince myself that it was simply a request for a chat. Sometimes the IRA leaders in the area would talk to me if there was need for a mediator with the security forces."

Father Pat's journey on foot took him to a street in which he knew all the inhabitants.

"There were no street-lamps working, and as I approached the corner, another person known to me as a member of the IRA, stopped me. He grabbed my arm and led me to a house which was at that time uninhabited."

As Father Pat entered the house, he was bundled into the hallway and the door was slammed shut.

"I was confronted by a masked man armed with a pistol. I'd seen people on the streets with guns but when one is being pointed at you in a confined space, it reminds you of your mortality. 'You've a job here to do, Father, and be quick about it,' he said and pointed to the top of the staircase where another masked man was positioned. I knew the voice behind the balaclava. When you've sat behind that confessional screen for so many years, you develop an innate recognition of voices. I stared into his eyes and he pushed me towards the stairs. 'What do you mean by a job?' I asked. 'You'll find out,' he replied. He laughed and told me it was my kind of job—'It's your kind of business,' he told me.''

Father Pat was escorted into a dingy bathroom where a middle-aged man was tied to a chair with two armed and masked men on either side of him.

"One of them said, 'He wants to make his confession.' There was something sick about the way they addressed me. One of them said, 'He's already made one to us and this is his last. You've got five minutes, Father. Don't try to be heroic or we'll kill both of you. Just get on with it.'''

Father Pat's eyes narrowed in anguish. He got up and paced the room, wringing his hands and marshalling the courage to describe the episode.

"It's hard," he said sitting down, his eyes lowered. "I froze when the bathroom door closed, I was suddenly dealing with evil and not just talking about it. The man in the chair was one of my parishioners. I remember looking at the bath filled with water wondering what they had done to him. He was stripped to a pair of wet underpants. His hair and body were wet so they'd obviously been holding him under the water. Looking back I observed so many things in a matter of seconds or perhaps I now just imagine that was so. Perhaps, because I have gone over it so many times in my head, I know so much that I didn't know then. He was badly bruised and his eyes were so swollen he could hardly see me. My first thought was whether I could get him out of there when the bathroom door opened. 'Remember, Father,' one of the gunmen told me, 'any funny business and you're both for it. Anyway, there's somebody out the back even if you could get him out the window.'''

The window, as Father Pat discovered, opened at the top but

not enough to allow a grown person to get through it. The victim was incapable of walking.

"I put my arm around him," said Father Pat. "It seemed the only loving thing I could do. His lips were swollen and I heard him murmur, 'Please help me, Father.'"

Father Pat's eyes filled with tears as he recalled that plea, and he couldn't go on for some minutes. I sat in silence waiting for him to compose himself.

"No one can know how I felt. There were two victims in that room, and one was about to die. I whispered in his ear that God was with him. It was as if I was saying something I knew was not true at a time when all he wanted was God to set him free. I asked him if he wanted me to hear his confession and he replied that he did. The thing that struck me most was that the sacrament of confession seemed to have the effect of transforming that room. 'I'm going to die. Isn't that right, Father?' I could only put my arm round him. He knew the inevitability of it and God was with him…of that I'm convinced. I wasn't so sure that God was with me. I felt so helpless. Leaving that room was a nightmare to live with."

On his way out of the house, Father Pat pleaded with the terrorist whose voice he had recognized. "This is against the law of God," Father Pat told him.

"You look after the law of God," replied the terrorist, "and we'll look after our business."

I asked Father Pat if that same terrorist had ever returned to the confessional.

"It's not a question I wish to answer."

"Why?"

"Because there are certain things only I can deal with," he replied. "However, I can say, and this has nothing to do with the confessional, I believe in my heart that the IRA killed an innocent man."

I asked Father Pat whether it was the duty of the priest to report his suspicions about the identity of the killers, and if a priest should answer a call to such a hideous event.

"For a priest, the confessional is not just that box in the Church. It extends into all aspects of life. In a conflict like this, a priest cannot be the judge, jury, or law-enforcer. Those roles would make everyone feel that a priestly confidence was worthless. I can comfort the dying, I can offer God's absolution, and I can confront violence with Christianity, but the moment I step outside of that framework, my role as a priest becomes compromised. Some of your readers will say that is a cop-out, and I would understand such a reaction. What is the alternative?"

I asked him whether excommunication was a real alternative. "The old chestnut! That's an outdated practice. Even Rome considers it that. It would have no effect on people who are convinced that what they are doing is right. It couldn't effectively be administered and to apply it in Ireland would mean having to apply it throughout the world. That would bring the Church firmly into the political arena and where would it stop? The Church knows there are conflicts in parts of the world where the use of violence is not easy to condemn. It's Protestants who keep referring to excommunication as though the Church could easily resort to that against people guilty of promoting heresies. The Church can only condemn the use of violence, not banish those who advocate or use it."

I referred him to the Church's Code of Canon Law issued by the Vatican in 1983, and in particular Canon 1397 dealing with offences against human life and liberty, which states:

> One who commits murder, or who by force, or by fraud abducts, imprisons, mutilates, or gravely wounds a person, is to be punished, according to the gravity of the offence with the deprivations and provisions mentioned in Can. 1336. In the case of murder of one of those persons mentioned in Can. 1370, the offender is punished with the penalties there prescribed.

Father Pat pointed out that Canon 1336 dealt with people in religious life and that the penalties included transfer to another office, dismissal from the clerical state, or the removal of privileges. These, he said, were expiatory and could affect the offender for a determinate or indeterminate period and were additional to any penalties the law of the country chose to impose.

He smiled at my reference to Canon 1370, went to a bookcase and read the following text from Canon 1370: "A person who used physical force against the Roman Pontiff incurs a *latae sententiae* excommunication. If the offender is a cleric, another penalty, not excluding dismissal from the clerical state, may be added according to the gravity of the crime." In the same canon less rigorous punishments were imposed on anyone who struck a bishop.

I wondered if, in theory, people committing murder effectively excommunicated themselves until such times as they renounced the use of violence.

Father Pat considered. "Hmm…yes, that could well be the case. For example, if someone came to confession, told me they were guilty of murder for political objectives and made it clear that they were likely to do it again, I would refuse them absolution and point out that they were in a state of sin and could not receive the sacraments. That would be a form of excommunication."

I suggested that if the Church pointed out that those in the IRA who were promoting, planning, or guilty of murder were, by their own actions, excommunicated, many people might be deterred from involvement in terrorism.

"No. Categorically, no. Firstly people don't come into confession and say, 'I've just killed a soldier, I would like absolution and I'm likely to kill again.' If someone asks for absolution for such a grave offence, the person is clearly sorry for what they've done,

> Life was fervid, enclosed, and catastrophic. The spiritual food consisted of the crucified Christ. His Passion impinged on every thought, work, deed, and omission, and sometimes in the wild fancifulness of childhood it was as if one caught sight of Him on a hill stretched out upon a Cross betwixt two thieves, with women at the foot of it, gnashing and weeping.
>
> —Edna O'Brien, *Mother Ireland*

and they have the right to absolution. It's not for any priest to interrogate the person to try and discover if they're likely or intent on committing the crime again. The priest will point out that it is one of the most serious sins in the eyes of God and by doing so is telling the person that God will not tolerate murder. By and large, I doubt if many priests find themselves with people confessing to murder or perhaps even making a confession if they are in an organization which promotes violence. There are a lot of people out there who'll one day need the confessional. Perhaps when it's all over, there'll be a lot of hard thinking by some. My advice is 'Don't assume that you'll have the time to repent.' The Church is clear on murder and anyone guilty of it who's been brought up a Catholic should be in no doubt about that."

As I left Father Pat I was in no doubt that his was a tortured soul. Perhaps, if one uses his imagery, the connection between his mind and soul was also frayed and might never be repaired. In his own words, he was "the living victim."

Martin Dillon worked for the BBC in Northern Ireland for eighteen years and has won international acclaim for his nonfiction books about Ireland, including The Shankill Butchers *and* The Dirty War. *He is often called on as one of the foremost authorities on global terrorism. He is co-author of* Robert Maxwell: Israel's Superspy: The Life and Murder of a Media Mogul. *This story was excerpted from his book,* God and the Gun: The Church and Irish Terrorism.

EDNA O'BRIEN

Escape to England

*She joins the great diaspora of those
who have left Mother Ireland.*

LEAVING IRELAND WAS NO WRENCH AT ALL. I TOOK THE MAIL BOAT, like most others, sat up all night, watched the drinking, the spilling, walked the deck, remembered how Mr. Thackeray and Mr. Heinrich Böll had come in by boat to write leisurely about it, remembered the myriad others, natives, who had gone out to forget....

The real quarrel with Ireland began to burgeon in me then; I had thought of how it had warped me, and those around me, and their parents before them, all stooped by a variety of fears—fear of church, fear of *gombeenism*, fear of phantoms, fear of ridicule, fear of hunger, fear of annihilation, and fear of their own deeply in-grained aggression that can only strike a blow at each other, not having the innate authority to strike at those who are higher. Pity arose too, pity for a land so often denuded, pity for a people reluctant to admit that there is anything wrong. That is why we leave. Because we beg to differ. Because we dread the psychological choke. But leaving is only conditional. The person you are is anathema to the person you would like to be.

But time changes everything including our attitude to a place. There is no such thing as a perpetual hatred no more than there is unambiguous states of earthly love. Hour after hour I can think of Ireland, I can imagine without going far wrong what is happening in any one of the little towns by day or by night, can see the tillage and the walled garden, see the spilt porter foam along the counters, I can hear argument and ballads, hear the elevation bell and the prayers for the dead. I can almost tell what any one of my friends might be doing at any hour so steadfast is the rhythm of life there. I open a book, a school book maybe, or a book of superstition, or a book of place names, and I have only to see the names of Ballyhooly or Raheen to be plunged into that world from which I have derived such a richness and an unquenchable grief.

Edna O'Brien is the author of many books, including House of Splendid Isolation, Lantern Slides, A Fanatic Heart, The High Road, *and* The Country Girls Trilogy. *Born and raised in Ireland, she currently lives in London. This piece was excerpted from her book,* Mother Ireland.

PART FIVE

THE LAST WORD

✦ ✦ ✦

Tara

A traveler takes his leave of a country
that has touched his core.

I CAME TO THE HILL OF TARA AS A MAN SHOULD AT SUNSET, AND alone, to say good-bye to Ireland. The sun was low in the west and soon the night mists would fall over the grasslands of Meath. Five broad ways once led to the Hill through all the provinces; but now there is nothing but the wind in the grass and the sound of sheep. Ireland is full of old unhappy things that strangely shake the heart; and this mound of earth is one of them, lonely, remote, and withdrawn like "something left on earth after a judgment day." The figure of St. Patrick, mitred and crozier in hand, stood against the sunset. He made the Sign of the Cross over Ireland. Near him an old stone leaned upward from the grass, the Lia Fail.

And as I stood there in this queerly alive place, memories of Ireland came to me, little happy pictures sharp as in sunlight: the homes of Ireland, the kindness, the laughter, the music, cabins of the West white on the hill, the smell of turf fires, the light throbbing in the sky, lapwings tumbling over wild marsh-land, the stone walls, the green light shining on the edge of peat seams, the wild wind of the moor, and all the little winding roads among the hills.

When my feet first trod Irish soil I felt that I had come to a magic country and now, as I said good-bye, I knew it truly as an

351

enchanted island. That minor note which is like a vibration in the air, something that lives in the light and in the water and in the soil, runs through every Irish thing, but, like the cry of a bat, it is too high to be heard. But a man is conscious of it everywhere.

Some day, I thought, a great Irishman will stand upon this hill and make faith with Ireland. He will take the story of his country in strong hands and give it to the world. He will love the past of Ireland as much as he believes in her future. In him the unhappy Irish trick of looking backward instead of forward will spend itself, and Ireland, sure of her future, will forget old wounds. And this man will do for her what Walter Scott did for Scotland: he will fuse two races and unite his country and make it whole. He will bring to Ireland the love and affection of the world. I like to think of him as a blend of north and south, a mingling of Catholic and Protestant. The southerner in him will watch the past and the northerner will reach forward into the future.

Ireland of the Sorrows is no more. The Ireland of romantic nationalism, the beautiful tragedy queen among nations, has gone, let us hope for ever. Ireland has emerged from the Celtic twilight into a blaze of day. In spite of her ventures, and she has lost no time in proving to the world that she can govern and embark on great enterprises, it may be that she is feeling, perhaps, that disillusion which a sleeper experiences when he awakens from an heroic dream into cold reality. But that will pass. The future is with Ireland. The sun sets, and the Hill grows dark. The shadows have fallen over the fields of Meath. The air is grey with night. St. Patrick rises up over the mounds of Tara, his hand uplifted. And in the silence and darkness I listen again for that hidden music. It is not for my ears. I hear nothing but the night wind in the grass; and I say good-bye to Ireland.

H. V. Morton was born in 1892 and died in 1979 in Cape Town, South Africa. He was the author of many wonderful travel books, including In Search of Ireland, *from which this piece was excerpted.*

By Elgy Gillespie

WHAT YOU NEED TO KNOW

Still lost in the damp Atlantic mist, yet looming large in cyberspace, these days Ireland is no longer lagging in time. It's thriving, swaggeringly youthful, cosmopolitan—and often anything but Catholic and Irish. The hills of Connemara are still green, the dry-stone walls still mossy, but there could be a brand-new villa with a satellite aerial smack dab in the middle. About time, say the locals. Above all, the islanders are confident, and often more prosperous than their English neighbors. The emigrants of the '80s have come home to roost with their new entrepreneurial ways and sophisticated tastes. Prices have risen with the advent of the euro, sometimes shockingly so, and tourism figures have een sliding. Yet Ireland's natural people-pleasing charms are still sung all over the world.

You'll have all kinds of other surprises, too. Your taxi driver can be a Bosnian refugee, your waiters will be Spanish or Italian, rarely Irish. And since when did all the Irish take to mobile phones and BMWs and start talking about that little place in Tuscany, you may ask? They often find fault with the "Emerald Tiger," as millennial Ireland is known. They say the rising tide of the booming '90s economy "lifted all yachts," in President Mary McAleese's phrase, rather than all boats. But that didn't mean anyone wanted to go backward. Nor does it mean the mainstays of life here—endless talk, the "crack," that social promiscuity, the pub, and the music and the pint—are any different. Even if returning Irish sometimes feel like gobsmacked tourists, strangers in their own land, they take the memory of a score or more heartfelt encounters away with them again and wonder is it exactly this they miss? "Tiger" Ireland has not lost generosity or sociability, always her greatest asset; and her natural friendliness is drawing in more people than ever before.

If you're new to Ireland, there are a few things we ought to tell you about first, like how to get there, what to bring, and what to expect.

353

THE NEXT STEP

THE BASICS

- Silly though it is to generalize, it's safe to say strangers will talk to you, whether you're on a train or beside them in a bar. They may buy you a drink, in which case you are welcome to buy one back—this is "a round." On the other hand, the weather might be bad and they might have a hangover the size of Chicago and merely grunt. In other words, take it easy and take nothing personally.

- Punctilious time-keeping is not an Irish vice. It has started to catch on slowly in business circles, but being a little late—a mere ten to fifteen minutes or so—is common.

- It's going to rain. Possibly it's going to never stop raining again. On the other hand, you might just be miraculously fortunate and strike the heat wave of the decade. If you bring a raincoat with a hood or an umbrella that doesn't blow out and get some rainy-day friends, you'll be all right.

- Ireland became ruinously expensive around the same time that it became more sophisticated and prosperous. It's so popular now that you'll find everything that was easy before—finding a table to eat in a restaurant, a place to park, a seat in the Abbey—a lot harder nowadays. Have second choices, don't micro-plan, go with the flow.

- Don't try to strip at a stag party in Temple Bar. Dublin's party town image is so ferocious these days that hordes of would-be bridegrooms and their mates come over for the weekend from next door to drink themselves senseless and get tied to lampposts with pants around their ankles. The natives finally lost their humor about this one morning when three naked, trouserless men were found on one block.

- Sometimes people who did not grow up in Ireland feel a burning need to lecture on Irish politics or perhaps even morals to the natives. Go ahead, don't let anyone stop you. But why not ask a few questions instead?

- The euro has officially taken over as the national currency of Ireland.

- It's a very sorry state of affairs to have to accuse the Irish of racism, but immigrants have reported outbreaks of racist remarks and worse—usually the victims are asylum-seekers with darker skins. Customs and

immigration have been accused of detaining and deporting foreigners under the same bias. Most people are terribly embarrassed by this, but it persists.

Where is Ireland?

Bouncing off the northwest outline of Europe into the Atlantic, Ireland is a mere eleven miles away from Scotland at its nearest point, the port of Larne in Northern Ireland. It's the westernmost, most maritime outpost of Europe, parallel with Wales, Scotland, southern Scandinavia, and the "next parish over" to Nova Scotia in Canada. This explains why summer nights are very white—it's light until past 10 P.M. in June, when people hardly sleep and party madly; conversely, inhabitants feel less lively in winter, when the energy level drops in proportion to the available daylight.

GETTING THERE

Ireland's literal isolation amid the gales meant that until recently, getting here was a long and dreary slog. That's all changed, and coming and going can be relatively cheap, too. Direct flights from major American cities by major American airlines are numerous. Dublin's own Ryanair (the no-frills airline) transformed European leisure travel with online and e-ticket booking to smaller airports from Scandinavia to Calabria—Dubliners now pop across to London for lunch. Always wanted to see the Faroes? Here's your chance. But never book by phone and always book ahead and be ready for the return flight to be a lot more expensive.

Direct Aer Lingus flights from the West Coast of the U.S. over the North Pole put Ireland a mere ten hours away, around six from the Eastern cities of New York and Boston, or eight from Chicago. They no longer have to land in Shannon Airport first as they used to, although they might stop there briefly on the way back. Dublin is handling as many transatlantic flights as Shannon now, and smaller airports like Cork, Galway, Belfast, and even Knock, Farranfore, and Killarney are handling more continental traffic.

Traditionalists still reach Dublin or its southern suburb Dún Laoghaire by ferry from Holyhead on the tip of Wales, a trip of two to three hours.

HE NEXT STEP

Other ferries leave from Pembroke and Fishguard in South Wales for Rosslare, in Wexford. The ferries are run by Irish Ferries (353-1-661-0715; www.irishferries.com) and Stena Sealink Line (353-1-204-7777; www.stenaline.ie). The journey from Holyhead has been trimmed down to a fraction of what it used to be and now takes place in floating casinos that bear no resemblance to the "cattle boats" of yore. Brittany Ferries ply Roscoff to Cork (from fourteen to eighteen hours, they claim; www.Brittany-Ferries.co.uk), while Irish Ferries take Cherborg to Rosslare. Both trips can be rough and much longer than advertised, but are a lot of fun and a great value if you qualify for a Youth Eurail ticket.

The Border Crossing

Since 1921, the northern six counties of Ireland have stayed within Great Britain, while the southern twenty-six counties became the Republic of Ireland with its own constitution. But crossing the border poses no problems to visitors, and tourism has been increasing in the North since the peace process began. You can walk around Belfast, Derry, and Armagh without constantly throwing up your arms to be searched, and there is less on-the-ground security than in most airports these days. In general, visitors are made even more welcome and greeted with even more friendliness north of the border—you may never leave. West Belfast is a Catholic stronghold reached by "peoples' taxis" and the Protestant equivalent is the Shankill or East Belfast. Neither place is especially scenic, but you will not be made unwelcome, although you may meet blunt inquiry—and why not? In any case, the Good Friday Agreement and peace process brokered by President Clinton has held, if fitfully at times.

HEN TO GO/ WEATHER

Nobody comes here for the weather; there's too much of it—and nobody does anything about it, to borrow the famous saying. The most popular months are July and August, when events like the Royal Dublin Horse Show or music festivals or *fleadhs* around the island draw crowds, and days are extra-long. If nature perchance bestows a sultry spell, the inhabitants become Mediterraneanized, giddy would-be Italians wandering about in

cutoffs. Sometimes they are in denial and do that anyway, rain or no rain.

A heat wave over here may merely mean temperatures sometimes soar into the high 60°sF. The mean average temperature is 64°F in summer, dropping to the low 40°sF in winter, when snow flurries may occur although snow rarely lasts. If you come in spring or in autumn, you may be just as likely to eat your lunch outdoors or to hunker down around a turf fire. If you like the races, come in spring. If you want to stay up all night, come in June, but if you want culture and relaxation at the Dublin Theater Festival or Wexford Opera Festival, try October or November.

The times you should avoid, practically speaking, are the big public holidays when everything shuts down. People tend to hibernate after Christmas, and winter shuts down a lot of tourist-related businesses. An early Easter can also shut things down for four days.

What Should I Wear?

Dress codes are simply not a problem—unless you visit one of the nudist beaches that have taken over small pieces of the coastline. No need to worry about suits and ties unless you're a CEO or a government minister, although socially conscious Dubliners like to spiff it up for occasions. What you'll need against the elements is a jacket and sweater, plus rain gear. Since you can get whatever you need in Dunnes Stores (the Irish equivalent of Penneys or Mervyns), why not take as little as possible? Your best bet is rain gear and a tough umbrella that won't blow inside out in a gale.

VISAS/PERMITS

Americans and other nationals need up-to-date passports; remember, it takes around five weeks to renew or apply for a U.S. passport, and security measures post-9/11 may have complicated arrivals here, too. But most visitors don't need visas. Visitors from the U.K. don't need a passport either. If your country of origin is not European, America, Australia, Canada, or New Zealand, and you're applying from the U.S., check with the Embassy of Ireland, 2234 Massachusetts Avenue, NW, Washington, D.C. 20008, 202-462-3939. For Northern Ireland write to the Embassy of Great

Britain, 3100 Massachusetts Avenue NW, Washington, D.C. 20008, 202-462-1340, or to the nearest consulate.

𝒞USTOMS AND ARRIVAL

The same regulations apply as to all European Union countries when you arrive here from anywhere outside Ireland and the United Kingdom, which means you can bring in 200 cigarettes, 1 liter of spirits, 2 liters of wine, 50g of perfume and 250ml of toilet water plus goods to the value of 175 euros if you arrive from America. If traveling from Britain or Northern Ireland, however, no duty-frees can be imported (they used to be available on the ferry boats, but they have been nixed). Agricultural items often require special clearance and you may be asked not to bring in fresh produce, food, or seeds that came from a farm.

Getting Around Ireland

Dublin Airport is approximately seven miles north of the city center. If you arrive in Dublin and see a bus with "Busaras" or "An Lar" on the front outside the air terminal, it's going to the main bus station or O'Connell Bridge in the heart of Dublin. Take it unless carrying heavy luggage, because it will be much cheaper than a taxi all the way into town. There are taxis in the rank outside Busaras, many buses to outlying areas, and a DART rail station for the main rapid-transit trainline nearby. You can also catch shuttle buses to the main rail stations to the West and South from here.

Cars can be necessary evils. Renting a car starts at a punitive $150–300 per week, and desks representing all the firms confront you in the airport, with the smaller, cheaper local firms, too. Inclusive package-deal rentals are the best deal; all you need is a current driver's license. Take out collision insurance as well as the mandatory third-party, since it's a tricky place to drive, and do specify unlimited mileage—gas is expensive—and return with the tank full. Consider making a reservation before you leave home—often you can get a better rate. And yes, you drive on the left side, although you may notice everyone ambles from side to side, and often the roads are too narrow to have more than one lane anyway. The speed limit is 30 mph in town, 70 mph on freeways.

Traffic's a nightmare, the roads are clogged, parking often involves buying pesky parking disks from newsagents, the accident rate is shockingly high—especially late on a Saturday night. Furthermore, the fines for drunken driving are out of this world—and although the trains aren't quite up to TGV standards, you'll enjoy them for their leisurely pace and landscape viewing opportunities. They don't go everywhere, but you can hire bikes at stations or bring them with you, or hire a car at the other end—or alternatively rent a horse-drawn gypsy caravan, a cruiser, or a barge. Since driving can be a nightmare in Ireland, why not opt for a low-budget rail card or the equivalent cheap bus pass that can take you everywhere the train can't?

Rail and Bus Travel Deals

Single railway tickets can be expensive, but Irish Rail (Iarnród Éireann) can offer you two great deals that can be bought ahead of time in the United States. The "Irish Rover" is valid in both northern and southern Ireland and can be used on five days out of a fifteen-day holiday. To find a similar deal for the bus network, which extends much farther than the train routes, there's an Emerald Pass. Purchase tickets and check schedules on the Web at www.irishrail.ie (Irish Rail) and www.buseireann.ie (Bus Eireann).

Eurail Passes are valid here too, and are a good idea if you are coming from the Continent since they cover the ferry ride from France. The Eurail Youthpass is an especially good deal at $401 for fifteen days of rail travel. Full-time students can get Travelsave stamps for discounts on tickets.

Other Alternatives

As well as buses, there are a few internal flights—Galway to the Aran Islands for one—and ferries to outlying islands, such as the Great Skellig in Kerry or Tory off Donegal. But it's the bicycle that has proven to be the sturdiest friend of those in search of the wilder, less traveled Ireland, for despite its rugged terrain, most of the island is ideal for cycling. Not only can you hire bikes around the country, you can take them everywhere on the train; and Raleigh Rent-a-Bikes lets you drop them off at a different stop, too.

HE NEXT STEP

ℋEALTH

Although you don't need any shots, a traveler's medical insurance plan is never a bad idea. Hospitals and medical care are good here, but heaven forbid that you have some kind of emergency and need coverage on the spot.

Emergency hospital care is available free for visitors, including STD clinics.

Any other hospital care is free for E.U. passport holders, but not for non-E.U. members.

Travel Insurance and Assistance

We recommend that you buy an insurance policy to cover any health problems that might occur during your trip. Several companies in the U.S. and Europe provide emergency medical assistance for travelers worldwide, including twenty-four-hour help lines. Travel agents and tour companies can recommend policies that can work for you.

𝒯IME

Ireland follows Greenwich Mean Time or (GMT), which means that it is five hours ahead of American Eastern Standard Time and one hour behind continental Europe. Thus, when it is noon in Ireland, it is:

4 A.M. in San Francisco
7 A.M. in New York
12 P.M. in London
1 P.M. in Paris
8 P.M. in Hong Kong
9 P.M. in Tokyo
10 P.M. in Sydney

Business Hours

Monday to Friday, from around 9 A.M. to 5 P.M. is the norm; but although Ireland is changing, it is still somewhat relaxed compared to other countries.

$\mathcal{M}$ONEY

The official currency is the euro. There are seven euro notes in denominations of 5, 10, 20, 50, 100, 200, and 500. There are eight euro coins in denominations of 1 and 2 euros, as well as 1, 2, 5, 10, 20, and 50 cents. You can change money in any Irish bank, either the Bank of Ireland or the Allied Irish Bank, or any ATM which belongs to the Cirrus or Plus network. Find out ahead of time from your local bank which network will work for your card. Bring a spare card hidden in a safe place and a small amount of cash plus some traveler's checks just in case—plastic works everywhere but cards do get lost or stolen, so you need a back-up.

- You don't have to tip everywhere here, since a tip is often included in the charge on a meal check; a waiter would expect about 10 percent or more if your check doesn't specify an included charge.
- On the other hand, you do tip taxi dricers a couple of euros.

$\mathcal{P}$OLICE

- The *gardai* or Irish police are large country boys, usually friendly towards tourists. Lately they have had a lot of drug problems to deal with and have lost some native charm and trustfulness as a result; but unless you look as though you might be smuggling heroin you should get on very well with them if—God forbid!—you have to call on them for help.

$\mathcal{E}$LECTRICITY

Appliances run on 240 volts AC, 50 cycles, which means you will need to bring an adapter with a three-point flat-pin plug. You can buy them in the U.S., but it may take some searching around, and airport duty-frees tend to have them, so why not pick one up in transit?

$\mathcal{M}$EDIA: LOCAL NEWSPAPER AND RADIO

The Irish Times is the daily paper of record and there is also the *Irish Independent*, the *Sunday Tribune, Sunday Independent, The Examiner, Sunday*

ᴛHE NEXT STEP

Business Post, and various local papers. *In Dublin* is the "What's On" weekly
and provides listings for theater and movies and information about shopping, galleries, museums, and more. For rock gigs, see *Hot Press.*

When you arrive, go to the tourism office in the corner of the arrivals
lounge, and browse the bookstands; they have all kinds of useful leaflets
and brochures and maps, many of them free. Want to do a literary walking
tour? Pub crawls? Guided rock star tour? Check the brochures here.

Dublin is blessed with several great bookstores, all of which are strong on
books of Irish interest: Eason's, Waterstone's, Hanna's, Hodges Figgis, and
many more.

Local radio is known as RTE (Radio Telefís Éireann) and is amazingly full
of talk; it will plug you in sooner than anything else can. Ireland has four
TV stations and one in the Irish language but you'll also find all the
English stations here. For a mellow background, pick Lyric FM for classical or jazz music.

ᴛOUCHING BASE: POSTAGE, PHONE, FAX, AND E-MAIL

The main General Post Office is in O'Connell Street, 705-7000, Mon.-Sat.
8 A.M.-8 P.M., Sun. 10:30 A.M.-6:30 P.M. Local post offices are open Mon.-
Fri. 10 A.M.-5:30 P.M., Sat. 9 A.M.-1 P.M., and have green "An Post" signs.

Irish post offices can often supply you with phonecards. These are useful for making calls from public phone boxes. You can buy them from
machines or from sweet shops, stationers, or corner convenience stores.

Do not let Irish phones get the better of you; it will be a hard fight but
they will be irksome if you use change because transatlantic calls are tricky
without calling card numbers, phone cards—or a kind friend who will let
you use theirs via an operator who tells you how much it knocks you
back. And "knock" may be the word; phone calls are expensive here,
which means people have a whole different phone protocol.

At the same time, you see people on cell phones everywhere and at all times. You may find it easier to buy a pay-as-you-go cell phone at one of the numerous mobile phone boutiques. Fax machines can be found in hotels, some post offices, some copying shops, and there are cybercafés in Dublin, Cork, and Galway. All this can turn out to be not as easy as it sounds. Eircom Ireland dispenses cell phones. There is an Eircom store in South King Street next door to the Gaiety Theatre where you can get prepaid phones.

CULTURAL CONSIDERATIONS

CUSTOMS OF THE COUNTRY

- People are pretty easygoing here. If you arrive on the dot of the appointed hour and your friend is ten minutes late, that's Irish time. Relax and don't get your knickers in a twist.
- A word about "rounds" in pubs. As mentioned earlier, it's not that nobody minds being thought a fool here, but the locals hate to be thought cheap even more. So while they are absolutely delighted to be generous towards you, the logical follow-up is, well, to respond in kind.
- "Travelers" is the polite name given by the Irish to the dispossessed who were, through no fault of their own, left to wander the roads of Ireland by horse-drawn caravan in order to eke out a living through dealing in horses and mending pots and pans—it was this last trade that earned them their older, less polite name of "Tinkers." Travelers now are mainly settled, or have motorized trailers. Concentrated in the Irish West, they have their own language (Shelta) and culture and customs. Their tradition is mostly oral and musical. While their advocates continue to fight for a better deal for them, they are making a transition into the newer world across the sea and into conventional housing at last, but still suffer a glaring social injustice that can be as inhuman as it may be romantic-seeming.

THE NEXT STEP

- Dublin has become like any other capital city in that petty crime exists here, along with drug problems and all the other evils that beset a rapidly changing population. Always lock your valuables in the trunk if driving. Have a back-up credit card or checks somewhere safe. The criminals are part of the growing drug problem here; and places to avoid include the side streets off O'Connell Street late at night, though the problem is not confined to any one spot or area. Watch out for a swarm of small children hanging around your knees, too; sadly, they are often also a risk. Trouble spots exist in Belfast, Derry, Cork, Galway, and Limerick. The island is generally less crime-free than it used to be as a result of its growing sophistication. Just don't leave valuables on view in a car, keep your credit cards apart, and put your passport and money in an inaccessible pocket.
- Recent influxes of Eastern European immigrants, particularly Romanian refugees, have resulted in a new immigrant problem and lots of hearbreaking city center begging..
- As a rule, the topics of The Troubles in Northern Ireland and abortion are the two most sensitive issues in any conversation. Just a warning; you could be sadly wrong in your guesses about your audience's feelings.

EVENTS AND HOLIDAYS

Banks and most shops are closed on: New Year's Day or January 1; Saint Patrick's Day or March 17; Easter weekend (March or April); May Day Holiday (first Monday in May); June Holiday (first Monday in June); August Holiday (first Monday in August); October Holiday (last Monday in October); Christmas Day (when public transport also stops); Saint Stephen's Day or Boxing Day (December 26); and remember that some major holidays have a sort of domino effect, especially in winter.

Sundays are still days when most shops are closed, but not newsagents or corner convenience stores. Try not to arrive on Good Friday, when people shut down for at least four days over Easter and even a drink is hard to find; ditto for Christmas. After Saint Stephen's Day, you might as well

be asleep since nothing is on except the races or an occasional movie. Saint Patrick's is now joyously celebrated with street theater, weather permitting; it used to be rather solemn and wet, but now it's a free-for-all.

January

- Sales continue: Dublin shoppers get their Grafton Street bargains, although nobody bothers to line up all night any more.
- National Gallery, Merrion Square: the classic collection, including the Old Masters, get the benefit of January's northern light this month (661-5133; free).

February–March

- February 1 is Saint Bridget's Day and is increasingly celebrated again by women, since she is their patron saint.
- Ash Wednesday is when the faithful mark the start of Lent—and their foreheads.
- Six Nations Rugby Tournament in Lansdowne Road, Ballsbridge (668-4601). Sadly, Ireland rarely wins, but that doesn't stop anyone from cheering the matches.
- March 17 is Saint Patrick's Day. This day continues to evolve into a bigger and better piece of street theater every year—nowadays featuring Jamaican steel bands and Galway's Macnas troupe or similar street theaters.
- Alternative Miss Ireland: comediennes and drag-artists don swimwear and evening wear for this send-up of a beauty pageant at the Red Box night club in Harcourt Street, (478-0166).

March–April

- Dublin Film Festival, ten days of new releases and brave little "indie" movies.
- Easter is a joyous reawakening throughout the country.
- Irish Grand National occurs on Easter Monday at Fairyhouse Races, (825-6167).

THE NEXT STEP

May

♦ Trinity Ball and May Rag Week. The students of Trinity College put on their penguin suits and long dresses in order to drink too much all night long in their city center campus. While the pranks may not be as wild as they were in the era of J. P. Donleavy's '50s novel *The Ginger Man*, they still manage to party all night long—and no, it isn't easy to climb over the wall.

♦ Listowel Writers Week in County Kerry. For over a quarter of a century this small but broadminded town has welcomed every kind of poet and writer and bohemian under the aegis of its special reputation for producing writers, most recently John B. Keane and Bryan MacMahon.

♦ Pentecost Sunday is also known as Whit because it coincides with Whitsuntide. This religious holiday is now sanctified by the European Union into a long weekend with a Monday bank holiday, sometimes as late as the first weekend in June.

June

♦ June 16 is Bloomsday, the day when James Joyce is commemorated by literary figures, who meet in the places he mentions in *Ulysses*, starting at the Martello Tower in Sandycove.

♦ Mid-June is the Dublin Writers Festival. Notorious for its large numbers of well-fed scribblers, Dublin has its own Writers Museum in Parnell Square where this festival throws occasional events.

♦ Festivals of Music in Great Irish Houses take place through June and July all over the country and wed wonderful music with glorious architecture.

July

♦ Saint John's Night is often celebrated with bonfires in the West and around the countryside.

♦ July 12 is known as the "Glorious Twelfth," the day when the Orangemen march all over Northern Ireland.

♦ Dublin's Temple Bar summer events season in Meeting House Square offers open-air music and cinema.

- The Fleadh Ceoil traditional music festival tours different towns around the island every year.
- Horse races in Killarney are very popular and bring horse lovers to this tourist-crammed town in Kerry.
- Galway Arts Festival is a mixture of mayhem, new music, theater, comedy, and street happenings.
- Mayo's Croagh Patrick Pilgrimage lures penitents to climb the mountain near Louisburgh barefoot on the last Sunday.

August

- The Royal Dublin Horse Show draws the world of horseflesh and showjumping to Ballsbridge for international events like the Aga Khan Cup.
- Kilkenny Arts Week is a varied program of theater, music, and dance to this well preserved medieval town with its castle, cathedral, and Design Centre.
- Dublin Regatta fills Dublin Bay with sails.
- Mid-August brings the Puck Fair to Killorglin, Kerry, a festival for a billy goat who is crowned king for a day in this small town!
- Ascension Sunday is a religious holiday celebrated by Catholics with a traditional Mass.

September

- The Liffey Descent is a canoeing race down the River Liffey from Straffan to Islandbridge, Dublin.
- The Liffey Swim usually takes place on the third weekend in September, when burly swimmers brave the murk of the "Whiffey" for a splash.
- All-Ireland Football and Hurling Finals are played on the second and last Sunday in the month in Croke Park, Dublin.

October

- Dublin Theatre Festival at the beginning of the month brings scores of exciting productions from all over the world to every performance space, and includes a fringe program of many more.

ℐHE NEXT STEP

- Comedy Festival celebrates the rising generation of Irish comedians led by the likes of Ardal O'Hanlon of "Father Ted," Tommy Tiernan, and many more.
- Rugby series begins at Lansdowne Road.
- Dublin City Marathon. Runners take in the main points of the city for this annual race.
- Galway Oyster Festival draws lovers of the famous bivalve to Oughterard, Clarinbridge, and other spots in the West.
- Cork Jazz Festival is held toward the end of the month and features the famous names of international jazz.
- Ballinasloe Horse Fair. A rambunctious County Galway festival that draws horse fanciers from all over the land to buy horses and ponies—after checking their teeth and finer points first.
- Kinsale Gourmet Festival. Many fine restaurants in this pretty West Cork seaside town specialize in seafood, and compete to outdo each other at this time of year.
- Hallowe'en (or *Samhain*) is the Irish All Souls Night.

November

- Wexford Opera Festival sometimes starts at the end of October, runs for two weeks, and always features three little-known works that merit revival in the small Victorian theater of this small fishing town.
- Belfast Festival at Queens University has been running throughout The Troubles for more than thirty-five years, with artistic activities centered upon the university campus at Malone Road.
- Dublin Antiques Fair usually takes place at the Mansion House on Dawson Street and provides browsing.

December

- Circus and fun fairs for children.
- Pantomime or Christmas theater shows (mainly for children).
- After Christmas, sales at main shopping areas.
- The Races. Most Dubliners have no reason to get out of bed after Saint Stephen's Day other than the races in Naas and Leopardstown where everybody has a "flutter" (a bet).

* Mumming festivals in County Galway, near Woodside.
* December 26 is Saint Stephen's Night. Mummers dress up and go door to door in Kerry, Dublin, and West of Ireland. Mummers, Wrenboys, and Strawboys are leftovers from a medieval tradition, going from door to door after Christmas and singing "Rise up landlady and give us a treat!"

IMPORTANT CONTACTS

The airport tourist desk is a useful first port of call when you need accommodation, and there are branches in every larger town marked with giant white "I"s for "information." You can also ask for free information from the American branches of the Irish Tourism Board, which is An Bord Failte in Irish.

Bed and breakfasts are listed in a special brochure distributed by Bord Failte, as are hotels. Good dining guides are the Bridgestone Guides by John and Susan McKenna.

The ireland.com site is a useful portal site to begin to look for everything; it takes you to *The Irish Times* and to information sites of all kinds.

☞MPORTANT TELEPHONE NUMBERS

Police 999 or 112 for police (*gardai*, pronounced gard-ee), fire, ambulance or rescue emergencies

Beaumont hospital (main hospital in Dublin) 809-3000

Directory assistance 1190 (Ireland); 1197 (U.K); 1198 (international)

Weather information 1550-122-1121

ACTIVITIES

☞FF THE BEATEN TRACK

Go west, or south, or northwest if you want less company. You can still get thoroughly lonely up in the Wicklow hills just half-an-hour south of

ᴛHE NEXT STEP

Dublin—the Wicklow Way can be reached from the end of a Dublin bus route. But much of Ireland is filling up rapidly—West Cork has become a mini-Riviera of cosmopolitanism, tiny Dingle and the Kerry coastline is bustling, Galway and Killarney are tourist meccas, so are the Aran Islands. But there are many other islands to look over, each and every one a beauty, from Bere Island in West Cork to Tory Island in stormy Donegal waters and Rathlin, off Antrim's coastline.

The North is very unspoiled, mainly because The Troubles have kept it tourist-free until recently; and harsh weather has protected County Donegal well. Camping can be wet here, so be prepared; but hiking is easy and rewarding. Wandering around Donegal is feasible from the end of a Lough Swilly bus ride out of Derry city: ask for the right maps at the tourist office.

For touring the south or southwest, would you consider a horse-drawn caravan? A motor-cruiser of your own up the River Shannon? Or a barge down the River Barrow? Just keep moving on, and if you have the stamina to tour Ireland by bicycle, grab a copy of Eric Newby's *Round Ireland in Low Gear* first, so you know what you're letting yourself in for.

ꝰUN THINGS TO DO

• Belfast

Next to the Queens University campus is the Ulster Museum, which can legitimately claim to be perhaps the best on the island for many categories, among them salvaged Armada gold, and very early fossils, and local modern art. The Tropical Ravine in the Botanical Gardens next door has lost all its windows repeatedly from bombs over the last decades, yet remains weird and wonderful. The Crown Bar on Victoria Street and Kelly's Cellars off Royal Avenue continue to be the best-loved pubs.

• Cork

Few visitors can resist playing the ancient Bells of Shandon Steeple. Go ahead and play: the locals are used to it and put up with it with grace.

Of course you need to kiss the Blarney Stone in Blarney Village outside

Cork City, easily reached by bus and a little less hair-raising than it used to be.

In picturesque Cobh, you can visit the new Heritage Center overlooking the harbor and dedicated to the emigrants of the past who left for the New World from here; the statue outside says it all.

Visit Youghal on the East Cork coastline to see where Walter Raleigh lived while introducing tobacco and potatoes to Ireland. A short trip inland takes you to Ballymaloe House for Sunday brunch; this is the cradle of Ireland's new cuisine.

◆ Dublin

Just walking about is the thing most people enjoy most, around Dublin's compact Left Bank in Temple Bar, or along Grafton Street near Dublin's O'Connell Bridge, or into the Liberties just west of Dublin Castle's walls off Thomas Street—all full of street life. The news has probably reached you that pub life is important too. You can engage in all kinds of pub crawls in Dublin, from a James Joyce Pub Crawl to a Literary Pub Crawl, and even a musical or comedy pub crawl. Of course, you can also go by yourself; the tourist board will direct you and even give you maps if you want directions. There are comedy clubs, nightclubs, cybercafés, coffee houses, open air music events—and if all else fails, Bewley's Oriental Tearooms is a warm spot to hang out in, any branch.

You should visit the Book of Kells; it's in the Old Library of Trinity College, where a page gets turned each day, and you can see a lot of other interesting old manuscripts in the same ancient and lovely building. More historic sites beckon too, like Christ Church Cathedral, Saint Michan's Church off the Dublin quays, Newman House, the Bank of Ireland, the Customs House, the Four Courts, and Dublin Castle's nooks and crannies. Don't forget the fascinating Marsh's Library, Writers Museum, and the Print Museum. Just walk around and look.

◆ Galway

Galway's narrow streets are bursting with bustle and life, and Spanish Arch and Shop Street and the quays are easily visited on foot. You will also enjoy the drive around the lakes on its doorstep to Oughterard and Clarenbridge, where you can also take in oysters and stout at festival time. The rugged Connemara coast past the Twelve Bens possesses its own spell. Some of Ireland's best-loved chefs operate here too—Gerry Galvin at Drimcong, for one.

The Aran Islands has its own particular appeal as part of the "Gaeltacht" or Irish-speaking Ireland; and its Dún Aengus hill fort atop a massive cliff is one of the most impressive ancient sites in the land.

◆ The Northwest

Donegal's Grianan of Aelach is another PreChristian hill fort that is curiously shaped yet retains an indefinable air of romance. It's within a stone's throw of Derry City and easily reached by city bus.

Sligo's heathery Ben Bulben is an outcrop indelibly attached to the memory of Ireland's best-known poet, William Butler Yeats. Sligo town is full of reminders of his links to the town.

◆ The North

The northern coast of Ireland from Donegal to Antrim boasts a string of long sandy beaches, one after another, with rollers that are often high enough to surf. Best-known beauty spots include the Mussenden Temple, the Carrick-a-Rede rope bridge, and the celebrated Giant's Causeway, a freakish formation of the local basalt and granite that has given it that unique "organ pipes" appearance and spawned many a local preChristian myth, too.

The Mountains of Mourne are gentle hills that offer pleasing prospects and pretty little towns like Rostrevor or Kilkeel.

The Boyne Valley has Ireland's most important megalithic remains, notably Newgrange with its cruciform-shaped passage graves. Several similar and equally interesting passage graves survive nearby that are not as popular with tourists.

♦ Kerry and Clare

The Great Skellig's vertiginous craggy face rises sheer from the Atlantic billows eleven miles from the shore, and is very difficult to land upon in most winds and weather; but it's worth the trouble. George Bernard Shaw's observation that it was the most interesting site and "part of our dream world" is still true today. Early Christians founded a monastery here that survived until the Vikings; after this, it fell into disuse and its beehive huts were deserted. There are few more interesting places for bird-watchers or amateur historians or simply visitors with a yen for spiritual experiences. Many boats leave for Skellig from Valentia Island, which is just off Cahirciveen and reached by the long bridge or ferry; there is even a Skellig booking office in Carhirciveen, and a Skellig visitors center at the bridge to Valentia.

The Ring of Kerry is a little crowded these days but you can still enjoy the circuit by foot or jaunting car or bike, weather permitting.

Near Dingle, Mount Brandon makes for good hiking and climbing, even when you can't see in front of your foot because the weather is so bad.

Listowel is a small North Kerry town that never fails to entertain the visitor. Of all its pubs, John B. Keane's is easily the most popular with visitors.

Clare is renowned for the lively music scene in its small seaside towns, such as Kilrush, Milltown Malbay, Ennistymon, and Doolin.

The Burren is an eery landscape of limestone next to the village of Doolin that harbors some spectacular megaliths including a prime dolmen, and a unique botany found nowhere else outside the Alps.

Yeats's tower near Gort is a sacred pilgrimage for poetry fans.

Near the Burren are the Cliffs of Moher, mighty faces of sheer rock that rush down into a turbulent sea crashing below.

THE NEXT STEP

♦ Limerick

Much targeted as the city where Frank McCourt of *Angela's Ashes* grew up, Limerick has fine architecture, the richly endowed Hunt Museum, and some fine Georgian architecture.

♦ Kilkenny

A magnificent medieval city picturesquely sited upon the Nore, its Design Center, castle, and Saint Canice's Cathedral are all worth visiting. Perhaps just trying out its pubs (popular with hurling teams) and walking around is the best way to enjoy it.

♦ Wexford

Again, just walking around can be the most fun. A small but pleasing fishing town, it fills up around the Opera Festival with people in evening tails and ball gowns.

Performing Arts

Nobody has failed to find a play to suit their tastes yet, either at the historic Abbey and Gate theatres, the more popular Gaiety and Olympia, the Method-oriented Focus Theatre, or sundry smaller venues. The Ark is a children's theater, and the Lambert Puppet Theatre in Monkstown has an excellent record of pulling in the smaller set, too. The National Concert Hall is the temple of classical music, while Dublin's grand opera company runs twice a year at the Gaiety. No shortage of cinemas, and in summer there are open-air movies in Temple Bar.

Galleries

If you like galleries and museums, the National Gallery with its native painters, impressionists, and Old Masters, the National Museum with its many treasures, James Joyce's Tower in Sandycove, Castletown House, the Museum of Modern Art, the Marino Casino, and even Kilmainham Jail all beckon. The National Museum has several sections, including Collins Barracks, and contains the wonderful Celtic gold collection of lunulae and collars, the early Christian vessels, the Georgian silver, the costumes of

yore. The somewhat dusty old Natural History Museum retains its own moldy charm.

Outdoors

The DART or small rapid-transit train follows the coastline and will take you to beaches and small harbors, from the fishing village of Howth down to the sandy expanse of Killiney. If you like open air, there's the tree-filled expanse of Phoenix Park, a present from Charles II to his mistress Nell Gwynne and where the Pope celebrated Mass in 1980. A lot tinier, but convenient and full of ducks, St. Stephen's Green is at the end of Grafton Street.

ADDITIONAL RESOURCES

IRELAND ONLINE

- ◆ Accommodations:
  www.karenbrown.com/ireland
  www.townandcountry.ie
  www.irelandyha.org
- ◆ Transportation:
  www.irishrail.ie
  www.raileurope.com
  www.irishferries.ie
  www.stenaline.ie
- ◆ Tourism Resources:
  www.ireland.travel.ie
  www.shamrock.org
  www.discovernorthernireland.com
  www.irelandnow.com
- ◆ News and Entertainment:
  www.ireland.com

THE NEXT STEP

www.unison.ie
www.rte.ie
www.dojo.ie/musicbox

- ◆ Outdoor Activities:
  www.irelandflyfishing.com
  www.interknowledge.com/northern-ireland/ukifish1.htm
  www.travel.yahoo.com/pltravelguide/398875
  www.heritageireland.ie
  www.gorp,com/location/europe/ireland.htm

- ◆ History:
  www.stonepages.com/ireland
  www.luminarium.org/mythology/ireland

- ◆ Art and Culture:
  www.islandireland.com
  www.entertainment.ie

- ◆ Current News:
  www.WorldTravelWatch.com
  www.countrywatch.com
  www.usembassy.ie

RECOMMENDED READING

Adargh, John. *Ireland and the Irish: Portrait of a Changing Society*. London: Penguin Books, 1995.

Böll, Heinrich. *Irish Journal*. Evanston, Ill.: Northwestern University Press, 1967.

Butler, Hubert. *Escape from the Anthill*. Dublin: The Lilliput Press, 1986.

Butler, Hubert. *Grandmother and Wolfe Tone*. Dublin: The Lilliput Press, 1990.

Cahill, Thomas. *How the Irish Saved Civilization: The Untold Story of Ireland's Heroic Role from the Fall of Rome to the Rise of Medieval Europe*. New York: Doubleday, 1995.

Cahill, Thomas. *The Great Shame: And the Triumph of the Irish in the English-Speaking World*. New York: Doubleday, 1998.

Carson, Ciaran. *Last Night's Fun: In and Out of Time with Irish Music*. New York: Farrar, Straus and Giroux, 1997.

Chambers, Anne. *Granuaile: The Life and Times of Grace O'Malley*. Dublin: Wolfhound Press, 1988.

Collins, Eamon, with Mick McGovern. *Killing Rage*. London: Granta Books, 1997.

Craig, Patricia, ed. *The Oxford Book of Ireland*. New York: Oxford University Press, 1998.

Crowley, Elaine. *Cowslips and Chainies: A Memoir of Dublin in the 1930s*. Dublin: The Lilliput Press, 1996.

de Valois, Ninette. *Come Dance with Me: A Memoir 1898-1956*. Dublin: The Lilliput Press, 1992.

Dillon, Martin. *God and the Gun: The Church and Irish Terrorism*. Great Britain: Routledge, 1990.

Donleavy, J. P. *A Singular Country*. New York: W. W. Norton & Company, 1989.

Dunne, Seán. *The Road to Silence*. Dublin: New Island Books, 1994.

Eagleton, Terry. *The Truth About the Irish*. Dublin: New Island Books, 1999.

Evans, E. Estyn. *Ireland and the Atlantic Heritage: Selected Writings*. Dublin: The Lilliput Press, 1996.

Evans, E. Estyn. *The Personality of Ireland: Habitat, Heritage and History*. Dublin: The Lilliput Press, 1992.

Farmar, Anna. *Traveller: An Autobiography of Nan Joyce*. Dublin: Gill and Macmillan, 1985.

Fegan, Melissa. Literature and the Irish Famine 1845-1919. Oxford: Oxford University Press, 2002.

Fennell, Desmond. *A Connacht Journey*. Dublin: Gill and Macmillan Ltd.,1987.

Flower, Robin. *The Irish Tradition*. Dublin: The Lilliput Press, 1994.

Helliwell, Tanis. *Summer with the Leprechauns: A True Story*. Nevada City, Calif.: Blue Dolphin Publishing, Inc., 1997.

Igore, Vivien. *A Literary Guide to Dublin*. London: Methuen, 1994.

Kavanagh, P. J. *Voices in Ireland: A Traveller's Literary Companion*. London: Mohn Murray Ltd., 1994.

Kelly, Sean, and Rosemary Rogers. *How to Be Irish (Even If You Already Are)*. New York: Villard Books, 1999.

Kirby, Michael. *Skelligside*. Dublin: The Lilliput Press, 1992.

Laxton, Edward. *The Famine Ships: The Irish Exodus to America*. New York: Henry Holt and Company, Inc., 1996.

MacLaughlin, Jim. *Travellers and Ireland: Whose Country, Whose History?* Dublin: Cork University Press, 1995.

Mathieu, Joan. *Zulu: An Irish Journey*. New York: Farrar, Strauss & Giroux, Inc., 1998.

McCourt, Frank. *Angela's Ashes: A Memoir.* New York: Scribner, 1996.

McFadden, David W. *An Innocent in Ireland: Curious Rambles and Singular Encounters.* Toronto: McClelland & Stewart Inc., 1995.

McKenzie, Richard. *Turn Left at the Black Cow: One Family's Journey from Beverly Hills to Ireland*. Dublin: Roberts Rhinehart Publishers, 1998.

Miller, Kerby, et al. *Journey of Hope: The Story of Irish Immigration to America*. San Francisco: Chronicle Books, 2001.

Moloney, Ed. *A Secret History of the IRA*. New York: W. W. Norton, 2002.

Moorhouse, Geoffrey. *Sun Dancing: A Vision of Medieval Ireland*. Orlando, Fla., 1997.

Moriarty, John. *Turtle Was Gone a Long Time: Crossing the Kedron*. Dublin: The Lilliput Press, 1996.

Morton, H. V. *In Search of Ireland*. London: Methuen & Co. Ltd., 1930.

Neville, Peter. *A Traveller's History of Ireland*. New York: Interlink Books, 1998.

Newby, Eric. *Round Ireland in Low Gear*. London: Lonely Planet Publications, 1987.

O'Brien, Conor Cruise. *Ancestral Voices: Religion and Nationalism in Ireland*. London: Poolbeg Press Ltd., 1994.

O'Brien, Edna. *Mother Ireland.* New York: Plume Books, 1999.

O'Connor, Joseph. *The Irish Male at Home and Abroad*. Dublin: New Island Books, 1996.

O'Connor, Joseph. *The Secret World of the Irish Male*. Dublin: New Island Books, 1994.

O'Donohue, John. *Anam Cara: A Book of Celtic Wisdom.* New York: HarperCollins Publishers, Inc., 1997.

O'Faolain, Nuala. *Are You Somebody? The Accidental Memoir of a Dublin Woman.* New York: Henry Holt and Company, 1996.

O'Toole, Fintan. *Black Hole, Green Card: The Disappearance of Ireland.* Dublin: New Island Books, 1994.

O'Toole, Fintan. *The Life of the Land: Irish Identities.* London: Verso, 1997.

Perkins, Sonya (ed.). *The Irish Today: A Celebration of Ireland and the Irish Diaspora.* London: Cadogan, 2000.

Raftery, Barry. *Pagan Celtic Ireland: The Enigma of the Irish Iron Age.* New York: Thames and Hudson, 1994.

Raymo, Chet. *Honey from Stone: A Naturalist's Search for God.* Minneapolis: Hungry Mind Press, 1987.

Robinson, Tim. *Setting Foot on the Shores of Connemara.* Dublin: The Lilliput Press, 1996.

Robinson, Tim. *Stones of Aran.* Dublin: The Lilliput Press, 1995.

Ryan, Alan. *A Harvest Original.* Orlando, Fla: Harcourt Brace & Company, 1999.

Scherman, Katharine. *The Flowering of Ireland: Saints, Scholars, and Kings.* New York: Barnes & Noble Books, 1981.

Seoighe, Manchín, ed. *The Irish Quotation Book: A Literary Companion.* New York: Barnes & Noble Books, 1992.

Solnit, Rebecca. *A Book of Migrations: Some Passages in Ireland.* London: Verso, 1997.

Somerville, Christopher. *The Road to Roaringwater: A Walk Down the West of Ireland.* London: HarperCollinsPublishers, 1993.

Tall, Deborah. *The Island of the White Cow: Memories of an Irish Island.* New York: Atheneum, 1986.

Tóibín, Colm. *Bad Blood: A Walking Along the Irish Border.* London: Vintage, 1994.

Tóibín, Colm. *The Sign of the Cross: Travels in Catholic Europe.* London: Jonathan Cape, Ltd., 1994.

Vega, Janine Pommy. *Tracking the Serpent: Journeys to Four Continents.* San Francisco: City Lights Books, 1997.

Wall, Eamonn. *From the Sin-E Cafe to the Black Hils: Notes on the New Irish.* Wisconsin: University of Wisconsin Press, 2000

THE NEXT STEP

Williams, Niall, and Christine Breen. *The Pipes Are Calling: Our Jaunts Through Ireland*. New York: Soho Press, Inc., 1990.

Wilson, Brian. *Dances with Waves: Around Ireland by Kayak*. Niwot, Colo.: The O'Brien Press, 1998.

Wilson, David A. *Ireland: A Bicycle and a Tin Whistle*. Belfast: The Blackstaff Press, 1995.

Yeats, W. B. *Fairy and Folk Tales of Ireland*. 5th ed. Channel Islands: Guernsey Press Company Ltd., 1995.

"THE NEXT STEP" WAS COMPILED BY ELGY GILLESPIE AND THE STAFF OF TRAVELERS' TALES.

Index

Index of Contributors

Acknowledgments

We would like to thank our families and friends for their usual forbearance while we are putting a book together. Thanks also to Lisa Bach, Susan Brady, Deborah Greco, Raj Khadka, Jennifer Leo, Natanya Pearlman, Tara Weaver, Cynthia Lamb, Judy Johnson, Trisha Schwartz, Elgy Gillespie, Michele Wetherbee, Maureen O'Reilly, Maureen Chevins, Maureen and Kerry Kravitz, Tim and Margaret Sullivan, Timothy O'Donnell, Maggie O'Reilly Ciskanik, Kate O'Reilly Doyle, Anne Mary O'Reilly Vieira, Frank O'Reilly, Angelique Syversen O'Reilly, Anne O'Reilly, Tim O'Reilly, Eugene Mc Cabe, Fran McKeagney, and Orla Carey and Ruth Moran of the Irish Tourist Board.

Selection from *Dances with Waves: Around Ireland by Kayak* by Brian Wilson copyright © 1998 by Brian Wilson. Reprinted by permission of O'Brien Press.

Selection from "Fiddlin' Around in Ireland" by Linda Watanabe McFerrin published with permission from the author. Copyright © 2000 by Linda Watanabe McFerrin.

Selection from "From Ireland with Music" by Andy Yale reprinted from the November/December 1996 issue of *Islands* magazine. Copyright © 1996 by Islands Publishing Company. Reprinted by permission.

Selection from "Gone Fishing" by Lee Gotschall-Maxon published with permission from the author. Copyright © 2000 by Lee Gotschall-Maxon.

Selection from *The Great Hunger: Ireland 1845-1849* by Cecil Woodham-Smith copyright © 1962 by Cecil Woodham-Smith. Reprinted by permission of HarperCollins Publishers, Inc. and Penguin Books Ltd.

Selection from *Here's Ireland* by Harold Speakman originally published by Dodd Mead and Company, Inc. Copyright © 1925.

Selection from *In My Father's Time* by Eamon Kelly copyright © 1976 by Eamon Kelly. Published by The Mercier Press, Cork, Ireland.

Selections from *In Search of Ireland* by H. V. Morton copyright © 1930 by H. V. Morton. Reprinted by permission of Methuen & Co. Ltd.

Selection from *An Innocent in Ireland: Curious Rambles and Singular Encounters* by David W. McFadden copyright © 1995 by David W. McFadden. Reprinted by permission of McClelland & Stewart Inc. The Canadian Publishers.

Selection from "Insights on Ireland" by Margaret Lynn McLean published with permission from the author. Copyright © 2000 by Margaret Lynn McLean.

Selection from *The Irish: A Character Study* by Seán O'Faoláin copyright © 1949 by The Devin-Adair Company. Reprinted by permission.

Selection from "An Irish Diaspora" by Larry Habegger published with permission from the author. Copyright © 2000 by Larry Habegger.

Selection from "Irish Ironies" by John Boland published with permission from the author. Copyright © 2000 by John Boland.

Selection from *Irish Journal* by Heinrich Böll copyright © 1967 by Leila Vennewitz. Reprinted by permission of Joan Daves Agency for Verlag Kiepenheuer & Witsch, and Leila Vennewitz.

Selection from "Irish Pleasures" by Laura Strehlau published with permission from the author. Copyright © 2000 by Laura Strehlau.

Selection from "An Irish Story" by Rick Wilber published with permission from the author. Copyright © 2000 by Rick Wilber.

Selection from *The Island of the White Cow: Memories of an Irish Island* by Deborah Tall copyright © 1986 by Deborah Tall. Reprinted by permission of the Stuart Krichevsky Literary Agency, Inc.

Selection from "Links with Tradition" by Larry Habegger published with permission from the author. Copyright © 2000 by Larry Habegger.

About the Editors

James O'Reilly, president and publisher of Travelers' Tales, wrote mystery serials before becoming a travel writer in the early 1980s. He's visited more than forty countries, along the way meditating with monks in Tibet, participating in West African voodoo rituals, and hanging out the laundry with nuns in Florence. He travels extensively with his wife, Wenda, and their three daughters. They live in Palo Alto, California.

Larry Habegger, executive editor of Travelers' Tales, has been writing about travel since 1980. He has visited almost fifty countries and six of the seven continents, traveling from the frozen Arctic to equatorial rain forest, the high Himalayas to the Dead Sea. In the early 1980s he co-authored mystery serials for the *San Francisco Examiner* with James O'Reilly, and since 1985 their syndicated column, "World Travel Watch," has appeared in newspapers in five countries and on WorldTravelWatch.com. As series editors of Travelers' Tales, they have worked on almost seventy titles, winning many awards for excellence. Habegger regularly teaches the craft of travel writing at workshops and writers conferences, and he lives with his family on Telegraph Hill in San Francisco.

Sean Joseph O'Reilly, editor-at-large and director of international sales for Travelers' Tales, is an editor of many Travelers' Tales books, including *The Road Within, Testosterone Planet, The Ultimate Journey, Pilgrimage,* and *The Spiritual Gifts of Travel.* An active member of the Society of American Travel Writers, he is also the author of the shocking and controversial book *How to Manage Your DICK: Redirect Sexual Energy and Discover Your More Enlightened, Evolved Self.* He lives with his wife, Brenda, and their six children in Arizona.

TRAVELERS' TALES

THE SOUL OF TRAVEL

Footsteps Series

THE FIRE NEVER DIES
One Man's Raucous Romp Down the Road of Food, Passion, and Adventure
By Richard Sterling
ISBN 1-885-211-70-8
$14.95

"Sterling's writing is like spit-fire, foursquare and jazzy with crackle...."
—*Kirkus Reviews*

LAST TROUT IN VENICE
The Far-Flung Escapades of an Accidental Adventurer
By Doug Lansky
ISBN 1-885-211-63-5
$14.95

"Traveling with Doug Lansky might result in a considerably shortened life expectancy...but what a way to go." —Tony Wheeler, Lonely Planet Publications

ONE YEAR OFF
Leaving It All Behind for a Round-the-World Journey with Our Children
By David Elliot Cohen
ISBN 1-885-211-65-1
$14.95

A once-in-a-lifetime adventure generously shared.

THE WAY OF THE WANDERER
Discover Your True Self Through Travel
By David Yeadon
ISBN 1-885-211-60-0
$14.95

Experience transformation through travel with this delightful, illustrated collection by award-winning author David Yeadon.

TAKE ME WITH YOU
A Round-the-World Journey to Invite a Stranger Home
By Brad Newsham
ISBN 1-885-211-51-1
$24.00 (cloth)

"Newsham is an ideal guide. His journey, at heart, is into humanity." —Pico Iyer, author of *Video Night in Kathmandu*

KITE STRINGS OF THE SOUTHERN CROSS
A Woman's Travel Odyssey
By Laurie Gough
ISBN 1-885-211-54-6
$14.95 —★★★—

ForeWord Silver Medal Winner
—*Travel Book of the Year*

THE SWORD OF HEAVEN
A Five Continent Odyssey to Save the World
By Mikkel Aaland
ISBN 1-885-211-44-9
$24.00 (cloth)

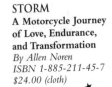

"Few books capture the soul of the road like *The Sword of Heaven*, a sharp-edged, beautifully rendered memoir that will inspire anyone." —Phil Cousineau, author of *The Art of Pilgrimage*

STORM
A Motorcycle Journey of Love, Endurance, and Transformation
By Allen Noren
ISBN 1-885-211-45-7
$24.00 (cloth)
—★★★—

ForeWord Gold Medal Winner
—*Travel Book of the Year*

Travelers' Tales Classics

COAST TO COAST
A Journey Across 1950s America
By Jan Morris
ISBN 1-885-211-79-1
$16.95

After reporting on the first Everest ascent in 1953, Morris spent a year journeying by car, train, ship, and aircraft across the United States. In her brilliant prose, Morris records with exuberance and curiosity a time of innocence in the U.S.

THE ROYAL ROAD TO ROMANCE
By Richard Halliburton
ISBN 1-885-211-53-8
$14.95

"Laughing at hardships, dreaming of beauty, ardent for adventure, Halliburton has managed to sing into the pages of this glorious book his own exultant spirit of youth and freedom."
—*Chicago Post*

THE RIVERS RAN EAST
By Leonard Clark
ISBN 1-885-211-66-X
$16.95

Clark is the original Indiana Jones, relaying a breathtaking account of his search for the legendary El Dorado gold in the Amazon.

THERE'S NO TOILET PAPER...ON THE ROAD LESS TRAVELED
The Best of Travel Humor and Misadventure
Edited by Doug Lansky
ISBN 1-885-211-27-9
$12.95

Humor Book of the Year
—Independent Publisher's Book Award

ForeWord Gold Medal Winner—Humor Book of the Year

TRADER HORN
A Young Man's Astounding Adventures in 19th Century Equatorial Africa
By Alfred Aloysius Horn
ISBN 1-885-211-81-3
$16.95

Here is the stuff of legends —tale of thrills and danger, wild beasts, serpents, and savages. An unforgettable and vivid portrait of a vanished late-19th century Africa.

UNBEATEN TRACKS IN JAPAN
By Isabella L. Bird
ISBN 1-885-211-57-0
$14.95

Isabella Bird was one of the most adventurous women travelers of the 19th century with journeys to Tibet, Canada, Korea, Turkey, Hawaii, and Japan. A fascinating read for anyone interested in women's travel, spirituality, and Asian culture.

Travel Humor

NOT SO FUNNY WHEN IT HAPPENED
The Best of Travel Humor and Misadventure
Edited by Tim Cahill
ISBN 1-885-211-55-4
$12.95

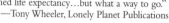

Laugh with Bill Bryson, Dave Barry, Anne Lamott, Adair Lara, and many more.

LAST TROUT IN VENICE
The Far-Flung Escapades of an Accidental Adventurer
By Doug Lansky
ISBN 1-885-211-63-5
$14.95

"Traveling with Doug Lansky might result in a considerably shortened life expectancy...but what a way to go."
—Tony Wheeler, Lonely Planet Publications

Women's Travel

A WOMAN'S PASSION FOR TRAVEL
More True Stories from A Woman's World
Edited by Marybeth Bond
& Pamela Michael
ISBN 1-885-211-36-8
$17.95

"A diverse and gripping
series of stories!"   —Arlene Blum, author of
Annapurna: A Woman's Place

A WOMAN'S WORLD
**True Stories of
Life on the Road**
Edited by Marybeth Bond
Introduction by
Dervla Murphy
ISBN 1-885-211-06-6
$17.95

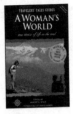

——— ★ ★ ★ ———
*Winner of the Lowell Thomas
Award for Best Travel Book—
Society of American Travel Writers*

WOMEN IN THE WILD
**True Stories of
Adventure and
Connection**
Edited by Lucy McCauley
ISBN 1-885-211-21-X
$17.95

"A spiritual, moving, and
totally female book to take you
around the world and back." —*Mademoiselle*

A MOTHER'S WORLD
Journeys of the Heart
Edited by Marybeth Bond
& Pamela Michael
ISBN 1-885-211-26-0
$14.95

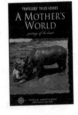

"These stories remind us
that motherhood is one
of the great unifying forces
in the world"   —*San Francisco Examiner*

Food

ADVENTURES IN WINE
**True Stories of
Vineyards and Vintages
around the World**
Edited by Thom Elkjer
ISBN 1-885-211-80-5
$17.95

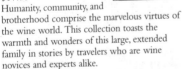

Humanity, community, and
brotherhood comprise the marvelous virtues of
the wine world. This collection toasts the
warmth and wonders of this large, extended
family in stories by travelers who are wine
novices and experts alike.

FOOD (Updated)
A Taste of the Road
Edited by Richard Sterling
Introduction by Margo True
ISBN 1-885-211-77-5
$18.95

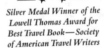

——— ★ ★ ★ ———
*Silver Medal Winner of the
Lowell Thomas Award for
Best Travel Book—Society
of American Travel Writers*

HER FORK IN THE ROAD
**Women Celebrate Food
and Travel**
Edited by Lisa Bach
ISBN 1-885-211-71-6
$16.95

A savory sampling of stories
by some of the best writers
in and out of the food and travel fields.

THE ADVENTURE OF FOOD
**True Stories of
Eating Everything**
Edited by Richard Sterling
ISBN 1-885-211-37-6
$17.95

"These stories are bound to
whet appetites for more
than food." —*Publishers Weekly*

Spiritual Travel

THE SPIRITUAL GIFTS OF TRAVEL
The Best of Travelers' Tales
Edited by James O'Reilly and Sean O'Reilly
ISBN 1-885-211-69-4
$16.95
A collection of favorite stories of transformation on

the road from our award-winning Travelers' Tales series that shows the myriad ways travel indelibly alters our inner landscapes.

THE WAY OF THE WANDERER
Discover Your True Self Through Travel
By David Yeadon
ISBN 1-885-211-60-0
$14.95
Experience transformation through travel with this delightful, illustrated collection by award-winning author David Yeadon.

PILGRIMAGE
Adventures of the Spirit
Edited by Sean O'Reilly & James O'Reilly
Introduction by Phil Cousineau
ISBN 1-885-211-56-2
$16.95

——— ★★★ ———
*ForeWord Silver Medal Winner
— Travel Book of the Year*

A WOMAN'S PATH
Women's Best Spiritual Travel Writing
Edited by Lucy McCauley, Amy G. Carlson & Jennifer Leo
ISBN 1-885-211-48-1
$16.95
"A sensitive exploration of women's lives that have been unexpectedly and spiritually touched by travel experiences.... Highly recommended."
— *Library Journal*

THE ROAD WITHIN
True Stories of Transformation and the Soul
Edited by Sean O'Reilly, James O'Reilly & Tim O'Reilly
ISBN 1-885-211-19-8
$17.95

——— ★★★ ———
Best Spiritual Book—Independent Publisher's Book Award

THE ULTIMATE JOURNEY
Inspiring Stories of Living and Dying
James O'Reilly, Sean O'Reilly & Richard Sterling
ISBN 1-885-211-38-4
$17.95
"A glorious collection of writings about the ultimate adventure. A book to keep by one's bedside—and close to one's heart." —Philip Zaleski, editor,
The Best Spiritual Writing series

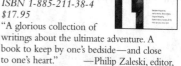

Adventure

TESTOSTERONE PLANET
True Stories from a Man's World
Edited by Sean O'Reilly, Larry Habegger & James O'Reilly
ISBN 1-885-211-43-0
$17.95
Thrills and laughter with some of today's best writers: Sebastian Junger, Tim Cahill, Bill Bryson, and Jon Krakauer.

DANGER!
True Stories of Trouble and Survival
Edited by James O'Reilly, Larry Habegger & Sean O'Reilly
ISBN 1-885-211-32-5
$17.95
"Exciting...for those who enjoy living on the edge or prefer to read the survival stories of others, this is a good pick."
— *Library Journal*

Special Interest

365 TRAVEL
A Daily Book of Journeys, Meditations, and Adventures
Edited by Lisa Bach
ISBN 1-885-211-67-8
$14.95

An illuminating collection of travel wisdom and adventures that reminds us all of the lessons we learn while on the road.

THE GIFT OF RIVERS
True Stories of Life on the Water
Edited by Pamela Michael
Introduction by Robert Hass
ISBN 1-885-211-42-2
$14.95

"*The Gift of Rivers* is a soulful compendium of wonderful stories that illuminate, educate, inspire, and delight."
—David Brower, Chairman of Earth Island Institute

FAMILY TRAVEL
The Farther You Go, the Closer You Get
Edited by Laura Manske
ISBN 1-885-211-33-3
$17.95

"This is family travel at its finest." —*Working Mother*

LOVE & ROMANCE
True Stories of Passion on the Road
Edited by Judith Babcock Wylie
ISBN 1-885-211-18-X
$17.95

"A wonderful book to read by a crackling fire."
—*Romantic Traveling*

THE GIFT OF BIRDS
True Encounters with Avian Spirits
Edited by Larry Habegger & Amy G. Carlson
ISBN 1-885-211-41-4
$17.95

"These are all wonderful, entertaining stories offering a *bird's-eye view!* of our avian friends."
—*Booklist*

A DOG'S WORLD
True Stories of Man's Best Friend on the Road
Edited by Christine Hunsicker
ISBN 1-885-211-23-6
$12.95

This extraordinary collection includes stories by John Steinbeck, Helen Thayer, James Herriot, Pico Iyer, and many others.

THE GIFT OF TRAVEL
The Best of Travelers' Tales
Edited by Larry Habegger, James O'Reilly & Sean O'Reilly
ISBN 1-885-211-25-2
$14.95

"Like gourmet chefs in a French market, the editors of Travelers' Tales pick, sift, and prod their way through the weighty shelves of contemporary travel writing, creaming off the very best."
—William Dalrymple, author of *City of Djinns*

Travel Advice

SHITTING PRETTY
How to Stay Clean and Healthy While Traveling
By Dr. Jane Wilson-Howarth
ISBN 1-885-211-47-3
$12.95

A light-hearted book about a serious subject for millions of travelers— staying healthy on the road—written by international health expert, Dr. Jane Wilson-Howarth.

THE FEARLESS SHOPPER
How to Get the Best Deals on the Planet
By Kathy Borrus
ISBN 1-885-211-39-2
$14.95

"Anyone who reads *The Fearless Shopper* will come away a smarter, more responsible shopper and a more curious, culturally attuned traveler."

—Jo Mancuso, *The Shopologist*

GUTSY WOMEN
More Travel Tips and Wisdom for the Road
By Marybeth Bond
ISBN 1-885-211-61-9
$12.95

Second Edition—Packed with funny, instructive, and inspiring advice for women heading out to see the world.

SAFETY AND SECURITY FOR WOMEN WHO TRAVEL
By Sheila Swan & Peter Laufer
ISBN 1-885-211-29-5
$12.95

A must for every woman traveler!

THE FEARLESS DINER
Travel Tips and Wisdom for Eating around the World
By Richard Sterling
ISBN 1-885-211-22-8
$7.95

Combines practical advice on foodstuffs, habits, and etiquette, with hilarious accounts of others' eating adventures.

THE PENNY PINCHER'S PASSPORT TO LUXURY TRAVEL
The Art of Cultivating Preferred Customer Status
By Joel L. Widzer
ISBN 1-885-211-31-7
$12.95

Proven techniques on how to travel first class at discount prices, even if you're not a frequent flyer.

GUTSY MAMAS
Travel Tips and Wisdom for Mothers on the Road
By Marybeth Bond
ISBN 1-885-211-20-1
$7.95

A delightful guide for mothers traveling with their children—or without them!

Destination Titles:
True Stories of Life on the Road

AMERICA
Edited by Fred Setterberg
ISBN 1-885-211-28-7
$19.95

FRANCE (Updated)
Edited by James O'Reilly,
Larry Habegger &
Sean O'Reilly
ISBN 1-885-211-73-2
$18.95

**AMERICAN
SOUTHWEST**
Edited by Sean O'Reilly
& James O'Reilly
ISBN 1-885-211-58-9
$17.95

GRAND CANYON
Edited by Sean O'Reilly,
James O'Reilly &
Larry Habegger
ISBN 1-885-211-34-1
$17.95

AUSTRALIA
Edited by Larry Habegger
ISBN 1-885-211-40-6
$17.95

GREECE
Edited by Larry Habegger,
Sean O'Reilly &
Brian Alexander
ISBN 1-885-211-52-X
$17.95

BRAZIL
Edited by Annette Haddad
& Scott Doggett
Introduction by Alex
Shoumatoff
ISBN 1-885-211-11-2
$17.95

HAWAI'I
Edited by Rick &
Marcie Carroll
ISBN 1-885-211-35-X
$17.95

CENTRAL AMERICA
Edited by Larry Habegger
& Natanya Pearlman
ISBN 1-885-211-74-0
$17.95

HONG KONG
Edited by James O'Reilly,
Larry Habegger &
Sean O'Reilly
ISBN 1-885-211-03-1
$17.95

CUBA
Edited by Tom Miller
ISBN 1-885-211-62-7
$17.95

INDIA
Edited by James O'Reilly
& Larry Habegger
ISBN 1-885-211-01-5
$17.95

IRELAND
Edited by James O'Reilly,
Larry Habegger &
Sean O'Reilly
ISBN 1-885-211-46-5
$17.95

SAN FRANCISCO
Edited by James O'Reilly,
Larry Habegger &
Sean O'Reilly
ISBN 1-885-211-08-2
$17.95

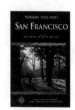

ITALY (Updated)
Edited by Anne Calcagno
Introduction by Jan Morris
ISBN 1-885-211-72-4
$18.95

SPAIN (Updated)
Edited by Lucy McCauley
ISBN 1-885-211-78-3
$19.95

JAPAN
Edited by Donald W. George
& Amy G. Carlson
ISBN 1-885-211-04-X
$17.95

THAILAND (Updated)
Edited by James O'Reilly
& Larry Habegger
ISBN 1-885-211-75-9
$18.95

MEXICO (Updated)
Edited by James O'Reilly
& Larry Habegger
ISBN 1-885-211-59-7
$17.95

TIBET
Edited by James O'Reilly,
Larry Habegger, & Kim
Morris
ISBN 1-885-211-76-7
$18.95

NEPAL
Edited by Rajendra
S. Khadka
ISBN 1-885-211-14-7
$17.95

TUSCANY
Edited by James O'Reilly, &
Tara Austen Weaver
ISBN 1-885-211-68-6
$16.95

PARIS
Edited by James O'Reilly,
Larry Habegger &
Sean O'Reilly
ISBN 1-885-211-10-4
$17.95

Politicaly moterated distortio
Perplexing shool   defiant

Tortuoas

My Mortal World was not paelled
w/ my eternal world.